Pirates on the Chesapeake

PIRATES ON THE CHESAPEAKE

Being a True History of
Pirates, Picaroons, and Raiders on Chesapeake Bay
1610 - 1807

Donald G. Shomette

Tidewater Publishers

Centreville, Maryland

For my son Kyle

Library of Congress Cataloging-in-Publication Data

Shomette, Donald.
Pirates on the Chesapeake.

Bibliography: p.
Includes index.
1. Chesapeake Bay (Md. and Va.)—History.
2. Pirates—Chesapeake Bay (Md. and Va.)   I. Title.
F187.C5S48   1985   975.5′18   85-40532
ISBN 0-87033-343-7

Manufactured in the United States of America
First edition, 1985; fifth printing, 1997

Contents

Acknowledgments

On a rainy Saturday afternoon in the fall of 1980, while examining several rolls of microfilm of early nineteenth century Maryland newspapers at the Library of Congress, I encountered, quite by accident, several news reports of the capture of a French pirate vessel in the waters of the Patuxent River in 1807. It was, I later discovered much to my amazement, an incident that had been entirely forgotten by the chroniclers of tidewater history. I brought the data to the attention of a close friend and associate, Ralph E. Eshelman, who, as Director of the Calvert Marine Museum at Solomons, Maryland, was deeply interested in any historical information relating to the maritime heritage of that particular river system. At his urging, I later delved deeply into that long-forgotten but intriguing episode of Chesapeake history, and as a consequence, the keel of this volume was eventually laid.

Of course, such an undertaking as this could never be completed in a vacuum, and numerous individuals and institutions have provided every form of assistance and inspiration. I would first like to thank Dr. Ralph E. Eshelman, for suggesting that I undertake this project, and the Calvert Marine Museum for permitting liberal usage of the transcriptions pertaining to the "Othello Affair," now housed there. I would like to extend a note of deep appreciation to Adriana M. Breheny for her translations of the Cornelius Evertsen papers and logs from the Dutch. These writings, published in Holland, which to my knowledge have never before been translated into English, add enormous depth to our knowledge of the history of the Dutch naval incursions into the Chesapeake in the seventeenth century. The Evertsen papers were filled with archaic word forms, nautical slang, and obsolete terms which Mrs. Breheny handled with astonishing competence. I would like to thank my long-time friend and associate, Dr. Fred W. Hopkins, Jr.,

Graduate Dean of the University of Baltimore, and Orva Heissen-buttel, for their critical readings of the various drafts of this work, and for the excellent suggestions they have provided for its improvement. A word of sincere appreciation must also be extended to Jennifer Rutland for her preliminary editing of an often intimidating, bulky manuscript, and for typing the final draft.

As it would be impossible, in the space allotted, to thank every member of the major institutions that have lent their valuable time and guidance to me during my research for this book, I would at least like to acknowledge a key few. Among this number are counted the superb staff of the Manuscript Division of the Library of Congress in Washington, the Research Library, Colonial Williamsburg, in Williamsburg, Virginia, and the Public Record Office, in London.

I would be remiss if I did not mention the debt of gratitude I owe to those who have tilled much of the ground I now tread upon, in particular Hugh Rankin and Arthur Pierce Middleton. Their thoroughly superb works on pirates and the colonial maritime history of the Chesapeake have served both as models and inspiration for me during the occasionally trying episodes encountered in producing this work. I must also pay homage to that most classic chronicler of buccaneer history, without whom the world might have ignored the Age of Piracy. Writing under the nom de plume of Captain Charles Johnson, Daniel Defoe produced *A General History . . . of the Most Notorious Pirates* which still stands as not only a literary classic, but a basic source work for anyone investigating the rise and fall of piracy in the Western Hemisphere.

And finally, I would like to express my gratitude to my wife Carol for her encouragement, understanding, and patience throughout the creation of this book.

Pirates on the Chesapeake

I

Prologue: Unhallowed Creatures

The chill of the English spring was still heavy on the Thames River on May 15, 1609, as the Virginia Company's supply fleet raised anchor off Woolwich and prepared to sail with the tide. With relative ease the crowded, stubby little boats slipped past the gray river world of muck and pilings, passing familiar navigational landmarks and riverfront towns such as Greenhithe, Swanscombe Marsh, Tilbury, and Gravesend. The covey of ships that sailed from the English coast, after stopovers at Plymouth and Falmouth for additional supplies, livestock, and passengers, eventually numbered nine vessels. It was to be the largest single English fleet ever sent to America, and it was bound for the relief and resupply of the company's struggling young colony of Virginia, which had been ensconced since 1607 upon the banks of the James River. And with it went nearly five hundred determined settlers bent on strengthening England's precariously established toehold on the North American continent.

The reasons why so many people dared to hazard their lives and fortunes aboard the cockleshell fleet (several vessels of which would not survive the voyage) to reach a land fraught with unknown dangers, in which most would neither prosper nor survive, forms the very fiber of the brave, oft-told saga of English America's beginnings. Their objectives were as varied as their numbers. Yet from the outset, the motivations of the colony's founding fathers were held suspect by England's arch rival in the New World, Spain. Spain feared that the Chesapeake Bay region, in which England's footing had been established, was meant to serve only as a base from which piratical excursions against Spain's American empire might be launched with impunity.

As early as February 23, 1609, Pedro de Zuñiga, the Spanish Ambassador to England, had written to King Philip III on the subject. "They have proposed," he said with deep concern,

> that all the pirates who are out of this kingdom will be pardoned by the King
> if they resort there [Virginia], and the place is so perfect (as they say) for
> piractical excursions that Your Majesty will not be able to bring silver from
> the Indies without finding a very great obstacle there, and that they will ruin
> the trade of Your Majesty's vassals, for that is the purpose of their going
> [there].[1]

Imperial Spain's economic and territorial paranoia was, in the years following the defeat of the Spanish Armada and the empire's decline from the role of pre-eminent naval power in Europe, certainly warranted in regard to her trade and treasure. Pedro de Zuñiga was well aware that deep within many an English mariner—given the right circumstances—beat the heart of an English privateersman. During the last half-century, English privateersmen, eternally considered as pirates (and with some justification) by the Spanish, operating in the English Channel, the West Indies, and elsewhere, had been a constant menace. When the likes of a Sir Francis Drake was loosed upon the high seas, Spain trembled. The settlement attempt in Virginia, as a potential base from which destructive piratical attacks might be launched, was thus viewed by Zuñiga as an important and dangerous move in the chess game of colonial empire. Indeed, the Spanish had been concerned about such moves by both the English and the French since the middle of the sixteenth century. At the very least, the homeward route of the Spanish treasure fleets bound from Cuba and riding the Bahama currents occasionally as far north as Hatteras, placed the infant Virginia colony on the Chesapeake in a strategic position from which raiders might easily sally forth to intercept the flotas. Not only was Spain's hegemony in the Americas at stake, but the very fountain from which her power flowed, namely, the gold and silver of the New World, was in potential jeopardy.

That Spain should view English intentions with a jaundiced eye requires some appreciation of the national pride the former held for its discoveries and conquests in the New World, and the consequent haughty attitude those accomplishments had engendered regarding other nations. "Whoever is conversant with the Portugal and Spanish writers," observed the astute English chronicler Richard Hakluyt, "shall find that they account all other nations for pirates, rovers, and thieves, which visit any heathen coast that they have sailed by or looked on."[2]

Yet Zuñiga's suspicions concerning English objectives were not without some foundation. In early summer of 1609, in fact, a proposition was made by Sir Richard Moryson to the Earl of Salisbury, that Irish pirates be exported to Virginia. Ireland had become a sink of piratical activity, and the move would not only rid the British Isles of such brigands but would utilize the New World as a ready-made dump for undesirables who might actually assist in its settlement. If allowed to settle in Virginia, the pirates would be useful in defending the colony in its infancy, and, if disturbed, "in relieveing their wants." The proposal, it might be assumed, would have certainly seemed provocative to Zuñiga had he been aware of it.[3]

The English, however, sought to avoid conflict. Unfortunately, though the leader of the Virginia Company's expedition, Sir Thomas Gates, had been instructed to avoid any provocations or confrontations with the Spanish, neither he nor the company directors could have predicted just how accurate Zuñiga's assessment would prove. Less than a year after the fleet's departure from England, the first piracy in Chesapeake history was hatched, not, ironically, as a result of any planned effort, but as a consequence of the terrible sequence of events in Virginia's birth that has come to be called the "starving time."

By the fall of 1609, the colony, beset by political upheaval, Indian attacks, famine, disease, and weak leadership, was rapidly degenerating into total chaos. Ony two of the original nine vessels that had sailed from England remained in the Chesapeake. Starvation, laced with cannibalism, desertion, a breakdown in civil authority, and idleness, all but guaranteed the colony's failure. And, as one contemporary chronicler of the descent into piracy later wrote, "Unto idleness, you may join treasons wrought by those unhallowed creatures that forsook the Colony, and exposed their desolate brethren to extreme misery." Twenty-eight or thirty of the colonists, apparently belonging to a company under the command of Captain Francis West, younger brother of Lord De La Warr, who had been dispatched upon a perilous mission to trade with the Indians, were to prove the instrument of the plunge into the abyss. Having successfully obtained a quantity of corn from the Indians, a seditious core among them began to conspire to seize their ship, *Swallow*, one of the two vessels remaining in the colony. They persuaded some of their comrades, cajoled others, and forced the remainder of the company to join in their evil endeavor. George Percy, the sickly president of the colony (in the absence of Gates, who had been shipwrecked, and Captain John Smith, the former president who had returned to England after a freak gunpowder explosion had nearly killed him), recorded the bitter birth of piracy on the Chesapeake.

They stole away the ship. They made a league amongst themselves to be

professed pirates, with dreams of mountains of gold, and happy robberies.
Thus, at one instant, they wronged the hopes, and subverted the cares of the
Colony, who, depending upon their return, fore-slowed to look out for
further provision. They created the Indians our implacable enemies, by
some violence they offered. They carried away the best ship, which would
have been a refuge in extremities. They weakened our forces, by subtraction
of their arms and succors. They are the scum of men, that failing in their
piracy, that being pinched with famine and penury, after their wild roving
upon the sea, when all their lawless hopes failed, some remained with other
pirates they met upon the sea. The others resolved to return to England,
bound themselves by mutual oath to agree all in one report, to discredit the
land, to deplore the famine, and to protest that their coming away, pro-
ceeded from desperate necessity.[4]

The Jamestown settlers, after being reduced to barely sixty miserable
skeletons subsisting on roots, herbs, acorns, walnuts, berries, and a
little fish, were finally relieved on May 24, 1610, when two ships hove
into view in the river. The vessels were *Deliverance* and *Patience*, built by
Sir Thomas Gates and Captain Christopher Newport at Bermuda,
where they were wrecked aboard the flagship *Sea Venture* nearly nine
months before while en route to the Chesapeake. Had Gates not
arrived, the Jamestown settlers would have all perished within ten
days. The colony, Gates informed the hollow-eyed survivors, would
have to be abandoned, for he had brought only enough provisions to
feed them for sixteen days. On June 7, the dejected colonists filed
numbly out of their crumbling settlement and boarded the ships lying
in the James.[5]

In far-off England, Pedro de Zuñiga, unconvinced that Spain's rival
would give up its purchase in the New World, had already written to
King Philip III: "I believe that they would again send people out,
because, no doubt, the reason they want that place is its apparent
suitability for piracy."[6]

Zuñiga was not incorrect in at least part of his assumption, for as
Gates and the Jamestown colonists dropped downriver they encountered, on June 8, off Mulberry Island, the vanguard of salvation, a
relief expedition commanded by Lord De La Warr. England *would*
hold on to her settlement. And piracy would flourish, indeed, not only
on the Chesapeake, but throughout the Americas for the next two
hundred years.

II

Grevious Crimes of Pyracie
and Murther

When Sir Francis Wyatt arrived in Chesapeake Bay in October
1621 aboard the ship *George* with a fleet of eight vessels to assume
command as Governor of Virginia, he found a colony in a reasonably
well-ordered and prosperous state. Peace had finally been established
with the Indians, imminent starvation no longer threatened, the menace of possible Spanish intervention had subsided, and a staple crop—
tobacco—had been developed for export. Immigration was on the
upswing. During the past year a total of twenty-one ships, employing
more than four hundred sailors and carrying thirteen hundred men,
women, and children, had, for the most part, arrived safely. And there
was plenty of room for all. Under the 1609 Virginia Company charter,
the colony officially embraced territory which extended two hundred
miles north and two hundred miles south of old Point Comfort at the
mouth of the James River, and stretched "from sea to sea"—from the
Atlantic to the Pacific.[1]

Governor Wyatt had received numerous instructions from the
Crown, issued on July 24, to guide him in the management of Virginia.
Principal among them were orders "to punish pyracies" and "to build
fortresses & blockhouses at ye mouths of Rivers" for the defense of the
colony.[2] The directions concerning piracy and defense were not ill-
considered, for the menace to colony shipping, not only by pirates but
by foreign nations nominally at peace with England, had of late become
very real. Although attacks had not yet been carried out in Chesapeake
waters, they were common on the high seas, and the occasional interdiction of colony shipping was becoming a problem.

The most recent incident had been an attack on Captain Nicholas
Elfry's 45-ton ship *Tygre*, chartered by the Virginia Company in Sep-

tember 1621 to carry "divers Passengers, and other goods and merchandize from London" to the colony. En route the ship had been overtaken by a "Turks man-of-warre" filled with pirates. *Tygre* was plundered of her provisions, sails, tackle, anchors, hourglass, and compass. Two English boys were taken prisoner. Fortunately, another English ship had appeared before further harm could be done, and the Turks sailed off. The pirates were unaware that two slaves, one French and the other an Irish lad named Walter Deane, had made their escape from their ship to the Virginiaman before it sailed away. Captain Elfry befriended Deane, took him into his crew, and, after calling at Virginia, sailed for Bermuda, where the youth was permitted to settle.[3]

Problems with the Spanish, who were always fearful of English encroachment upon their territorial jurisdiction and of trade monopolies in their own colonies, also persisted. Heavy-handed challenges to Virginia-bound shipping in American waters were on the increase. Only the year before, though Spain and England were at peace, a 160-ton Virginia Company ship called *Margaret and John,* mounting eight iron cannons and a small falcon gun, commanded by Captain Anthony Chester and carrying eighty passengers, including the Virginia Company treasurer, the Earl of Southampton, and his deputy, John Farrar, barely survived a desperate sea fight against two large Spanish warships. Blown off course into the West Indies, the ship endured a bloody six-hour engagement before finally escaping.[4]

Although what happened to both *Tygre* and *Margaret and John* were typical of the dangers faced by Virginia shipping on the high seas, such difficulties were not the only ones colony sponsors had to cope with. Occasionally, the very Englishmen hired by English companies to carry supplies to the infant colonies decided on their own to free-lance in piracy and caused considerable embarrassment to the government, nourishing Spanish fears that the Chesapeake would yet serve as a base for buccaneering. One such would-be buccaneer who succumbed to the call was Captain John Powell, master of the trim little bark *Hopewell.* While on colony business, Powell thought nothing of stopping and seizing foreign shipping on the high seas for his own enrichment. In 1619, after having experienced numerous adventures and mishaps while sailing under the flag of the Somers Island Company, Powell found gainful employment by bringing the first load of black slaves to Virginia. His standing with the Virginia Company directors based upon his brief plunge into piracy, however, was certainly not good. In 1623, when the company was asked to permit him to trade in the colony, permission was denied, the company fathers noting that they were "afraid Capt. Powell should go to the West Indies" to again try his hand at piracy.[5]

Fortunately for Governor Wyatt, outright attacks on vessels plying the waters of the Chesapeake had yet to develop into a major concern. Yet interdiction of Virginia shipping on the high seas and the willingness of English mariners, such as Powell, who were occasionally given to dabbling in piracy, were problems that threatened to spread eventually to the very sands of the tidewater itself. As the Virginia colony grew and thrived, it was virtually inevitable. The vast distance between the power centers of Europe with all their turmoils, and the frontiers of the New World were consoling to some, but the sea, as one historian so aptly put it, was in fact "the highway of imperial ambition rather than a barrier to it." And, on the seas as in the undefended colonial frontier environment of the Chesapeake, lawlessness and the constant threat of attack by a host of assailants was the price to be paid for planting the seeds of empire. For that very reason, the unprotected waters of Virginia, and, later, of Maryland, were destined to suffer what would seem an endless series of incursions ranging from independent pirates, privateers, and assorted freebooters to the powerful navies of Holland, Spain, and France. Few would have suspected, however, that the first serious damage would be inflicted by loyal, honest Englishmen upon themselves.

One of those who had sailed for Virginia aboard *George* with Sir Francis Wyatt was a thirty-four-year-old stockholder in the Virginia Company, a hearty, pugnacious, well-educated man named William Claiborne. Claiborne had been a friend of Captain John Smith in London, and through political connections had secured a three-year appointment as surveyor in the colony "to survey the planters' lands and make a map of that country."[6] Possessed of courage, industry, and resolve, Claiborne, viewing the Virginia Capes for the first time, could little guess that he would one day be branded a pirate, nor could he foresee the turmoil his singular enterprises would inflict upon the political geography and future of the entire tidewater region.

William Claiborne's ascendancy in the Virginia colony was rapid. By 1624 he had become a member of the Governor's Council, and the following year, termed "a person of quality and trust," he was appointed secretary of state for Virginia. An activist not simply content with acquiring large amounts of land (which he did, in great gulps), he sought permission from the Governor to explore to the head of the Chesapeake and any parts of Virginia lying between north latitudes 34 degrees and 41 degrees, and to trade with the Indians.[7] On April 27, 1627, permission was granted, and he was soon sailing northward on

the pristine waters of the Bay, examining with a keen eye its vast
unsettled shore.[8] It was undoubtedly during this voyage that Claiborne
first sighted the level, fertile fields and forests of Kent Island. Perhaps
reminded of his native Kent in England, he gave the great island its
name. Here, he envisioned, would be the perfect base for an Indian
fur-trading empire. Nearly three quarters of the way up the Bay, close
enough to the mouth of the Susquehanna River to have access to the
northern tribes, yet within several days sail from Jamestown, the site
was superb for a trading post. By 1628 he was actively trading with the
Indians and laying the foundations for his enterprise.

Within three years, having tested the waters and found them to his
liking, Claiborne returned to England to secure financial support for a
major trading operation on the Chesapeake. It apparently took little
effort to convince a rich and powerful London merchant named William Cloberry of the advantages to be had in the Indian fur trade. Soon
Claiborne was a one-sixth partner in a new stock company formed by
Cloberry to exploit the trade, and was given full managerial authority.
It was at this time that he learned of a colonizing effort being formulated by one George Calvert, Lord Baltimore, an influential peer who
was intent on staking out his own portion of the New World for a
Catholic colony. The fact that Baltimore sought to found his own
colony immediately to the north of Virginia must have caused the
ambitious Claiborne no small discomfort. Yet he persevered. Through
the advantageous connections provided by Cloberry, he was issued, on
May 16, 1631, a royal license, signed by William Alexander, secretary
of state for Scotland, "to trade and traffic of corne, furs or any other
commodities . . . make discoveries for increase of trade," and to freely
conduct said trade with his ships, men, boats, and merchandise "in all
sea-coasts, rivers, creeks, harbors, land and territories in or neare those
parts of America for which there is not already a patent granted to
others for trade."[9]

Claiborne wasted little time. Twelve days after securing the license,
he set sail from Deal, England, aboard the ship *Africa* with a cargo of
trade goods valued at more than thirteen hundred pounds sterling,
some twenty indentured servants, a linen maid, and a cripple "to read
prayers." Two months later he landed at Kecoughtan, Virginia.[10]

By late August 1631 Claiborne had arrived at Kent Island with one
hundred men, a place "unplanted by any man, but possessed of the
natives of that country." With little fanfare, he purchased the island
from the Indians and promptly proceeded to occupy the land by
building dwellings and mills, laying out gardens, planting orchards,
and stocking farms with cattle. Within a year the island was being

represented in the Virginia Assembly.[11]

While William Claiborne was systematically establishing a base for his trading empire on the Chesapeake, Lord Baltimore continued pressing King Charles I for a charter to establish a new colony north of Virginia. The colony was to be named Maryland, in honor of Queen Henrietta Marie. Though George Calvert died in April 1632, his efforts were not in vain, for soon afterward the King affixed his seal to the charter, which was then granted to Calvert's son Cecilius, Second Lord Baltimore, on June 20, 1632.[12]

The territorial borders assigned to Lord Baltimore's planned colony, unfortunately, clearly overlapped those which had been granted to the Virginia Company, and which were claimed by Virginia. And right smack in the middle of it all lay Kent Island. Aware of Claiborne's trading settlement, Lord Baltimore at first took a conciliatory stance toward the Virginia secretary of state's establishment. He directed his brother and governor of the yet-to-be-established Maryland colony, Leonard Calvert, to deal firmly but courteously with Claiborne. It was to be made quite clear to him that Kent Island lay within Lord Baltimore's patent. Claiborne would be permitted to continue his trading operations, and Baltimore was "willing to give him all the encouragement he cann to proceede." However, Leonard Calvert was directed to insist that trading would only be permitted under a license from Baltimore, a demand which, if agreed to, would establish Cecilius Calvert's authority over Kent Island.[13]

When word of Baltimore's charter arrived in Virginia, the colony planters were enraged over the challenge to their colonial borders, protesting the action in a petition to the King. On July 3, 1633, however, the Council of State waffled on the issue by leaving "Lord Baltimore to his patent and the other parties to the course of law according to their desire."[14] The unwillingness of the King or his council to rule directly on the matter would, in a very short time, lead to charges of piracy, bloodshed, and the first naval engagement between English-speaking peoples in the New World.

On February 27, 1634, two tiny vessels, the 300-ton ship *Ark* and the 250-ton pinnace *Dove*, bearing the first settlers for Lord Baltimore's new colony of Maryland, arrived off Point Comfort in the Chesapeake. It was undoubtedly with some trepidation that they did so, for Baltimore's instructions had specifically forbade either a visit to Jamestown or anchoring off the Virginians' new fort at Point Comfort. "We expected here every hower," wrote one of the colonists, the Jesuit priest Father Andrew White,

to be staid by the [Virginia] Councell, desireing noethinge more then our
ruine. At this time Captaine Claborne was there from whome we understood
the Indians were all in armes to resist us, having heard that 6 Spanish ships
were a comeing to destroy them all. The rumour was most like to have
begunne from himselfe.[15]

The Maryland colonists were treated kindly by Governor of Virginia
John Harvey despite the outright hostility of the Virginia Council, for
they carried letters from both the King and the Earl of Portland,
Baltimore's treasurer. The Governor, indeed, seemed eager to lay
aside the challenge to Virginia's territorial jurisdiction and assist the
colonists, albeit more out of a desire for personal gain than out of
simple humanitarianism. It seemed that the Governor was assisting the
colonists in hopes of benefiting from Baltimore's help "to receive a
great summe of money due to him out of the exchequer."[16]

Claiborne, having met with Calvert, immediately requested the
opinion of the Council of Virginia as to "how he should demean
himself in respect to Lord Baltimore's patent and his deputies, now
seated in the bay; for that they [the Marylanders] had specified . . . that
he was now a member of that plantation, and therefore should relinquish all relations and dependence on this colony." The Council stoutly
reassured him that the island remained a part of the Virginia colony.[17]

It was then that William Claiborne, Secretary of State of Virginia,
determined to resist Lord Baltimore's claim of authority over Kent
Island. And it was then that Claiborne's real troubles began.

When Leonard Calvert's band of colonists finally began to establish the
settlement of St. Mary's City astride a picturesque bluff overlooking a
broad, quiet tributary of the Potomac which they dubbed St. Mary's
River, they did so confident in the knowledge that they had rather
easily secured the friendship of the local Indians, a tribe belonging to
Algonquin stock. But by the summer of 1634 signs of suspicion, dis-
trust, and occasional hostility began to appear among the neighboring
Patuxent Indians. The settlers at St. Mary's, greatly concerned over the
mysterious change, abandoned their domestic chores and set about
providing for their defense. It was soon related by a Virginia fur trader
named Henry Fleet that a rumor had been spread among the Indians
that the colonists were "Waspaines," or Spaniards that had come to kill
them. Fleet claimed that the rumor was started by none other than
William Claiborne.[18]

Incensed, the Maryland colony made formal complaint to Governor
Harvey. Claiborne was immediately placed under bond and confined
to Jamestown and the custody of Captains Samuel Matthews and John

Utie until the charges could be investigated. Both Maryland and Virginia appointed commissioners to meet with the Indians at their village of Patuxent, on the Patuxent River in Maryland, on June 20, 1634. The commissioners from Virginia were Thornton Hinton, William Pierce, Matthews, and Utie; those from Maryland were George Calvert and Frederick Winter. Claiborne, the principal of the controversy, was, of course, also present. As a consequence of the meeting at Patuxent, William Claiborne was vindicated, and it was soon revealed that Henry Fleet, jealous of the accused's well-organized competition for the fur trade, had lied to the Indians.[19]

Claiborne's exoneration was followed by a letter from the Lords of Trades and Plantations, written on July 22 to the Council of Virginia, supporting the rights of the planters to enjoy their estates as they had under the Virginia Company charter. The King himself, having been petitioned by the worried principals of William Cloberry and Company for protection of their possessions on Kent Island, had declared in a letter to Lord Baltimore, written on October 8, that it was contrary to justice and the intent of the grant to the Calverts that the Kent Islanders be dispossessed. Furthermore, the King directed that they should continue to enjoy full freedom of trade and instructed Lord Baltimore not to disturb or molest the island settlement in any way.[20]

Unhappily for Claiborne, news of the charges from which he was exonerated on June 20 reached Lord Baltimore in September—without the refutation that had cleared him. Lord Baltimore was outraged. Notwithstanding the King's instructions to the contrary, he sent word to Governor Calvert that if Claiborne continued to trade without a license, he was to be arrested and thrown into St. Mary's jail and his plantation on Kent Island confiscated.[21] Arresting a secretary of state of a powerful neighboring colony, however, was no simple matter. Thus, Lord Baltimore brought pressure to bear in England that obliged Governor Harvey to promise his full support to Maryland. Opposition to the already unpopular Harvey in Virginia and the Maryland colony was growing. Trade between the two colonies was nonexistent. Some Virginians vowed that "they would rather knock their cattle on the head than sell them to Maryland."[22]

Despite Harvey's support of Lord Baltimore, William Claiborne resolved to stand fast. He prepared his dominion for armed resistance, at the same time expanding operations on the island. He imported more servants, cleared more land, and erected more houses. And Cloberry, reassured by the King's support, sent more goods to trade with the Indians.[23]

The island was menaced, not only by white enemies, but by fierce

Indian foes as well. Now, Kent Island fell victim to actual assault by hostile Susquehannocks and Wicomeses. Three islanders were killed before the attack could be repelled. The islanders rushed to prepare their defenses against both white and red enemies by erecting two fortifications: Kent Fort was soon under construction near Kent Point, and a second work, dubbed Crayford Fort, was built near Craney Creek.[24] Claiborne did not ignore his naval defenses, and a pinnace, named *Long Tayle,* was built and turned over to the command of Captain Thomas Smith, and manned by twenty men.[25] With activity of this sort escalating, and hostility in both the Maryland and Kent Island camps intensifying, it was not surprising that a flash point would soon be reached. In the spring of 1635 events began to move with dizzying swiftness.

As the small Maryland pinnace approached Palmer's Island (now known as Garrett Island), near the head of the Chesapeake, neither her commander, Sergeant Robert Vaughn, nor his second, John Tomkins, were aware of the misfortune lying in wait for them. Their cargo consisted of "a great quantitie of trucking commodities," undoubtedly intended for the Indian trade, which Maryland sought to encourage. Although the record is incomplete as to how the ensuing affair began or was carried out, what is clear is that one John Butler, brother-in-law and agent of William Claiborne, seized the pinnace, its cargo, Vaughn, and Tomkins, probably for invading the trading dominion of the Kent Islanders, and carried his prisoners to Kent. The seizure of the pinnace became the first documented act of "Pyracie" on the waters of the Chesapeake Bay.[26]

Claiborne quickly released the Marylanders, undoubtedly to carry word back to St. Mary's of his resolve to resist Maryland's incursions, and continued to direct his trading activities as if nothing had happened. On April 5, Captain Smith sailed *Long Tayle* on a trading voyage to the Indian village at Mattapany, on the shores of the Patuxent River in St. Mary's County. In retaliation for the taking of their own pinnace and the capture of their men, the Marylanders, led by Captains Fleet and Humber, promptly seized *Long Tayle.* Smith was ordered to produce a license for trading from Lord Baltimore; he presented not a license but copies of the King's commission and a letter confirming it. The Marylanders scorned the papers as false and proceeded to confiscate both the vessel and its cargo. Captain Smith was released to make his own way home.[27]

Enraged and provoked by the confiscation of *Long Tayle,* the Kent Islanders, who now had severely reduced means of securing provisions, sought revenge. Claiborne issued a special warrant to Lieutenant Ratcliffe Warren to seize any vessel belonging to St. Mary's. A sloop named *Cockatrice* was fitted out, armed, and manned with a crew of fourteen men. Governor Calvert, well aware of the vengeance of which his foes were capable, armed and readied two vessels of his own, the big trading pinnaces *St. Helen* and *St. Margaret.* These were placed under the command of his most trusted colony officers, Captain Thomas Cornwalyes and Cuthbert Fenwick.[28]

On April 23, a little more than two weeks after the confiscation of *Long Tayle,* while cruising in the Pocomoke River on the lower Eastern Shore, Lieutenant Warren sighted *St. Helen* and prepared to take her. Suddenly, he was surprised by the appearance of *St. Margaret,* which was under the personal command of Cornwaleys. Undismayed by the odds, the Kent Islanders closed and attempted to board and take the enemy commander's pinnace in hand-to-hand fighting. A brisk battle ensued, during which Warren and two of his men, John Belson and William Dawson, and William Ashmore of *St. Margaret* were killed and several others wounded. *Cockatrice* was soon captured. The first naval engagement between English-speaking peoples in the New World was over quickly. The first blood of naval combat on the waters of the Chesapeake Bay had been spilled.[29]

Surrender of *Cockatrice* was, for William Claiborne, a bitter pill to swallow. Revenge would be all the sweeter. He promptly dispatched another armed vessel, this time under the command of Captain Thomas Smith, to cruise about the mouth of the Pocomoke. On May 10 Smith fell in with Cornwaleys in the harbor of the great Wicomico. Though details of the engagement that followed were not recorded, there was bloodshed. The battle apparently ended in favor of the Kent Islanders, for Cornwaleys's corn, furs, trading goods, and possibly the vessel itself were confiscated. Captain Smith had exacted a measure of revenge for the humiliation of *Long Tayle*'s seizure a month earlier and the surrender of *Cockatrice.*[30] Flushed with success, Claiborne dispatched Captain Philip Taylor in another vessel to the Patuxent to recapture *Long Tayle.* But once again the tables were turned, and Taylor was himself taken.[31]

Even as the battles on the Pocomoke were being fought by Claiborne's lieutenants, the leader of Kent Island was at Jamestown maneuvering for support against Governor Harvey. Governor Calvert, having failed in his efforts to capture Claiborne, now demanded from the Governor of Virginia his surrender. The unpopular Harvey, however, was unable to comply, for he was faced with nothing less than open insurrection by the people of Virginia for his support of Baltimore's efforts to bring down the Kent Islanders. Harvey was soon seized and sent to England to face charges for actions inimical to Virginia. In his stead, Captain John West was elected by the Virginia Council as Acting Governor on May 7, 1635.[32] An uneasy truce now prevailed between St. Mary's and Kent Island.

In December 1636 Kent Island was visited by one George Evelin, a man who had recently acquired a sixth share in Cloberry and Company. At first the purpose of his presence was anything but suspicious to Claiborne and his followers. When the first shipment of goods and servants arrived in February of the following year, however, it was learned that Evelin had been given power of attorney by Cloberry, and command of the Kent Island operation. Claiborne was instructed to return to England to explain his actions and adjust his accounts. Active to the last, however, he moved quickly to establish a permanent plantation and trading base under the command of Captain Thomas Smith on strategic Palmer's Island, at the head of the Bay and in the heart of Maryland territory, to expand the company's fur trade. Before leaving, he prepared an inventory of company property and secured from Evelin a bond not to sell or assign away Kent Island or its goods.[33]

No sooner were Claiborne's sails over the horizon than Evelin began to violate the bond into which he had entered, and opened direct personal negotiations with Calvert. Courted by the wily Governor at St. Mary's City, Evelin soon transferred his allegiance from Cloberry and Company to Lord Baltimore. In return for his promised efforts to "secure the good will and influence of several of the most popular among the servants of the Island" by giving them their freedom or bribing them with tobacco, Evelin was appointed by Calvert as Commander of Kent.[34]

The allegiance of the Kent Islanders to Lord Baltimore, despite the new commander's best efforts, was not easily secured, for he was believed by the very people he sought to confirm as allies to be a traitor and turncoat. Soon Evelin had virtually wrecked the Cloberry operation by selling the company goods to the islanders, to Virginians on the James, and to Marylanders at St. Mary's. Precious little, in fact, was ever utilized for its intended purpose; the Indian trade and island commerce came to a crushing halt. The threat of starvation among the islanders loomed large, and Evelin was almost universally despised at Kent. Two of Claiborne's trusted agents, John Butler and Thomas Smith, led the resistance against the traitor, and soon became marked men by the Maryland leadership. The islanders remained adamant in their refusal to betray their allegiances. In a last-ditch effort, Evelin was sent to take peaceful possession of the island with a commissioner from St. Mary's. He addressed the assembled population of the island at Kent Fort and was soundly rebuffed.[35]

Governor Calvert, whose fortunes against the Kent Islanders in the past had not been good, was reluctant to employ force of arms in installing Evelin to command without instructions from his brother in England. In the late fall of 1637, however, intelligence arrived suggesting that a possible attack upon the colony by Susquehannock Indians to the north was in the offing. The Maryland Council, fearing that the Virginians might supply the Indians with guns via the trading post at Palmer's Island, determined that both Kent and Palmer's islands would have to be subdued once and for all.[36]

Immediately Calvert gathered together a force of about twenty musketeers and placed them under the command of Cornwaleys, while taking personal charge of the expedition. Near the end of November 1637 he set sail from St. Mary's for Kent Island, intending to apprehend the leaders of the opposition, Smith and Butler, "and by the example of theire punishm^t. to reduce the rest to obedience." The winter weather, however, failed to cooperate, and though the Governor remained at sea for a week, he was unable to cross the Bay.[37]

In early February, Calvert learned that the Susquehannocks, encouraged by Captain Thomas Smith, still intended to make war against St. Mary's. Under Smith, the Kent Islanders had fortified Palmer's Island and were preparing to reinforce the place with additional men and supplies. Calvert resolved to act immediately. Another expedition was prepared, with thirty musketeers under Cornwaleys, with Calvert in the lead, and accompanied by Evelin.[38] The Marylanders, this time, crossed without mishap, arrived at the southernmost end of Kent Island, and landed a little before sunrise near Captain Claiborne's house, which was "seated wthin a small ffort of Pallysadoes." Though the gate facing the sea was barred, one of the Governor's company, possibly Evelin, was acquainted with another entrance, and the Marylanders took the fort by surprise and without opposition. Though a search for Butler and Smith, "the cheif incenduaries of the former seditions and mutinies upon the island," failed, Calvert was not deterred. He promptly rounded up all of the persons in the fort and secured them from escape. He then set off upon a march, prisoners in hand, towards Butler's plantation (called The Great Thicket) some five miles distant, and directed his pinnace to rendezvous with him at Craford, Evelin's seat on the island. At a half-mile distance from The Great Thicket, he dispatched an ensign named Clerck with ten musketeers to surprise and take Butler and bring him to Craford. The capture was conducted successfully and without mishap. Calvert then directed his sergeant, Robert Vaughn, with six musketeers to Thomas Smith's plantation at Beaver Neck, across a small creek and opposite Butler's plantation. Smith was also captured. He and Butler were imprisoned aboard the pinnace and charged with the crime of piracy.[39]

Governor Calvert, having severed the head of opposition from the body, issued a proclamation of general pardon to all Kent Islanders (except Butler and Smith) who submitted to Lord Baltimore's government within twenty-four hours. Kent Island submitted en masse. Governor Calvert then directed that the islanders would have to accept Lord Baltimore's patents for lands upon the island, and that new boundaries would be surveyed and laid out in the spring. Captain Evelin was left in command, and the two resistance leaders, Smith and Butler, were brought back to St. Mary's under a close, heavy guard.[40]

Leonard Calvert sought clemency for Butler, taking him from the sheriff's custody and into his own home to attempt to win him over to Lord Baltimore's side. If he could successfully secure the influential Butler's support, the population of Kent Island might follow suit. Indeed, if all went well, the capable Butler might even be groomed for a command on the island. Smith, who had commanded two of Claiborne's ships, was another matter. It was he, and another Kent Islander, Edward Beckler, who were charged with the death of William Ashmore during the April 23, 1635, Battle of the Pocomoke. Smith, it was clear, could not be treated so generously. An example had to be made. Thus, in March 1638, he was indicted, found guilty, and sentenced to be hanged for piracy and murder—the first conviction for piratical acts in Chesapeake history. Governor Calvert, hoping that his point had been made and that mercy would temper allegiances, issued a stay of execution for Smith, and the condemned was released on bail.[41]

Smith was not to be tamed. Returning to Kent Island, he raised a revolt against the Maryland government. A second expedition was fitted out, again bringing Calvert and fifty musketeers to the island. Kent Fort was reinforced with several cannons, and all of Cloberry's goods and indentured servants were removed. The company was ruined. Again Smith was captured and brought to St. Mary's under guard. This time, no mercy was granted, and he was hung by the neck—not as a pirate, but as a rebel.[42]

John Butler, converted to the Maryland cause, no doubt as much by an appreciation for the dramatic shift in the balance of power as by Calvert's persuasion, was appointed on May 27, 1638, to the post of

Captain of the Militia Band of the Isle of Kent. His authority, ironically, included the mustering of inhabitants capable of bearing arms to repel pirate invasions and Indians, and to suppress mutiny and civil disorder.[43]

Captain William Claiborne, disgraced by charges of the Maryland Assembly on March 24, 1638, of "grevious crimes of pyracie and murther" for the April 23, 1635, affair on the Pocomoke, became a wanted criminal and outlaw in the Maryland colony. As a consequence, all of "his lands and tenements which he was seized of . . . goods and chatteles which he hath within this Province" were forfeited to Lord Baltimore.[44] Despite the inevitable petition which Claiborne submitted to King Charles I, the crown was unwilling to consider the issue and referred it to the Lords Commissioners of Plantations. Fortune continued to frown on the former Virginia Secretary of State, for in April 1638, the commissioners ruled in Lord Baltimore's favor. With such powerful political forces in England supportive of Maryland, and with Kent and Palmer's islands firmly in Governor Calvert's hands, the Governor of Virginia withdrew support from William Claiborne entirely. The islands belonged to Maryland.[45]

III

The Plundering Time

In the winter of 1641-1642, Captain Richard Ingle, a native of Redriff, Surrey, England, and master of the good ship *Eleanor of London,* entered the waters of the Chesapeake Bay, bound for St. Mary's City. Aboard his vessel he carried as passenger Captain Thomas Cornwaleys, veteran of the Kent Island conflict, and one of the Maryland colony's most prominent citizens, returning to his estate after spending several months in England. Ingle was no stranger to the Chesapeake, having plied the Virginia trade for nearly a decade, and on occasion he had hauled freight for his friend Cornwaleys.[1] Neither he nor Cornwaleys could have suspected that within two years they would soon be playing opposite roles in a tragic episode that would come to be known in tidewater history as the Plundering Time.

Cecil Calvert, Lord Baltimore, was undoubtedly happy to see his brother Leonard, the Governor of Maryland. It had been eight years since Leonard had landed in the Chesapeake to found the Maryland colony on his brother's behalf, and now he had returned to England on matters of the greatest concern. There were important moves afoot that needed to be discussed and considered, not the least of which was the terrible schism developing between England's Anglican King Charles I and the largely Puritan Parliament. Civil war was almost certain to break out, and the Catholic Lord Baltimore's position was deemed precarious at best. Though the Calverts had been deeply bound to Charles for his support of their colonial endeavors, they knew that if the King were overthrown, the Maryland Charter, in which their very authority rested, might well be revoked. Baltimore had learned over the years to cope with the Anglican King, but he was astute enough to realize that if he wished to maintain control of Maryland, he would henceforth be obliged to tread a very narrow path between the two contending forces. For the moment he could ill afford to tilt toward one side or the other, and wisely resolved to maintain a neutral position throughout the turbulent days ahead, both for his own benefit and for the peace and prosperity of his colony. But peace and prosperity in Maryland in the days to come would become a most rare commodity.

When civil war erupted in England, King Charles was hard pressed from the outset by the Roundheads of Parliment, and it was clear that the loyal colonies on the Chesapeake, for the most part, would have to fend for themselves. Yet he did take time to dispatch orders to Maryland to seize any Parliament ships and goods in the colony, along with their traitorous companies.[2] Giles Brent, the Acting Governor of Maryland in Leonard Calvert's absence, whose political wisdom was far less astute than that of either Lord Baltimore or Governor Calvert, eagerly cast about in an effort to fulfill the royal command. When Richard Ingle returned to the Chesapeake in January 1644 as master of the pinnace *Reformation,* he was destined to find himself, from charges leveled against him by one William Hardige, the unhappy subject of Brent's overzealous dedication to the Crown.[3]

Hardige was a Maryland tailor who had frequently been involved in suits for debts to Thomas Cornwaleys and others. It was surprising then to no one when, about the middle of January, the boatswain of the good ship *Reformation* filed suit against Hardige for tobacco (then the equivalent of hard cash), returnable by February 1.[4] It is uncertain whether Hardige's resentment over the suit (as Cornwaleys later charged) was the motivating factor in his subsequent actions, but he lost no time in informing Maryland authorities that *Reformation*'s master, and friend to Cornwaleys, Richard Ingle, had recently uttered treasonable words against the King. Hardige informed the Attorney General of Maryland John Lewger that in March or April, 1642, he had heard Ingle state, at both Kent Island and at St. Mary's, that he was a "Captaine of Gravesend," for the Parliament and against the King. In February, at Accomac, Ingle had been commanded in the King's name to come ashore, or so Hardige alleged he had been told by Ingle. He had refused to do so in the name of Parliament, and, standing with "his curtelaxe drawn, said, he that came aboard he would cutt off his head."[5]

Hardige's accusation was just the kind of information Brent had been looking for. Three days later a warrant was issued to Hardige by the colony secretary to arrest Ingle upon charges of high treason.

Adding insult to injury, Ingle's friend Thomas Cornwaleys was force-fully instructed to assist the tailor in his duty "to use all means for apprhending of Ingle, & to keep it secrett." Brent directed St. Mary's Sheriff Edward Packer to seize *Reformation* and all of the goods aboard and to take an inventory of the ship's furniture, tackle, and goods belonging to Ingle or in his possession. A proclamation was to be published and tacked to the mainmast of the ship:[6]

> *These are to publish & proclayme to all persons as well seamen as others that Richard Ingle master of this ship is arrested vpon highe treason to his Majesty & therefore to require all persons to be aiding & assisting to his Lordships officer in the seising of this ship, & not to offer any resistence or contempt thervnto nor be any otherwaies aiding or assisting to the said R. Ingle, vpon p[er]ill of highe treason to his Majesty.*[7]

On January 18 the unsuspecting Ingle was arrested and taken into custody by Sheriff Packer, and *Reformation* and all of her goods were seized. A guard under the command of one John Hampton, a planter, was placed aboard the ship with express orders not to permit Ingle aboard under any circumstances without a warrant from the Lieuten-ant Governor.[8] Since the complaints against him were likely to result in "great demurrage to the ship, & other damages and encombrances in the gathering of his debts," Ingle was extended the right of bail, placed at one barrel of powder and 400 pounds of shot as a bond to guarantee his or his attorney's appearance in court on February 1.

Incredibly, despite Giles Brent's specific instructions and the con-stant presence of Sheriff Packer, Richard Ingle had soon boarded *Reformation* and escaped in a most controversial manner. Packer ex-onerated himself by noting that he had no prison "but his owne hands" with which to confine the alleged traitor, and had been obliged to guard him personally. He later testified that he had supposed "by certaine words spoken by the Secretary" that Brent and the Council had decided to permit Ingle to board his ship. When Captain Corn-waleys and James Neale (one of the Council members) came from a Council meeting and escorted Ingle aboard *Reformation*, he had ac-companied them.[9] Cornwaleys later explained his actions in the affair by stating that he understood the charges against Ingle to have been "of no importance but sugggested of mere malice of the accuser william hardige." He further claimed it was his understanding that Ingle was permitted aboard the ship with the full consent of Brent and the Council.[10]

When Ingle, Neale, Cornwaleys, and Sheriff Packer boarded *Refor-mation*, Cornwaleys instantly put the guard at ease. "All is quiet and peace," he told Hampton, and then persuaded him to turn over his rapier to the gunner of the ship and to order the guard to lay down their arms and disperse. Dutifully, Hampton, a simple planter, followed Cornwaleys's directions. After all, when the most influential citizen of the colony, in company with a member of the Council and the sheriff of the county, coming directly from a meeting with the Acting Governor, directed it, who was he to object?[11]

Suddenly Ingle and his men seized the weapons and the ship. Packer was helpless to stop them. It was later charged that the captain of *Reformation* and at least three of his men—William Durford, John Durford, and Frederick Johnson—fell to beating and wounding the guards before executing their escape.[12] Then, after setting Cornwaleys and his party ashore, the ship's anchor was raised, and *Reformation* glided gracefully down the St. Mary's River.

Brent was undoubtedly furious over the fiasco, and immediately suspended Sheriff Packer. Sworn in in his place was one Robert Ellyson. Ellyson's first act, on January 20, was to issue a warrant for Ingle. Ingle was to turn himself in before February 1 to answer charges of treason, and any person that might bear witness to such crime was directed to present his information to Attorney General Lewger.[13]

Ingle was most certainly angered at his arrest, but had enough presence of mind to make an effort to deny his accusers the means of pursuit. As Ellyson prepared the warrant for his arrest, Ingle brought *Reformation* to anchor in St. Georges Creek, at the entrance to St. Mary's River. There, he fell upon and captured several vessels belonging to one Henry Bishop and several others, seized their guns and other goods, and then, in a vindictive rage, "did threaten to assault & beate downe the dwelling houses of the inhabitants of this colony yea even the Leiutenant Gen: pyratically & mutinously."[14] It was not a hollow threat.

At St. Mary's City, despite the fact that Ingle was no longer available to answer charges against himself, namely, those of carrying out "certaine treasonable & pyraticall offences," Attorney General Lewger formally proceeded to present the charges against him to a jury. On January 29 at a pretrial hearing, William Hardige was summoned to give evidence of the charge of high treason and related in full his accusations.[15] On February 1, a jury of twelve was empaneled to hear Hardige's and the others accusations.[16]

Attorney General Lewger, stating that the court had power to consider treason beyond the jurisdiction of the province to determine whether Ingle should be tried in England, presented three bills for the jury to consider. The first addressed Hardige's charge that Ingle drew arms against the King in the name of Parliament while at Accomac.

The second claimed that he, "by the instigaōn of the divell, & example of other traitors & enemies of his majestie" levied, wore, and bore arms against the Crown, and had accepted and exercised command of a captainship for the town of Gravesend, a Parliament stronghold, against the King. The third bill addressed a charge that Ingle, while riding in *Reformation* near St. Clement's Island in the Potomac River, spoke malicious and scandalous words against Prince Rupert, the King's Lieutenant General in England, calling him a "rogue and rascall."

The charges were admittedly weak and impossible to prove. Not surprisingly, the jury returned each of the bills *Ignoramus.*[17]

The same day, a second jury was empaneled to evaluate the charge that Ingle had broken away from Sheriff Packer by force. Again the jury returned *Ignoramus.*[18]

Later in the afternoon, the first jury was recalled and handed two more bills. The first was to determine whether Ingle had, in April 1643, while at Mattapanian, on the south side of the entrance to the Patuxent River, stated "that Prince Rupert was Prince Traitor & Prince rogue, and if he had him aboard the ship he would whip him at the capsten." Again the jury returned *Ignoramus.* The second bill alleged that on March 30, 1643, Ingle had stated, while aboard his ship in St. Georges Creek, that King Charles I "was no king neither would be no king, nor could be no king, unless he did joine with Parlament." To this charge, the inquest could not agree on a decision and adjourned at 7:00 P.M. until the following Saturday, February 3.[19]

On Saturday, Attorney General Lewger discharged the jury, and the bill was given to another, which returned it *Ignoramus.* Despite the consistency of the returns, Lewger persisted. On February 5, yet another jury was summoned, once more to address the charge that Ingle had uttered treasonable statements while in St. Georges Creek, but this jury could not agree and was discharged.[20]

On February 8, Lewger finally introduced a charge that would stick. Ingle was accused of the "crimes of pyracie, mutinie, trespasse contempt & misdemeanor" for the seizure of vessels and goods belonging to Henry Bishop and others in St. Georges Creek on January 20. The proceedings were not conducted without great bias, for one of the jurymen was Bishop himself and another was Nicholas Cossin, a planter whom Ingle had sued for tobacco due him the preceding year. This time the finding was against Ingle, and he was impeached.[21]

It was a hollow—and ultimately fatal—victory for the Maryland government. Aside from securing the bail left behind and ordering seizure of all goods and debts in the colony due Ingle, there was, considering the embarrassing manner in which he had escaped, precious little to gloat about. John Lewger immediately demanded 600 pounds of tobacco in payment for some plate and a scimitar Ingle had procured from him, for which Cornwaleys quickly agreed to pledge security. Another £1,123 sterling was still outstanding.[22]

Lewger then turned his attention to the four men who had allegedly permitted the "Rescous and Escape of an offendor imprisond for highe Treason." Neale was temporarily suspended from the Council, but, probably owing to his influential position, was not prosecuted and was later reinstated. Hampton and Packer, too, were charged but not prosecuted, undoubtedly because of their direct familial relationship to the attorney general, although the former sheriff of St. Mary's was never to regain his job. Someone, however, had to be punished, and Thomas Cornwaleys became the scapegoat. He was obviously the most instrumental person involved in the fiasco, and was charged, prosecuted, and levied a fine of one thousand pounds of tobacco (valued at five pounds sterling) to be paid to the attorney Thomas Wyatt, commander of Kent Island, in behalf of a debt owed by Governor Calvert. It was the highest fine the law allowed, and was easily paid by the wealthy planter.[23]

The overall cost to Thomas Cornwaleys was to be much greater than the fine of a thousand pounds of tobacco. Feelings against him were strong, and within a short time had grown to such proportions that he was compelled, for his own safety, to flee St. Mary's County. Leaving his estate in the hands of his factor, Cuthbert Fenwick, he joined Richard Ingle aboard his ship, still lying in St. Georges Creek. In March, it was said, Ingle departed for London, then in open rebellion against the King and the seat of Parliament's forces, to join the "enemies & rebels" against the Crown. Soon after his arrival, according to some sources, the master of *Reformation* testified before a Parliamentary committee concerning Cornwaleys' losses sustained in the interest of Parliament and attesting to his loyalty to their cause.[24]

Aside from the excitement of the Ingle affair, which everyone assumed had ended with his flight to London, the Chesapeake tidewater at first experienced mercifully few ripples from the far-off conflict in England. Both the governments of Maryland and Virginia had remained royalist, and trade with the King's largest stronghold, the port of Bristol, was brisk, though even occasional visits by Parliament ships, in Virginia at least, were tolerated.

Occasionally, however, the proximity of both Parliament and royalist vessels in the tidewater at one time was bound to result in open hostility. Such was the case on a fine spring day in 1644. It was unhappily to be the signal for one of the worst massacres in colonial Virginia history to begin.

On the morning of April 15, a Dutch herring buss drifted lazily down the James River from Jamestown. As she approached Blanck Point, her master, David de Vries, fresh from a courtesy call on William Berkeley, Virginia's new governor, spied a large Bristol flyboat and decided to come to anchor nearby. Shortly afterward, with the onset of flood tide, the Dutchman noted two large, unidentified ships sailing upriver toward the Bristolman, and then come alongside her. Suddenly, the two ships broke out the ensigns of Parliament and simultaneously opened up with blistering broadsides on the unsuspecting flyboat. De Vries watched with excitement as men scurried about the decks of the Parliament ships unsuccessfully attempting to grapple the royalist to board and take her in hand-to-hand combat. Though the intense fire from the Parliament ships brought down some spars and blocks, the surprised royalist captain did not lose his head, and immediately began cutting his cables. With the aid of the river currents, he was able to work his craft out of reach, and by poling and rowing pushed the ship well up into a shallow creek beyond Blanck Point where his deeper-draft attackers could not go.[25]

"Lying there out of musket range," de Vries observed in his journal, *the royalist plied a gun so smartly that his foes could not launch their small boats to board her, nor avail themselves of further broadsides. Both parties kept up a desultory fire by single cannons which, however, did considerable damage to all three, and caused many casualties.*[26]

The battle was keenly watched, not only by de Vries, but by Indians along the shores. It was a curious and fascinating thing to them—Englishmen fighting Englishman. The message was not lost.

By dusk, neither side had gained the upper hand. The London ships, realizing that their surprise attack had failed and that the countryside was by now fully aroused, dropped far down the river and came to anchor. There, de Vries, a neutral, boarded the larger of the two ships and spent an entertaining evening with her officers discussing the fight. He was told in the course of conversation that they had sought to buy tobacco in Virginia, but that the planters were all royalists and refused to sell them any. Rather than return home to London empty-handed, they had decided to compensate themselves by attacking and seizing the Bristol ship—a most costly exercise for both sides. The following morning de Vries visited the Bristolman and learned that she had suffered terribly from the heavy gunfire. One unfortunate Virginia planter, aboard at the time to buy trade goods, had been caught in the surprise attack and was killed by a cannonball.[27]

De Vries departed Virginia soon afterward, but none too soon for his own good. On Holy Thursday, April 18, three days after the engagement, an Indian uprising, hatched in the mind of the aged but wily Chief Opechancanough, an influential Indian leader determined to kill every Englishman in Virginia, sprang to life. More than five hundred settlers were massacred. It was later reported in Massachusetts that a captured Indian had stated that the moment for the uprising had been deemed ripe when "they understood that they were at war in England, and began to go to war among themselves, for they had seen a fight in the river between a London ship, which had been for parliament, and a Bristol ship, which was for the King." The entire colony's survival was in jeopardy. Now, even Parliament was sensitive to the terrible danger to the royalist colony. On August 26, the House of Commons granted permission to several persons to transport arms, munitions, clothes, and victuals, custom-free to the Chesapeake "for the supply and Defence and Relief of the Planters." Ultimately, Governor Berkeley, a cavalier loyal to the Crown and dedicated to Virginia, was able to mount a series of expeditions against the Indians, defeat them, and capture Opechancanough. The setbacks and hardships to the colony, caused by the overflow of civil war into Virginia, however, had been monumental.[28]

In October 1644 Richard Ingle was still smarting from the affair in St. Mary's months before, but now fully committed to the cause of Parliament. He was also apparently convinced, because of the still fluid state of trade in the Chesapeake, that he might return to Maryland. This time, however, he would carry the force of arms, for he had secured for *Reformation* one of the first letters of marque and reprisal granted by Parliament, and, by his commission, was authorized by the Lord High Admiral of England "to seize and take all ships and vessels with their goods and company, in or outward bound, to or from any place" hostile to Parliament or which had been found to "have traded with any of the Inhabitants of such place since their desertion of the King and Parliament . . . "[29] Only recently, petitions to the House of Lords had been submitted and approved to interrupt the trade of the Dutch, who had been siphoning off much of the American commerce. Such actions opened up even more avenues for any ambitious Parliamentarian so inclined. For Richard Ingle, he could trade if he wished, but he could also make war.[30]

Ingle's friend Cornwaleys remained in England when he sailed, but was apparently determined to keep his options open for a possible return to Maryland after the war ended, and resolved to continue his trading as before. He entrusted Ingle with a cargo of shoes, stockings, woolen and linen cloth, and other goods "useful in that country," valued at two hundred to two hundred and fifty pounds in England, and consigned to his factor in St. Mary's, Cuthbert Fenwick.[31]

By September 1644, when Governor Leonard Calvert had returned to Maryland, Parliament was in virtual control of the government of England, though outwardly maintaining that its acts were those of itself and the King. Upon his arrival, Calvert barely had time to assess the situation in the colony before his old nemesis, Captain William Claiborne, now elevated to Treasurer of Virginia and again a member of the Virginia Council of State, decided the moment was ripe to forcefully reassert his claim to Kent Island. Claiborne sailed to the island with ten or twelve men and "stirred up the inhabitants with his own company and seven or eight others" brought from Chicacoun, Virginia, to rebellion. First the home of Giles Brent, Lieutenant Governor and now Commander of Kent Island, was seized. Then Kent Fort was taken, and Claiborne's authority over the entire island was quickly reestablished.[32]

Leonard Calvert responded cautiously by dispatching a secret reconnaissance expedition of eight men under the command of two loyal Marylanders, Mark Phypho and John Genalles, to discover Claiborne's strength, whether there were any ships of force present, and what disturbances had been committed.[33]

Within a short time Calvert's problems had more than doubled. Several days after dispatching the reconnaissance, on December 29, Richard Ingle arrived in Maryland waters aboard the armed letter of marque ship *Reformation* bound for St. Mary's. Though the Protestant captain carried articles of trade ostensibly intended for Thomas Cornwaleys' factor, revenge served as his true guide. While in Virginia he harangued his crew, many of whom had been taken aboard there, "to go up in the quality of a man-of-war to Maryland to plunder the Papists." He informed his men of his commission from Parliament, read a line or two of it to them, and contracted with them "for a sixth part of all the pillage for their adventuring of their lives with him."[34]

Soon after *Reformation* entered Maryland waters, Ingle learned that a Dutch ship, *Speagle,* was in the St. Mary's River at St. Inigoes trading. In "a rage and fury" he turned his own vessel about and prepared to return to Accomac, Virginia. Why he was upset by the presence of a Dutch ship can only be conjectured. In view of the events that followed, it would appear that he was deeply concerned that the ship, apparently a vessel of some force, might help Calvert defeat his real objectives—to extract revenge and plunder the colony—before his surprise was complete. Before he departed, however, he dispatched a letter to key Protestants in Maryland designed to build support for his actions within the colony, which made his intentions crystal clear. He informed them "of a Commission which he had from Parliament to plunder all Papists and root them out of Maryland (terming them by the title of vermin) and to plunder all them as would take up arms with him." He closed by informing them that there were two more ships carrying commissions from Parliament in other sections of the tidewater also preparing to swoop down upon the hated Catholics.[35] This last statement, in light of later events, appears to have been pure balderdash designed to excite the support of local Parliamentarians and to frighten royalists, for no such vessels ever appeared.

Governor Calvert was painfully aware of the recent turn of events in Parliament's favor as a result of the climatic Battle of Marston Moor in which royalist forces were soundly defeated. Yet he was still ignorant of Ingle's piratical intentions and quickly sought to mollify him by forgetting all of the unseemly events relating to the piracy conviction. He enlisted the support of the influential Jesuit priest Father Thomas Copely, "one of the chiefest inhabitants of the Province." Two letters were drafted, one by Calvert, and the other by Copely. Cornwaleys' agent in Maryland, Cuthbert Fenwick, an obvious choice as go-between, was directed to pursue *Reformation* into Virginia to deliver the letters to Ingle. Before undertaking the mission, however, Fenwick took the precaution of hiding much of Cornwaleys' silver plate in the forest until the potential turmoil of impending events subsided. The factor prepared for the voyage to Virginia by sending one Thomas Harrison, a servant whose indenture had been purchased from Ingle by Cornwaleys sometime earlier, and another servant, Edward Matthews, to assist a third, Andrew Monroe, in bringing a small pinnace near to the Cornwaleys manor house to prepare for the trip. Apparently one of Ingle's supporters, Monroe stoutly refused to bring the pinnace in.[36]

Before Fenwick could sail, Ingle again appeared, this time his crew enlarged by a dozen "of the most rascally fellows of desperate fortunes he could get in Virginia." The factor dutifully presented him with the letters, which graciously invited him to return to Maryland and assured him "of all free and friendly trade." The sea captain read the documents, then stuffed them into his pocket. He informed the factor grimly that "they came to late," and imprisoned him in the ship's roundhouse.[37]

With deliberation, borne of a thirst for revenge as much as duty to the Puritan cause, Ingle sailed into St. Mary's River about the second week of February 1645. With little difficulty or commotion, he quietly landed and captured St. Inigoes Fort, a small earthen work commanding the water approach to St. Mary's City. The fort, which served primarily as a refuge in case of Indian attack, had been armed with little more than a battery of small cannons, called "murtherers," and a few muskets,[38] and was apparently either undefended or lightly manned when taken.

Whether or not Ingle had joined forces with Claiborne at the time of the advance into the St. Mary's is unknown, though shortly after Christmas, the latter had proposed to the Kent Islanders that he go with twenty of his men and a force of islanders to capture Governor Calvert and the fort protecting St. Mary's.[39]

Ingle next moved upriver to St. Inigoes Creek, approximately three miles below St. Mary's City. Here, he fell upon and captured *Speagle*, "saying it was because he feared the inhabitants of Maryland would use it against him." After carrying the ship and installing his mate, a Virginia carpenter named John Durford, as commander, he politely informed the Dutch captain that his ship would be given back to him later. The promise seemed to lack conviction as Ingle pushed ahead with the next phase of his invasion—a direct assault on St. Mary's City itself.[40]

The capital of Maryland, totally unprepared for the attack by Ingle and his two ships, fell with barely a whimper on February 14. Lieutenant Governor Brent and Attorney General Lewger were among the more prominent citizens surprised, taken captive, and held prisoner aboard *Reformation*.[41] Lewger had apparently been taken while near naked. The capture of Leonard Calvert was prevented only by his timely flight and exile in Virginia.[42]

Ingle then moved to quell all possible hopes of opposition rallying against him. The one remaining potential strong point on the western shore was none other than the new manor house of Thomas Cornwaleys on St. Inigoes Creek. In the house, which was apparently being utilized as the colony arsenal, were stored "200 iron guns, [and] several hand guns" valued at £20. Lying at anchor in the adjacent creek was the spanking-new pinnace which Andrew Monroe had refused to move, replete with rigging, cables, anchors, small guns, pots, kettles, bedding, carpenters' tools, and a small boat with oars, valued at £250. There was also a shallop with mast, sail, and oars, and two small boats, altogether valued at £30. If he could take these vessels, his flotilla would be the largest armed force afloat on the Chesapeake, and if he could occupy the house, he would possess a formidable garrison for the protection of his forces ashore, and from which he might conduct forays at will against Catholics throughout the colony.[44]

Ingle summoned Cuthbert Fenwick, whom he had held prisoner overnight, to his great cabin. The two men were soon drinking and laughing loudly. Fenwick, apparently hoping to make the most of the camaraderie and their mutual association with Cornwaleys, requested leave to be put ashore. Ingle sobered instantly, informing his companion that he would be permitted to land only after he signed a warrant, a note to his wife, the acting mistress of Cornwaleys's house, for the delivering up and use of Cornwaleys's pinnace, house, and arms. The captain assured the factor that none of the goods or the house "would be spoiled or damaged" and vowed to "keep indemnified" for Cornwaleys and "to wrong nobody that was in the house," promising to look after his friend's property carefully. Finally, Fenwick agreed and signed the document, urging Ingle, even as the ink dried, not to forget his pledge.[45]

"Nay," Ingle assured him solemnly, "if I have promised, I will be as good as my word."

He then summoned two watermen to take Fenwick ashore in a wherry. At the same time he quietly ordered a party of seamen, led by John Sturman, a cooper, to go ashore in the ship's boat, seize Fenwick, and bring him back after the warrant had been delivered.[46]

Within a short time a landing party under the command of John and Thomas Sturman and William Hardwick prepared to occupy the estate of Captain Thomas Cornwaleys, and all memory of the solemnly pledged agreement between the captain and the factor faded as the privateersmen wandered about the home of the richest man in Maryland.

In the hallways they discovered cupboards filled with spices, wax, drugs, candles, shoes, and an iron-bound chest containing satin damask petticoats laced with gold and silver. There were Turkish carpets and great chests filled with quilts, curtains, cushions, and linens. In the parlor were magnificent inlaid chairs and table, an enormous cypress chest valued at £130, and ornate Flemish wall hangings, curtains, and carpets. By the fireplace lay a great pair of andirons, tongs, bellows, and sundry items of convenience. In other rooms they discovered shelves of books, tapestries, deep feather beds, boxes of porcelains and china, exquisite carpets, brass and pewter, and fine silver plate. In the servants' quarters and in adjacent outbuildings were the more mundane artifacts of daily life: a smith's forge and tools, ironware, carpentry tools, ploughs, yokes, a wain, chains, and cables. In the fields there were more than 120 head of cattle, innumerable goats, sheep, swine, and horses. There were dozens of valuable hogsheads of tobacco. The household staff consisted of three black slaves and numerous indentured English servants. And, most happily for the thirsty privateersmen, there was a great store of beer, wine, and "strong waters." In all, Ingle was now commander of an estate whose goods alone were valued at £2,623. Thomas Cornwaleys, even on the Chesapeake frontier, had been a man accustomed to a "splendid manner of living."[47]

Cornwaleys's estate was immediately garrisoned, and after a brief inspection, Captain Ingle returned to his ship. In his absence the privateersmen began living in fashion and "in all riot" off the manor's abundance. Indiscriminate plundering became the rule. The silver plate hidden by Fenwick in the nearby forest was soon discovered and divided into eight parts, with the chief of the garrison taking a full share. The pillage of the manor was carried out with vigor, as the raiders

> plundered and Carryed away all things in It, pulled downe and burnt the pales [fences] about it, killed and destroyed all the Swine and Goates and killed or mismarked allmost all the Cattle, tooke or dispersed all the Servants, Carryed away a Great quantity of Sawn Boards from the pitts, and ript up Some floors of the house . . . Thomas and John Sturman forst themselves of the . . . house as theire owne, dwelt in it Soe long as they please and at their departing tooke the locks from the doors and ye Glass from the windowes and in fine ruind his whole Estate to the damage of . . . at least two or three thousand pounds.[48]

When Ingle returned, rather than condemn the action of his men carried out against the property of a former associate, he "did send for all the remainder of the goods that was in the house and gave order to set the house on fire."[49]

Thus commenced a time of severe hardship for Catholic Maryland lasting for nearly two years. For the Jesuit missionaries in the colony it was a period of privation and death. Father Roger Rigby, living with the Patuxent Indians on the Patuxent River, and Father John Cooper, residing at St. Inigoes, were forced to flee for their lives across the Potomac to Virginia. Both died there the following year, some said, at the hands of Ingle's ruffians. Father Bernard Hartwell, also of St. Inigoes, apparently went into hiding, but he too died, in 1646, a refugee from the privateersmen to the very end. Father Copely of St. Mary's City, and the venerable Father White, ensconced among the Indians at Port Tobacco, were captured and sent to England in chains to face charges of treason.[50]

More than two thousand pounds sterling worth of church property was seized or destroyed. At St. Mary's City, St. Inigoes, and Port

Tobacco all of the church and house furnishings, including rich tapestries, silver plate, gold, diamond, ruby, and sapphire jewelry (undoubtedly sacred vessels and vestments employed in church services), and a sizable library of books were stolen. The chapel house at St. Mary's was burned to the ground, and sixty cattle dispersed. Hogs and other livestock disappeared, along with twenty-one indentured servants. Over twenty thousand pounds of tobacco, six hundred bushels of Indian corn, all of the wheat, peas, oats, and barley, as well as two large boats and thirty pounds of beaver skins, were stolen.[51]

Ingle moved swiftly and resolutely with little resistance against many prominent Marylanders. The plantation of Giles and Margaret Brent on Kent Island was plundered (undoubtedly with the aid of William Claiborne) of a pinnace, grain, tobacco, furniture, jewelry, silver, account books and records, and eight servants. The estates of other prominent citizens, such as Thomas Gerard of Colton's Point, were pillaged to the point of ruination.[52]

The mode of robbery followed a pattern that was to become familiar in the weeks and months that followed, continuing well after Ingle's departure. A party of Ingle's men would suddenly appear without warning at a plantation and demand tobacco, corn, or other commodities actually or allegedly owed to Thomas Cornwaleys or his factor Cuthbert Fenwick. If opposed, they would seize the commodity in question and haul it off to *Reformation* without giving a receipt. Occasionally, when protests were made, Ingle would order the goods forcibly seized and the tobacco barn or warehouse in which it had been stored burned to the ground. In time, the raiders made little pretense, confiscating goods without offering any excuse whatsoever.[53]

Ingle sought to cloak his vindictive plundering beneath a mantle of political loyalty and duty to Parliament. He required all colonists to take an oath against Lord Baltimore and King Charles. With a single exception, every Catholic in the colony refused. As a consequence, many were forced to flee for their lives and seek refuge in Virginia. Before the reign of terror had run its course, the population of Maryland would be reduced from four hundred to one hundred settlers, the Great Seal of the Province of Maryland was lost, and many of the official records of the colony destroyed.[54]

Captain Ingle did not forget to reward his Protestant supporters in Maryland, many of whom continued to pillage their neighbors' property well after his departure. Frequently, plundered property was provided for the "relief" of those settlers "well affected to Parliament," most commonly in the form of confiscated cattle, which were redistributed on the hoof with relative ease. Those that bore register marks, such as at St. Inigoes, where the right ear was cropped and the left ear was slit, were simply altered by "putting more slits in the ear, or by cropping of the ear still closer to the head and then slitting it, or cutting off both ears" to mask the original owners' marks.[55]

About the first week of April 1645, even as some Maryland Protestants began to prepare their own defenses "in a certain fortified citadel" of earth in the vicinity of St. Mary's against a possible reinvasion by Leonard Calvert, Captain Richard Ingle sailed for England, having remained in Maryland waters for fourteen weeks. He took with him as a prize the Dutch ship *Speagle,* which he had once solemnly pledged to return to its master, and the rich and varied fruits of his season of untempered plundering.[56] Maryland was left to its own devices, without a government (save for the Claiborne establishment on Kent Island), and a handful of Protestants scattered about the lower western shore to tame the land.

Finally, in the latter part of 1646, Governor Leonard Calvert, with the aid of Virginia's Governor William Berkeley, was able to raise a force of Virginians and exiled Marylanders to retake St. Mary's City and the colony. Pledging both his and the proprietor's estates to pay for the troops, Calvert crossed the Potomac River unopposed. His entry into a nearly deserted capital was unresisted. After almost two years of anarchy, the western shore of Maryland was restored to its former masters.

In 1649 members of the Maryland Assembly wrote a letter to Lord Baltimore, in which they recalled the bitter fruits of the colony's worst trial of survival to date.

> *Great and many have been the miseries calamities and other Sufferings which your Poor distressed People Inhabitants of this Province have sustained and undergone here since the beginning of that Heinous Rebellion first put in Practice by that Pirate Ingle and afterward almost for two years continued by his Complices and Confederates in which time most of your Lordships Loyal friends here were spoiled of their whole Estate and sent away as banished persons out of the Province those few that remained were plundered and deprived in a manner of all Livelyhood and subsistance only Beginning under that intollerable Yoke which they were forced to bear . . .* [57]

Though years of struggle lay ahead for the Lords Baltimore in achieving their claim to Kent Island, reestablishing the colony's prosperity, and inducing order, the Plundering Time of Richard Ingle was finally at an end.

IV

Dutch Capers and Crimson Raiders

S ir William Berkeley, His Majesty's Royal Governor of Virginia, appeared grim as the Council members filed by pairs and singly into the General Court chambers at Jamestown on June 20, 1665. Present were Thomas Ludwell, the court's able secretary and confidant to the Governor, and Colonels Miles Cary, Thomas Stegg, Thomas Swann, and Nathaniel Bacon. There was the former Governor of Virginia, now Councillor, and General of the Militia Richard Bennett, as well as George Reed, Francis Willis, and the patrician farmer Theodoric Bland. Also present was the powerful John Carter, whose arrival in the colony in the 1640s after the outbreak of civil war in England had not hindered his rise in colony affairs in the least. Carter was a curious sort, a planter noted for owning one of the largest libraries in the colony devoted to morality and the afterlife. He was already well on his way to laying the foundations of one of Virginia's most powerful dynasties.[1] All of these men had been summoned by the Governor from their various estates and plantations to discuss a most urgent matter—the outbreak of war between England and the States-General of Holland.

At fifty-eight years of age, William Berkeley had been Governor of Virginia off and on for nearly twenty-three years and had weathered well the violent political storms of the past. A cavalier of the first rank, he adamantly supported the monarchy of Charles I and stubbornly defied the reign of Oliver Cromwell, though it had meant the loss of office. With the assumption of Charles II to the throne in 1660, Berkeley again found himself Virginia's executive, albeit in a colony beset on all sides by perils, ranging from Indian raids to grasshopper plagues and economic depression. The days ahead, if past events were any indication, would prove to be as turbulent as any in the young colony's history.

Berkeley and the Council were well aware of the nature of the phenomenal political and military emergence of Holland at the conclusion of the bloody Thirty Years War in 1648 as a powerful national entity with the largest merchant marine and trade network in all of Europe. Both were cognizant of British national objectives, which had been bluntly and forthrightly stated by General George Monck. "What we want," the general admitted, "is more of the trade which the Dutch have."[2] The British Navigation Act of 1651, which sought to further that objective, had thrown down the gauntlet of economic—and, ultimately, military—warfare to the States-General.

As a consequence of the challenge, the First Anglo-Dutch War erupted in 1654. The cause of that indecisive, costly struggle had unfortunately remained unresolved, and the peace that followed was unstable at best. England continued to press forward, grasping for a greater share of the commercial pie, ever challenging the prosperity and naval superiority of Holland. Despite the transition from the Cromwellian era to the monarchy of Charles II, the national navy of England (now the Royal Navy) continued to grow. By the outbreak of the second war, the fleet was over 230 ships strong.[3] England refused to flag in her headlong race down the highway of imperial and economic ambition. A second Anglo-Dutch war was inevitable.

Throughout it all, little, if any, thought had been given to the colonial backwater of the Chesapeake region. This time it would become painfully evident that Dutch attentions would focus on the now rich trade between the Chesapeake colonies and England.

On January 24, 1665, the King issued a directive to Governor Berkeley to place Virginia on a war footing, and in a posture of defense "against the attempts and invasions of his most unjust enemies the Dutch now at war with him and his subjects." The order unfortunately failed to reach the Governor until June 3, more than four months after its initial issuance. Despite the delay, Berkeley was alarmed about the danger of possible Dutch attack and summoned the Council "to advise and consider of the best way of securing the said colony and ships trading thereunto."[4]

Debate in the Council chamber was never more serious than it was over the matter of defense, for the colony was woefully ill-equipped to protect the Chesapeake, much less the long miles of island-studded, sparsely-inhabited coastline. Weapons of every kind were in extremely short supply, and those that were available were in poor condition. Nothing better illustrated the inadequacy of the colony's defense capabilities than the general orders issued on June 21. The untried militia were directed to immediately muster in their respective meeting places—not to train, but to survey their arms. Any weapons found to be unusable—and there were unquestionably many—were to be repaired. The smiths of the colony were directed "to fix all such arms as shall be brought unto them any other work in their hands notwithstanding and to do the said work at such reasonable rates as the courts held in their respective counties shall judge fit."[5]

All militia officers were directed to stand ready to march on two days' notice. To better defend the shipping, all vessels in the colony were ordered to anchor only in one of four designated places: in the James River off Jamestown; in the York River off Tindall's Point; in Corotoman Creek on the Rappahannock; and at Pungoteague on the Eastern Shore. Hawsers were to be run ashore so that the ships at those places might be hauled up at the first sign of danger. Ten men out of every company of county militia were to be dispatched with tools and provisions to the designated anchorages to construct platforms for artillery batteries "and lines for small shott to defend the said ships." Work would begin in September and was to be completed with all possible speed. Since Virginia was very nearly bereft of ammunition and ordnance, Berkeley was requested by the Council to implore the Crown to supply the colony's wants. In the meantime, permission was sought to remove two guns out of every ship coming into port to furnish the batteries. The guns were to be returned to the ships upon their departure.[6]

Virginia was beset by difficulties on every front; not the least of these was the state of economic depression caused by low tobacco prices in Europe. For the time being, the Governor was obliged to scrape by on minimal military provisions. He was thus able to order only two hundred pounds sterling worth of emergency powder and shot ("Calvier and pistoll bullets and high swan shott") by the first ships returning to the colony from England. After careful consideration, it was decided to abandon a derelict fortification erected in 1640 at Point Comfort and bring its fourteen cannons, at public expense and at all possible speed, upriver for the defense of the capital at Jamestown. Finally, the militia commanders were instructed to hold their troops to "stand and remain ready to march" to the four principal anchorages at the first alarm.[7]

Governor Berkeley, given even the difficulties in hand, was not pessimistic about the outcome of a potential invasion. There could be no question about Dutch naval superiority. But should the Dutch enter the Chesapeake, Virginia's 1,500 dragoons, 2,500 "able men with snaphances," and a reserve of 3,000 to 4,000 militiamen (albeit poorly armed) left little doubt in the Governor's mind that the colony could be defended ashore. While some militia would hold fortifications and others would defend the shipping against boarding parties, enemy landings could be readily frustrated by roving companies of dragoons. The Governor had the utmost confidence in the militia's ability to strangle an inland invasion attempt. "I shal not doubt," he wrote optimistically, "to encounter with as many strangers of what nation so ever they are when they are out of the protection of their Great Gunns which they can never manage halfe a mile within our thicke woods." His able secretary, Thomas Ludwell, was of a like mind and noted in a letter to Lord Arlington in August that the enemy might certainly burn Virginians' houses by the waters, but the militia would make any "longer march too dangerous for them unlesse their purchasse were greater then they can expect here."[8]

The matter of maritime vulnerability was as much of a concern as any that faced the government. Virginia-bound vessels were severely undermanned owing to impressments by the Royal Navy while in European waters. Such poorly manned ships stood a good chance of meeting "with Dutch Men of Warr in the Channell, or else Where, on their returne for England." It was only a matter of time until similar attention would be paid to the Chesapeake by enemy warships and privateers (or "capers"). Orders had already reached the colony that no ship would be permitted to depart unless she had three more vessels in company, but without convoy escorts such measures proved marginally valuable at best.[9]

Though Berkeley was concerned with the possibility of a Dutch privateer or naval descent on the colony, he was equally distraught over the small but growing menace of piracy which was beginning to plague the sea-lanes of North Ameria. The Governor underscored that concern by noting that the waters were "so full of pirates that it is impossible for any ships to go home safely."[10]

In October, war preparations were temporarily forgotten and the issue of piracy brought to the fore when an English ship commanded by a certain Captain William Whiting arrived in the colony. Whiting, it seemed, had handily attacked, captured, and plundered a Spanish ship. Since England and Spain were, for the moment at least, at peace and technically friends, the captain was accused of piracy and arrested. His ship, lying at anchor in the Elizabeth River, was seized. Aboard, investigators discovered a number of Indian slaves who had been taken from the Spaniard and held as prisoners. The accused was committed to the custody of the sheriff of Jamestown until a preliminary hearing could be convened in November. The hapless slaves, "declared free

Indians and accordingly to have their liberties," were set free. After a preliminary hearing, Whiting was sent to England, aboard the first ship leaving the colony, to face trial in Admiralty Court.[11]

The toll of shipping bound from the Chesapeake for England had risen sharply, though every measure possible short of providing armed convoy guardships had been taken to ensure the safety of commercial vessels. As a consequence several influential London merchants heavily involved in the tobacco trade had requested, first in 1662 and again in 1664 and 1665, assistance in protecting that trade. In June 1665 the Privy Council finally acted by instructing the Admiralty to provide a convoy of Royal Navy warships to sail out of English waters, "beyond soundings," to meet the inward-bound tobacco fleet and convoy it safely home to England.[12] Simultaneously, the governors of Maryland and Virginia were instructed to order all ships leaving the Chesapeake to "associate and returne in Company for their better security."[13]

The tobacco fleet, despite such precautions, suffered several losses to Dutch warships on the homeward-bound voyage. Some merchantmen, which had ignored the convoy orders, suffered the consequences and not a few were captured. In November the Crown issued instructions that no ships trading in Virginia would be allowed to sail until April of the following year, and even then must sail only under convoy of an admiral and other officers appointed by the Governor. It was expected that such a timely imposition would permit enough ships to gather together to provide an adequate defense against enemy attack. Berkeley grimly pointed out to the Crown that even when both the Maryland and Virginia fleets were drawn together, the whole would still be inadequate in numbers and force to defend themselves against a single 30-gun man-of-war. Even a heavily armed privateer or pirate might wreak great damage. Nevertheless, orders were orders, and the Governor was obliged to give leave for the sailing of the convoy on or after April 15.[14] Berkeley's predictions came true when one of the fleet, a large Bristolman called *Alexander,* with 600 hogsheads of tobacco, was captured on the homeward bound voyage by a Dutch caper after a two-hour running fight.[15] It would not be the last time Berkeley's overruled concerns would be borne out.

The Virginia government's decision to fortify and protect key anchorages with batteries, including the river anchorage off Jamestown, and to abandon the derelict fort at Point Comfort was not without substantial merit. But when royal officials in England learned of the measure, they adamantly insisted that the eroding fort at the mouth of the James be reconstructed and strengthened, completely sabotaging Berkeley's own plans to protect Virginia's maritime interests. The Governor and the Council argued that a fort at the mouth of the river was useless since the entrance was "soe large that any Enemy Shipp may ride out of all possible dainger of the greatest Cannon in the world." They begged at least to be allowed to finish the fort and redoubts at Jamestown, the heart and center of the colony.[16] The King and Council were unmoved.

The Virginia Council followed the King's directive, though not without great misgivings about the "misinformation some Persons whose Particular interests carry them against the more publick concernments of this country and the merchants trading hither." In March 1666 the Council reiterated its deep concern about the order, noting that the fortification at Jamestown could be constructed at a fifth the cost of the one at Point Comfort and would be far more useful to the defense of shipping there. They sarcastically noted in the Council records that Point Comfort was

> the only place on the mouth of this river where we conceive it to be of no defence at all because ships cannot hale [sic] on shore but they will be exposed to the violence of all the winds of three quarters of the compass and the place so remote from all assistance that it cannot be defended but by a constant garrison in full pay to the almost insupportable charge of the country.[17]

Still, the Crown's decision stood. On March 29, 1666, the Governor and Council grudgingly instructed the sheriff of Nansemond County to impress forty men to work upon the fort at Point Comfort. They were to be joined by thirty men from Lower Norfolk County, twenty-five from Warwick County, and twenty from Elizabeth City County. A house forty feet long by twenty feet wide was to be erected at the site for the accommodation of the laborers. Every ship then riding in the James River, or ships that might later enter the river, would provide one carpenter, with provisions and tools, to work for a period of two weeks upon the construction of the fort. The artillery, which had already been removed to Jamestown for the defense of the anchorage there, was ordered restored to the Point Comfort fort. The duties collected were to be paid in the form of powder, lead, and iron shot, and "if any of them have any more powder to spare than what will be due from them that they sell it to the country for what it cost them with thirty percent advance upon the first charge." The justices of Warwick, Elizabeth City, and Upper and Lower Norfolk counties were given the jobs of providing a supply of axes, saws, and other tools necessary for the felling of pine trees at Point Comfort, and of managing the payment of twenty pounds of tobacco per day for the laborers employed.

Carts, oxen, and other necessaries were to be impressed as needed, with the owners receiving a "reasonable" rate for their use. The works at Jamestown were simply to be filled in with earth and forgotten.[18]

Work upon the Point Comfort fort progressed slowly, without benefit of engineer, impetus, or enthusiasm. In late June 1666, the perceived peril became real when a Dutch caper sailed into the Chesapeake and captured two merchantmen with ease. The frantic colony government believed the lone ship to be the vanguard of a larger force which was expected to arrive shortly to invade the colony.[19]

The government reacted with a vigor born of desperation. The labor force of twenty men then employed on the fort construction were, in a panic, armed and placed under the command of a Major Powell. Concerned that the as-yet-unmounted artillery might be captured, Berkeley ordered it buried beneath four feet of earth and the burial site defended by the twenty armed laborers. The Elizabeth City County militia under Colonel Leonard Yeo was to be immediately mobilized and readied to march to the relief of the fort at an hour's notice. Colonel Miles Cary was to dispatch a supply of powder and shot to Yeo, while the colony was placed on alert. Meanwhile, Major General Richard Bennett was directed to summon all of the colony's militia commanders and county justices of the peace to his residence to determine the exact state of defense and to prepare for the mobilization of all boats and sloops fit for service in Virginia to repel expected enemy landings. If any boat impressed into service needed repair, Bennett was authorized to press either carpenters or smiths to work immediately upon the vessels, and to seize whatever cordage or sails were available for their outfitting at the public expense. Major General Robert Smith was authorized to seize all available powder and shot from any merchants and planters not in imminent danger of attack to supplement the colony's sparse munitions supplies. All ammunition was to be forwarded to Bennett, who was to manage the dispersal of the commodities entrusted to him sparingly. Though their regions were not immediately threatened, militia officers of the York River and the Eastern Shore were placed on standby alert.[20] Thus had a single Dutch raider mobilized the entire colony of Virginia for an invasion that failed to materialize.

The vulnerability of the colony's defenses was apparent. On July 10, 1666, the Council met again, in frustration, and passed a resolution it hoped would bear immediate fruit.

Whereas *it doth appear to us by experience that tho' we build a fort according to his Majesties royal commands which we are now upon and*

*shall Perform with all possible speed yet by reason of the openness and large
extent of the several rivers within this colony it will be impossible to defend
the ships trading hither without so many forts as we are not able to build nor
garrison It is therefore upon mature deliberation on the premises* ordered
that the Right Honourable the Governor be desired most humbly to suppli-
cate his Majesty to command one of his frigates to attend here for the better
defense of the ships aforesaid and we shall be always ready to supply her
with our best assistance in what ever she shall have occasion for.[21]

Further supplications for military aid reached Whitehall in early
1667, when a representation by Francis Moryson was read before the
Privy Council, noting that Virginia stood in great need of artillery and
arms, and requesting that twenty culverins, demi-culverins, and sakers,
with powder and shot, and one hundred "Horse Arms" for the dragoons be sent immediately. Moryson reiterated the Virginia Council's
resolution of July 10 in a petition requesting that a frigate be appointed
to sail from England by the middle of February "to ride in Chesapeake
Bay to secure the Shipps Trading thither." On January 11 the petition
was granted and the Lord High Admiral was authorized and instructed
to dispatch a frigate to the Chesapeake by the requested date.[22]

For the first time in its history, the Chesapeake Bay would have a
Royal Navy guardship on permanent station, a practice which would
continue, off and on, until the American Revolution more than a
century later.

The British Admiralty was hard pressed, in the early days of 1667, to
provide a guardship for Virginia. English interests in European waters
were sorely threatened by the powerful Dutch fleet commanded by
Admiral Michiel Adriaanszoon De Ruyter, and the far-off Chesapeake
undoubtedly rated less consideration than the imperiled English
Channel. Yet the danger to England's Chesapeake trade—and revenue—was tangible, and after deliberation, the Lord High Admiral
dispatched one of the few expendable relics of the navy of Charles I, a
46-gun frigate called *Elizabeth*.[23]

Elizabeth, originally a vessel of 474 tons displacement, had been built
at Deptford, England, in 1647 as a 32-gun ship,[24] and by 1667 she had
seen service during the reigns of Charles I, Oliver Cromwell, and, now,
Charles II. She had passed through the English Revolution and the
First Anglo-Dutch War intact, but at the outbreak of the Second Anglo-
Dutch War she was apparently in such poor condition that her value in
European waters would have proved limited at best. Service as a guard-
ship in the colonial backwater of the Chesapeake was perhaps, in the
Admiralty's view, the only duty for which *Elizabeth* was now suited.

Thus, in February she sailed westward to serve out her days on what would henceforth be called the Virginia, or Chesapeake Station.

The crossing for *Elizabeth* was turbulent, and upon her arrival in the Chesapeake in the spring she had become "soe disabled in her Maste and Leakey in her Hull as that she could not keep at sea," and was immediately tied up for repairs.[25] Her sad plight would cost the colony dearly, for Virginia defenses were little more advanced than they had been during the previous fall. The Crown had sent only ten cannons (two culverins, two demi-culverins, and six sakers) rather than the requested twenty to Jamestown. Upon his arrival, *Elizabeth*'s commander found that the redoubts designated for construction on the York, the Rappahannock, and the Eastern Shore were empty and useless because all of the colony's old cannons were still emplaced or buried at Point Comfort.[26]

Virginia was ripe for any enterprising Dutch raider that happened along, and Admiral Abraham Crijnsen, or Crimson, as the English called him, was as capable a Dutch naval commander that ever sailed in search of a fight. In late May the admiral approached the Virginia Capes with four men-of-war, which included *Prince William,* the flagship of 38 guns, two of 24 guns, one of 18 guns, and a small 8-gun dogger.[27] At each ship's foremast flew the state flag of Holland and from each poop the "bloody" red flag of war. Drum and flag decorations on their sides and the deadly long guns perforating their hulls left little doubt as to their purpose.[28] Crimson had already captured Surinam from the English and, as one historian so aptly put it, he was cruising up the American coast "looking for trouble."[29]

On June 1 Crimson fell in with and captured a small shallop, *Pauls Grave,* off the Virginia Capes. Interrogation of the shallop's hapless master, Nicholas Bodrum, and his crew provided the Dutchman with exciting information: the Chesapeake tobacco fleet was at that moment assembling in the mouth of the James River and the guardship *Elizabeth* was laid up in repair three leagues upriver.[30] Crimson quickly determined to first attack the guardship and then to seize the rich tobacco fleet. The main event feared by Berkeley was about to begin, but not before a preliminary round.

As Crimson brought his fleet into the Chesapeake, he encountered and attacked a lone London merchantman bound from Tangier to Virginia commanded by Captain Robert Conway. Conway valiantly resisted the Dutch assault, though wounded himself, for a full two hours before being overpowered. His gallant defense, against insurmountable odds, throughout the action deeply impressed the Dutch

commander. Out of "his noble disposition" Crimson rewarded his
enemy for his courage by giving him *Pauls Grave,* on the understanding
that he shepherd the fleet into the James.[31]

On June 4, Crimson quietly entered the Chesapeake and anchored.
On the following morning his warships raised English colors and, led
into the James by the merchantman, approached the anchored tobacco
fleet, an even score of merchantmen awaiting only a few stragglers to
join them before sailing for England. For the fox to enter the henhouse
undetected, Crimson continued his ruse by having soundings and hails
to other ships cried out in English. Slowly the warships crept up the
James past the unfinished fort, entirely unsuspected by the
merchantmen.[32]

As the squadron approached the guardship, the ruse was abandoned. Captain Lightfoot, commander of *Elizabeth,* was ashore "with
his wench that he carryed with him from England," allegedly attending
a wedding. Fewer than thirty men remained aboard ship, all entirely
unaware of their peril. Suddenly, the James was shattered by the
booming of cannons as Crimson's squadron poured three quick broadsides into the guardship's hull and closed to board. Though several
seamen aboard *Elizabeth* sought to resist but a single cannon was fired in
her defense before the ship was abandoned.[33]

While a prize crew secured their capture, the remainder of the
invaders dropped back down the river to Hampton Roads and quickly
began to snap up the stunned fleet of merchantmen lying at anchor.
Though it was later acknowledged that several of the ships might have
saved themselves by escaping into the shoally maze of the Elizabeth
River where Crimson's deep-draft warships might not have dared
venture, all were so paralyzed by surprise and fear that the Dutch
victory was total. The Crimson raiders were now masters of the entire
lower James River, and the Virginia Governor's worst fears were being
realized.[34]

Sir William Berkeley was both enraged and grief stricken when news
of the disaster reached him. Yet he was not a man to panic. He
immediately took stock of his military assets. The fort at Point Comfort
was, of course, totally useless, and none of the other forts was even
armed should the Dutch attempt other anchorages. There were three
fat merchantmen in the upper James and nine more anchored in the
York. If these ships could be quickly manned and armed, he reasoned,
there might still be time to attack and defeat the Crimson raiders and
secure the tobacco fleet again. Should the enemy decide to ascend the
James, the shipping there—and the capital of Virginia itself—stood
little chance of surviving. In a plan born of desperation, Berkeley

decided to man the York River fleet "being the nearest to the enimy and hasten to them and fight them."[35] Simultaneously, the ships in the James would descend to attack from above, thereby engaging the Dutch in the narrow confines of the river in a pincers movement. Offensive action seemed to be the only hope, even though the merchantmen stood little chance unless they could close and board the warships, thereby utilizing superior numbers of men.[36]

Three regiments of militia, approximately nine hundred men, and the crew of *Elizabeth* were directed to march to the York to board and man the nine vessels there. Artillery from a number of smaller ships, combined with that already aboard the big ships, made the fleet surprisingly more heavily armed than the entire Dutch squadron. At Jamestown, a fourth militia regiment manned the three largest merchantmen there, and the ships were rapidly fitted out with artillery in the same fashion as those on the York. Everyone was filled with a zeal and lust for battle.[37]

Berkeley's plan called for the York River fleet to round Horseshoe Shoals and the peninsula and make its way into the James, thereby blocking the Dutchmen's escape to sea. At the same time, the James River fleet would drop down to attack the foe from the rear. The Governor resolved to personally command the operation from aboard the largest vessel in the York River fleet. He was joined aboard by a number of the Council members and approximately forty gentlemen, planters, and officers. The mortified captain of *Elizabeth* had little choice but to join in the plan and "very passionately resolved to hazard himself in the Admirall with the Governor and the rest of his Company." The elderly Berkeley, seeking to instill fighting spirit in his men by example, declared his intention to lead them to victory or die in the attempt.[38]

At Hampton Roads, Admiral Crimson displayed little interest in leaving the Chesapeake principally because his squadron was in great want of water. Several landing parties were dispatched ashore immediately after the capture of the tobacco fleet to obtain that most precious commodity. The Virginians, for once, were prepared, and at every point the Dutch landing parties (whose interests lay in plunder and provisions as well as water) were driven off in sharp skirmishes. General Bennett, in command of the lower James forces and in defending the shores of Elizabeth City County, behaved admirably, leading his forces bravely and securing "as much affection . . . as ever men did" from his troops.[39]

Crimson's problems lay not only in a shortage of water, but also in a shortage of manpower. He had captured an entire fleet of twenty ships and a man-of-war, but he now found himself totally incapable of manning his rich prizes. *Elizabeth* was still in no condition to sail and, before she could even dare the open seas, she would require the completion of the major overhaul that had been underway when she was captured. The admiral thus found it necessary to burn five or six of the merchantmen and the guardship.[40]

On the York River, Governor Berkeley's plan to attack the Crimson raiders was meeting with unexpected resistance. The captains of the nine merchantmen, whose initial zeal for the enterprise had been loudly proclaimed, were rapidly growing cold to the idea. They began to produce excuses for not sailing. Every hour saw new delays, and a growing feeling of helplessness settled over the Governor.[41] In the James, Admiral Crimson had undoubtedly been made aware of the gathering opposition. He had inflicted serious damage on Virginia's and England's tobacco commerce, and though he could not take with him as many prizes as he had captured, the rewards for the fourteen or fifteen vessels already in hand would certainly be great. Though bold, he was not insensitive to his situation. With the threat of well-organized opposition in the York being an immediate reality, and with the determined resistance against landing parties ashore in the James already proven, Admiral Crimson finally decided to leave the Chesapeake in triumph before it was too late. The humiliation of Virginia and the English, he happily reflected, had been total. He would suffer no discredit for discreetly departing the Chesapeake with his prizes.[42]

Ironically, an ocean away, a similar bold attack, planned by Admiral De Ruyter (albeit on a much grander scale) was about to precipitate the next peace. On June 22, a massive Dutch naval squadron of sixty-eight vessels entered the Thames estuary, broke the chains blocking the Medway, and, in a masterful stroke, captured eighteen Royal Navy warships, including the onetime flagship of the fleet, the 90-gun *Royal Charles*. Thirty-nine days later, hostilities were suspended by the Treaty of Breda. But for Virginia, though no one knew it, the war was already over, for on June 11, 1667, Crimson sailed triumphantly out of the Chesapeake never to return.

V

Cleare Their Shipps for Fight

The Dutch raid on the Chesapeake had been a humiliating defeat for Virginia, but it was quickly, perhaps mercifully, forgotten in the wake of the crushing English debacle at the Medway. Unaware for some time of the peace that followed, the Virginia government moved quickly to regroup its paltry defenses in the event raiders such as Crimson should return. Colonel Yeo was empowered to impress whatever men and materials would be necessary for expediting the construction work on the fort at Point Comfort. A chief gunner, Gowing Dunbar, was appointed to command the fort's artillery "when and as soon as the same shall be planted and made." A sloop in the public service, commanded by one Christopher Gould, was directed to carry down to the fort from the charred hulk of *Elizabeth* "all such great guns as can be weighed and got out of the said ship with sufficient help of men and materials which he [Gould] is hereby empowered to press and take."[1] Ship departures were delayed until June 27 owing to the possibility that enemy vessels might still be lingering about the capes.[2] As far as Virginia was concerned, the war emergency was still very real.

The confusion wrought by the Crimson raid had inspired some Virginia opportunists to less-than-meritorious deeds. One such individual, a justice of the peace, Nicholas Smith of Pagan Point, "did plunder or agree with some persons to plunder the ships in the late extremity of the *dutch* invasion of this country." Though looters like him could not be ignored, Smith's activities deserved special attention from the government. Apparently not wishing to arouse disfavor among his appointed officials whose excesses were less public, Berkeley fined Smith fifty pounds plus clerk's and sheriff's fees, a stiff penalty for the times, and ordered him to return all plundered goods. All fines levied were to go to the construction of Virginia's coastal fortifications.[3]

The renewed construction at Point Comfort was destined to be short-lived. In November Council Secretary Thomas Ludwell outlined a tale of woe which could not fail to frustrate the staunchest colonist and which made the Dutch attack pale by comparison. Prior to the Dutch raid, the country had been subjected to a terrible hailstorm, with hailstones as large as turkey eggs, which killed most of the livestock and cattle. Then came the Dutch. Barely days after Crimson and his raiders departed, forty days of continuous rain destroyed whatever lay standing in the fields that had not been destroyed by the hailstorm. On August 27 a terrible hurricane, lasting twenty-four hours, and accompanied by lighning and thunder struck the colony. "The waves," wrote Ludwell,

> [were] impetuously beaten against the Shoares and by that violence forced and as it were crowded up into all Creeks, Rivers and bayes to that prodigeous height that it hazarded the drownding many people who lived in sight of the Rivers, yet were then forced to climbe to the topp of their houses to keep themselves above water. [The waters] carried all the foundation of the fort at point Comfort into the River and most of our Timber which was very chargably brought thither to perfect it. Had it been finished and a garrison in it, they had been Stormed by such an enemy as noe power but Gods can restraine . . .

In its fury, the tempest drove ships aground, blew down nearly ten thousand buildings, flattened all of the colony's Indian corn and tobacco, fences, and other structures. Those hogs and cattle which had been fenced in and had survived, were soon running loose about the fields devouring what little the storm had spared.[4]

The dreadful tempest had produced, amid its destruction, one positive result for Governor Berkeley: a temporary resolution to the conflict over the best coastal defense for Virginia. With the total erosion of the Point Comfort fort and the obligation to the Crown that went with it, Berkeley was now free to proceed with his own fortification program at Jamestown and at strategic points at or near the mouths of Virginia's important rivers. The works at Tindall's Point at Gloucester on the York River and Corotoman on the Rappahannock were enlarged, and two new redoubts, at Nansemond on the James and at Yeocomico on the Potomac, were erected, all at great expense and less than skillfully. Unfortunately, the strong fort planned for the defense at Jamestown was soon far behind schedule, and the redoubt planned for Pungoteague was apparently altogether abandoned. Charges for each fort's construction were to be borne by the counties on the rivers that were to be defended. Each of the forts was to mount at least eight great guns, have walls ten feet thick and ten feet high, and contain a "court of guard and a convenient place to preserve the magazine."[5]

Though Berkeley initially pursued the construction program with vigor, the often unfinished products and incumbent maintenance problems were a source of continual frustration. Erosion of the crude mud-and-dirt riverfront structures was an ever-present problem. By June 1671, most of the works were eroding faster than the government could repair them. "We have," the Governor explained in exasperation, "neither skill or ability to make or mainetaine [the forts] for there is not now so farr as my inquiry ran [or] ever was one Ingeneir in the Country soe that wee are at continuall charge to repaire unskillful and inartificiall buildings of that nature."[6]

Arming the works was equally frustrating. The guns from the wreck of *Elizabeth,* originally intended for the Point Comfort fort, were now to be used to defend the five new redoubts. Unfortunately, they were found to be unserviceable, and the guns that had once been buried at the Point Comfort site were so rusty and scaly that they were deemed equally useless. But when peace came, all appeals for military aid fell upon deaf ears, and both construction and maintenance programs ground to a dismal halt.[7]

By early 1672 England and the States-General again found themselves on the brink of war, and Virginia's Chesapeake defenses were still incomplete, naked and exposed. Immediately upon the outbreak of the third Anglo-Dutch War, an event which this time lined up England and France against a weaker States-General, the King directed Berkeley to place the colony in the best possible defensive posture. It was a task which was nothing short of monumental. In early February the King and Lords Commissioners of Plantations were informed by Thomas Grantham that the colony was simply "unable to defend itself through want of ammunition." There was not even enough powder at the Tindall's Point redoubt to charge a single piece of ordnance. It was absolutely certain, said Grantham, that only by providing a speedy supply could the danger of surprise attacks—such as the Crimson raid of the last war—be prevented. Grantham proposed that the Crown provide him with protection for a ship and men and he would personally deliver the ammunition and the King's dispatches to Virginia without charge.[8]

On March 25, 1673, Governor Berkeley reiterated Virginia's precarious position in a letter to the Lords Commissioners for Trade and Plantations. He reviewed not only the effects of the disastrous winter of

1672-1673 in which more than half of the colony's cattle (which had grown quickly after the reduction of several years earlier) had been lost, but also the effects upon the Virginia trade as a result of the war. Few ships were even reaching the colony, and those that did were bringing in less than a fifth of the goods and tools necessary for Virginia's survival. He concluded by informing the commissioners that Virginia was in "extreme want of ammunition" and begged their intercession with the King to supply a small quantity.[9] There were, in fact, barely enough arms in the colony to supply one of every ten Virginia militiamen. And the situation was rapidly degenerating.

In April the Virginia government received the unhappy news that "severall of the Shipps of Warr belonging to the States Gen[ll] are designed Against this Place." The Governor and Council immediately sought to place the colony defenses on alert and ordered all militia officers to muster their forces. Because of the weapons and munitions shortage, all commanders were directed to "take Care that the Armes [which] shall bee in any Howse more than the people Listed Can use be secured for those who shall be found wanting in Armes." And, once again, all arms which were not in good condition were to be immediately repaired. The militia was authorized to requisition all powder, shot, and arms found in any stores and warehouses, and then be "Ready to March upon the first summons."[10]

For the first time, Berkeley was deeply concerned about the implications of a general call-up. With every able-bodied man serving in the militia to guard the colony's waterways, "Wee leave at our backs as Many Servants (besides Negroes) as their are freemen to defend the Shoare." And along the entire frontier there were the Indians to worry about. Freemen, faced with the twin dangers of Indian attack and slave revolt, were understandably fearful of leaving their homes and estates unprotected. At least one-third of the single freemen "whose labour Will hardly maintaine them," as well as those who were in debt, Berkeley felt, were ripe for revolt should the Dutch gain the slightest advantage during an invasion. Keeping a force in being was next to impossible. Troops could not be quartered for very long in any one place owing to the difficulty of storing provisions in the hot, moist climate, and infestations of vermin made large-scale food stockpiling impossible. Public storehouses were out of the question.[11] And the very provisions that were necessary to feed the troops were at the moment extremely short in Virginia. "There were many more difficulties . . . for diseases this Winter before haveing destroy'd at least Fifty thousand Cattell and their Owners to p[r]serve them having given them almost all their Corne Brought Soe great A Scarcity of provision amongst us as men Could not have bene kept long together." An attack at this time, "when all mens Cropps both of tobacco and Corne lay hardest upon their Hands (being much in the woods by reason of the great Raines which fell Some time before)," could be disastrous.[12]

Though the Governor could raise twenty regiments of foot and twenty troop of horse, he entertained strong misgivings about the capabilities of the Virginia militia under combat situations. He noted that since his soldiers had been well exercised, but had for many years "bene unacquainted with dainger, Wee cannot with much Confidence rely on their Courage against an Enemy Better practized in the hazards of Warr."[13] Others of the Council were awed by the military acumen of the Netherlanders and made no secrets about it. They feared the Virginians might even be forced to fly to the mountains "and leave this country and our estates a prey to the invaders."[14]

The danger of a sudden Dutch raid (if not a full-scale invasion) on the shipping in the roads was, in light of recent intelligence, substantial. Notwithstanding the defensive capabilities of the largely unarmed river forts, which were limited at best, the Governor ordered that upon the first alarm, the militia was to place fifty men and their arms aboard each ship in Virginia waters "to serve as small shott to defend the said Shipp till further Order can be taken for their Better Defense."[15]

Sadly, all of the forts were by now in utterly miserable shape. The shabby, eroding York River works at Tindall's Point, for instance, were in no condition to resist the slightest attack, despite earlier orders for their repair. Stopgap measures were all that could be hoped for. Thus, directions were given that the guns be protected by "Cannon Basketts," or baskets filled with earth and placed around the guns to form a wall, or some other makeshift cover.[16]

Unlike the other four river forts, the Jamestown works, which were to have been constructed of brick, were as yet little more than specifications in a contractor's notebook. The constructors hired by the government to build the works, Major Theodore Stone, William Dromond, and Matthew Page, had failed to assemble more than a few piles of bricks and other materials, and had, in fact, not even begun the actual construction work on the fort. With the colony pressed by the threat of attack, and the defenseless capital now totally "Exposed to the Attempts of the Enemies," the three contractors were chastised with threats of dire punishment unless the works were completed. The government finally agreed to let them have a second chance. A new agreement "to finish the said Worke, & New substantiall Carriages for all the Gunns now in James Citty" was drawn up. Notwithstanding the new contract, by the end of May the contractors had failed to make

notable progress in their project, and the few bricks they had manufactured were of such poor quality that they were deemed utterly
useless. The government could do little but withhold payment and
schedule a June meeting to decide what to do next.[17]

Flagging morale lifted on June 20 with the long-awaited arrival of
two English frigates under the command of Captains Cotterell and
Gardner, which were to escort the tobacco fleet back to England. The
two warships had arrived none too soon, for the great merchant fleet
was already assembling for the perilous convoy home and had been
entirely defenseless. Delays in assembling were bound to occur, especially after many of the vessels had been loading in Chesapeake waters
for six months or more. Soon after the guardships arrived, Captain
Cotterell visited Jamestown and informed the Governor and Council
that, for want of wood and water and other necessaries, he could not be
ready to sail homeward with the tobacco fleet until July 15. The York
River fleet, the Governor was then informed, would, alas, be unready
to sail until that date, and the Maryland tobacco fleet had yet to be
heard from. There were five ships still loading in the Rappahannock,
and two more up Bay. A total of twenty-two ships would thus be
delayed in joining the fleet and would have to sail home undefended
unless an extension for the official departure time was granted, far too
many to be left behind by the convoy. The delay was acceptable to the
government, despite stringent orders for sailing having been preset by
the Privy Council.[18]

The delay would cost Virginia dearly, for a Dutch descent on the
Chesapeake was already being formulated in the minds of two of the
States-General's boldest mariners, Cornelius Evertsen the Younger
and Jacob Binkes.

Cornelius Evertsen the Younger came from a long line of prominent
Dutch Zeeland mariners. His illustrious family could boast of no less
than five admirals and a commodore in the last three generations.
Evertsen himself was a man of commanding countenance, with a large
nose and full, almost cruel lips that pointed downward at the corners in
a perpetual sneer. His thick, usually furrowed brow, long flowing hair,
glaring eyes, and dark hint of a moustache added to an already imposing visage. Evertsen's daring, occasionally intemperate, demeanor and
sagacious courage had earned for him a reputation as one of the ablest
naval commanders in the Netherlands.

Born in 1628, the son of the noted Admiral Jan Evertsen, Cornelius
Evertsen the Younger (one of three Evertsen admirals to bear the
name Cornelius) had followed in the tradition of his seafaring fore-

bears. He had fought zealously at Scheveningen and at the Texel during the last Anglo-Dutch war, commanding a division of ships. He had served under de Ruyter at the Medway and on the Thames in 1667. After the capture of the English flagship *Royal Charles* during the latter operation, Evertsen was placed in command of the prize by de Ruyter. She was the noblest prize taken by the Dutch naval forces to that time, and it was a singular honor to be given command to bring her home.[19] Evertsen had fought actively throughout the Second Anglo-Dutch War, both in Europe and the West Indies. He had earned distinction at the Battle of Solebay, and during one engagement had been wounded so badly that his survival was thought unlikely.[20]

At the outset of the Third Anglo-Dutch War, Cornelius Evertsen was 44 years old, and anxious for action. When command of an expedition to the West Indies to harass British shipping and colonial commerce was offered to him, he accepted. His command consisted of a tiny squadron of six Flushing warships. These were: the 46-gun flagship *Swanenburgh*; the 20-gun pinnace *Schaeckerloo*, Captain Paschier de Witte; the ketch *Sint Joris (St. George)*, Captain Cornelius Eeuwoutssen; the snow *Zeehond (Sealion)*, Captain Daniel Thijssen; the hoeker *Eendracht (Concordance)*, Captain Maarten Andriessen; and *Suriname (Surinam)*, Captain Evert Evertsen, son of Francis Evertsen. Though manned by only 587 seamen, mariners, and "militia" or landsmen,[21] it was a force strong enough to drive the English to despair. In the West Indies, Evertsen was joined by a smaller but no less dangerous squadron commanded by a daring Friesian captain named Jacob Binkes. Binkes had been attached to the Admiralty in Amsterdam, and like Evertsen, had been dispatched to the West Indies on a mission of harassment.

Binkes possessed a less imposing visage than Evertsen. His light-colored hair and eyebrows accentuated a fairly high forehead and eyes that betrayed the weight of command in the creases beneath them. His complexion was sallow, with cupid lips, an aquiline nose that flared at the nostrils, and a double chin. Yet he was no less a leader than the Zeeland admiral he served alongside of. Together, Evertsen and Binkes had wrought hell and havoc amid English colonial interests in the Caribbean, culminating in the complete surrender of the island of St. Eustatia on June 8, 1673.[22] Finally wearied of the West Indies, the two Dutchmen turned their attention, and their fleet, northward.

Their next target would be Virginia.

A dry hot wind blew out of the south on the morning of July 10 as the Dutch squadron of nine warships and their prizes approached the gaping mouth of the Chesapeake Bay. Six miles below Cape Henry and a mile from the barren, sandy shore, the wind died and the fleet lay becalmed in four and one-half fathoms of water. Aside from the little cluster of warships, the sea was flat and featureless without a sail to be seen.[23] There was little to suggest the bustle of activity generated by the great Virginia tobacco fleet assembling at that moment in Hampton Roads, less than twenty miles away, or of the smaller Maryland tobacco fleet plodding down the Chesapeake to join them. And there was less to indicate that Virginia was prepared for the crisis that was shortly to befall her.

Late in the afternoon, a small breeze bestirred *Swanenburgh's* limp sails. Without fuss the Dutch squadron raised anchors and began to creep cautiously northward toward the entrance to the Chesapeake. The following morning, July 11,[24] the flagship spotted two unidentified sails coming out of the Bay, but upon being discovered, one of the vessels, a small shoal-draft ketch, made for the shallows of Smith's Island. Evertsen instantly took up the chase, but soon gave up and came about, intimidated by the shoally waters. The other tidewater vessel escaped back into the Bay. Toward evening, the admiral, having lost sight of Binkes and several of his ships and prizes while in pursuit of the ketch, entered the Chesapeake with six warships and came to anchor.[25]

The second Dutch raid on Virginia and the Chesapeake was about to commence.

On the morning of Saturday, July 12, as the sky lightened in the east, the Dutch fleet raised English colors and prepared a subterfuge reminiscent of Admiral Crimson's exploit in 1667. Within a short time, *Swanenburgh's* lookout observed eleven English merchantmen, two warships, and several small craft coming towards her from the James. Evertsen remained anchored, confidently assuming the English had been taken in as before, and awaited to administer the denouement.[26]

The English had not been fooled in the least. Warned on Friday by coast watchers that four Hollander ships of war, from 30 to 44 guns, one 6-gun ship, one fireship, and three Flushing ships, from 30 to 46 guns, had entered the Bay, Berkeley's forces quickly girded for battle. Captain Cotterell was immediately informed and "p^rsently Comanded Severall Masters of the abler Merchant Shipps in James River on Board, and order'd them to Cleare their Shipps for Fight, and press'd as many men as they thought fitt out of the Weaker Shipps."[27]

Despite earlier misgivings, the Governor's thrown-together fleet seemed not in the least apprehensive over the security of nearly forty sail of Virginia merchantmen anchored in the James, bolstered by the confidence of the two Royal Navy commanders, Cotterell and Gardner. If the Virginia flotilla could only hold back the Dutch long enough, the commanders reasoned, the merchantmen in the James might easily escape upriver or beneath the fort at Nansemond, weak as that might be.[28]

Unfortunately for the English, their plan had failed to entertain the element of chance, for suddenly, as if on cue, before the entire James River flotilla could be readied for battle, eight sail of the Maryland tobacco fleet were spotted bearing down on the Dutch from up Bay. They were ignorant of the enemy's ruse and unconscious of the extreme danger they were in. It readily became apparent that the Maryland ships could only be saved by instant action on the part of Cotterell's flotilla. Thus, the two Royal Navy warships, taking with them six of the armed merchantmen, sailed boldly out of the James to give battle.[29]

Evertsen and Binkes continued at anchor "in hopes that [the English] would come towards us," but as the collision range between the two forces narrowed to a quarter of a mile, the English battle fleet suddenly turned and headed back toward the James to draw the invaders away from the Maryland fleet. Four of the armed tobacco ships promptly ran aground, and a fifth scurried ahead of the remaining pack for safety. Led by Evertsen in *Swanenburgh,* the Dutch immediately raised anchor and took off in hot pursuit of the two warships and the sole armed merchantman in their way. For the moment, the Maryland tobacco fleet was ignored.[30]

Over the next three hours, a running battle between the two unevenly paired squadrons continued, with the pursuing Dutch gradually closing the gap. Captain Grove, commander of the lone armed tobacco ship still in the fight, was soon forced aground, leaving the two Royal Navy ships to fend off the entire Dutch fleet. As both Evertsen, with his six largest ships, and his quarry approached the James, Captain Gardner, mistakenly believing Grove to be free, and in need of help, "judging that the enemy (if he checkt them not) would be in with [the] merchant ships riding in the James river," courageously tacked his ship, bringing her across the path of the Dutch. Evertsen, "fearing that he was going to sea," followed with his fleet, and within a short time, *Swanenburgh* had come up on her quarry. For at least an hour, Gardner fought the Zeelander, alone and with untempered zeal, though "all his greate maste and his fore topmast [were] desperately wounded, and most of his rigging shot." At last, finding Grove's ship still aground and unable to continue the fight much longer, the Englishman again skillfully came about. As the Dutch admiral noted with some chagrin, Gardner "choked off our wind" and, against all odds, successfully disengaged. Through the brave, though desperate, expedient of drawing off the Dutch from the Maryland tobacco fleet, Gardner had saved all but one of the Maryland ships.[31] But more important, the daring, hastily contrived naval defense had bought the English merchant fleets precious time, time to withdraw out of harm's way, and time for Virginia's militia to organize its shore defenses.

Evertsen, so close to victory, was not about to give up. A running pursuit to overtake the heavily-laden Maryland fleet which waddled slowly toward the James was soon on again, with both sides trading shots from a distance. During the early evening *Shaeckerloo* and a prize snow came up the Bay and joined the fray. Observing several armed Virginia tobacco ships still aground and deserted, Evertsen ordered twenty men from *Swanenburgh* transferred to the snow to go over and take possession of them. By evening the Dutch pursuit had slowed to a cautious crawl owing to the dangers of the shoally waters about the mouth of the James and the deep draft of many of the Dutch warships.[32]

Soon after sundown, Captain Binkes fell in with, captured, and boarded a large English pinnace, probably Grove's ship, which he at first supposed to be the Vice Admiral of the James River flotilla. Evertsen immediately attempted to come up with the two ships to talk, though the battle was still hot. Suddenly, *Swanenburgh* ground to a halt on a sandbar in eighteen feet of water, "which we didn't know and couldn't see because of the dark." Finally, about 8:15 P.M., the shooting stopped, and, judging it too dangerous to resume pursuit into the river in the night, the Dutch fleet came to anchor near its stranded admiral. The admiral devoted the better part of the evening to freeing his flagship, which "with greatest difficulty . . . came loose again."[33]

On the morning of the 13th, as the Dutch prepared to resume the contest, a ship was observed floating in the Chesapeake, apparently abandoned by her crew. Presuming her to be unmanned, Evertsen dispatched *Zeehond* to bring her in. The vessel proved to be the pinnace *Pearl* laden with tobacco, which was promptly transferred to a shallop commanded by a Captain Boes. Also captured was a large boat belonging to Colonel Custis which was en route down the Bay to deliver letters, and "knowing no better that we were English," it was snapped up with ease.[34]

Even as the two new prizes were being taken, several ships in the Dutch squadron prepared to enter the James. At 11:00 A.M. *Swanenburgh* moved to again join the vanguard, but she was soon stymied by a midday Chesapeake calm. Evertsen ordered the shallop of Captain Boes fitted out with oars and manned. If he couldn't sail to fight the English, he brazenly resolved to tow his ship up to attack. The King's ships, anchored near the mouth of the Elizabeth, into which they retreated to refit with ropes and sails, "did their best to get rid of us," noted *Swanenburgh*'s journal, "but they seeing we were coming very close, retired to the Elizabeth River, which is very narrow and full of oyster banks so that it was impossible to pursue her there without experienced pilots."[35]

Though Evertsen and Binkes lacked knowledgeable pilots, they did have a number of English prisoners, two of whom were seamen with a passing familiarity of the James and Elizabeth.[36] The Dutchmen, attentions now riveted to at least thirty-four merchantmen fleeing before them into the James, pressed after them. This time, their progress was frustrated by alternating calms and contrary winds. Toward evening, as they poked cautiously up the James, four of the squadron ran aground between the mouth of the Elizabeth and the Nansemond. Two of the ships were soon freed, but the other two, including Binkes's ship and *Suriname*, were stuck fast. Wisely, the admiral brought the remainder of the squadron to a temporary anchor to protect the stranded warships. The Dutchmen watched in disgust as eleven or twelve fat merchantmen escaped into the Nansemond and came to anchor beneath what appeared to be a substantial fort. A score or more ships were seen running up the James to Jamestown.[37]

The Dutch had certainly cornered their quarry, but bagging them was a wholly different matter. Evertsen was on the proverbial horns of a dilemma. To hazard a penetration into the Nansemond was to tinker with disaster, for it was "a very narrow and perilous river full of banks." The dozen or so merchantmen boxed within were apparently well-defended by an imposing earthen fort. The Zeelander was unaware that the works were defended by little more than a company of militiamen and no artillery. To press up the James with the free ships would leave the two grounded men-of-war at the mercy of the two Royal Navy frigates holed up in the rear in the Elizabeth River. Evertsen decided to remain where he was until the two warships were freed, but to dispatch three of his smallest vessels upriver in pursuit of twenty-two merchantmen flying before him.[38]

With great effort, the Dutch pursued both objectives. The two warships, after several days labor, and the unloading of all ammunition aboard, with the assistance of the other vessels in the squadron, were finally freed. Farther upriver, the fleeing Englishmen were not so fortunate. Five of the merchantmen ran aground before reaching the security of the defenses at Jamestown. Soon, the Dutch were upon them in *Zeehond, Schaeckerloo,* and Captain Boes's shallop. Unable to free all but one of the unfortunate merchantmen, four of the English vessels were burned, and the fifth, a large pinnace called *Madras,* was carried back down the James as a prize, just as Captain Binkes's ship was freed from its own imprisonment.[39]

When Captains de Witte and Boes reported to Evertsen, they informed him of the difficulties encountered upriver. After taking the five stranded Englishmen, they had labored to free them by throwing overboard the rich cargoes of tobacco with which they had been laden. The English sought to deny them a sixth vessel, a "large flute" which had grounded, by setting her afire. Following suit the raiders then burned all but *Madras.* De Witte and Boes informed their commander that from intelligence provided by prisoners, the five ships which had been destroyed carried between 3,600 and 3,700 "vats," or hogsheads, of tobacco.[40]

On Thursday, having been in the James for nearly five days, Evertsen interrogated the two English sailors whom he had been employing as pilots. He asked them if it was possible to bring his lightest ships into the Elizabeth to attack the King's ships, or into the Nansemond to take the merchantmen ensconced there. The two seamen pleaded that they were not very familiar with the James, at least not enough to sail heavy warships through its waters. If the Dutch fleet attempted the Elizabeth and should run aground, they would be in great peril of losing their ships. As for the Nansemond, they pointed out that that waterway was simply too shallow to permit the large warships passage, and that to enter would require crossing a bar of only thirteen feet in depth. The river channel was barely two ship lengths wide, and then only in a few places at that. It was learned from an English traitor who had boarded the fleet at night "that a number of trees had been chopped and thrown in the deep to prevent entry." That the English were preparing to come out and fight again, however, was not certain until the traitor informed the Dutch that an express had been sent to the York River where a number of large ships still lay at anchor. They had been directed to unload their cargoes, clear themselves for action, and make ready to attack.[41]

On the following morning Evertsen and Binkes, having evaluated the situation, "approved and resolved" to take leave of their anchorage on the James, undoubtedly to prevent becoming bottled up in the river by the English naval force preparing on the York. They promptly dropped down to the mouth of the river to join the prizes which had been captured during the operations on the Chesapeake and in the

James. Soon after coming to anchor near the prizes, the lookout on *Swanenburgh* spotted a sail, "a flute laden with tobacco," making her way down the Bay, entirely unaware of the turbulent events which had recently transpired. A shallop was sent out from *Suriname*, and the vessel was quickly taken. Her dazed skipper could only say that "He didn't know any better that we were English."[42]

When *Swanenburgh* rejoined the gaggle of prize ships clustered together in Hampton Roads, Evertsen discovered that a small sloop, bound from Staten Island, had been picked up coming into the Bay on the 19th. Aboard the vessel was a certain Captain Carteret and his wife who had taken passage for England. Upon examination, it was determined the vessel was involved in smuggling.[43] The master, Samuel Davis, was interrogated closely about English strongpoints on the seaboard, and especially about those of Holland's former enclave, New York City. Evertsen and Binkes pressed their captive on the condition of New York's defenses, promising him the return of his sloop and cargo if he would reveal the true state of the city. Davis was adamant in his story that the place was in a strong state of military readiness, well supplied with arms and munitions, and resolute in its desire to repel all invaders. Davis, unfortunately, was rebutted by one of his passengers, one Samuel Hopkins from Arthur Kill, in New England. Another passenger, a professor, claimed Davis was totally incorrect. New York, he said, was in no condition to defend itself. There were few cannon mounted, and those that were were on rotten carriages. There were few men in arms in the city fort. The governor of the place was absent, and New York was totally incapable of repelling an attack.[44] Evertsen and Binkes were intrigued by the prospects.

On Sunday, the Dutch spent the better part of the day preparing their prizes for sea, making repairs to the injured prize *Pearl* which had lost her steering and suffered other damages, and transferring prize crews to their respective charges. When Evertsen took muster, he found his prize fleet consisted of seven vessels: the pinnaces *Peace*, *Elias*, *Pearl*, and *Madras;* the large pinnace ship *John and Martha;* the flute *Posthorse;* and the little flute ship *Benjamin*.[45]

The following day Captain James Carteret and his wife were put ashore, and the fleet raised anchor to move farther out from the James. That evening, the boat which had taken the Carterets ashore returned with several sailors and an English major to negotiate a prisoner exchange. Evertsen agreed to turn over as many Englishmen as he had onboard on the condition that all Dutchmen in English hands ashore be turned over to him. An exchange was agreed upon. The English prisoners were placed aboard Colonel Custis's boat taken days earlier and released.

On July 22 the Dutch fleet raised anchor and prepared to leave the Chesapeake for good. Before departing, however, they fell in with a small ketch which was promptly taken up by *Schaeckerloo*. The vessel had come down from the head of the Bay with 400 hogsheads of tobacco bound for New England. The vessel was quickly examined and then released after the skipper swore an oath that "Neither his ship nor any of his goods on board belonged to the English but only to his factors."[46] Why Evertsen and Binkes were willing to permit such a rich prize to go is unrecorded. It is possible that with their manpower stretched to the limit in manning their own fleet as well as the seven prize ships already in hand they were unwilling to strain or weaken their companies any more. It is also possible that they did not wish to be delayed in their departure any further, for Evertsen and Binkes now had even greater prey in mind.

Tantalized by the information provided by the passengers aboard Captain Samuel Davis's sloop concerning the defenseless state of New York City, the two Dutch commanders had decided to attack and capture the very city their forebears had founded nearly half a century earlier and had only recently turned over to English control. On July 23, with a stiff breeze to propel them, they set sail from the Virginia Capes bound northward. Eight days later they brought their fleet into a half-moon formation before a small fort at the foot of Manhattan Island, "Let flye all their broad sides & in ye smoake landed 500 men" and took New York by storm.[47]

Though no one could have foreseen that the war was destined to last less than one more year, Virginia was thoroughly demoralized. In the wake of their attack, Evertsen and Binkes had left the seeds of panic and confusion. The Secretary of the Council of Virginia Thomas Ludwell promptly dispatched a letter to the British Secretary of State Lord Arlington begging immediate assistance. The capture and destruction of a major portion of the tobacco fleet, he wrote, had forced him

> to implore yor Lordships assistance towards His Matie when our declarations shall be presented to the Councell table, that the true state of our p^{r}sent condicōn being waighed and our inability to defend our selves considered and the consequence of saueing soe considerable a plantacōn, wch imployes soe many shipps, spends soe much of the manufacture of England, and brings soe great a revenue to the Crowne being duely valewed, His Matie may be graciously pleased to afford us that protection wch wee cannot give our selves.[48]

When the official report of the invasion was dispatched, Governor Berkeley and the Council reinforced Ludwell's plea for support while capably pointing out the inherent weaknesses of the Virginia defenses, and justifying the colony government's own views on such matters. When the enemy appeared, the militia, weak and poorly armed, nevertheless turned out and "appeared Soe ready in Every place that the Enemy desended not on the Land though they wanted water to great Extremety." The loss of shipping, Berkeley proudly noted, had not been due to lack of protection (for all the vessels that had sought the security of the forts at Nansemond and Jamestown had been saved), but due to unfortunate groundings. Anticipating a rebuttal from the King that the James River fleet might have been saved by a fort at Point Comfort, Berkeley and the Council presented their reasons for not constructing one after the last effort had failed. They were against a fort at Point Comfort

because it being A direct Chanell and A great Tide, A Shipp may ride in Safety in the Bay till it hath A Good Wind and upon A Tide may runn by A better Fort then all the Wealth and Skill of this Countrey can build.

Such a fort would only secure the James, and would need at least forty or fifty cannon to be effective. The cost of constructing a work there, at a place "which affoards not Soe much as A Foundation to build on, much less any Materialls," he estimated would be fifteen thousand pounds sterling. The entire public revenue of Virginia did not exceed two thousand pounds per year. To garrison such a work would place an additional financial burden on the colony that only the levy of additional taxes and duties might lessen. Virginia was simply unable to pay for the defenses she needed.[49]

The destruction or capture of a large portion of the Chesapeake tobacco fleet was a terrible embarrassment to the Crown, and pointed up the colony government's long-standing inability to defend itself. All of the colony's efforts to build forts and raise money for armaments had resulted in dismal humiliation at the hands of the Dutch. In the days, weeks, and months that followed, disaffection with the Governor's handling of Virginia's defenses snowballed. When the assembly authorized the county courts to raise new taxes in October to defray expenses in rearming local militias, a tax revolt broke out in Lawn Creek Parish. The revolt was eventually quelled, but Berkeley's management of colony defenses, and general unhappiness with his administration resulted in the outbreak of open rebellion in 1676. Though the rebels, led by Nathaniel Bacon, were stamped out the following year, William Berkeley was recalled to England in disgrace, where he died before defending his actions before King Charles II.[50]

VI

Commotions, Tumults, and Disturbances

O n a bright summer's day, an observer standing on the high marl banks of Tindall's Point on the north shore of the York River could easily view the comings and goings of shipping at the river's mouth, three miles to the southeast, and on the Chesapeake Bay beyond. But no one noticed the nondescript ship that came to anchor at the river's entrance on a certain day in June 1682. Scant attention was given to several small boats from the ship, their oars dipping deep into river waters, as they crawled spiderlike toward the point. It is doubtful that anyone even suspected their ultimate intentions, for immediately after touching upon the beach at Tindall's, they descended with unopposed vigor upon two plantation homes, one belonging to Mrs. Rebecca Leake and one to John Williams, and forced entry into them. The robbers rifled and plundered the two houses of "a considerable quantity of goods, monies, & plate" and then vanished as quickly as they had appeared.[1]

The Council of Virginia was deeply upset over the raid, but more worried

> that ye Pyrate doth still continue roving within ye Capes, with intent to commit and perpatrate ye like villanies and robberies on some other [of] the Inhabitants of this Colony, or that ye s[ai]d Pyrate waites with expectation to take small vessels, sloops & shallops, as they come in and out of this Colony.[2]

The Council acted swiftly. Colonel William Cole,[3] a member of the Council since 1675, was handed the task of bringing the freebooters to heel, or at least preventing further depredations. He was instructed to impress a pink, ship, bark, or ketch, or any vessel "he shall think most fit to convert" for the job along with rigging, tackle, and furniture. The vessel was to be held in a state of readiness to receive aboard as many men as necessary to take up pursuit of the pirates should they appear again. The colonel was authorized to victual his vessel with twelve barrels of pork and other provisions, which were to be secured from whomever he could find to provide them.[4]

Cole's pirate chaser, manned by eighteen officers and men, proved to be but a temporary expedient. The only positive thing that could be said about the measure was that the vessel might provide timely warning should a pirate ship be spotted. With such a small crew, and a vessel naked of artillery, little more than an early warning against such raiders could be hoped for. Colonel Cole's efforts ultimately yielded little in the way of protection for Virginia, for the raiders of Tindall's Point disappeared without a trace.

In Maryland the pirate menace had become something of a state matter when the rather shocking intelligence arrived informing the government that the rovers intended to surprise "the Person of the Right Honourable the Lord Proprietor and with him the Magazine kept at Mattapony [Mattapany at the mouth of the Patuxent] for the Defence of the Province." Though the attack failed to materialize, both the upper and lower chambers of the Maryland Assembly voted to provide a convenient guard for the defense of the governor and the security of the magazine. By November, the move had cost the colony 39,900 pounds of tobacco.[5]

Not long afterwards, the pirates turned up in Rhode Island, where five of them were captured. The Governor of that colony obligingly dispatched the prisoners to Virginia, that "they might have their tryalls where they had perpetrated such villanyes." Immediately upon their arrival, they were committed, "well loaden with Irons," to the Middlesex County jail. Irons, however, were apparently not enough, for the five brigands escaped almost immediately. "Hue & Cryes being issued through all parts of ye Country for their seizing & apprehending," a massive manhunt was launched. Two of the men, William Harrison and John Manly, were quickly recaptured and hauled off to the Jamestown jail to await trial. The remainder escaped entirely. The General Court of Virginia brought a grand jury decision in *Billa vera*, and a petit jury decision of guilty was handed down against the two pirates, though they were deemed the "least guilty" of the five. On November 28 both were sentenced to be hanged by the neck until dead.[6]

The sequence of events that followed the verdict produced some of the most bizarre behavior exhibited by pirates on record. On the evening of December 5, the day before the execution, the two convicts petitioned Lieutenant Governor Sir Henry Chicheley for two days' reprieve because one of the prisoners, a Polish seaman, wished to be baptized. The reprieve was granted, and the baptism was performed. On December 8, the warrant for the execution (which was to be carried out the following morning) was signed and delivered to the hangman. That night, Harrison and Manly again freed themselves of their irons and escaped by removing two iron bars from one of their cell windows.[7] When the escape was discovered, "Hue & Cryes issued to all parts of ye County but wrought no Effect, not ye least advice being received which way ye Convicts went." The escape was a complete success.[8]

Incredibly, three nights later the fugitives voluntarily returned to the jail, "went in att the same place they went out," and in the morning sent for the sheriff. They merrily informed the stunned officer that they had effected what they had intended—a mission which will forever remain a mystery—and were now prepared to submit to their sentence.[9]

Never before in the history of Virginia had such a thing happened. The act "so wrought upon the hearts of many well Disposed Christians" in the colony, including the President of the Council, that several petitions were submitted to the Lieutenant Governor begging that the two men again be saved from the gallows. On December 13, with the advice of the Council, Chicheley granted a full reprieve, with final judgment pending the King's pleasure. Nearly two years later Governor Francis Howard, acting on instructions from the Lords Commissioners of Trade and Plantations, extended to the redeemed pirates a full pardon with the assurances that they would never resort to their old practices again.[10]

Despite the unique twist of events surrounding the Tindall's Point affair, the problem of vigilance and defense against future piratical incursions into the Chesapeake persisted. Temporary, stopgap measures such as those employed against the raiders could not be considered effective in monitoring piratical activities in the tidewater, much less to suppress the pirate trade. The next Governor of Virginia, Lord Culpeper, advocated a singularly strong naval defense. A "good vessel will . . . restrayne the unbridled liberty of Privateers pyrates (for the most part) who have of late been troublesome then to the noe small terror of the Inhabitants, and begun formidably to infest the seas thereabouts, Even to the disturbance of the trade with England."[11] Indeed, the Chesapeake, without regular naval protection, stood on the brink of becoming a haven for privateers sailing under legally granted commissions as well as for those pretending to carry commissions.

Disturbed by "the piratical practices depredations and insolencies of private men of War and others pretenting [sic] Commission" King Charles II had been obliged to issue a decree on March 12, 1683, addressing the problem. Among other things, it forbade English men-of-war to rove "so near our Coasts as to give any occasion of fear to our Merchant Ships." Ships not specifically employed in trading and fishing voyages were to be detained, and foreign privateers were altogether forbidden from selling their prizes in British or colonial ports. Trade with foreign men-of-war, friend or foe, was strictly prohibited, and the King's subjects, unless licensed, were restricted from sailing in either military or merchant vessels of any foreign nations "upon pain of being reputed pirates and punished as such."[12] For Virginia the effects of the decree were minimal at best.

In the Chesapeake tidewater, far from the center of English government, there was a certain tolerance—indeed, an affinity among the rural population of the Bay for pirates and privateers with whom they occasionally bartered and traded. In July, a company of twenty pirates commanded by a certain Captain Wright arrived in Virginia in a bark from the island of Tortuga and settled peaceably on the Eastern Shore, apparently without the least opposition.[13] Yet the Tindalls' Point Raid, though only a pinprick against the general population, was another matter, for it produced an exacerbating effect upon the Council far more reaching than the scope of the actual crime itself. The Council finally recommended, "as ye last result," a measure that had been supported from the outset by Lord Culpeper. In mid-March 1683, after frequent meetings, the Council agreed that it was absolutely necessary for the peace and safety of the government that additional soldiers be placed on the tiny force already maintained by the colony, but

> more especially, that there should be care taken to preserve ye Dominion of ye water, as ye best, and indeed only means, to hinder & prevent all commotions, tumults and disturbances on land, and to secure Trade against Pyrates, that now begin to infest it.

A small land force of twenty soldiers was requested by the Council. For naval defense, a sloop of sixty tons and ten guns, fully rigged and fitted, and manned by a master, mate, gunner, and fifteen able seamen was thought to be the minimal acceptable deterrence against piracy on the Bay's waters. The vessel would cruise about the Virginia Capes "untill his Majesty shall give directions for a better ship, which they doubt not, but he will be pleased to doe next year."[14]

The little sloop *Katherine* was eventually secured for the job and was to be "maintained at the Charge of the Country."[15] Command was assigned to one Captain Roger Jones, an officer who had come to Virginia with Culpeper and had taken up residence near him at Green Springs. The captain was apparently a man of some means and rank and had lived in London before coming to the colony. His personal coach was emblazoned with the ancient Welsh family coat-of-arms of the family Ap John, which was early seated at Nottinghamshire, where he had been married, and owned valuable estates.[16]

Despite his station, Jones's appointment and his eventual conduct while in that office gave birth to a flurry of rabid accusations against him. Not the least of these was that rather than securing the Chesapeake from pirates, he frequently consorted with and profited from them. Others suggested that he had enriched himself more than he should have from the emoluments of the office he held. Though *Katherine* was to be manned and sailed by eighteen officers and men, Jones managed to secure only eight men as crew but constantly drew salaries for twelve,[17] a practice which was not uncommon by Royal Navy standards of the day, but one which was frowned upon by certain elements in the Virginia provincial establishment where such things were considered crass.[18] Yet the double standard practiced by frequently self-serving government officials from the Governor on down certainly did little to provide an example.

Nevertheless, at the onset there seemed to be every hope of success for the antipirate endeavor. On May 28, 1683, Jones received his commission, and on June 11 he asked for and received permission to press "soe many lusty Young men, both Seamen and others" as would be necessary to fill out his complement.[19] In light of the events that were to follow, the fielding of *Katherine*, given a more aggressive, honest commander, would have been timely. Her usage unhappily would prove far from advantageous in Virginia's infant war against piracy.

In mid-April 1683, a company of sea rovers under the command of Captain John Cook arrived in the Chesapeake with two prizes captured in the West Indies. One of the prizes was a French merchant ship laden with fine wines which had been taken only shortly before off the Isle of Vacca. Seeking security and refuge in the isolation of Accomac County on the Eastern Shore, the pirates proceeded to fit out the better of their two prizes, a vessel of eighteen guns, "with Sails, and every thing necessary," for what was to be a long and daring voyage. The French wines were readily traded with the amicable locals for provisions, naval stores, and other necessities.[20] When Captain Jones arrived to investigate, it was later charged, he struck his colors to the pirates and chose to be captured rather than to fight. But as soon as the pirates discovered him to be "a well-wisher to them," he, his company, and *Katherine* were released, and a quantity of wine and other commodities were presented to him as a "gift." Ultimately, Jones was accused of "advising, trading with & sheltering severall Pyrates & unlawfull Traders, instead of doeing his duty in Seizing them," a charge that would hound him throughout his career.[21]

Captain Cook and his company had secured not only respite and resources with which to refit their prize as a pirate ship (dubbed *Revenge*), but time in which to lay plans for a bold expedition around the Horn to the South Seas, and a cruise against the rich, treasure coasts of Chile and Peru. Able recruits were enlisted from Captain Wright's pirate company (which had arrived at Accomac the preceding April and chafed from boredom and inaction), "and as many more engaged in the same Design," recorded one of their party, "as made our whole Crew consist of about 70 men." Having provided themselves with every necessity for such a perilous adventure, the pirates then agreed upon "some particular Rules, especially of Temperance and Sobriety, by reason of the length of our intended Voyage." On August 23, 1683, *Revenge* set sail on a cruise destined to have significant impact upon the history of English navigation, for portions of her company were fated to carry out no less an achievement than a full circumnavigation of the globe.[22] Others would return to Virginia five years later to face a different sort of adventure—a most uncomfortable flirtation with the gallows.

Several days after Captain Cook departed for the South Seas, his ship was stricken by a week-long tempest. The constant south-southeast wind which blew directly into her teeth drove *Revenge* far off course. One of Cook's veteran seamen later recalled that the storm "drencht us like so many drowned Rats, and was one of the worst Storms I ever was in."[23] They had weathered one hurricane only days earlier while in Virginia, one which had slashed across the lower Chesapeake tidewater with awesome impact. "It hath pleased ye Almighty God," the Virginia Council recorded of that tempest,

> on ye twelveth day of this instant August to raise up & excite soe great a gust both of wind and raine, that it hath in all probability destroyed ye greatest part of Indian Corne growing on ye ground and great quantities of wheat by ye unhappy falling of houses.

Damage had been so great that the prospects of famine forced the government to forbid the export of such staples as corn, wheat, grain, and other commodities until the following summer.[24] The storm, which undoubtedly blotted out the government's concerns about the buccaneers on the Eastern Shore, had left Virginia virtually defenseless against piratical incursions. Fortunately, Cook had departed for richer hunting grounds. Captain Jones, however, was now obliged to contend not only with accusations of consorting with known pirates, but with the difficulty of repairing his ship, which had been severely damaged by the storm while lying in the York River. *Katherine*'s masts had been terribly injured, and damage to other sections of the vessel were equally serious.

Though after the tempest Jones couldn't defend the Chesapeake, the Virginia Council resolutely did its best to make it difficult for raiders to negotiate the hazardous waters of the Bay. On August 30, the government, undoubtedly with the buccaneers Wright and Cook in mind, noted that Virginia "hath been many times exposed to great hazard and danger by Privateers too frequently restoring hither, and many continue in ye like." As a result, the colony was "lyable to greater danger, if some course be not prescribed, whereby to prevent their Coming in, and improving their knowledge of our rivers and Harbours." Hence, the Council issued orders strictly prohibiting anyone from piloting any vessel whatsoever that was suspected of being a privateer into any river, creek, or harbor within the colony. Any such questionable vessel that came to anchor in colony waters would be immediately boarded by the nearest justice of the peace to discover who had piloted her in, and to make arrests as needed.[25]

By winter, the danger of pirate or privateer incursions had, it was felt, lessened to such a degree that the continued—and expensive—services of *Katherine*, a "Vessel not answering ye expectation & designe" of the government, was deemed no longer necessary. The controversy over Captain Jones' reputed soft spot for pirates no doubt contributed to that decision. On November 29, he was relieved of command, the sloop was discharged from service and laid up, and her munitions, arms, rigging, and sails were sent to be stored "att middle Plantation."[26] Less than three months later, Virginia would welcome a forceful new Governor, and a new bout against piracy would be initiated.

On February 21, 1684, Francis Howard, the Baron Lord Effingham, read his commission as Governor of Virginia, dated September 23, 1683, before the Executive Council sitting at Gloucester on the York River.[27] Though history would record the new Governor as an overbearing, imperious autocrat who exhibited little regard for the Virginia House of Burgesses, and even less for the "odious" public at large, Howard arrived in the colony with grim determination to succeed against pirates where others had failed.[28] At first blush, the new Governor appeared willing and prepared to argue for the strengthening of the Chesapeake's naval defenses. He was well aware of the accounts of infestation of the tidewater by these "low-lifes" prior to his administration and was determined to prevent the same from besmirching his own.

Howard wasted little time after his appointment in improving Virginia's naval defenses. It was time for the Royal Navy to take a hand in matters, he felt, and at the King's expense rather than that of the colonies. In October 1683 he proposed to the Privy Council in England "the great want of a small Fregat in Virginia, as well to give countenance to his Majestys Authority, and to prevent any future Insurrections there, As for securing his Majestys Customs, and opposing the Pirates that have lately infested that Coast." He capably justified the request by simply noting that the revenue of Virginia "exceeds that of all the other plantations put together" and thus deserved the attention. On October 31 the Privy Council concurred with the Governor's proposal and directed that a Royal Navy "Man of Warr Ketch" be equipped and fitted out with a crew of forty men. Though placed under the command of the Governor of Virginia, the vessel might also receive instructions from the Governor of Maryland, in whose colony local piratical activities had been reported.[29] The ship selected proved to be the tiny 79-ton ketch *Quaker,* Captain Thomas Allen commanding, which had been purchased by the navy in 1671.[30] Though certainly not a frigate, she was better than the *ad hoc* defenses of earlier times, and Howard appeared pleased.

Less than four months after presenting his commission as Governor, and now armed with a permanent guardship, Howard issued, at the direction of Charles II, a proclamation putting teeth in his war against piracy. The proclamation was specifically designed to prohibit the trading, harboring, or corresponding with any pirates or privateers whatsoever. There would be no repeat in his administration of the charges leveled against Captain Jones, for the abominable trade with pirates, he admonished, must be stopped.

The proclamation noted that entertaining and harboring of privateers and pirates was not only dangerous, but hazardous to the peace and welfare of the King's subjects. Any intercourse with pirates and privateers, as well as those suspected of having unlawful designs was strictly forbidden and was to be reported on to the authorities immediately. All commissioned officers in the colony were authorized

> *to raise such a Number of Men well Armed, as they shall find needfull for ye defence of their parts, from Attempts of any Privateers or Pyrates, until he, or they can receive fitt Orders . . .*

Furthermore, anyone found harboring, entertaining, trading with, or corresponding with any pirates or privateers after the publication of the proclamation, on June 19, 1684, would be "prosecuted as Notorious Offenders, and shall be lyable unto such paines, punishments, and penalties, as the Law shall be Judged against them."[31]

To the majority of pirates, despite the take-command attitude of the new Governor, as evinced by his proclamation, such efforts presented little more than idle threats. The buccaneers that roamed the Chesapeake were hardly impressed by such bluster or by the tiny guardship, and continued with their merry business of trading with the locals, and occasionally plundering a few homes along the Bay's periphery and shipping on its waters. Worse still was the increase in the home-grown variety of pirates. The most notable of these during the Howard administration was a particularly evil sort named Roger Makeele, who not only based his operations out of Watts Island, near Accomac County, but apparently developed a loosely-knit confederacy of local picaroons from the surrounding islands. Makeele's activities would grow to such proportions as to alarm not only the government of Virginia but that of Maryland as well.

The boat that put out from the Choptank River on Maryland's Eastern Shore in mid-January 1685, though only sixteen feet long at the keel, carried a cargo of twenty thousand pounds of tobacco which promised to improve immeasurably the fortunes of her master, one Richard Stevens. The voyage down the Bay was undoubtedly expected to be without incident, for as everyone in the tidewater knew, pirates only sailed Chesapeake waters in the spring and summer.[32]

As evening approached on January 20, Stevens and his crew of two neared Watts Island, a small, sandy islet east of Tangier Island and off the Bay side of Accomac County, Virginia, where it was decided to put in for the night. Within a short time, the three weary seamen were ashore, huddled around a warm fire. As the last glow of twilight turned to night, seven men suddenly appeared from the surrounding darkness. Stevens instantly recognized the leader of the party as Roger Makeele, an old acquaintance of his, and "a person of not onely evill fame, but certainly of very bad life and conversation." Accompanying Makeele was his lieutenant, a man named Smith, and at least three Watts Islanders belonging to the plantation of a certain Mr. Jenckins.[33]

Makeele's intentions were instantly apparent as two of his men seized the little tobacco boat. Enraged at their temerity, Stevens jumped up and "laid hands on the grapling" but was violently grabbed by Makeele and thrown into the water. Stevens and his men, unarmed and outnumbered by a body of brigands carrying guns and swords, were powerless to resist. The pirate leader ordered the boat to put off. One of Makeele's men and one of the islanders embarked aboard a shallop, one of two pirate vessels riding nearby in the darkness, and set off in company with the tobacco boat.[34]

With "many threatening words, and daunting expressions in company with [the] other two Islanders," Makeele remained on the beach with his captives for nearly two hours. Finally, the shallop returned, having deposited the tobacco boat on a nearby island. Two of the Watts Islanders were then directed to maintain an armed vigil on the beach for the remainder of the night to protect the pirate's vessels and guard the prisoners. The remainder of the men, with Makeele and the "Overseer of the Island," then retired to a house situated nearly a mile away.[35]

The following day Stevens and two of his men were permitted to visit the house and found the pirates drinking rum and brandy and feasting on mutton and turkey. The rovers scoffed as their hungry captives begged for food and drink, and for two days and nights forced them to fast. Finally, Makeele ordered one of the islanders to set the three prisoners ashore on the mainland. A small boat, which had been hidden among the underbrush, was launched, and Stevens and his men were embarked. Within a short time, they were landed in a remote marsh where, despite the winter cold, they were stripped of their clothes in "payment" for the trip and released. Stevens managed to reach civilization in Accomac to report the piracy to the local authorities, while his two crewmen, Richard Baily and a man named William (possibly a slave or indentured servant) made their way to Dorchester County.[36]

Barely two weeks had passed after the capture of Stevens's tobacco boat before Makeele, operating from his base on Watts Island, nearly struck again. This time, the intended victim was a sloop bound from the western shore of Maryland for the Eastern Shore of Virginia, laden with eight hundred to nine hundred pounds of goods. The sloop had come to anchor innocently enough under the lee of Watts Island, ignorant of the danger that lay before her. Two of the crew went ashore, where they chanced to encounter Makeele and his party. With seeming magnanimity, the pirate extended an invitation to the entire crew to join them "and refresh themselves with fresh provisions." Beef and mutton from recently slaughtered animals hung nearby, and the temptation was undoubtedly great.[37]

Fortunately for the sloop and her crew, a certain Thomas Ley, whose own vessel, laden with plank and other lumber, lay at anchor nearby. Ley's vessel, deemed "a bad sloope," had escaped the attention of the pirates, possibly because of its condition, but Captain Ley was well aware of Roger Makeele's nefarious intentions. He "well knew said Makeele, and pceiveing [sic] his designe to betray the strangers on shoare, took opportunity to acquaint them of the danger, and practice of said Roger . . . whereupon they repaired on board, and gott to Sayle."[38]

Though the merchant sloop and her crew saved by Ley fortuitously escaped the clutches of the pirates, Makeele's depredations had only begun. In the weeks that followed, his confederacy of pirates spread about the islands of Accomac and were soon threatening any shipping going up or down the Bay. Makeele and his compatriots did not limit their robberies to the Chesapeake or to white men. Indians on the Eastern Shore were among those plundered of guns, furs, and other goods. The pirates struck often, "violently assaulting plundering and robbing" innocent citizens of both Maryland and Virginia, and those passing to and from the tidewater by land and sea.[39]

By February the situation had degenerated to such an extent in Maryland that the Governor's Council, meeting at St. Mary's City, ordered that a letter be sent to Governor Howard requesting that he use all of the means in his power to help suppress and apprehend the pirate and his brigands. In Maryland itself, warrants were issued to the "several sheriffes of this Province & to apprehend the said Makeele and his Confederates or any of them wheresoever they shall be found within their respective Bailywicks limitts & precincts." Maryland authorities were directed to conduct a thorough search for the pirates upon land and sea, and when found they were to be arrested on sight and placed in custody to await trial.[40]

Such efforts proved to be in vain, for Makeele continued to elude authorities, conducting his raids with apparent impunity. Near the beginning of March, he and his band descended upon Isle of Wight County in Virginia. They came by water, robbed the home of one Nicholas Smith, and then vanished. The Virginia authorities, believing that Makeele was "supposed to be roving to and againe in the bay, in expectation of more booties," were whipped into a near-panic. On March 10 Governor Howard met in session with the Council at Nominy to determine a course of action. The Governor, making use of the newly-armed naval forces, directed Captain Allen, commander of the ketch *Quaker,* to "saile into ye bay and cruze about and search all parts therein for ye aforesaid Roger Makeel and ye other his Complices." To insure that neither that pirate nor any other such notorious offenders escaped justice, two additional sloops were manned and sent to assist *Quaker* in her quest.[41]

With pressure building to secure his capture, Makeele abandoned the Watts Island base and began to utilize the shallow sounds and rivers of North Carolina as a frequent refuge, much to the chagrin of royal authorities in Virginia. The neighboring colony to the south of the Old Dominion (as Virginia was then beginning to be called) was already earning a reputation as a pirate haven, one in which Governor and Proprietor Seth Sothel held a certain affinity for sea rovers of Makeele's ilk.[42] Governor Howard, having grounds to believe the pirate to be in North Carolina, followed protocol and dispatched a formal letter to Sothel requesting him to conduct a search in his colony to apprehend and return the buccaneers to Virginia jurisdiction. Howard agreed to cover the costs incurred, but he need not have bothered, for Sothel simply ignored the request. Howard was not prepared to impugn North Carolina's territorial jurisdiction by explicitly ordering Captain Allen to invade the colony in search of the pirates, but he did direct him "in case, It shall happen, that it bee discovered, in what place they are, to use all endeavours to bring them into this Governm[en]t in order to have their legal tryals."[43]

Whether or not Allen took the hint is unknown, for Howard's success at repressing the Makeele raids is only implied. The Governor was, however, able to report later in the year that "some Pilfering Pyrates have done damage to the Inhabitants, but I have taken the Chiefest and executed them."[44] Though we can only conjecture that Makeele was brought to justice, his depredations on the Chesapeake had ceased. The effectiveness of Howard's campaign against the pirates was, on the surface at least, a success. But the effectiveness and performance of the guardships on the Virginia Station was another matter.[45]

Not long after the arrival of *Quaker,* Governor Howard's force of pirate chasers was increased substantially by the addition of another Royal Navy vessel, His Majesty's ketch *Deptford.* Though the Crown had resolved in 1686 to send a fifth-rate man-of-war of thirty guns and a hundred men, *Deptford* was all that could be spared. Built in 1665 at Deptford, England, the 89-ton burthen, 10-gun warship was only slightly larger than her younger sister.[46] Sadly, her master, Captain John Crofts, was totally ineffective as a commander. Governor Howard, who had little respect for practically everyone, scorned both Crofts and Allen. "My footman would make as good captains as they," he once complained, with some justification. Of the two mariners, however, Crofts was by far the worse. He had come into the colony "Belching out a thousand oaths . . . to get an estate, and that he would have one before he left." His cruelty to his officers, whom he frequently beat until they were black and blue, was enhanced by an overfondness for the bottle.

Domestic quarrels with his shrewish wife were of legendary proportions.[47]

Captain Crofts hated Howard with a passion usually reserved for enemies in the heat of combat. In numerous letters to Admiralty Secretary Samuel Pepys, he accused the Governor of discouraging His Majesty's naval commanders on the Virginia Station in the performance of their duty and encouraging unfree and unfair trade. Outraged at the accusations, Howard summoned both Crofts and Allen before him in Council on February 2, 1688, but Crofts refused to appear. Complaints against the absent commander abounded, while support for the Governor in this matter, as expected, was plentiful. The Surveyor General of Customs Patrick Meyne reported of frequent charges of "Injuries Offered to Masters and Merchants of Shipps Traders into Virginia, by Crofts." Captain Allen supported every charge placed against his fellow captain, and disavowed every accusation the captain made against the Governor. The entire affair, unfortunately, had little more effect than to cloud further already turbid waters, and scant benefit to the public good resulted. In the end, Howard refused to act, feeling that if he complained of the performance of the King's officers, his complaints might be interpreted as suggestions that he did not need their services in the first place.[48]

Nevertheless, Governor Howard's and the Virginia government's aggressive attitude toward piracy and privateering was unusual for the English colonies of the Atlantic seaboard, most of which were like North Carolina, which welcomed pirates, either overtly or covertly. Many merchants were driven to dealing with pirates by the very policy that sought to establish British mercantile supremacy. Colonial merchants, unable to compensate for the limited goods available to them through normal outlets as a result of the limitations imposed by the English Navigation Acts of 1651, compensated for their lack of world market goods by buying them from pirates. By the late 1680s, Rhode Island, Boston, and New York had become hotbeds of pirate trading. Governor Sothel of North Carolina was typical of many autocratic colonial chief executives who were soft on pirates in more ways than one. Having once been captured and ransomed by Algerian pirates, he had later openly traded with their kind, sold privateer commissions for twenty guineas each, and thought nothing of occasionally seizing the property of honest merchants while at the same time branding them as pirates.[49] In Pennsylvania it was reported by one of the King's customs officers:

> They walk the streets with their pockets full of gold and are the constant companion of the chief in the government. They threaten my life and those

who were active in apprehending them; carry their prohibited goods publically in boats from one place to another for a market; threaten the lives of the King's collectors and with force and arms rescue the goods from them. All these parts swarm with pirates, so that if some speedy and effectual course be not taken the trade of America will be ruined.[50]

Howard fully intended to purge Virginia and the Chesapeake of pirates despite the prevailing attitudes in other colonies. On February 2, 1688, he was pleased to present to the Executive Council the most recent command of the King, that "all Pirats, and Sea Rovers, their Confederates and Accomplices, with their Shipps, Goods & plunder" be seized and imprisoned until they might be prosecuted.[51]

Within less than a few months, Howard would have the opportunity of achieving at least part of his wish, though under the most extenuating of all possible circumstances.

VII

Pieces of Eight and Silver Plate

Admiralty Secretary Samuel Pepys held a guarded opinion of Admiral Sir Robert Holmes, the man King James II had assigned to rid the West Indies and adjacent seas of pirates and privateers. He recognized Holmes as a useful, though somewhat "rash, proud coxcombe" whose high opinion of himself was equalled only by his self-serving cunning. The admiral was indeed an egotistical man. He had once captured a vessel in which the Italian-made torso of the Sun King, Louis XIV, was being conveyed to France for the modeling of the head. Holmes retained the unfinished marble work and eventually crowned it with his own august features.[1] Despite such vanities, Pepys saw much of value in the officer.

> He seems to be very well acquainted with the King's mind, and with all the general factions at Court and spoke all with so much frankness that I do take him to be my Lord's good friend, and one able to do him great service, being a cunning fellow, and one that can put on two several faces and look his enemies in the face with as much love as his friends.[2]

In May 1687 King James renewed the earlier proclamation of Charles II against piracy, issued in March 1684, but offered a unique alternative to assist in its success—pardons for all buccaneers who turned themselves in under certain conditions of the decree. The edict, entitled "A Proclamation for the more effectuall reducing and suppressing of Pirats and Privateers in America," was issued on January 20, and officially published on January 22, 1688.[3] Intent on putting muscle behind the order, the Crown commissioned none other than Sir Robert to sail for the West Indies with a squadron to rid the seas forever of the piratical scourge. The admiral embarked with strong personal inducements to insure his success. Not only was he granted all profits from his and his agents' seizure of privateer and pirate vessels, but his personal authority in matters relating to his mission was to supersede that of all the English colonial governors in America.[4]

Assisted by Thomas Lynch, his zealously active deputy, and keeper of the King's Privy Seal and a corps of agents, Holmes pursued his objectives with the resolution of a school of piranha stripping a carcass. His ships cruised about the isolated coasts, inlets, and islets of the Americas frequented by pirates, making sudden, and occasionally indiscriminate, descents on suspected vessels. Through his network of agents, Holmes waged a heavy-handed campaign of hectoring designed to dismantle the growing affiliations between governors and local councils and the buccaneering brotherhood. Though his efforts ultimately failed to shake the dirt loose from the roots of the colonial establishments,[5] his initial operations in the Chesapeake tidewater met with support from the Howard administration, where the guardship force was beefed up by the addition of a third vessel, HMS *Dumbarton*. No one would have guessed how fortuitous the arrival of that frigate would prove to be, or how quickly Howard's support of Holmes would degenerate into conflict.

The tiny shallop scudding down the Chesapeake on that warm summer day of June 22, 1688, would have seemed innocent enough to the casual observer, but for Captain Simon Rowe, the commander of *Dumbarton*, charged with protecting the tidewater against pirates and privateers, nothing was too insignificant to bear investigation. Rowe's ship, anchored near the mouth of the James, was a sixth-rate, 191-ton former Scottish vessel, the largest Royal Navy warship to be assigned to the Virginia Station since the ill-fated *Elizabeth*, nearly two decades earlier. Relatively new to the service, having been commissioned in 1685, she was manned by a crew of seventy and carried eighteen guns, certainly enough to intimidate the likes of the little boat approaching from up the bay. As the shallop neared the James, Captain Rowe could not have guessed the controversy he was about to set in motion by ordering her to come to.[6]

There were four men aboard the shallop, three whites and a black, as well as three large sea chests and, apparently, several bundles of personal belongings. Closer investigation, however, produced the startling discovery that could not have failed to excite all aboard the warship. The chests were heavily laden with a fortune in pieces of eight, silver plate, and other valuables. The four men in the shallop, who identified themselves as Edward Davis, Lionel Delawafer, John Hinson, and Peter Cloise, were instantly seized and secured on suspicion of piracy.[7]

Rowe knew little of the notoriety or past history of his unhappy guests, but the treasures they possessed spoke volumes about their deeds. After the suspects were clamped in irons and shipped off to Jamestown, Captain Rowe, Colonel Cole of the Council, and one John Johnson drew up an inventory of the contents of the sea chests and other belongings. Under the heading "Lionell Dellawafer" was listed the following:

> *In one Bagg, 37 silver plates; two scollops; seven dishes, silver lace, some cupps broken. Plate weighing bagg, string and all, 74 lb.*
>
> *Three baggs of Spanish money marked L.W., containing 1100 dollars thereabouts.*
>
> *In a chest marked L.W., a peece of cloth and some old things, with old broken Plate and some little Basons, weighing in all 84 lb.*

Among Edward Davis's belongings were three bags of Spanish money, principally pieces of eight; a parcel of broken silver, weighing 142 pounds, in a small chest; "ffower pairs of silke stocking, A few Remnants of Lynnen Damnified"; several paper books (possibly logbooks); two suits of clothes; and miscellaneous other items.

John Hinson's chest contained similar riches—two bags of Spanish money containing 800 pieces of eight; one chest of broken silver plate weighing 106 pounds; remnants of linen and cloth; some clothes; and pieces of varicolored ribbons.[8]

Soon after their arrival in Jamestown, the four suspected pirates were brought before Lord Effingham and several members of the Council for questioning. Lionel Delawafer, who was cross-examined first, claimed that he had been in the West Indies for several years, and that he was a common resident of Jamaica. He used to go out with traders to trade with the Spanish and "sometimes with the privateers, but said he never was a privateer himself nor belonged to any." When asked to explain how he came by his plate and money, he replied that he had acquired it over a period of years by trading with privateers and Spaniards. Barely three months earlier, he volunteered, he had left Jamaica for Barbados, and from there traveled to Bermuda on a trading voyage. From Bermuda he had traveled to Pennsylvania, "thence to the head of the Bay, thence in a shallop to New Point Comfort and then were bound for Elizabeth River and in the way was seized by Captain Rowe." He denied having known Davis for long, or to have ever seen him before Bermuda, but he had been well acquainted with John Hinson for four or five years and knew him to trade with the privateers and Spaniards. When questioned about the treasure in the trunks, he acknowledged owning "one of the chests and a Bagg containing about 160 lb. weight of plate, and in three baggs about 1100 pieces of eight, 500 of which were sent by him to one William Grinton living in Lyn Haven, being left him by one Timothy Rion [or Lion] dec^d.," along with a chest full of clothes and sundry other items of little value.[9]

John Hinson's testimony followed Delawafer's account closely; although he espoused his own innocence of privateering all the while. He too, he said, had never seen Edward Davis before their meeting in Bermuda.[10]

The black, Peter Cloise, whom Davis claimed as his property, told an entirely different story. He had, he testified to the Governor, lived among the Spaniards until taken from them by Davis nine years before. He had frequently sailed with his master aboard the 14-gun ship *Emanuel,* aboard which the latter had held command, and which was manned by over one hundred seamen. *Emanuel,* it seemed, had taken quite a number of ships and plundered "many towns in Spain" (later found to be the Spanish Main). The most damning evidence against the three white prisoners was Cloise's statement that they had all sailed together as comrades for some time.[11]

Despite Cloise's deposition, the prisoners maintained that it had been their objective to go to Lynnhaven and "there to set themselves downe." They had passed through both Pennsylvania and Maryland peaceably enough, having secured certificates signed by two justices of the peace. Before their journey had been so rudely interrupted by Captain Rowe, they claimed, they had already met with Captain Thomas Allen of HMS *Quaker,* who also provided them with a certificate of immunity.[12]

Despite the certificates allegedly secured (which, Governor Howard blandly pointed out to the Council of Trade and Plantations in Whitehall, were nothing more than passes from Maryland showing that they were not runaway servants), it was only later asserted that Allen had never even encountered the travelers. The Governor had little doubt that the prisoners were, in fact, privateers. On July 9, 1688, he issued a writ instructing the jailer of Jamestown to commit the men "to James Citty Gaol for suspition of pyracy," where they would await the Crown's pleasure.[13]

Davis, Delawafer, and Hinson, having adamantly denied the charges of piracy, were now indeed upon the horns of a dilemma. They stood little or no chance of benefitting from the King's proclamation, by claiming a pardon unless they admitted to being pirates. Yet to admit it after being arrested was to risk losing not only their substantial treasures and goods to the likes of Sir Robert Holmes and his agents, but their lives as well.[14]

In light of what seemed a hopeless predicament, the four prisoners could not have helped but reflect upon the amazing odyssey which had begun five years earlier and which now seemed about to end in fatal ignominy.

In August 1683, when Captain John Cook sailed in the good ship *Revenge* from Accomac, Virginia, for the South Seas, he took with him a seasoned company of seventy veteran privateersmen well experienced in crossing swords with and plundering the hated Spanish. Cook's quartermaster and second in command had been Edward Davis and his surgeon was Lionel Wafer. Years later, upon his return to Virginia, Wafer would attempt to mask his identity by changing his name to Delawafer. All three men, despite testimony provided in 1688, had already spent years in the West Indies and in the South Seas roving and raiding under the command of such notable buccaneers as Captains Bartholomew Sharp, Coxton, Wright, and Yanky. They had attacked and taken towns and ships, crossed the steamy jungles of the Isthmus on Panama on foot, were befriended by savage jungle natives, and wrought unending chaos on the Spanish colonists of Tierre Firme.

John Cook was a native "cirole" of the West Indian island of St. Christophers (now St. Kitts), born of European parents and reared in an environment from which the only true escape was the sea. His peers saw him as a "sensible man" who had spent the better part of his life as a privateersman. Cook had risen to piratical prominence first as quarter-master under the Dutch privateersman Yanky (who held a French commission to cruise against the Spanish), and then to the captaincy of one of Yanky's prizes, taken near the island of Tortuga. In assuming command of the prize, he had been joined by as many of Yanky's men "as were so disposed," including his indefatigable accomplice Edward Davis, only to be attacked, plundered, and marooned on the Isle of Vacca soon afterward by French pirates commanded by a certain Captain Tristian. Cook, Davis, and six or eight of their company, however, were made prisoners onboard Tristian's ship and carried to Pointe à Gravois. Neither Cook nor Davis were men who accepted surrender easily, and while the French captain and many of his men were ashore, they recaptured their ship, sent the remainder of the crew ashore, and stood away immediately for the Isle of Vacca to rescue their marooned comrades. Revenge against the French was all the sweeter when, en route, they encountered and seized a ship recently arrived from France which was laden with a cargo of wine. "They also took a Ship of good force, in which they resolved to embark themselves, and make a new Expedition into the South Seas, to cruise on the Coast of Chili and Peru." But they resolved to sail first to Virginia where they might in safety fit their new prize, appropriately dubbed *Revenge*, with sails and secure the necessities for the long hazardous voyage around Cape Horn.[15]

In Virginia, Cook and Davis were joined by many of Captain Wright's company who had arrived the preceding year. One of these was a particularly intelligent, if dour looking, diarist and adventurer, thirty-one-year-old William Dampier. Born in 1652, a farmer's son, at East Cocker, near Yeovil, England, Dampier had been apprenticed early in life to the master of a Weymouth ship and had voyaged to France, Newfoundland, and Bantam. During the Second Anglo-Dutch War he had enlisted and fought as a foot soldier under Sir Edward Spragge. He later engaged in a variety of professions, from managing a plantation in Jamaica to trading around the islands of the West Indies and working in the logwood trade on the Bay of Campeche. In late 1679, while on a trading voyage to Jamaica, he threw in his lot with a squadron of buccaneers assembling under Captains Coxton, Sawkins, Sharp, and others who were planning an attack on the Spanish treasure port of Porto Bello on the Isthmus of Panama.[16]

Dampier not only joined up but marched with the pirates across the Isthmus of Panama, participated in the attack and capture of the city of Santa Maria, assaulted and seized a fleet of eight ships in a daring nighttime sortie in canoes, raided the town of Pueblo Nova, captured and burned the city of La Serena, weathered several mutinies, hiked back across the Isthmus, cruised the Caribbean, and finally retired with his meager spoils to Virginia with Captain Wright. His stay in Virginia was not an easy one in light of his buccaneering past and the official crackdown by Virginia authorities. When Captain Cook prepared for another cruise of the South Seas, Dampier was ready and eager to go.[17]

The Eastern Shore of Virginia served the pirates well as a base from which they might refit their vessels, take on supplies, and prepare for their certainly perilous voyage. When Cook, Davis, and their men departed from Virginia shores, it was to begin a piratical adventure to the storied South Seas for which it would be difficult to find parallel. Although Cook was destined to die on the arduous voyage, Davis, Wafer, Dampier, and Hinson would go on. Ultimately, they would be joined by other pirates with similar objectives, and their tiny band would swell by the hundreds. Dampier, in a milestone voyage, would participate in a circumnavigation of the globe and live to publish his tale. Davis, aided by his trusted friend Lionel Wafer, would lead in Cook's place, conducting a campaign of raiding and marauding the

rich South Seas coast of Spain's American empire. They would discover islands and visit lands unknown to Englishmen, from the frozen
isles in the Straits of Magellan to the sweltering jungles of the Isthmus.
They would chart new passages through uncharted seas, sack towns
and cities, and ransom wealthy captives. Davis would ultimately command a grand pirate army of a thousand men, French and English,
black, white, and mulatto, with a fleet of ships that would dare the
heavily armed flotillas of the Spanish South Seas fleets. They would
carry out daring overland marches through the jungles of Central
America to strike the Spanish when they least expected it, and impose a
reign of panic and terror from Panama to Chile. And finally, their
coffers filled with plunder, they would return to the Atlantic via the
perilous Straits of Magellan, and then sail triumphant into the West
Indies.[18]

For Davis, Wafer, and Hinson, their return would provide an opportunity to retire with their accumulated booty, upon which they
might live like lords for the rest of their days. In the West Indies they
met one Captain Edward Carter in a Barbados sloop and booked
passage for Philadelphia, their pirate band having divided to go their
own separate ways. About the middle of May, 1688, after nearly five
years of buccaneering, the three pirates and Davis's slave entered the
mouth of the Delaware, landed, and carried their treasure and belongings overland to the head of the Chesapeake. There they secured a
shallop, and mindful of their former stay in Virginia, bolstered by the
King's pardon which dangled before them, sailed for Point Comfort
where they intended to settle down to the life of the gentry.[19]

It was then that their troubles really began.

On August 6, as Edward Davis, Lionel Wafer, and John Hinson languished in the Jamestown jail, the royal proclamation of January 22,
1687/88, was published in Virginia. It offered, among other things, full
and gracious pardons to any pirates or privateersmen who surrendered within a year of its issuance (18 months if they were in isolated or
distant areas when the news reached them) and provided adequate
security for good behavior in the future. At this juncture, the pirates
managed to secure the legal assistance of one Micajah Perry. Perry
wisely suggested that they change their tactics and apply for the pardon, even though it meant a virtual admission of guilt. On August 16
Davis, Wafer, and Hinson, taking Perry's advice,

> petitioned his Excellency that they might be admitted, to the benefitt of his
> Majesties Gracious Proclamation, upon which they affirmed they came in,
> And the Proclamation being published the 6th day of August, they ap-

prehended themselves to be within the Gracious mercy of that Proclamation.[20]
The petition ended with claims for the restoration of the confiscated goods. Among Wafer's goods were (according to Wafer) 1,158 pieces of eight; 162 pounds of plate and 1½ ounces of gold; several suits of clothes; and £40 worth of silk and cloth. Davis's list now included not only plate, coins, and goods, but one "Negro Man," undoubtedly Peter Cloise.[21]

Three days after the pirates' petition, Governor Howard dispatched Rowe's inventory of the confiscated treasures to Lord Sunderland, along with a letter gloating over the prisoners' admissions of piracy.[22] It had not been until Davis, Wafer, and Hinson had produced a virtual confession that the Governor informed them of the decree of the court: they had been taken into custody by a government representative and had not surrendered of their own volition, and as a consequence had failed to meet the required terms of the proclamation. Howard, however, could do little until the King's pleasure was known. Trial of the pirates in Virginia, it seemed, was out of the question, for the Crown, outraged at the friendly treatment many pirates had enjoyed in the American colonies, had forbidden such proceedings unless sanctioned by the King's principal pirate chaser, Admiral Holmes.[23]

In October 1688, Howard received instructions from Lord Sunderland to prosecute the prisoners and turn their treasure and goods over to Holmes.[24] For the first time, the Governor balked. Try the prisoners he might, but turning over the treasure before the pirates were prosecuted was something else. As one chronicler later noted, nothing was done at all, the delay owing, perhaps, to the fact that the official suppressors of piracy "were apt to demand help 'in no way respectful terms,'" and were so important and influential that they could and would act quite independently of authority.[25]

Though his clients remained in jail, the astute Micajah Perry continued pressing their case. In March 1689 he sent another petition (which was quite remarkable in its understatement) to the Commissioners of Trade and Plantations.

For some years the prisoners had been in the South Seas, and having procured a small quantity of plate and other goods, designed to spend the remainder of their days honestly and quietly. So in May 1688 they arrived at Pennsylvania and after some stay procured a pass and took boat for Patuxent river, where they surrendered to Captain Thomas Allen.

Perry related the account of the arrest of his clients by Captain Rowe and pleaded for the pardon, "which they sought when they surrendered," and the return of their treasure, which they stated was worth £2,316.19s.

On April 18 another petition was sent to the Virginia Council of State and to its President Nathaniel Bacon in which the buccaneers reiterated their entire case and "humbly prayed that they might be inlarged, and their Mony plate and Goods delivered unto them." The Council replied, citing Lord Sunderland's letter, by saying that they, or any other persons apprehended for piracy, would be prosecuted according to law "at such time & in such Manner as Sir Robert Holmes or his Agent shall desire."[26]

Captain Thomas Berry, recently appointed to the command of HMS *Deptford* over the irascible Captain Croft, had been designated by Sir Robert as his agent in Virginia. Thus, immediately after receiving the petition of April 18, the Council dutifully notified Berry of the need for him to "be acquainted with the Petition before Proceedings could be had." Before the captain could respond to the Council's summons, the pirates submitted yet another petition on April 23, reiterating that of April 18 and moving "that they might have a hearing, and the benifitt of his Majesties Gracious Proclamacōn." The Council delayed action, informing the prisoners that Berry was expected in town soon and that it was absolutely necessary to know what orders he had received from Sir Robert before proceeding.[27]

When Berry finally reached Jamestown and presented himself to the Council, he reviewed the petitions with a jaundiced eye and then bluntly informed the stunned councilmen that according to his directions from Sir Robert, he could not proceed with any trial of the accused pirates until the plate, money, and other goods which had been taken with them by Captain Rowe were delivered into his hands. Though no one was willing to say so publicly, jurisdiction over the treasure was taking precedence over the administration of justice. A letter from Berry addressed to Governor Howard, however, sought to smooth any ruffled feathers the Virginia government might have in that regard. "I have power to ask you to release them if found fit objects for mercy, being provided with funds to ship them to England for the King's pardon." Governor Howard, still miffed at Sir Robert's assertion of authority over his own, refused to give ground, since the prisoners, he reiterated, had formally declared that their objective in coming to Virginia was to surrender and seek the benefit of the King's amnesty. "Therefore," he replied, "though I believe them to be great villains, I do not think it right to try them until the King's pleasure is known."[28]

With Governor Howard's departure for England (for reasons unrelated to the piracy issue) the dispute over custody of the booty continued, although the war of words was now between Berry and the Council. Though the money had been "by his Excellencies Order, and direction safely Secured and ready to be produced when the matter should be adjudicated," everyone wanted a share of it. Berry demanded it in behalf of Admiral Holmes. Captain Rowe, it was discovered, had kept some of the treasure, apparently aboard his ship, and refused to release it in defiance of court subpoenas. And the Council, which maintained custody of the bulk of it, wasn't turning it over to anyone until word from the King arrived or until some other viable solution appeared. The Council continued to defy Berry's authority on the grounds that the pirates hadn't been seized, but had surrendered voluntarily. Berry, too, was adamant, refusing to permit prosecution. The legal standoff continued while Davis, Wafer, and Hinson languished in their cells.[29]

On April 29, after more than ten months of imprisonment without benefit of bail or trial, the three buccaneers once more petitioned the Council, again reiterating their case and begging for the return of their treasure. This time, the Council, undoubtedly softened by the words of good lawyer Perry and the intransigence of Berry, and once again able to assert its own authority in the absence of Governor Howard, ordered the prisoners' release on giving security of five hundred pounds sterling for good behavior. The treasure would still remain in the Council's custody, but Davis, Wafer, and Hinson were to be permitted to go to England to receive a pardon or face trial according to English law. Each man was allowed thirty pounds to defray the cost of the voyage. The sum was to be taken from the treasure, as would all charges incurred for their imprisonment, food, and other fees for the prevous ten months.[30]

Davis, Wafer, and Hinson had not rested in their attempt to recover their goods from the Virginia government and from Captain Rowe. Several suits were filed against the captain "for wrongfully forceing their Estates from them." Rowe contemptuously failed to appear before the court and ordered several witnesses (members of his crew) to do likewise. The President of the General Court of Virginia Nathaniel Bacon then informed him that the three buccaneers had entered an account of debt against him for four thousand pounds sterling and were suing for an additonal two thousand pounds sterling in damages for their case. Again Rowe was summoned by the sheriff of Elizabeth City County to appear in court on April 5, 1690. Again he balked. And again he refused to let his men appear, though they had been lawfully subpoenaed. The court could do little more, for officers of the Royal Navy in the late seventeenth century were practically immune from civil law, especially in the colonies, and answered only to the Admiralty. Helpless to force Rowe to appear before it, and deeming it "not convenient to cause ye men belonging to their Maj[es]ties Ship to be brought from her," the court empowered four men—Captain Anthony Armestead, William Wilson, Bertram Servant, and Captain Thomas Allamby—to take depositions from anyone the complainants designated. But Rowe simply continued his campaign of obfuscation, and despite the best efforts of the court, the suit was doomed to failure.[31]

Although the order for their release had been issued in late April, the three buccaneers remained incarcerated in the Jamestown jail at least through May and June, for on July 8 another official letter was dispatched to the Lords of Trade and Plantations, once more detailing their legal odyssey and requesting instructions. Soon afterward, they were finally released on bail, albeit against the wishes of certain influential Virginians who saw them as a menace to decent citizens of the colony. In September, the redoubtable Philip Ludwell, no longer a member of the Council of State, but a Virginian with considerable political clout, enumerated a list of grievances in the colony. Among the items on the list was the case of

> three men who came in June 1688 from the South Sea to surrender under
> the King's proclamation but were imprisoned without bail or trial, and their
> goods detained until the Governor's departure, when they were released to
> the great danger of the community.

Davis, Wafer, and Hinson, though finally at liberty, were, if anything, more destitute than dangerous; they "punctually observed" the guidelines set for their bail. Unable to secure even the smallest portion of their treasure despite the promise of the Council, they were unable to support themselves. Again, on October 23, they submitted another in the seemingly unending stream of petitions for their effects. Again, the petition was refused until the King's pleasure was known.[32] Not until the winds of change had swept the far-off shores of old England would their own fortunes be destined to improve. But breezes had already begun to blow.

In 1688 King James II, whose unbalanced reign had threatened the religious and political harmony of England imposed by his predecessor and brother Charles II, was forced to abdicate in a bloodless coup known as the Glorious Revolution. James's eldest daughter Mary and her Protestant husband William of Orange were invited by a number of English nobles, both Tories and Whigs, to accept the crown. William readily accepted the challenge and landed at Torbay with an army. Though few Englishmen were enamoured with him, England's leaders and populace supported William out of simple hatred for the tyranny of James. The King was forced to seek refuge in Catholic France, and in 1689 Parliament declared the throne of England vacant. Shortly thereafter William and Mary were crowned King and Queen, and a new political order began to permeate the realm. Part of that new order included an active, diligent, and highly competent chief executive of Virginia.

On November 14, 1689, Captain Francis Nicholson was commissioned by King William and Queen Mary at Westminster as Lieutenant-Governor of Virginia, to serve as chief executive in the colony in Governor Howard's absence in England. Nicholson took command in May 1690, presenting his commission to the Council of State at Jamestown on June 3.[33] He was destined to become one of Virginia's most competent governors of the colonial era, and the colony's most ardent pirate fighter until the administration of William Spotswood nearly two decades later.

One of the first orders of business on Nicholson's agenda was to address the lingering problem of what to do with Davis, Wafer, Hinson, and the treasure. The buccaneers greeted the new executive with another petition, and again the Council was obliged to review the case. Nicholson, upon personally examining the buccaneers, saw the law quite clearly and acted with deliberate decision by ordering the money, plate, and goods sent to England to be delivered to Sir Robert, along with a request for the Crown's "Opinion what was requisite and Necessary to be done therein." Since no answer to Micajah Perry's petitions to the Lords Commissioners of Trade and Plantations had been received, Nicholson, on his own authority, ordered that three hundred pounds be retained in Virginia to pay for debts incurred by the buccaneers. Any funds remaining after the debts were paid would be sent to England. Davis, Wafer, and Hinson were given permission to return home to defend themselves and their claim to the booty. Another inventory of the treasure was ordered to be made by Council clerk William Edwards in the presence of Council members Ralph and Christopher Wormeley and Colonel John Armestead, and delivered up to Secretary William Cole. The treasure was then to be taken by the councilmen and placed aboard *Effingham,* "a Shipp of good Force," commanded by Captain John Purvis, and sent to England. Nicholson then turned his attentions to that portion of the treasure held by Captain Rowe. The captain was sternly directed to produce an inventory of the goods in his custody which had been seized from the pirates and to deliver it to Secretary Cole, who was to "Secure the said things, till direction be given, what shall be done with them."[34]

In July 1690 Lionel Wafer and John Hinson watched with no little interest from the home of Ralph Wormeley as the bulk of their troublesome treasure was loaded aboard one of Captain Purvis's boats for carriage to *Effingham*. Though now free on bail, they were heavily in debt for food, clothing, and shelter, and, despite the Council's repeated assurances that they would be allowed thirty pounds each from the treasure for their voyage to England, no funds had been made available. They were now absolutely destitute and were forced to petition the Council for the promised funds to clear their debts and pay for passage home to secure a trial or pardon and defend their ownership of the treasure.[35]

On July 26, 1690, the Council finally decided that if Wafer and Hinson could agree with their creditors that 100 pounds would clear their debts and pay passage, they would be permitted to leave for England, and the bills would be paid from the booty. The Council cleverly stipulated, however, that only when they were aboard ship were they to signify to whom the money was to be paid, thereby avoiding any embarrassing confrontations. Edward Davis apparently had already cleared himself of his debts and secured passage to England alone to defend himself and to save his share of the treasure. Wafer and Hinson resolved to follow at all costs, and within a short time, they too were at last aboard ship bound for home to join their companion.[36]

Writing of his travels in later years, Lionel Wafer preferred not to take note of his tedious and unhappy stay in the tidewater. "There I thought to settle," he recalled, "But meeting with some Troubles after a three Years residence there, I came home to England in the Year 1690."[37] But his problems—and those of his companions—were not over. Soon after reaching home, they drew up yet another petition, this time to King William III himself, again reiterating their tale of woe. Misfortune had followed in their tracks, for owing to the capture of some papers by the French, examination of their case in England had been delayed. Though they had made inquiry of Governor Nicholson for their goods (undoubtedly meaning those held by the Council and Captain Rowe) after arriving in England, they had been unable to learn whether or not he had given orders for their shipment to England. They feared it was but a pretext for depriving them of their property. "We beg for pardon," they beseeched the King, "and restitution of our property."[38]

The King adroitly sidestepped the matter, referring the issue to Lord Effingham. Howard, still obliquely opposed to Sir Robert's claim to the treasure by virtue of the commission he held, yet wishing to be done with the whole affair, acknowledged that Davis, Wafer, and Hinson were notorious pirates, but added, "I beg the Treasury to take over the goods, and acquit me of them."[39] Sir Robert, about to be foiled in his claim if the Treasury assumed authority over the booty, refused to be denied his just due, and was peeved that some of the treasure was still in Virginia. His displeasure was made quite clear to Effingham, who, in turn, transmitted the Admiral's concern to Nicholson. "I find S[r] Robert Holmes is dissatisfied at yo[r] detainder of Plate & Money in Mr. Wormeleys hands," and duly directed that the remainder, in both the Council's and Captain Rowe's possession, be sent to England.[40]

The Virginia Council, on receipt of Effingham's letter in March 1691, delayed action until late the following month. On April 21, the Council finally directed Secretary Cole, "in whose possession those few things that could be discovered in Cap[t] Rowes Custody," to ship the goods to Howard aboard the frigate *Experiment*.[41] Of the total of three hundred pounds in Spanish money and ten pounds of plate initially left in Ralph Wormeley's possession, two hundred pounds remained. The Council directed this portion of the treasure to be placed aboard HMS *Wolfe* "or some other good ship," consigned to Howard, and dispatched to England after all "Just fees and Claimes are settled and paid."[42]

In England, Admiral Holmes, irate over the disposition of the booty, was equally concerned over the proximity of Davis, Wafer, and Hinson to the center of royal authority and the treasure. He was aware that many cold-blooded buccaneers had found supporters and influence at the highest levels of government in the colonies, and he was undoubtedly concerned that Davis and company might manage the same in London. He now demanded that they be returned to Virginia to face trial—far away from the money and access to the King's ear. The demand was ignored, as the admiral's authority and influence in the issue continued to erode. Yet Holmes wasn't the buccaneers' only nemesis. The Spanish Ambassador had been busy for some time preparing a dossier against them, and the Dutch Ambassador was equally anxious to see the pirates punished. Although Davis apparently attempted personally to placate the latter, the ambassador, "having grevious things against him," was far from friendly.[43]

Yet Davis, Wafer, and Hinson were not without their sympathizers and supporters at court, and fate began to bend in their favor once again. Two of their principal accusers, Captain Thomas Berry and the Spanish Ambassador, had died suddenly. In January 1691, a member of the British aristocracy, Lord Sydney, whose interest in the case may only be surmised, requested a meeting with the new ambassador from Spain to learn if he would object to the treasure being restored to the three buccaneers. The Lords of the Treasury offered their own favorable opinion, one long awaited by Davis and company, that the buccaneers had indeed gone to Virginia with the intention of surrendering, and they had full rights to the goods for which they were applying. In February the Lords Commissioners of Trade and Plantations fully concurred.[44] The King's pardon and the return of the treasure to the buccaneers seemed only a matter of time; Sir Robert Holmes had been defeated.

In April the Virginia Council was sent instructions to send all of the remaining property of the three men to England, but affairs dragged on with remarkable slowness. In May the buccaneers submitted another petition to the Lords Commissioners of Trade and Plantations for their goods and money which were now being held by the Commissioners of Customs. Nothing happened. Again, in June, and once more in July, new petitions were presented urging dispatch since the petitioners were now "threatened with a miserable fate in prison."[45]

Sir Robert Holmes, however, refused to be silenced. In August he wrote from Bath claiming "certain silver" in the custody of the Treasury and declaring the acts of robbery by Davis and his men to be unparalleled. He deeply regretted that Davis was "countenanced in England, where the gallows is too good a reward for him."[46]

The following month, September, yet another petition was submitted, this time to Queen Mary. "Captain John Purvis," the buccaneers wrote, "who brought our silver from Virginia, tells us that if his bill of lading for same be returned to him he will deliver us what money he has in his custody, provided he receive quittance for that which he delivered to the treasury." Again nothing happened.[47]

At what point Edward Davis, Lionel Wafer, and John Hinson encountered Dr. James Blair, or indeed whether they ever met him face to face at all, is unknown. The consequences of their unusual relationship, however, were significant for all parties. Blair was a remarkable man, an educator and clergyman, born in Scotland in 1655 and educated there. In 1685 he had traveled to Virginia after serving as an Anglican rector near Edinburgh, and in 1689 he was appointed by the Bishop of London as commissary in Virginia, the highest position one could aspire to in the colonial church. In 1691 Blair had returned to

England with a mission of momentous import—to promote the establishment of a college in Virginia. With crusading zeal, he spearheaded a major campaign to secure support for the college. A royal charter was obtained, the royal grant including quitrents from twenty thousand acres of land in Virginia. As a concession, the college was to pay a symbolic rent to the Crown of two books of Latin verse annually. Despite the good will of the King and Queen and the support of the government and aristocracy in Virginia, more money was needed, and Blair traveled to London to badger the prosperous mercantile community for donations.

Perhaps it was coincidence, but more than likely it was Blair's shrewd nose for money that brought the clergyman and the pirates together. Davis and his men had been dangling by a legal thread for years, with practically anyone in authority dipping into the treasure on the slightest excuse. Yet the will of the Lords Commissioners of Trade and Plantations and the Treasury had been made known. Admiral Holmes was no longer a viable force with which to be reckoned in the issue, and Governor Howard had disavowed any further concern in the matter. All that was needed, apparently, was a little nudge of the King and Queen. And Dr. James Blair was apparently the man to do it—for a price.

How the deal was arranged is unknown, but in December the buccaneers submitted their last petition. Less than three months later, on March 10, 1692/93, the King, meeting in Council at Whitehall, issued the final word in the affair.

Upon reading the Peticon of Edward Davies, John Hinson and Lionel Delawafer, humbly praying that their Money Plate, Jewells and Cloathing, Seiz'd as Pirats goods in the year 1688 by Capt. Rowe Commander of the Dunbarton Frigatt in Virginia may be restored to them, and it Appearing by the Report of the Right honorable the Lords Commissioners of the Treasury that ye Petitioners by writing under their hands had own'd themselves to be Pirats & had Claim'd the Benefitt of a Proclamacon issued by the late King James for Suppression of Pirats and Privateers in America, by force or Assurance of pardon but had not strictly comply'd with the Conditions of the said Proclamacon and the Petitioners being Willing that the Sum or Value of three hundred pounds of the goods belonging unto them and now lying in their Majesties Warehouse together with the fourth part of what shall be recovered belonging to the Petitioners from the said Captain Rowe or his Executors shall be employ'd towards the Erecting a Colledg or free Schoole in Virginia or such other Pious or Charitable uses as their Majesties shall direct. It is this day Ordered in Councill as it is hereby Order'd that the Money, Plate, Jewells and other goods belonging to *the said Petitioners and seiz'd by Captain Rowe now lying in their Majestys Warehouse or wherever the Same may be found be forthwith Restored to the Petitioners the Sum or Value of three hundred Pounds only Excepted, which together with the fourth part of what remains in the hands of the said Captain Row or his Executors or which shall be recovered from them as belonging to the Petitioners is to be dispos'd of towards the Erecting of A Free Schoole or Colledg in Virginia in case the same shall be founded by grant from their Majesties and if the same shall not be so founded as aforesd to such other pious or Charitable uses as Their Majesties shall direct the petitioners giving good Security to answer the fourth part of what shall be receiv'd or recovered from the said Captain Rowe or his Executors to be Applied as Abovemencon'd, and the Right Honorable the Lords Commissioners of the Treasury are to give all necessary directions herein.*[48]*

And thus it came to pass that the College of William and Mary, the second free college in English America, was established, with a significant portion of its first endowment raised from pirate booty.

VIII

Profligate Men

Throughout the long controversy over Davis, Wafer, and Hinson, the Chesapeake Bay remained relatively free from piratical invasions owing principally to the protection provided by HMS *Dumbarton*. By 1691, however, the Bay's weather, the ever-present shipworms, and general wear and tear had destroyed the guardship to such an extent that she was no longer seaworthy. As a consequence the man-of-war was intentionally beached and broken up. Her big guns were hauled ashore and mounted in a battery at Tindall's Point, and her sails and rigging employed as replacements for other Royal Navy vessels calling in the tidewater.[1]

Dumbarton was replaced briefly by a merchantman of three hundred fifty to four hundred tons chartered by the Royal Navy in late 1690 for convoy duty to Virginia. This vessel, *Wolf*, was commanded by Captain George Purvis and manned by a crew of thirty-three. Armed with as many as twenty guns, she took her departure from England on December 20, 1690, and arrived off Cape Henry on March 16, 1691. Her visit to the Chesapeake was noteworthy for only one thing: on the day following her arrival, while en route up the Bay to the Rappahannock, she ran aground on a shoal midway between the York and Rappahannock rivers. After a week of struggle, and with the assistance of local mariners, she was finally freed; the bar upon which she grounded is known to this day as Wolf Trap Shoals. After an otherwise uneventful stay, *Wolf* departed Lynnhaven for England on June 20, 1791.[2]

By fall another guardship, HMS *Henry Prize*, a sixth-rate, 24-gun vessel, was on station. Captured from the French in 1690, the 246-ton guardship was 86 feet in length and 25½ feet abeam.[3] She was described as "a very Sharfe [sharp] Ship an ill Roader a poor ship for riding at anchor, and pitches very dangerously in an open Roade." She possessed "a very Sharpe Deepe body" which made cleaning her more of a chore than English seamen were used to with English-built hulls.[4] Her commander, Captain Richard Finch, proved to be as timid and complaining an officer as Purvis had been poor at sailing.

In October 1691 Finch complained of having to pay for pilotage services while cruising the Bay and claimed such costs should be borne not by the Royal Navy but by Virginia. He demanded that a sloop be built to assist him in the revenue service and applied to the Governor and Council for funds. Affronted by the navy officer's imperious demands, they informed him that the colony neither possessed nor could raise the money, and that the navy must, at any rate, pay for its own pilotage. Finch proposed to the Council that instead of cruising about the Chesapeake, he take station at the mouth of the York River, where he could monitor all ships arriving and departing from the Bay. If "it should happen that any Enemies that he is not able to deale with should come in," he could immediately sail upriver to the protection of the Tindall's Point battery. Judging from Finch's own description of his vessel as an "ill Roader," to have remained at anchor in the mouth of an estuary such as the York would have been the worst of all possible choices. Nevertheless, the Council agreed, simply (one suspects) to quell his constant complaining.[5]

Conditions aboard the guardship were miserable. Not only was she a poor, leaky sailer, but her crew was in great discomfort. Throughout the winter of 1691-1692 they were so ill-clothed that they were obliged to beg for relief from the Royal Navy convoy ships *Assurance, Conception,* and *Aldbrough* in April 1692. It is not surprising that the guardship's crewmen were frequently prone to desertion, many of them running off to the sparsely populated Carolinas.[6] By April the hull of *Henry Prize* (which had lain constantly at anchor) had become so riddled by shipworms that the only way to save her was with immediate careening and cleaning. By June, however, work had failed to start owing to a lack of carpenters. Finch complained, and the Council agreed to authorize the captain to impress the necessary men. But even then it was feared that the ship would not be ready to escort the annual tobacco fleet into the Atlantic by July; and she would certainly be of no use in protecting the Bay from pirates or other enemies.[7]

Apparently, *Henry Prize* was a hopeless case, for in January 1693 she was laid up, unable to perform the duties for which she had been sent to Virginia, as she was now "disabled by the want of Cables and Anchors." Desperate to have some form of protection, Nicholson and the Council beseeched Finch to at least hire a sloop or some other small vessel, put to sea, and start doing his job until a replacement from England arrived.[8]

The Governor of Virginia was undoubtedly frustrated by the inability to keep a man-of-war constantly cruising about the Bay, but he was also keenly aware of the vulnerability of Virginia's isolated coastal areas where guardships rarely cruised. Experience had already shown that pirates and smugglers had made extensive use of the lonely backwater channels of the seaboard side of the Eastern Shore, and unless something was done, such activities were likely to continue. In the spring of 1692 he invited the four burgesses representing Northampton and Accomac counties, who were then in Jamestown, to attend a Council meeting and present their views on the matter and provide the Council with their firsthand knowledge of the situation.

On April 28 the burgesses met with the Governor and Council and were asked whether they felt that there would be any injury to the inhabitants of their counties "if noe Ships or Vessells whatsoever should be permitted to goe into the Little Rivers and harbours on the Seaboardside of the Eastern Shore," an area "Enemyes and falce Traders" were known to frequent. The burgesses declared that such an action would not be harmful. With Nicholson's prompting, the Council thus ordered a prohibition of all maritime traffic on any of the rivers or harbors along the Atlantic Coast of Virginia's Eastern Shore, with the sole exception of Smith Island River, where legal traders and merchantmen frequently called on first arriving in the colony. The Council also ordered the courts of Northampton and Accomac to find fit and proper ways to monitor all shipping "to prevent any Mischief that may happen by the Suddain arrivall of an Enemy from Sea." Princess Anne County had been maintaining a lookout named Adam Hays on the county's Atlantic coast for some time at the expense of the General Assembly, and, it was undoubtedly hoped, Accomac and Northampton might see fit to follow suit.[9]

Nicholson continued to do his best to protect the Chesapeake from the scourge of piracy, a trade which thoroughly disgusted him. "I confess," he once wrote,

that I have always abhorred such sort of profligate men and their barbarous actions; for such they are the disgrace of mankind in general, and of the noble, valiant, generous English in particular, who have the happiness of being governed by so great a King.[10]

In 1694 the able chief executive of Virginia was appointed by the King to the governorship of neighboring Maryland in the place of Edmund Andros. He carried with him to that colony his hatred of piracy, and an intolerance for the leaders and merchant communities of other English American colonies who openly winked at, and occasionally outright supported, pirates. In Massachusetts pirates had been permitted to fit out expeditions and sell their prize cargoes openly. Condemned buccaneers were, on occasion, even permitted to purchase their freedom. Rhode Island had become a refuge and clearinghouse for pirate booty. Connecticut, whose governors were elected annually, tolerated the rovers because the chief executives frequently feared the political opposition of the powerful merchant community which traded with them. New York's Governor Benjamin Fletcher, his secretary, the collector of customs, and even the Royal Navy guardship captain on station there, were widely known to be in league with the freebooters. Protection and privateer commissions could be had for a price, and Fletcher himself had been seen publicly consorting with known and notorious pirates. The buccaneers frequented the lonely coasts of New Jersey and Delaware, where they could careen their ships and trade freely with the natives. The sparsely populated colonies of North and South Carolina, however, were reported to be rapidly becoming the principal pirate sanctuaries on the Atlantic coast. In South Carolina, where wealthy pirates could walk the streets in the open, and the poorer sort, unable to pay their way, were frequently hung, their presence was common. It was in the shallow sounds of North Carolina, which had become "a Receptacle of Pyrats," that the infestation was becoming a menace to the Chesapeake. The Carolina sounds had become, according to one royal official, Edward Randolph, a place "which receives Pirates, Runaways and Illegal Traders" of the lowest sort.[11] And it semed that everyone along the coast had a stake in their nefarious commerce. On January 24, 1698, when a new 10-gun, 154-ton Royal Navy advice boat named *Swift* ran aground south of Currituck Inlet, she was beset by a horde of local inhabitants who blatantly seized and burned papers thought to connect them with piratical activities.[12]

But for Francis Nicholson, new Governor of Maryland, the principal concern regarding pirates now came to focus on neighboring Pennsylvania. In that colony the buccaneers had found a steady and powerful friend in Governor William Markham. Not only did Markham's administration wink at the presence and commerce of the pirates (many of whom were involved in lucrative operations in the Red Sea and Madagascar), it permitted, and even assisted, several of their number or their supporters to rise to positions of political prominence. One pirate, James Brown, a former member of the crew of Captain Avery, married Markham's daughter and gained a seat in the Pennsylvania Assembly. Another, Captain Robert Snead, purchased the post of justice of the peace. Admiralty Court Judge Robert Quary, former secretary of South Carolina, onetime acting governor of that colony and Justice of the Court of Common Pleas, had turned a blind eye to pirate commerce in South Carolina and was once suspected of trafficking with them.[13] Both Snead and Quary, however, having achieved a measure of respectability in Pennsylvania, and sensing a slight shift in the winds of fortune, quickly became antipirate zealots of the first rank.

In the fall of 1696, as a result of the excesses of the Markham administration in Pennsylvania, desperate appeals for help reached Nicholson from a number of Philadelphia merchants who feared the loss of their ships and crews to Markham's piratical associates. The streets of Philadelphia were filled with the robbers, who walked about openly, promoting their buccaneering voyages. They solicited seamen and servants, enticing them with offers of fabulous wealth that could be had in a very short time. Some suggested that a mariner might make as much as three thousand pounds in as little as three or four months as his share of a "privateering" voyage to the Red Sea. Merchants and shipowners were forced to compete with the pirates for the services of common seamen by paying up to four months' wages in advance. And because some pirates were not selective in their victims, insurance rates rose accordingly.[14]

One shipowner, Francis Jones of Philadelphia, who implored Nicholson's help, noted that he had a ship fitting out at Philadelphia bound for Maryland to take on tobacco for England, but was unable to keep his crew, which was being seduced away by a pirate named John Day, commander of the brigantine *Josiah*. Day was a buccaneer, smuggler, and embezzler well known on the Carolina coast, who was in Philadelphia openly recruiting and outfitting for a pirating voyage to the Red Sea. Jones, fearing not only the loss of his crew, but of his ship as well, to Day and his associates, had at first sought Markham's help. Markham did nothing, replying that *Josiah* was a well-manned vessel of force, and since he lacked men and arms to suppress Day and his men, "they would doe what they pleased." Day boasted publicly that he held a commission from Markham, and that any effort to secure his crew, which had been seduced away from other vessels, would quickly be overridden by his friend the governor. When several of the *Josiah*'s crew complained that the tiny brigantine wasn't big enough for the large number of men who had been enlisted in her company, the pirate captain soothed their worries by telling them that they should be patient, for "in a fortnight or three weeks time they would have a good

ship under foot & burne the Brigantine."[15] Day continued his successful recruitment, swelling the ranks of his company even further, by
promising shares of up to two thousand pounds in booty to each man.
For those who were picky about the nationality of their victims, he
promised to spare none but the English and to take the first vessel
met.[16]

Nicholson, who had watched the growing pirate population of Pennsylvania with alarm, and had frequently berated Markham for his
affinity for those in that profession, was outraged by the Day matter.
Considering it in the King's interest, as well as in the interest of
Maryland's commerce, he resolved to act where Markham refused to
act. He would put an end to "Capt Day & his Crew of Rogues" before
they could sail by sending a force of armed men into Pennsylvania to
stop and arrest them. The expedition, under the command of Lieutenant Young, was immediately successful, capturing Day and his crew.
Then came a report from Francis Jones, informing Nicholson that
"this Governm[t] that could not protect themselves from fifty Rogues
could presently raise men enough [under the command of a Major
Danielson] to resque those fellows from the Kings forces w[ch] were of a
greater number." When Lieutenant Young protested to Markham, the
Pennsylvania Governor threatened to throw him in jail for the seizure
of the pirates, whom he said "were honest men & that they were not
Seizable." Jones beseeched the lieutenant to visit the Governor again
with him and document the intentions and activities of the pirates. This
time Markham cautiously received the officer and Jones, who was
apparently armed with sworn depositions of seamen whom Day had
attempted to recruit for his pirating voyage. He promised to bring the
affair before his Council.[17]

While Markham procrastinated, Jones secured more depositions,
Young waited patiently, and Day, whose ship lay at Newcastle on the
Delaware, was warned by one of his men of a shift in the political winds.
The pirate immediately set sail, dropping down to Bombay Hook on
the Delaware, and commenced plundering the local inhabitants of
hogs and provisions before finally setting off on his intended voyage.[18]

Though John Day and *Josiah* would soon disappear into the mists of
history, the jurisdictional dispute that had erupted between the governors of Maryland and Pennsylvania over the invasion of the latter to
seize the pirates continued. Nicholson's anguish over the situation was
exacerbated by Markham's willingness to continue to embrace and
assist the rovers who arrived in his colony and who "walk the streets as
impudently as ever in defiance."[19]

By late June 1697 it was being reported "that a great many Privateers and Pyrates lay sheltering up and down the Province of Pennsylvania," where they were protected, harbored, aided, and assisted, often by open force and violence on the part of the government. Worse, they were being joined by members of the Royal Navy and "the looser sort of seamen and servants" from adjacent colonies. As many as a hundred Marylanders and Virginians had flocked to their ranks. Nicholson, fearing that such a population of vermin would flood overland into Maryland and infest the upper Chesapeake, ordered on July 1 that all civilian and military officers belonging to Cecil County, which lay on the Pennsylvania-Delaware border, and all masters of ships riding in county waters "be upon their guard and take particular care (more especially the Sheriff) to prevent disturbances, mischief or any attempts wch possibly may be made by the ^{sd} privateers & Pyrates & the Inhabitants & seamen running to them."[20] The tensions between Maryland and Pennsylvania would continue until 1699, when Governor Markham would finally be removed from office as a consequence of his excesses and associations with pirates.

Nicholson, despite his problems with Pennsylvania, could take some consolation in the knowlege that the lower Chesapeake was again well protected by a strong guardship, HMS *Dover Prize*, which had arrived to replace *Henry Prize*. Ironically, the man-of-war was commanded by an ex-pirate named Thomas Pound who had once been sentenced to death for his roving. His ship, a fifth-rate, 330-ton, 32-gun vessel, was substantial in size, 105 feet in length and 27 feet abeam, and had been taken into naval service in 1693. Pound, a native of Falmouth (now Portsmouth), Maine, had once cruised the New England coast aboard the pirate ship *Mary*, and during one particularly vicious hurricane in 1689, had even visited the Chesapeake to secure a safe anchorage in the York River. His visit came during the height of the Davis-Wafer-Hinson debates, while HMS *Dumbarton* had been careening, and thus rode out the storm in security. When finally captured in Massachusetts, he was saved from the gallows by the timely intervention of several citizens of influence from Boston. Pound became a reformed man and instantly gave up his buccaneering ways. He obtained a commission in the Royal Navy, assumed command of *Dover Prize*, and found himself patrolling against his former Brethren of the Coast.[21]

Pound remained on the Chesapeake Station for some time, effectively discouraging would-be pirates. In 1698 a new guardship of considerably lesser force, HMS *Essex Prize*, with a commander of somewhat less-than-aggressive tendencies, Captain John Aldred, arrived in Virginia. Aldred had received his orders, dated September 14, 1697, to sail for the Chesapeake, in company with the doomed advice boat *Swift*, bound for duty in Maryland waters as a revenue boat. In Aldred's instruction from the Admiralty lay the seeds of what would prove to be the most trying and bitter controversy between the Royal Navy and the government of Virginia to date. The directives, among other things, specifically prohibited the captain from impressing any men within or in sight of Virginia, or from any merchantmen lying in Virginia waters. To fulfill his manpower needs, he was to apply to the Governor, with whom he was to orchestrate his activities for the best interests of Virginia.[22] From the very outset of his arrival, John Aldred's relationship with the colony he was to protect was strained. When the aggressive enemy of all pirates, Francis Nicholson, arrived in 1698, having once more been appointed to assume the reins of government in that colony, the situation degenerated further. And with the following spring, a major new threat of pirate invasion only exacerbated an already fragile working relationship.

By April 1699, with Nicholson again firmly in control of the Virginia colony, important orders from the Lords Justices of England arrived. The Governor and Council were directed to be on the lookout for a buccaneer named William Kidd, commander of the ship *Adventure Galley*. Kidd, a former pirate-hunter commissioned to track down buccaneers off Madagascar and in the Red Sea, had himself gone on the account, taking and plundering numerous French, Moorish, and Portuguese ships as he went. He had run afoul of British authorities, however, when he had captured an Armenian ship called the *Quedagh Merchant*, a vessel nominally sailing under the flag of France, but which, as some historians intimate, was actually in the employ of the East India Company, and which complained loudly about Kidd's activities to British authorities.[23] The Lords Justices, at the East India Company's urging, directed all colonial governors to apprehend and secure Kidd and his associates, in order that they be "prosecuted to ye utmost rigor of law." Should they be seized in Maryland or Virginia they were to be held until further directives were issued by the King.[24]

On April 18, 1699, Nicholson dutifully directed the colony's militia commanders, sheriffs, collectors of customs, and naval agents and officers to be on the alert and to apprehend the rovers should they come into the colony.[25] Several days later, formal proclamations were issued in both Maryland and Virginia authorizing the capture of the pirates.[26]

Though alarms were soon sounded throughout the tidewater, actual fears of pirate incursions only escalated when word arrived from Captain Thomas Wellburn, Sheriff of Accomac County, that Kidd had arrived on the coast. Wellburn, it seems, had learned from Matthew

Scarburgh, Collector of Customs for the Eastern Shore, that he had been informed of Kidd's arrival on the Delaware by two ex-pirates, Peter Stretcher and one Lewis, from Hore Kill, a secluded pirate retreat near Lewes. They had been aboard his ship, a vessel of 42 guns, which was accompanied by an 18-gun sloop. There were, they reported, 130 pirates among them, although 5 or 6 had taken their leave, some going to Philadelphia and others shipping aboard a sloop belonging to one Andrew Gravenrod (later discovered to be bound for Maryland). The pirates were heavily laden with booty, and it was said that each of their company had a share valued at £4,000. Their ships carried "30 Tunns of Gold and Silver aboard." The pirate chief apparently felt himself secure on the hospitable waters of the Delaware, so much so that he had sent for his wife to join him, but she had reportedly refused. The most alarming news, however, was that "Kidd plyes often on ye Coast." The Chesapeake was, in the Governor's view, certainly threatened.[27]

By the time Nicholson had received word of the presence of Kidd on the coast, the sloop of Andrew Gravenrod had already entered the Bay and come to anchor in Maryland's Severn River. Aboard was a lone pirate, Theophilus Turner, who was intent on retiring quietly in the tidewater. The new Governor of Maryland, Nathaniel Blakiston, had already been alerted by Judge Quary that the sloop might visit Maryland, and when she finally came in, he was ready. The Governor immediately dispatched an agent, William Bladen, to board the vessel to investigate, and act if necessary. Gravenrod and Turner were immediately arrested, and four hundred pieces of eight confiscated from Turner's chest.[28]

Captain Gravenrod, upon being interrogated by Maryland authorities, claimed that he was merely a victim of circumstance. He had been chased a few days earlier by a ship of force four leagues off the Delaware Capes. His pursuer had fired a gun to bring him to, raised an ensign, and sent a boat after him. Hailing the boat from a distance, he was told that the ship was *Winchester* of London, Captain Stoat commanding. But when they carried him aboard, he found, to his surprise, that she was the pirate ship *Nassaw,* from Madagascar. The pirates had obliged him to take aboard Turner and two others with their chests. Though his two piratical compatriots soon afterwards transferred to two other ships at the Delaware Capes bound for England, Turner had chosen to stay with Gravenrod and disembark in the Chesapeake tidewater, where he undoubtedly hoped to lose himself in the general population. Blakiston, upon hearing their tales, released Gravenrod, who posted security, but retained Turner under arrest. The pirate, however, who was to be sent to England to be tried, "Shewed an Ingenuity in his Confession" that moved the Maryland Governor to recommend him to be a fit object for the King's mercy.[29]

Both Maryland and Virginia worried about reports that as many as sixty deserters, and more than a few pirates who had been captured and escaped from jail, were intending to swarm into the tidewater.[30] Yet by comparison, the presence of Captain Kidd and some three-score deserters from his crew that lingered in the vicinity had become a veritable nightmare for Robert Quary of the Vice Admirality Court of Pennsylvania. With the assistance of Governor Bass of New Jersey, he was able to apprehend four of the pirates at Cape May

> and might have with Ease secured all the rest of them, and the ship too, had this Government given me the Least aide or assistance, but they [did] not, or soe much as Issue out a Proclamation. But on the Contrary the People of the Government have Entertain'd the Pyrates, Conveyed them from place to place, Furnish'd them with Provisions and Liquors given them Inteli'gence and sheltred them from Justice, and now the greatest part of them are Conveyed away in Boats to Road Island. All the person[s] That I have Employed in Searching for and apprehending these Pyrates are abused and affronted and call'd Enemies to the Country for Disturbing and hindring honest men (as They are pleased to call the Pyrates) from bringing their money and Settling amongst them.

In total desperation, Quary dispatched an express to Governor Nicholson to send a man-of-war to the Delaware immediately. The Governor of Virginia responded by sending *Essex Prize* "to look About Sixty Pyrates (wch belonged to one Kidd) who came from Madagascar." As quickly as they had arrived, however, the buccaneers had disappeared. The Delaware was empty, for unbeknownst to either Nicholson or Captain Aldred, Kidd had sailed for Boston, where he was immediately arrested upon his arrival and shipped off to England for trial. On May 23, 1701, Captain William Kidd, one of the most famous rovers of the age, was hanged at Execution Dock.[31]

On the Chesapeake Bay, unfortunately, there would be no breathing spell, for the worst pirate invasion in its history was already underway.

IX

The Pirate with the Gold Toothpick

John James was an ugly, imposing man, severely disfigured by small-pox. He was of middle height, square shouldered, large jointed, with a blemish in his left eye that gave him a squinty, sinister visage. His speech was broad and thick. His demeanor toward prisoners was calculating and cool. He had a bold ego, as the more successful pirates tended to have, and he occasionally compared himself to the infamous Captain William Kidd.[1]

James was captain of the ship *Providence Frigate,* the command of which he had secured in the not uncommon manner of many pirates, through a mutiny against the vessel's previous commander, a ruthless Dutch buccaneer named Hynd. He had disposed of the Dutchman and fifteen of his comrades in typical pirate fashion, by marooning them on the Berry Islands, ten leagues to the leeward of New Providence in the Bahamas, and allowing them three small arms and a bottle of gunpowder with which to face their future.[2]

When James secured control of *Providence Frigate,* he had also taken over the right to a covey of victims that had fallen prey to Hynd while he was a marauder in the Caribbean Sea, from the Bay of Campeche to the Bahamas. Perhaps unwilling to chance the fate suffered by Captain Hynd, James took his little armada to New Providence, where his new flagship was careened, watered, and attended to. Four additional cannons were brought aboard, bringing the vessel's armament count to twenty-six guns. To encourage the island's residents to help refit the ship, he took hostages from among them. The work was carried out with great expedition. Having refitted, rearmed, and permitted his crew the customary, and all important pirate's frolic ashore, James disposed of his erstwhile flotilla in the most profitable manner possible, and sailed away in search of new prizes.

The successes and travails of *Providence Frigate,* renamed *Providence Galley* (and, when occasion suited, *Alexander*), after her departure from New Providence are largely unknown. Apparently, Captain James experienced a good deal of success, for when he approached the coast of Virginia in July 1699, he boasted of having several million pounds sterling in gold and silver aboard which had been taken from captured vessels.

What drove Captain James toward the Virginia Capes and the Chesapeake was not additional treasure, but the need for provisions, rigging, guns, and anchors. As *Providence Galley* began to cruise off the Virginia coast in mid-July, her string of successes remained unbroken. James's first victim in Virginia waters was the pink *Hope,* of and heading for London, which had sailed from the James River on July 23.[3] The capture proved to be a remarkable stroke of good luck for the pirates. Although the vessel itself was an inconsequential prize, the government documents found aboard could not help but tantalize the pirates. Among them were six months' worth of record books belonging to the guardship *Essex Prize.* These records contained strategic information on the weak status of Virginia's naval defenses. Such data seemed to suggest infinite possibilities to James. Interrogation of *Hope*'s crew further substantiated his information when he learned that at least two crew members had been aboard the little guardship that very day. They were undoubtedly knowledgeable about the infirmities of the ship, its size, weaknesses, and possibly even the somewhat temperamental personality of her captain. But most important, it was noted that *Essex Prize* was the only guardship available for the defense of the entire Chesapeake.[4]

James immediately realized the potential offered by the Virginia colony's weak situation, and was eager to profit from it. *Providence Galley* was far superior to the guardship in both artillery and manpower. Thus, the pirate captain boldly resolved to beard the lion in his den by directly attacking and capturing *Essex Prize* and plundering her of her valuable rigging, sails, anchors, cables, guns, and ammunition. The Chesapeake Bay, from the wide expanse of water between her capes, clear into Maryland, and all the shipping therein, would then be his for the taking.

The gale of July 24 was brutal. A severe storm of wind and rain lashed the Virginia Capes without mercy, driving right up the throat of the Chesapeake. HMS *Essex Prize* lay at anchor in four fathoms of water, five miles northwest of Cape Henry, to which place Captain Aldred had moved her at the onset of the tempest, gouging three anchors into the sandy bottom. At 3:00 A.M. the gale intensified. Despite the three-point anchorage, the guardship bucked with every sea. Suddenly, the small bower snapped. Aldred immediately directed the reserve best bower dropped to stabilize the vessel's position. The little warship then veered off by nearly a full cable length, and was then slowly brought up on the broken cable to face the sea.* The storm continued unabated. At about 4:00 A.M. the wind shifted dramatically. Aldred was obliged to cut away the sheet anchor or face a broaching sea. Again the ship veered a full cable length. Miraculously, the two remaining anchors held fast until the winds and sea began to dissipate.[5]

As the storm passed and order returned aboard *Essex Prize,* Aldred sent the longboat to Kecoughtan with letters for the Governor and to secure water for his ship. While ashore, the landing party careened and repaired the longboat, which had suffered from much neglect. By the evening of July 25 all had returned to normal.[6]

At twilight Captain Aldred noted the passage of the flyboat *Maryland Merchant,* of Bristol, Captain Richard Burgess commanding, outward bound with a cargo of tobacco. Nothing seemed out of the ordinary. At 1:00 A.M. the guardship shifted her anchorage into six fathoms of water approximately four miles west northwest of Cape Henry. Three hours later, as dawn began to lighten the eastern sky, a strange sail was spotted in Lynnhaven Bay, bearing down on the outward-bound *Maryland Merchant.*[7] His suspicions instantly aroused, Aldred directed that all sail be made for the stranger. As *Essex Prize* came up to within hailing distance, the stranger hoisted the King's colors and a blood-red flag to her maintop and fired guns without shot to both windward and leeward. As the guardship maneuvered for position and her own identity became apparent, the intruder unloaded a vicious full broadside. It was instantly clear that the stranger was not one of the King's ships. The challenge was promptly answered by Aldred—with interest.[8]

It was soon obvious that *Essex Prize,* with only sixteen guns and fewer than sixty men, was no match—despite her initial bravado—for the larger ship which, it was later learned, boasted twenty-six guns and one hundred thirty men. Cognizant of her advantage, the intruder immediately put on additional sail and, with an easterly wind, tacked and bore down on the King's ship. Aldred was now fully aware that he was battling a pirate ship of great strength. Hoping to draw the deep-draft attacker away from *Maryland Merchant,* which lay approximately three miles to the north, and into the shoally waters of the Virginia

---

*It was common practice to attach buoys or floats to anchor cables; in case the cable snapped the anchors could still be relocated and recovered.

shore, he also tacked. Onward came the pirate with bow guns firing, a shark in pursuit of a dolphin.[9]

In order to permit the Bristolman's escape to the north, Aldred recorded in his ship's log, "I kept a leading fight to ye So[wd] towards Cape Henry my master being well acquainted with ye shoals." But the wily pirate was not easily fooled and hovered just beyond the dangerous shallows. Finally, he tacked again and stood off. Aldred stubbornly refused to abandon the game of ghosting the foe but never fully committing *Essex Prize* to full combat.[10]

Incredibly, at this juncture, *Maryland Merchant,* instead of escaping into the shoally waters to the north, bore directly down toward the pirate, by "being to windward and sailing very well," in an attempt to get into the James River. Before the flyboat could get to the leeward of the intruder, the pirate fired a single shot at her. *Maryland Merchant* instantly struck. Her attacker ranged alongside and commanded her master and his company to come aboard in their ship's boat. The pirates then took the men from the boat and cut it loose, leaving the flyboat at anchor and unmanned, and once again put about to take up pursuit of *Essex Prize.*[11]

"Ye pyrate ship," Aldred later wrote, "being very clean, wronged me much." Worse, he saw his position as a compromising one. Having recently sent his longboat ashore with seven men to careen and water, his onboard complement was severely weakened. The enemy had superior firepower, manpower, and speed, and its intention of cutting *Essex Prize* out and boarding her was clear. If "he had so done," Aldred recorded in his own defense, "he would have over powered me with men."[12]

A council of war was held, and, upon the advice of his officers, Aldred resolved to continue the fight by using the only strategy feasible—to once more attempt to draw the pirate into the shoals. But again the pirate tacked off. *Essex Prize* followed her, but to no avail. The pirate, tiring of the cat-and-mouse game, and in possession of the superior sailer of the two ships, was by 11:00 A.M. far to the windward and out of shot range. Seeing pursuit as a hopeless, and perhaps fatal, task—especially as a lee tide was coming on—Aldred "thought it more service to make sail into ye shore to acquaint ye Governor thereof, to prevent his [the pirate's] doing any further damage and to make a stronge defence agst him." Damage to *Essex Prize* was minimal, primarily in her sails and colors. *Maryland Merchant* was left to the not-so-tender mercies of the pirate.[13]

Away from the scene of action, Aldred fired off an immediate report to Governor Nicholson, outlining the battle and the reasons for his abandonment of the fray. He was returning, he said in excuse of his actions, to prevent any other ships from sailing into the buccaneer's clutches and to secure as many landsmen as possible, with which he "may deal with him & may keep him from doing any more damage."[14]

With *Essex Prize* unwilling to continue the fight, the pirates turned their attentions to *Maryland Merchant*. Captain Burgess, when finally confronted by the squint-eyed, pockmarked buccaneer chieftain and his crew, was thoroughly intimidated. Yet he was at the same time impressed by the unexpectedly courteous demeanor of the pirate leader, who was explicit in his promise that "he designed no prejudice to the English Nation, as to their persons," but that his wants—which he promised to pay for rather than take by force—*would* be supplied.[15]

The pirates were full of boasts about their prowess and the rich prize they had onboard, a treasure in gold and silver worth three million pounds sterling. It was soon apparent that *Maryland Merchant's* provisions and sailing gear were far more attractive to the pirates than the meager personal wealth aboard the little merchantman. "They thought it not worth their while," Burgess later reported, "to take a gentleman's plate and money, value nigh £100, that was on board."[16] Instead, they proceeded to strip the flyboat of her mainsail, topsail, spritsail, best bower, cables, and one hundred pounds of dry goods. Eight of her crewmen were pressed into service aboard *Providence Galley*.[17] Before James was finished plundering the flyboat (without leaving the promised pay for merchandise taken), he asked his captive who he thought *Essex Prize* had been cruising in search of. "Captain Kidd," replied Burgess rather timidly.

"I am Kidd," boasted the pirate.

And Burgess believed him.[18]

Maryland Merchant was soon released, though in such a disabled condition that it was eventually driven helplessly aground on the shoals of Willoughby Point.[19]

On the morning of July 27, when the sloop *Roanoke Merchant*, belonging to Colonel Robert Quary sailed through the Virginia Capes, bound from Barbados for Annapolis, nothing seemed amiss. Her commander, Captain Nicholas Thomas Jones, saw little that seemed unusual when he noted the large ship anchored in Lynnhaven Bay, "under ye King's Colours, with Jack, Ancient, and pendant aboard." He took it to be one of His Majesty's men-of-war, probably the Virginia guardship, and thus took no measures to avoid passing close by her.[20]

Suddenly, two cannons roared an unwelcome salutation, followed by an order bellowed across the water for Jones to come aboard. With little alternative but to oblige, he did. Once onboard, he was greeted by the warship's commander, who informed him with a smirk that if *Roanoke Merchant* had failed to follow directions, she most certainly would have been sunk. Jones's suspicions, already aroused by the presence of a flyboat lying nearby which the commander boasted of having taken the day before, were further sharpened by the unmilitary attire adorning the ship's officers and crew. "I observed," he later recalled, "ye Company and Captain Him self to have gold chains about their Necks. Ye Captain had a gold tooth picker hanging at it."[21]

Interrogated by the warship's remarkably ugly commander, Jones readily divulged information about his lading, and upon request meekly produced clearance papers. The commander then informed him that he would be taking from *Roanoke Merchant* her provision stores of peas, pork, and tallow, "and what else he had occasion for." Relishing the stunned expression on the merchant captain's face, the commander then casually informed him that he was a pirate.[22]

Shortly afterward, as he was being escorted to a place of confinement, Captain Jones was approached by a pirate crewman named Lux, whom he recognized as a seaman who had once belonged to the New York brigantine *Charles,* a vessel which had also fallen prey to the pirates sometime earlier.[23] Lux soothed the somewhat distraught prisoner by telling him that the commander would not harm him, "otherwise than to take what he wanted or what he had a mind to." Placed in confinement, Jones would have no opportunity to see what the pirate commander wanted or had in mind.[24]

> The plunder of *Roanoke Merchant* was total, eventually including *sixteen barrel of porke, one Barrell of tallow, twenty nine Bushels of Beans, two Quoiles of Ropes, Six firelocks with all our Ammunicon, most of ye Carpenters tools, and diverse necessary Utensils for use, ½ Barrell of Tarr, & Balls of Rope Yarn, long line and Reckle, several Cask of Water, and a quantity of provision, by which about 30 or 40 barrels of Corn were damnifyed, fallen down to ye bottom of ye Sloop, likewise one barrel marked R.M. belonging to one Mr. Robert Mellam a passenger one Bear skin & one Bever skin.*[25]

The pirate chieftain enjoyed toying with his victim. Later in the day, he summoned Captain Jones to his cabin to reveal his identity and to inform him of what lay in store. He was, he boasted, none other than Captain John James, a Welshman from Glamorganshire, and his ship was *Alexander,* taken from "one Captn Watt [Rhett] of South Carolina about the Bay of Campeachy." After the brief introduction, he proceeded to make Captain Jones squirm and beg for mercy. Fingering his golden toothpick, the pirate loudly announced his intentions of impressing several of *Roanoke*'s crew—perhaps even Jones himself—into his own company and then burning their ship. Jones begged him to forego destroying the vessel, an act which would bring ruin upon the merchantman. Failing to move the buccaneer with begging, he tried another tack, and stoutly refused to join with the pirates. "Rather than go with him," he promised, "I would burn with the Sloop."[26]

Wearied of the game, Captain James ordered two of *Roanoke*'s crew to join his company. Mate John Lukas and seaman William Steeward were compelled to sign the pirate articles, though they "appeared very unwilling, begging and earnestly entreating ye Captain for their liberty, but all in vain."[27]

Captain Jones was ordered to go in his sloop to fetch water from *Maryland Merchant* (still at anchor nearby) and bring it back to *Providence Galley*. He timidly and promptly carried out the first part of the order, but a strong tide prevented his return to the warship. The pirates weighed anchor and promptly bore down on the little sloop. Captain Jones once more found himself detained aboard *Providence Galley*.[28]

At about 8:00 P.M. the pirate quartermaster, nominally the second-in-command, questioned Captain James as to whether or not it would be prudent to put to sea. Apparently, some of the crew were anxious to move on to easier pickings. Since the pirate's code required a consensus in such matters, a consultation with the entire ship's company was held to determine "what ye Company inclined to doe." Within a short time, they decided to put to sea. At 10:00 P.M. *Providence Galley*, glutted with provisions and extra sailing gear, raised anchor and set sail from Lynnhaven Bay for richer hunting grounds.[29]

As the ship got underway, the question of what to do with *Roanoke Merchant* was put to a vote. Captain Jones was given the opportunity to beg publicly for the return of his sloop and men. Finally, after repeated entreaties, the buccaneers agreed to release him and his sloop, but to retain most of his company.[30] Undoubtedly aware that the sloop captain and his few remaining seamen would relay, at the first opportunity, all intelligence possible to royal authorities, Captain James filled his prisoners' heads with frightening information. There was, he told John Martin, *Roanoke*'s master, another pirate ship, a consort sloop to *Providence Galley*. She had eight guns and fifty men and was lurking somewhere off the Chesapeake Capes, awaiting the right moment for her turn to visit the Virginia coast. The wily pirate chieftain adroitly refused to divulge any information as to his own destination or from whence he had come. His news was designed to intimidate and confuse the authorities, and it did so with incredible success.[31]

Captain Jones, humiliated by his experiences but relieved to have escaped unharmed, boarded his sloop, and with the few men left to him, stopped briefly to deposit a certain Mr. Pope, a merchant who had also been detained by the pirates, onboard *Maryland Merchant,* and then stood up the Chesapeake for Annapolis, anxious to be on his way lest the pirates change their minds. In Maryland, he reported the full story of his travails directly to the Governor, and then began the sad business of inventorying his losses.[32]

Providence Galley, commanded by the colorful pirate with the golden toothpick, made its way unhindered through the Chesapeake Capes.

For several days afterward, Captain John Aldred remained anchored off Castle Point, near Hampton, licking his wounds and replacing his ship's torn sails with new ones, ostensibly to bring her to "a readiness to engage [the pirate] again."[33] Finally, three days after the battle, on July 29, he dispatched *Essex Prize*'s master in an armed pinnace to Lynnhaven Bay to secure intelligence concerning the pirate's whereabouts and strength. The pinnace soon encountered the grounded *Maryland Merchant* and received from her master the grim details of the buccaneer's identity and strength, as well as a full account of her various captures. When the pinnace returned to *Essex Prize* at around midnight, she brought with her welcome word of *Providence Galley*'s departure and the not so pleasant news that her alleged consort was lingering somewhere beyond the Virginia Capes awaiting an opportune moment to conduct her own raid on the colony shipping.[34]

Aldred was undoubtedly worried at the prospect of having to once again do battle with the pirates. He was certain, too, that accusations would arise over his lack of success—some would say, spirit—during the engagement with *Providence Galley.* In his own defense he quickly composed a "certificate" of the weaknesses of the guardship and dispatched her master to call upon Governor Nicholson with it.[35]

"These are to satisfy," the certificate read, "Francis Nicholson Esq his Majty-Lieut & Govenr genrl and Vice Admiral of Virginia &c. yt his Majestys Ship Essex prize has one Deck with a small Fall fore & aft, 16 guns, Complement 60 men, and having no Steerage, she is but ordinarily provided to make a close fight, if forced off my Decks."[36]

The Governor's Council would accept the excuse without question, but Francis Nicholson's growing animosity toward Captain Aldred, fueled by the captain's apparent timidity in battle and unwillingness to seek information about the pirates until they had departed, had reached a new height.

The repercussions resulting from the attack on Virginia by *Providence Galley* were swift. Governor Nicholson convened an urgent meeting of the Council at Jamestown and testily laid before it letters from Aldred and related documents from Colonel William Wilson, militia commander of Elizabeth City County, concerning the pirate invasion. The Council moved quickly, for though the immediate crisis had abated, pirate landings in several colonies to the north, as well as on the Virginia coast—"to make their escape"—were probable. Expresses were sent to the governments of the northern colonies with descriptions of *Providence Galley* and her company of brigands and the crimes they had committed, in an effort to secure their apprehension and bring them to trial.[37]

The Council also reviewed Aldred's certificate on the condition of *Essex Prize* and readily agreed that the ship "is not of force sufficient to defend his Majestys Colony & Dominion agst attempts of pyrats or sea Robbers." They lamented, with Aldred, that, because it was impossible to secure enough men for a ship of war in an emergency without going to great expense, and because of a greatly dispersed population, "a pyrate or other Enemy may land and execute his intended Mischief, before any number of men can be gotten together, and put on board a Ship to oppose him." Of course, the root of the concern lay in the economics of the thing, for there was significant danger of loss to His Majesty's customs revenues from any tobacco ships that might be captured or destroyed.[38]

It was apparent to the Governor and Council that more force and better protection were necessary. The Council implored Nicholson to request the King to supply "a Ship of sufficient force to defend his Colony & Dominion agst pyrats, and yt there may be allowed to her a small Tender, which in case of Necessity, may serve as a fire Ship."[39]

The government, distraught over attacks on the shipping, was equally concerned about the possibility of pirate landings on the Virginia coast. Pirates could blend with the general population to escape punishment or conduct coastal raids to secure the provisions to enable them to continue their nefarious activities. Responding to this concern on August 9, Nicholson issued a decree directing the commanders of militia in the counties of Norfolk, Princess Anne, Accomac, Northampton, and Elizabeth City to appoint coast watchers, or lookouts, in each county to patrol their respective seacoasts until September 29. It was believed that after that date, with the onset of late fall, sea conditions and weather would diminish the likelihood of pirate activities in Virginia waters until spring.[40]

One watcher would march up and down the beach between Cape

Henry and Lynnhaven River. Another would patrol between Cape Henry and Currituck Inlet. A third would be stationed on remote Smith's Island, at the mouth of the Bay. A fourth was directed to patrol the shores of Northampton County, and a fifth, the beaches of Accomac. Each man was to watch for any ships and observe their courses and actions. If any boats sent ashore caused the slightest suspicion, the lookouts were instantly to notify the local militia commander, "who is hereby directed to take such Care, and give such Orders as shall be necessary for ye defence of his County." The commander was to give general notice of the landing to all other county militia commanders, as well as a full report to Governor Nicholson. Captain Aldred was also to be warned of "any Ship or Vessel yt shall be at Anchor or Cruising by the Capes, or upon ye Coast, if Suspected to be a pyrate."[41]

Despite these defensive measures, the wake left by *Providence Galley*'s invasion of the Chesapeake underlined the vulnerability of Virginia's exposed coast. Though no further incursions occurred during the summer of 1699, the susceptibility of isolated regions to landings was driven home with some impact in the fall, further accentuating Virginia's impotence.

On October 16, Colonel John Custis, commander of the Northampton County Militia, sent an urgent dispatch to Governor Nicholson informing him that a ship had anchored close to the beach on the back side of Smith's Island. Twelve men had come ashore and had killed and wounded several cattle, which they carried off. They surreptitiously departed in the night. It was unknown whether they had put back to sea or whether they were sailing into the Chesapeake. Custis, who promptly sent a man to the island to see what damage had actually been done, was certain that the party was a group of pirates.[42]

The colonel outlined for the Governor the difficulty and danger inherent in maintaining a watch on the isolated island, as well as the utility of such a place to roving bands of pirates. The island, he noted, was the only place where they might obtain provisions, water, and wood without opposition. They would never dare to land on the mainland, he assured the Governor, where a force could easily be mobilized to oppose them and where provisions were not to be as readily had or stolen as on Smith's Island. It would, in fact, "be very easy for more to come and victual, and water, & wood there, ye Isld being distant from ye Main better than a League, the lookers out not being able to come off, if [it] blows any wind, having nothing but Canoes." In any event, the lookout was in constant danger of being discovered and captured, and even if he should escape to the mainland to spread the alarm, the pirates, from their commanding position, could never be surprised. The colonel, undoubtedly with *Essex Prize* in mind, offered the suggestion that a small frigate be stationed in Smith's Island River where the pirates must bring their vessels to victual.[43]

Smith's Island had already been visited, well before the King's proclamation on piracy had reached Virginia and before the October landing, by "some Sculkers" who took on water. Custis expressed little doubt that more would soon be coming in search of fresh meat.[44]

The colonel's letter did not reach Governor Nicholson for a week. By this time the purported buccaneers were probably many leagues away. Nevertheless, Nicholson promptly ordered Captain Aldred to cruise about the Capes in the event the pirates might still be lurking. The captain quickly assured the Governor of his hearty desire for action, but excused himself from the mission, claiming that none of his company was familiar with the waters. The entire question became moot, however, for *Essex Prize* was going to refit in the Elizabeth River—or so Nicholson said in a somewhat apologetic letter to Custis. The best the Governor could promise was assistance when the ship was finally capable of putting to sea—whenever that might be.[45]

Nicholson's frustrating failure to blunt the impact of seaborne brigandry was again exhibited in the late fall, when a pirate named Henry King, once a Pennsylvania trader, seized and plundered the London merchantman *John Hopewell,* commanded by Captain Henry Munday, off the Virginia coast. Nine of Munday's company cast their lot with King and his crew. A letter (dated November 1699) was dispatched to Governor Nicholson by the owners of the ship with a list of names of the nine deserters and a request that, if they should land in Virginia, the government would apprehend them and bring them to trial.[46]

The government, of course, was powerless to do anything. The merciful advent of winter seas, however, brought relief from the rovers, who preferred the warmer West Indies. Spring would be another matter.

X

The Winter of Discontent

Governor Francis Nicholson had little use for slackers. Fortunately, his anger at Captain John Aldred's unwillingness to follow orders was tempered by his unhappy realization that *Essex Prize* was the only naval defense Virginia was likely to have for some time to come. Yet even after the pirate attack, Aldred's procrastinations and excuses continued. The Governor's fuse was burning dangerously short. Cordiality had long since evaporated, and incident after incident helped feed the sprouting buds of antagonism between the two men. When Nicholson ordered Peter Heyman, his trustworthy Collector of Customs for the Lower District of the James River, aboard *Essex Prize* to check the number of crewmen onboard, the captain refused to permit him to make the count. Later, in September, when Nicholson himself went aboard and demanded to speak with the captain, Aldred refused, obstinately remaining within his great cabin claiming to be a victim of "Country distemper." The infuriated Governor placed him under arrest and confined him to his cabin under guard. Released a week later, the captain ridiculed the Governor's measures as "silly, impertinent, and full of pride and vain glory" and bitterly complained about the Governor's conduct in a letter to the Admiralty in England.[1] These confrontations served to accentuate the precarious state of the colony of Virginia.

On September 12 an exasperated Nicholson ordered the little warship brought up from below the mouth of the James to Jamestown. Ten days later, the ship was still at anchor at the mouth of the river. Nicholson was furious. Aldred defended his tardiness with complaints. In addition to the "very weak and defenceless Condition" of his ship, as represented to the Governor after the skirmish with *Providence Galley*, she was now in want of gun carriages, iron work, and matches. What was worse, he claimed, was that only fifteen days' provisions were onboard and he had never been informed of where such stores might be procured on His Majesty's credit.[2]

Nicholson discussed the situation with the Council, which in turn decided that "forasmuch as by the said Aldred's rep'sentation . . . it appears to be very dangerous for the said Ship to lye below the mouth of the River," the vessel was ordered to immediately ascend the James and anchor off the mouth of Archer's Creek. There she was to lie, with Aldred and crew confined to ship, until further orders were issued. The captain was instructed to put his time to good use by preparing to attend the Governor's Council meeting in mid-October. There he was to present, in writing, an account of the ship's condition; whether or not she was fit to cruise in the Chesapeake and between the Virginia Capes; and, if not, what supplies and services would be necessary to ready her for such a cruise.[3] Nicholson, more comfortable in the Council chamber than on the deck of a ship, had a few personal bones to pick with the aberrant sea captain. One of these was the erratic manner in which Essex Prize had hitherto been victualled; another was the reportedly constant absenteeism of the captain, and his crew, from the ship, on the pretense of securing victuals ashore. The Governor suspected both as the reasons for the warship's failure to cruise when ordered.[4]

Aldred presented his report to the Governor and Council on October 18. In it, he complained that his ship was weak in the bow, causing severe leaking. The leakage resulted in serious damage to the ship's stores, particularly in heavy weather. Repairs, he stressed, were absolutely necessary, not only to the ship, but to her longboat as well. Six gun carriages were in shambles. He needed at least a hundred weight of matches, some planking, tar, and pitch, and, most important, credit to purchase these items.[5]

The Council, though in sympathy with the reported condition of the ship, was in no mood to coddle the captain, who now stood in great disfavor. His report was deemed unsatisfactory. A week later he was again summoned to answer a surly Governor and an unsympathetic Council, whose apparent sources of independent information were much better than the captain might have imagined. His official dressing down bordered on inquisitorial.

The captain, the Governor charged, had intentionally and unwisely distributed his ship's stores in widely separated sections of the country for storage, and in so doing had generally neglected the King's service. Essex Prize had lain entirely too long in the James, failing to cruise when ordered to prevent potential pirate incursions. For nearly half a year Aldred's men and the ship's boat had been employed at various tasks far from the ship on the pretense of victualling. The captain, his officers and men were as often as not lodged ashore when they should have been aboard their ship and ready for action. Frequently, the ship's company had been sent about the countryside, far from the ship, "which occasions great complaints by the Inhabitants of thefts by the seamen." And finally, the King's service and the safety of the colony had been prejudiced for want of a gunner aboard ship.[6]

All of these deficiencies, "His Excellency was pleased to say, he expected to be altered for the future."[7]

"Has the good captain anything to add?" asked the Governor.

"No," answered Aldred sheepishly.

Nicholson smiled, his points having been made before the Council. He then magnanimously promised to provide Captain Aldred with everything he needed and instructed the officer to sail as soon as possible for the Elizabeth River to apply for the requested articles and services. There Captain Samuel Bush and Colonel James Wilson would provide "such Creditt and other assistance" as would be necessary, as well as warrants for the impressment of carpenters and other workmen needed to repair the ship, the boat, and the gun carriages. Aldred, having "hitherto been very negligent in not giving his Excellency an account of his proceeding from time to time according to Orders," was sternly instructed to provide a record of his actions from the previous Christmas onward and to produce, in the future, a regular written report of his activities.[8]

Not long after the captain took his leave from the meeting chamber, the Council again took up the issue of securing a ship of greater force than *Essex Prize* for the colony's protection. Richard Lee, one of the Council members, noted that a larger ship was necessary not only for service during fair weather seasons (which were the most conducive to pirate activity) but also for cruising the Chesapeake throughout the winter, when a smaller vessel couldn't and when a surprise attack by buccaneers would be the most devastating.[9]

The colony's panic, caused by the *Providence Galley* invasion, had subsided, but the fear of possible future attacks had not. In late October, when news reached the Chesapeake that eight captured pirates (including two belonging to Captain Kidd's notorious crew) had escaped from prisons in New York City, Rhode Island, and New Jersey and were believed to be heading for Virginia, "attempting to take such Ships or Vessells as they can meet with," the Governor was forced to address the emergency. A proclamation was immediately issued strictly prohibiting anyone from harboring, entertaining, concealing, or corresponding with the escapees, or for that matter any pirates whatsoever, upon pain of prosecution as an accessory to piracy. Civil and military officers in the colony were again placed on alert, and loyal citizens were requested to attempt to apprehend any and all pirates. To sweeten the pot, a reward of twenty pounds sterling was offered for every buccaneer brought in.[10] Not one pirate was captured.

Again, in December, the government was informed that a company of ten pirates had taken the ship *Adventure,* of London, and her cargo, valued at thirteen thousand pounds sterling. It was suspected that the rovers were lurking about the Virginia coast "and may endeavor to conceal themselves by privily coming on Shore in this his Matys Colony and Dominion in hopes of being harboured by wicked and ill disposed Persons and so to avoid the just punishment due by Law."[11] A proclamation, with an offer of a reward, similar to that of October was issued, with equally unsatisfactory results.

The danger of pirate attacks was all too apparent, as was the solution for defense—stronger guardships. Yet the Crown had to be kept abreast of the degenerating situation. Thus, the Council formally appealed to the Governor to personally address the King. "Whereas of late many Notorious Robberies have been Committed by the Pyrates as well within this Colony as in other [of] His Maj[ts] Plantations on the Continent of America, whereby it appears that the dangers from those People do continually grow greater and greater, therefore His Maja[ts] Hon[ble] Council do pray His Excellency that he will please represent His Most Sacred Maj[ty] the great Mischeifs and p[r]judices, that are likely to ensure thereupon to the Colonies under His Obedience in America."[12] Nicholson, of course, was only too happy to forward the Council's concerns to the Crown.

The Governor's frustration with the colony's weaknesses and his simmering animosity toward Aldred again flared in November with news of the pirate landings on Smith's Island. *Essex Prize* was ordered to cruise in search of the invaders. Aldred said he would be only too glad to comply with the order, but that such a cruise would be impossible without a pilot familiar with the waters. Curiously, the captain devoted the second half of his reply letter to a diatribe against Colonel Wilson— a man the captain for some unrecorded reason despised with a passion—and his lady.[13] Nicholson fired back a scathing retort.

"You cannot but know," he wrote,

that you have bin in these partes long enough to be acquainted with the Coast (considering how very little space it contains) especially if you cruised the Bay last Summer according to my Orders to you given for that purpose,

and if after all yor Master is not capable of the Charge of so small a Ship, he
is not fitt to be Master, of any of His Maj^ts Ship[s]; however I cannot but
take notice to you, that I thinke it strange you should p'tend to careen yor
Ship in Smith's Island River last Summer without order, and yet now say
you want a Pilot for those partes; You have already had my orders about a
Pilot and must not expect any other; You may Impress a Pilot if you will take
care to pay him,

"and on that Condition," he cynically concluded, "you will never want One."[13]

The Governor was appalled at the character assassination of Lieutenant Colonel Wilson and his lady and severely castigated Aldred for stuffing an official letter "with such Billingsgate railing," which was as unfit for him to receive as it was unbecoming of the captain to send. Such material, he advised, was offensive to his office, and hereafter, he instructed, the captain would stick strictly to business or be answered "with the utmost Severity."[14]

Again Aldred delayed sailing, this time complaining of the need for more materials, the lack of which, he alleged, would prohibit him from putting to sea at all. The Governor was incredulous that the captain had failed to take these needs into account earlier, when he had the opportunity to secure such materials. He was also piqued over the captain's failure to send regular reports as ordered.[15]

"What remains for me to add," the Governor wrote in a hand brittle with rage,

is, that laying aside all excuses and delays, you do with all possible speed sail
with His Maj^ts Ship Essex prize undr yor command into Chisapeake bay and
there Cruise according to my former Orders to you in that behalf given, And
herein I require and Command you in His Maj^ts name not to fail, as you
answer the contrary at yor perill.[16]

Nicholson then directed Colonel Wilson and Peter Heyman quietly to monitor Aldred's activities, particularly his departures on and returns from cruises. Heyman was entrusted with the touchy mission of delivering Aldred's sailing orders.[17]

The Virginia government made no secret of its desire to improve the colony's naval defenses against pirates. Exasperated with Aldred, Nicholson and the Council toyed with the idea of employing His Majesty's advice boat *Messenger,* then stationed in Maryland, to cruise the lower Chesapeake. The little boat, commanded by Captain Peter Cood, possessed a displacement of barely seventy-three tons and mounted only six guns. The Council wisely decided that the vessel was simply too small and vulnerable to cruise the Bay during the winter months.[18] Nevertheless, Virginia needed any naval resources she could get to meet the expected spring onslaught of pirates. The Council was of the opinion that although *Messenger* would be of little immediate value, she would certainly be of great service for the defense of the coast and of the Chesapeake (if deployed with *Essex Prize)* during the coming season. The Council requested that Nicholson write the Governor of Maryland for the release of the boat for service in Virginia waters beginning in May, and to see that she was manned and fitted out in Maryland, since it would "not be possible to procure any supply of men after she comes hither." Most of the available seamen, it was assumed, would have already departed in homeward-bound vessels or would have been snapped up by *Essex Prize.*[19]

The guerrilla war between Governor Nicholson and Captain Aldred continued unabated throughout the winter. Every communication between the two men provided a new bone of contention, particularly when it related to such issues as impressment of seamen. Much to the Governor's dismay, Aldred had patently ignored standing orders concerning the pressing of both landsmen and local seamen. In February the captain pressed one Nathaniel Pope, an apprentice to a Virginia merchant, from the ship *John of Bristol.* Nicholson, probably upset by the pleas of the merchant, was obliged personally to order Pope's release. On another occasion, a man was pressed from an inward-bound ship commanded by a certain Captain Burford. The Governor, cognizant that merchantmen fearful of such actions were likely to take their trade elsewhere, tactfully instructed Aldred that

> *hereafter he is to be carefull that he do not presse a man from any Ship inward bound that being very prejudiciall to them in their loading but when ye Ships Sail outwards he is to take one man from every Ship having above twelve till he hath made up his Complyment of which he is not to fail for that after ye Ships now in ye Country are sailed he will not have no other opportunity to get men till ye next year.*[20]

On another occasion, the Governor received an urgent message from one John Harwood, captain of a merchantman called *Mary of London,* requesting that a carpenter be made available to fit his ship for sea. The Governor, always anxious to promote the business of the merchant marine for the benefit of the colony coffers, directed Aldred to loan the captain the services of George Stoakes, a Virginia ship carpenter whom Aldred had lately impressed aboard *Essex Prize* as a common sailor. Harwood was to have the loan of Stoakes for one month, after which he was to be returned to the guardship.[21] Stoakes was dutifully detailed to *Mary.* By March, Aldred had grown suspicious of his whereabouts, and upon investigation discovered that the car-

penter had deserted. Aldred, keenly aware of the Governor's disdain
for the impressment of local citizens, promptly replaced the deserter
with a landsman, one George Sykes.[22]

Governor Nicholson was duly irritated and brought the matter of the
impressments of Stoakes and Sykes before the Council. On March 11,
1700, he wrote to Aldred of the government's decision in the matter:
"It is the opinion of my Self and his Majestys Honourable Council here,
that You should impress no men, who have lived so long on shore,
when You may be Supplyed with as able, if not abler Seamen from ye
Ships which go out."[23]

Aldred simply ignored the order.

Despite the constant stream of orders and requests from Governor
Nicholson, it was not until February 1700 that *Essex Prize* again put to
sea on a cruise, albeit a very short one. Even at sea, Aldred's cascade of
complaints and pleas for cables, rigging, and other naval supplies did
not cease. The Governor did his best to placate the captain—lest he
generate new excuses for not sailing—and immediately directed that
cables and rigging salvaged from the wreck of HMS *Swift* stored at
Kecoughtan be placed at Aldred's disposal. Nicholson also assured his
reticent captain that as long as *Essex Prize* continued to cruise, he
"should not [be in] want [of] a Supply of any necessaryes that could be
procured for him in this Countrey."[24] When Aldred complained that
the ship's surgeon, Jonathan Keate, who had somehow managed to put
to sea without his chest, was in need of certain medical supplies, herbs,
and vegetables necessary for the health of the crew, Nicholson dispatched a quarter of his personal store to the ship.[25] Of course, it was
not easy to make good the Governor's pledge of cooperation. When
Aldred forwarded the bill for pilotage services to Wilson and Bush, as
instructed by the Governor, the bill was not honored, and the pilot,
Israel Voss, was obliged to petition the Governor for recompense.[26]

As the cold season pressed on, it must have seemed to Nicholson that
the Chesapeake weather and Captain Aldred were in collusion, for the
captain was obliged to return from his too-short cruise as a result of
turbulent seas. Safely anchored off Kecoughtan, Aldred began once
more to speak of the necessity of careening his ship "e'r ye worm comes
in." He needed, he said, more provisions and supplies. Yet when
carpentry and boatswain stores were ordered, neither the captain nor
his officers were available to sign for them.[27] His complaints were
becoming painfully repetitive to Nicholson, Wilson, and Bush.

By the end of March, the Governor of Virginia seemed to be at the
end of his rope with a vexing captain who responded to neither coax-

ing, bluster, nor direct orders. Yet he seemed the model of general restraint when he wrote Aldred that he was "heartily sorry yt his Majestys ship . . . hath done his Majesty so little service since I have had ye honour to comand here." He was quite unhappy that *Essex Prize* had spent more time lying at anchor at Kecoughtan than on patrol. He was equally disturbed that the captain and his men were usually ashore committing "disorders in ye night time" rather than cruising against pirates.[28]

Finally, the Governor issued an ultimatum to his errant captain that unless he set sail and cruised according to orders, the ship would be brought up to Jamestown and secured. The message was clear. "Fail not of complying with these orders," admonished the Governor, "as you will answer the contrary to."[29]

Aldred responded on cue, as expected. He was sorry to hear the Governor's complaints and claimed that lack of cables and rigging and the turbulence of the Chesapeake weather had prevented him from being at sea. He refuted the charge of disorders, "which I am an utter Stranger to," at Kecoughtan by either himself or his men. He claimed to have made strict inquiry into the matter and found that only one man had been drunk and he had recently been committed to the charge of Colonel Wilson for punishment. The other charges were shrugged off with various rebuttals. His reply ended with a promise to proceed on a cruise—when wind and weather permitted.[30]

Throughout the winter, Aldred's procrastination, querulous nature, and timidity held the door open for any pirate daring enough to test Chesapeake waters. Fortunately, none had chosen to do so. The rovers were likely to return in the spring, a fact of which the Governor of Virginia was painfully aware. The defense of the Chesapeake and Virginia and the protection of their overseas commerce, he realized, were entirely dependent upon sea power. Failure to maintain that power—or even an illusion of strength—was jeopardizing the safety of all. On March 18, 1700, Nicholson prepared for the impending spring onslaught by issuing a bravely worded proclamation which, in light of the realities of the colony's naval defense, possessed, for those in the know, something of a hollow ring.

Whereas his most Sacred Maty hath been graciously pleased to signify to me that he doth declare it to be his Royal will & pleasure that all such Pirates as shall be forwardest to surrender themselves and most ingenious in their Confession shall have the surest grounds to hope for his Royal mercy, and hath commanded me to intimate the same to all persons concerned. Therefore I Francis Nicholson Esqr his Matys Lieu^t and Governor General of his Colony & Dominion of Virginia by and with the advice & consent of his

Ma^{tys} hon^{ble} Council of State, Do hereby publish and make known ye same to all his Ma^{tys} good & Loving Subjects, and more particularly to all such Persons as have been any way guilty of Piracy. And I do also charge and command all his Matys Officers in Chief of the Militia Sheriffs, Justices of the Peace, Constable & all other his Ma^{tys} Officers civil & Military as also all good and Loving Subjects whatsoever that they use their utmost endeavours to take seize & apprehend all & every such Pirate & Pirates. And all such as may be justly suspected of Piracy or of being aiders or abettors therein or any way accessory thereto, and such persons safely to secure their effects whether Silver gold Jewels or other goods & Merchandizes and to give me immediate notice thereof, And I do likewise command all his Ma^{tys} Officers Civil & Military to take care to put in effectual execution all Laws of England Acts of Assembly Proclamations & all other publick Orders relating to Pirates and Privateers as they or any of them for any neglect therein will answer at their perills of the utmost Rigour and Severity of Law.[31]

As Governor Francis Nicholson's winter of discontent began to lapse into the spring of a new century, the miserable prospects of pirate invasions of Virginia's Chesapeake waters loomed larger than ever. Only a miracle, it seemed, might prevent the inevitable.

On the balmy afternoon of April 20, 1700, that miracle appeared, for the colony was finally blessed with the unexpected arrival of a sleek and powerful guardian, a 32-gun man-of-war called *Shoreham*.[32]

And close on her heels came the pirates.

XI

Bloody *Peace*

In December 1699, as Governor Francis Nicholson fumed over the slothfulness of Captain John Aldred, a tiny pirate sloop set sail from Pointe à Gravois, Hispaniola, in the West Indies.[1] The commander, a sagacious French buccaneer named Lewis Guittar, had only recently been elected to the captaincy of the sloop by her pirate crew.[2] It was a selection destined to bring Guittar and his company into one of the bloodiest confrontations with the forces of law and order in the piratical history of the Chesapeake Bay.

Within ten or twelve days of assuming command, Guittar met with an early and fateful success. While cruising the coast of Hispaniola, he fell in with his first victim, a small Dutch trader laden with linen for the Spanish trade. The pirates quickly snapped up the defenseless Hollander, and after plundering her of part of her cargo and a supply of brandy, they pressed her surgeon into service. The trader was then released.

The surgeon proved to be of great value to Guittar, for he claimed to have recently been cheated out of six or seven hundred crowns by the master of a Dutch merchantman engaged in the Surinam trade. With glowing descriptions of the merchantman's superb sailing qualities, he freely provided the buccaneer chieftain with information on the ship's whereabouts. His only desire, he said, was "to be revaged [*sic*] upon the Ma[st]er of the Shipp who had wronged him." Guittar, excited by the thought of a superior, swifter vessel than his own, acted immediately. He sailed to the Saltitudos (modern Ile de la Tortue), where the vessel was said to lie, located and took her, and, good as his word to the surgeon, set her master, Captain Cornelius Isaac, adrift in a longboat. There was, in view of her future employment, some irony in the ship's name—*Peace*. Guittar promptly dubbed her its French equivalent, *La Paix*.

Before Isaac and several of his company were left to their fate on the open seas, one of Guittar's crew, a Dutchman named John Houghling, who had been forcefully pressed against his will aboard the pirate sloop, requested that Isaac give him a "tickett" declaring his innocence of piracy to the world should he be taken. The captain agreed and scribbled out a document that Houghling would be obliged to lodge in his own defense less than half a year later. "We [the] underwritten," it read,

> *do declare that John Houghling is forced against his will to stay and remane upon the Ship LaPaix under the Comand of Lewis Guittar and have set our hands to witness it to ye end no body should trouble him or should pretend he was there by his own consent. Witness our hands*
>
> *Cornelius Isaac.*[3]

Guittar was apparently quite pleased with his sleek new prize, a vessel of about two hundred tons burthen. She was substantial in size—eighty-four feet in length, twenty-five feet abeam, and eleven feet deep in the hold. She possessed a single deck fore and aft, with a small forecastle and a "half" or quarterdeck extending to the mainmast. Capable of mounting at least twenty iron guns on carriages, she would, properly equipped and fitted, prove to be a force with which to be reckoned. *La Paix*, Guittar decided, would become his flagship.

After fitting out the new prize to their own peculiar needs, the pirates commenced a successful cruise of the West Indies, capturing at least four ships. Whenever resistance was encountered and the prey taken, a few unhappy victims were punished for their temerity by being hung from their own yardarms. Other victims were frequently given the opportunity to enlist among the pirates. Those that refused were occasionally hung, tortured, or set adrift. Depending upon the whim of the moment, some victims were released without any damage other than the usual plundering. *La Paix*'s crew began to swell, not only from those forced to serve or by volunteers, but also by picking up castaways and shipwreck victims.

On April 17 *La Paix* sighted the 100-ton Bristol pink *Baltimore*, Captain John Lovejoy commanding, en route from Barbados to Virginia. She had, in so doing, unwittingly picked up a trail that would eventually lead to her ultimate destiny. The pink, a much faster sailer than even Guittar's ship and a vessel type highly esteemed for its speed and maneuverability by the buccaneers, seemed a worthy prize regardless of what her lading might be. Guittar decided on a ruse to ensnare his swift victim. Wearing Dutch colors, "the pyrate made as if he had been in distress" so that Lovejoy lay back, innocently waiting for him to come up. Finally coming alongside, the pirate hailed her master and was informed where she was from and where bound. Then, without warning, *La Paix* fired a shot and killed one of pink's passengers, a merchant named James Waters. Captain Lovejoy struck his ensign immediately. Within a short time, he and several of his crewmen found themselves helpless prisoners in the pirate's hold.

Guittar decided that *Baltimore,* though unarmed, would make a worthy consort, along with a prize sloop already in hand, and directed his quartermaster and nearly a score of hands aboard to sail her. The prizemaster was instructed to steer a course, in company with *La Paix,* for Virginia. A cruise into the Chesapeake seemed a good diversion for a crew weary of the sweltering tropics, and there the little pirate flotilla might take on water and make much needed repairs to its ships and rigging. In the event the fleet became separated, a prearranged rendezvous point was selected, though *Baltimore* was strictly ordered "to tend upon them til they were wthin the Capes."

Several days later, as *La Paix* cruised northward, Guittar's spate of successes continued. Between eighty and one hundred leagues from Virginia, the three pirates fell in with and captured the sloop *George,* Joseph Forrest master, bound from Pennsylvania to Jamaica. Plundering of the ship began immediately, even as her company was being taken off and imprisoned aboard *La Paix.* Deeming the prize not worth saving, the buccaneers started a blaze in her cabin, bored a hole in her side, and abandoned her.

The following day, they were within only thirty leagues of their destination, Cape Henry, when a fat Virginia-bound brigantine, *Barbados Merchant,* of Liverpool, was sighted. Pursuit of the ship was soon underway. *Baltimore,* the fastest of the three pirates, rapidly outdistanced the flagship and came up with the intended victim alone. Though the little pink carried no heavy armaments, her complement had been increased to nearly sixty men. She would have little trouble overwhelming the brigantine's crew. Captain William Fletcher, *Merchant*'s master, saw no alternative but to surrender.

At the outset, the pirates treated Fletcher and his company with respect, and a congenial (if strained) atmosphere pervaded, even as the ship was being plundered. One of the pirates did his best by guile to entice *Merchant*'s crew to join the buccaneers. "You sail in a merchantman for twenty-five shillings a month and here," he boasted, "you may have seven or eight pounds if you can take it." But the brigantine's company remained adamant against signing the pirate articles. The friendly climate instantly evaporated, and the mood of the rovers became vicious. Captain Fletcher was seized, stripped of his clothes, and savagely beaten with the flat of a cutlass. Had not one of the buccaneers interceded, the captain would certainly have been killed on the spot. Thus "inspired," a carpenter and one seaman signed the articles. The remainder of the crew still refused to join. Determined to punish their captives for rejecting the articles, the pirates smashed the ship's compass, cut away a section of the rudder, took off all the ship's candles, and cut down the masts, sails, and bowsprit and cast them into the sea. Taking with them the ship's papers, books, and longboat, they then set *Barbados Merchant* and her unhappy crew adrift to face the prospect of a slow, agonizing death at sea. Fortunately, the rovers had been too anxious to depart, and failed to notice the foremast, sails, and rigging that were still tangled over one side of the vessel. After the pirate's departure, with the aid of a jury-rigged foremast and an ancient compass which had been overlooked during the general plunder, Captain Fletcher eventually managed to bring his brigantine safely into Accomac.

Having failed to come up with *Baltimore* as her crew stripped and plundered *Barbados Merchant*, Guittar brought *La Paix* about "to make the best of his way for the Capes [and] made a light for the pink to follow." But the pink took no notice, proceeding on her own merry way, never to be seen by Guittar again. She would continue to cause Virginians more than a few anxious moments well after *La Paix* had experienced her own moment in history.

On the morning of April 23, *Pennsylvania Merchant,* a brigantine commanded by Captain Samuel Harrison, en route from England to Philadelphia, lay becalmed about north latitude 37 degrees 38 minutes, approximately twenty leagues off Cape Henry. Harrison must have cursed quietly to himself when the wind died as he was standing in for the shore. By afternoon, however, a slight breeze had sprung up, just about the time the captain spied a ship wearing Dutch colors and attended by a small sloop. As the two oncoming vessels "clapt upon a wind" and hauled up their sails to get to the windward in an obvious attempt to gain the weather gauge, the brigantine's master became suspicious, perceived their intentions, and skillfully maneuvered to escape.

Sailing north with the pirates in close pursuit, *Pennsylvania Merchant* soon came up with and hailed the drifting wreck of *Barbados Merchant,* then attempting to jury-rig her foremast, but "had no time to help her." The momentary delay was enough for the pirates. Soon afterward, as dusk began to fall, they overtook the evasive merchantman and bid her strike her colors.

"Keep off or I will fire," replied a defiant Harrison to the shadowy form nearby.

Guittar was apparently unwilling to initiate a boarding attempt in the dark, and stood off. He remained close to his prey throughout the night, though Harrison sought desperately to elude him. Dawn found the two ships still within range of each other. Again the pirates ordered the merchantman to strike. This time, the demand was punctuated with gunfire. "I did not," Harrison later remarked, awed by the first closeup sight of *La Paix,* "think the [pirate] Ship had been so bigg over night." *Pennsylvania Merchant* struck immediately, and Harrison was ordered to board the rover. When asked why he had refused to strike his colors when first ordered, he innocently replied: "Because there was peace with all the world."

Shortly afterward, boats began plying back and forth between the pirate and her prize. The brigantine's crew were stripped of clothing and treated roughly while the thirty-one passengers aboard were systematically robbed. One unfortunate, Joseph Wood, was relieved of nine hundred pounds in cash and three hundred sixty pounds in bonds and papers. Not knowing what the papers were, only that they bore official-looking seals which appeared to be commissions of some sort, the pirates threw them around carelessly. Sails, rigging, tackle, blocks, apparel, and other goods—valued at two thousand pounds— were stripped from the ship and carried aboard *La Paix.*

As punishment for his evasive tactics, Harrison was informed his captors intended to burn the ship. Guittar, however, had sounder reasons. If he were to release the brigantine so close to Virginia, he feared that she might try to notify authorities in the colony, "where there was commonly a man of war." Harrison, in the meantime, was taunted by the crew, who informed him that he was a most fortunate man indeed, for when one of the Dutch ships they had encountered in the West Indies had resisted, several of the crew had been hung from the yardarm for their efforts. Unmindful of the pirates' dangerous mood, he pleaded for his ship. "I begged hard for her," he later testified, "but it was put to the vote and carryed for ye burning of her."

Soon after the passengers and ship's company were removed, John Houghling, whose earlier protests against piracy had vanished with *La Paix*'s string of successes, and who had become "a great Companion with the Captaine," was given the task of setting the prize afire. "It was," Guittar later stated, "the Pylotts doing he [Guittar] being no Artist himself." Entering Harrison's great cabin, Houghling began building a small fire, even as another pirate forced the brigantine's carpenter to

cut a hole in her side. The pilot, wearing Harrison's coat (which had
apparently been picked up in the cabin) and a pair of plundered
stockings, was in the last boat to leave *Pennsylvania Merchant,* which,
after nearly two days of captivity, was set adrift, aflame and sinking.

Guittar and his crew were elated over their evil accomplishments.
Shortly after the burning of *Pennsylvania Merchant,* the loot from the
capture was divided up on the quarter deck of *La Paix.* In the evening,
one of the prisoners was permitted on deck and observed that "a
parcell of the Pirates were very merry." One of their number, Francois
Delaunee, was particularly good at dancing. "I taking Especiall notice,"
the prisoner later recalled,

> *I highly Commended his daunceing. Another standing by hitt me on the
> Shoulder and told me there was one on board could daunce much better and
> then brot up one such I think did exceed. This action Seemed to me a
> Rejoyceing for the Success they had in their Villanies.*[4]

Early on the morning of April 28, as Guittar neared the Virginia
Capes intent on filling his water casks and rerigging his ship, two
merchantmen were spotted outward-bound from the Chesapeake
three or four leagues from Cape Henry. One proved to be the Belfast
ship *Indian King,* a beautiful Virginia-built vessel bound for London
and commanded by Captain Edward Whitaker. The other vessel,
Friendship, also of Belfast, was a smaller ship of barely one hundred
tons burthen, bound for Liverpool with a cargo of tobacco. *La Paix*
instantly gave chase to the larger of the two. When the pirate had crept
up to within a league and a half of her victim, *Indian King*'s master
began to "mistrust them to be Rogues and stood in againe" toward the
Capes. Before his ship had even trimmed her sails, however, the pirate
drew up his courses. "I takeing them to be honest men," Whitaker later
noted woefully in reviewing his mistake, "and so not minding to loose
so much time stood off againe to Sea. They came Jogging along without
Colours till they came within Shott of us then hoisted up a Dutch
Ensign." At that instant, when it was already too late, Whitaker recalled, "I Judged him a Rogue."

The pirate then took down the Dutch flag, ran up "his bloody
Ensign," and fired a warning shot at the merchantman. It was all that
was necessary, for Whitaker instantly lowered his colors. Summoned to
come aboard the pirate, he hoisted out a yawl and with four of his
company rowed to *La Paix.* Simultaneously, a yawl full of buccaneers
boarded *Indian King.* The mate, surgeon, crew, and passengers, their
hands tied behind them, "were violently and with force of armes taken
and Carried on board" the pirate ship. There, amid terrifying threats,

shouting, and wild gestures, they were robbed of their money.

Guittar interrogated the merchant captain about the country he had just left and whether or not there were any men-of-war there. Whitaker was entirely unaware of the arrival of HMS *Shoreham* and believed that only *Essex Prize* protected the Chesapeake. "I told him," he later reported, "that there was none that I knew of, Except a Small one [and] I heard she was gone home." The delighted pirate chieftain pressed his prisoner for information about what money and provisions were onboard *Indian King.* When Guittar left to turn his attentions upon *Friendship,* Whitaker was surrounded by the surly pirate crew, robbed, and thrown into confinement below deck along with several of his passengers.

It was about 10:00 A.M. when *La Paix* bore down on *Friendship* and fired a volley of small arms "at them in a Warlike manner." Captain Hans Hammil, commander of the little merchantman, who was standing by the mizzenmast when the first volley was fired, collapsed in a bloody heap. His ship struck instantly and hove to. The mate, John Calwell, was ordered aboard the pirate, which had soon dispatched a party of four of their own to take command of the prize. When Calwell and four of *Friendship*'s company reached the pirate, Guittar and John Houghling were standing on the quarterdeck.

"Was anyone killed?" queried the pirate chieftain.

Calwell replied that one man had been wounded.

"Who?" questioned Guittar.

"The master," replied Calwell.

Guittar appeared very sorry and offered to send his surgeon, but the mate informed him bitterly that it was already too late. The wound inflicted upon his captain was mortal. Houghling, in a macabre joke, feigned sympathy and consolingly asked where Hammil had been standing when shot.

"By the mizen shrouds."

"No," corrected the pilot, "he stood by the Mizen Mast and I fired the Gun that Shott him." With that, he burst into a fit of insane laughter and walked away.

After plundering *Friendship* of flour, provisions, and water, and transferring her crew to *La Paix,* the pirates finally entered the Chesapeake Bay with their prizes in tow. Standing into Lynnhaven Bay, they came upon several ships at anchor. One of Guittar's prisoners, Captain Whitaker, was questioned as to whether or not there were merchantmen. He could give no positive answer. Thus, Guittar decided to single out one of the finer looking ships as his next victim and soon bore down on her. She proved to be *Nicholson,* Robert Lurtine master, bound for London with seven hundred hogsheads of tobacco. The pirate, showing no colors, closed with his prey rapidly and soon came to within pistol-shot range. Lurtine hailed the approaching ship and asked the name of her home port.

"Out of the sea you Doggs," came a reply, accentuated by a volley of small shot.

Nicholson, valued at two thousand pounds sterling, which had been readying to sail when the pirate first appeared, instantly slipped her cable, loosed her canvas, "and made the best of way" to flee. For two hours the merchantman, a swift sailer, eluded her attacker, though *La Paix* somehow managed to keep to windward to prevent her escape. For two hours the guns of the pirate pounded her quarry to force submission. Finally, with his mainyard and main topsail shot away, Lurtine struck his colors and was ordered aboard the pirate ship. Pleased with his success, Guittar failed to notice the tiny pink running into the James, carrying word of the pirate's presence to Virginia authorities. Celebrations were apparently already in progress aboard *La Paix* when she hove to in Lynnhaven, for when the prize crew of nearly a score of men boarded their new prize, many were already drunk.

The pirates found *Nicholson* a ship very much to their liking. She was fast and maneuverable and could readily be converted to their needs. She would make a handsome addition to their growing fleet. First she had be be cleared "to fit & put her in a posture of defense." But work was somewhat retarded, for soon after boarding, the pirates discovered a supply of "strong Beer and some red wine on board" which they promptly began to consume. The more they drank, the crueler they became. Several of *Nicholson*'s company, apparently as punishment for their resistance, had their hands tied and were savagely beaten with tarred rope ends. A number of them were struck upon their backs with the flat sides of cutlasses; at least one was struck so hard that a cutlass broke. Not all of the pirates revelled in such amusements. When *Nicholson*'s gunner was brutally whipped, one of the pirates, the dancer Francois Delaunee, who had himself been forced to join the buccaneers, openly wept at the cruelty.

Interrogation of the prisoners brought worse torture upon *Nicholson*'s carpenter. When he revealed the "there was a man of warr in the Country and others said there was not," the pirates took the flint from a musket lock and slowly screwed the metal into his thumb. Tiring of this entertainment, they beat him mercilessly and "told him he should not lye the next time."

Despite the degenerating state of sobriety, the pirates wasted little time on such atrocities. Several prisoners aboard *La Paix* were put to work transferring sails and provisions from *Indian King* to *Nicholson*. Many of the latter's captive company were forced at sword point to begin hoisting the ship's cargo of tobacco from the hold and heaving it into the Chesapeake. One of the pirates, Cornelius Frank, brandishing his cutlass, threatened "that those that would not work all night" would be stabbed in the morning. By dawn 110 to 112 hogsheads of tobacco, some clothing, and several bolts of cloth which had failed to strike the pirates' fancy had been cast into the sea. But the work by this time had slowed to a crawl. Many of the buccaneers had fallen into drunken stupors. Most would soon be rudely awakened.

The Sunday evening of April 28 had passed pleasantly enough for Governor Francis Nicholson, who had been busy sealing letters at the home of Colonel William Wilson in Kecoughtan. Captain William Passenger, recently-arrived commander of HMS *Shoreham,* whose ship lay offshore in the James taking on water, had just stopped by briefly to pay his respects.[5] Only a few days earlier, the Governor had received, via Captain Passenger, the Admiralty Office's orders to put *Essex Prize* in the best condition possible for her return to England, and for her to take any merchantmen ready under convoy.[6] She was being replaced by *Shoreham,* a vessel of far superior strength with a commander of competence. Aldred had, of course, thought it absolutely necessary that his own ship be careened and refitted; he absolutely refused to consider setting a departure date.[7] He complained that he had no spare boats or men to notify every master of a ship in Virginia waters of the convoy's departure, and probably wouldn't have done so if he had.[8] Nevertheless, Nicholson was relieved, for Passenger seemed to be everything Aldred wasn't, and his ship (unlike *Essex Prize*) was well-armed and ready for duty.

Passenger's orders from the Admiralty had been explicit. Inasmuch as "the most dangerous time of the year for Pyrates comeing upon this Coast" was at hand, the good captain had been specifically ordered "to go out and Cruise in the Bay of Chisapeake and about the Capes thereof, for the Defense of this Colony against Pyrates, all which that you meet with, you are to take, sinke, burn or otherwise destroy, as you best can." Passenger's ship was certainly equal to the task. She had been built as a fifth-rate man-of-war at Shoreham, England, and was commissioned in January 1694. Displacing 359 tons, *Shoreham* was 103 feet in length, 28 feet abeam, and armed with 32 guns—a match for any pirate in the Americas.[9]

Buoyed by the big warship's presence, Nicholson and the Council had even sought to supplement *Shoreham*'s capabilities by ordering the purchase of a small sloop to serve as a tender. Such a vessel would be useful not only in watering and providing wood for the warship, but could also act as a scout in shallow creeks, small inlets, and shoally places *Shoreham* dared not go. She would, it was thought, be of additional value in surprising "any Pyrates boates, which shall be sent on Shoar in any private places." One such vessel, with a 27-foot keel and a 10-foot 6-inch beam, had already been offered to the colony by one Joshua Broadbent for a trifling 40 pounds sterling![10] The good will between Nicholson and Passenger already stood in stark contrast to the sad relationship between the Governor and Aldred.

As Nicholson, Wilson, and Passenger were passing the balmy spring afternoon in pleasant conversation, Captain Aldred burst into the house with terrible news. He had, he said, just come ashore from onboard a pink that had only hours before escaped from a pirate ship lying in Lynnhaven Bay. Passenger sprang up and (despite Nicholson's objections that he wait until morning, when he might call out the militia and dispatch warnings to ships in the area) "immediately went on board his Maj^tys Shipp the Shoreham and got her under Saile designing to goe downe in the night." The warship's watering party was recalled, and merchant ships in the vicinity were requested to send men to reinforce her crew. Though *Shoreham* was quite strong in terms of armaments, a great many of her complement were mere boys. She was, however, soon under sail and making directly for Lynnhaven Bay. Unfortunately, contrary winds and darkness hindered her progress. The pilot refused to guide her through the extremely shoally waters in the dark, and Passenger, in frustration, was obliged to bring her to anchor barely three leagues from the pirate fleet. Ashore, Nicholson readied the militia on the south shore of the James, but he yearned to be at the front of the fight and by 10:00 P.M., in company with Aldred and his friend and trusted Collector of Customs Peter Heyman, he had boarded the anchored warship.[11]

At 3:00 A.M. on April 29, HMS *Shoreham* weighed and carefully began to pick her way toward Lynnhaven Bay. An hour later, as night began to surrender to the gray of dawn, the ghostly outline of the pirate ship *La Paix* could be seen etched against the morning sky half a mile away.[12] The battle was imminent.

Lewis Guittar had been well warned of the oncoming man-of-war but chose to ignore the information. The preceding evening, as *Shoreham* had nosed her way down the James, Captain Whitaker of *Indian King* spotted her and taunted the pirate chieftain that there "was a great Shipp" on the move. Guittar scoffed, saying that "there is no man of Warr here and if it be a Merch^tman I will have him by and by." He gave the matter no further notice. The pirates aboard *La Paix* continued to bring sails and other plunder aboard and to take on water throughout the night without the slightest concern for the danger that would soon descend upon them.

With the dawn came the grim realization that the "great Shipp" was indeed a man-of-war. The prize parties distributed throughout the pirate fleet were immediately summoned back to the flagship, even as the moment of battle drew near. The grogginess of overindulgence for many was for the most part washed away by the urgency of impending battle. Two who failed to return, Cornelius Frank and Francois Delaunee, lay in the captain's and chief mate's cabins aboard *Nicholson* sleeping off their drunkenness. Aboard *La Paix,* nearly fifty prisoners were driven below into the ship's cramped hold and locked up for the duration of the fight, their fate now tied to that of the pirate ship.

Guittar's battle plan was simple: get to the windward of the better armed but poorly manned *Shoreham,* close, and board. Quickly, as *La Paix*'s topsails were loosened in the Virginia wind, the bloody red flag was hoisted. Passenger closed and fired a shot across her bow. The pirate refused to strike and returned the fire with interest. At about 7:00 A.M. the engagement became general, with the pirate maneuvering to get to windward, and the Royal Navy ship, her "Kings Flagg Ancient and Jack flying," constantly denying her the weather gauge in a ballet of bloody consequence. Broadside after broadside echoed up the Chesapeake as the two ships closed to within pistol-shot range, fired, and then separated. Though Passenger's men were too few to sail the ship and fire their guns at the same time, the big warship's superior firepower had a telling effect when employed. Yet neither side wavered in its resolve, despite the growing damage and casualties each suffered.

La Paix's pilot, John Houghling, a man who had garnered great esteem among his fellow pirates since the days of his capture by them, seemed to be everywhere during the fight. As the heat of battle increased, he cast aside the coat he had plundered from Captain Whitaker. At one point he inspected the prisoners in the hold, and when asked how the battle fared, he answered: "Dam her she is but a little Toad no bigger then we. We shall have her presently." The prisoners could determine little about what was going on topside, but one overheard Houghling to say he "hoped in a short time to get to windward of them and have the Doggs." It was a vain hope, for Captain William

Passenger was not about to relinquish the weather gauge.

The carnage aboard the crowded decks of *La Paix* was considerable. The dead, and even some of the more seriously wounded, it was later charged, were thrown overboard to make room for the living. Portions of a human skull whistled through the air as a volley of shot from *Shoreham* raked the pirate's deck. Yet the grisly fight continued. The shoreline of the nearby beaches was dotted with a few spectators; Charles Scarburgh, Collector of Customs for the Eastern Shore, called the battle "as Sharp a Dispute as I think could be between two ships."

Aboard *Shoreham,* Governor Nicholson inspired the crew with promises of gold (presumably to be taken from the pirates). Beside him on the quarterdeck stood Peter Heyman. Both men had participated in the battle with pistols when the ships closed to within range, recklessly exposing themselves to the pirate's gunfire. Elsewhere, John Aldred emerged from his chrysalis and behaved with courage as pistol shot and cannonballs crashed about him. But it was Captain Passenger, charged with managing the fight, even though the Governor was aboard, who "behaved himself with much Courage & good Conduct having to Deal with an Enemy under a Desperate choice of killing or hanging."

The king's forces were not without their own casualties. Between 1:00 and 2:00 P.M., as the two ships swung close together, Peter Heyman unleashed several rounds of pistol shot. Suddenly, a volley from the pirate ship whistled past the Governor and a volunteer, Joseph Maunsaged, only several feet away, and fatally struck the unfortunate customs officer standing between them.

Slowly but perceptibly, the superior firepower of *Shoreham* began to disintegrate *La Paix.* The pirate's masts, yards, and rigging were shredded "all to shatters," several guns were dismounted, and her hull was badly battered. The ship was fast becoming a floating wreck, and it was only a matter of time before Guittar would decide to draw out of range and disengage. Nearing the shore, he swung his helm hard to the lee, but as his ship grudgingly came about, she suddenly failed to respond. Her rudder had been shot off. Without bowlines, sheets, and braces to haul the sails, she was virtually powerless. And with a veritable storm of small shot and partridge shot raining upon her deck, her crew had been driven below and was unable to make necessary repairs. *La Paix* drifted aimlessly for a few minutes, her sails hanging limp and torn, then shuddered as she drove aground. Captain Passenger came to anchor nearby in three fathoms of water and patiently waited. At about 4:00 P.M., as a great quiet enveloped the Chesapeake, the bloody red flag of *La Paix* fluttered down, and the flag of truce was raised.

As his ship was so badly shot up, Guittar, with no hope of escape, might have surrendered outright, but he still had two negotiable assets: fifty innocent prisoners and the willingness of his crew to perish rather than face capture. Having already agreed to live and die together, the pirates resolved to blow up their ship with all aboard rather than to grace a noose in Virginia. A train of gunpowder was placed across the deck to thirty barrels of explosives. Guittar coolly informed his captives of his intentions less than an hour after *La Paix* had grounded. The terrified prisoners, led by Captain Lurtine, pleaded with the pirates to permit one of their number to swim to *Shoreham* and inform the King's men of their plight. One of the captives, Baldwin Mathews, agreed to go and leaped overboard, but instead of swimming to the warship, struck out for the beach.

The pirates, watching Mathews swimming to shore and safety, became edgy and began to chant, "broil, broil," meaning that they would all burn together unless quarter were granted. A second volunteer, John Lumpany, who had been a passenger aboard *Pennsylvania Merchant,* approached Guittar. The "Capt. of the Pyrates," he later testified, "bid me have a good courage & speak to this Effect. Tell the Commander in chief if he will not give me and my Men Quarter and Pardon I will blow the Ship up and we will all dye together." On deck, Lumpany bade the pirate captain adieu, left him at his cabin door, jumped into the Chesapeake, and swam to *Shoreham,* where he related the surrender terms to the Governor.

Nicholson responded promptly, scrawling out a reply in his own hand between 4:00 and 5:00 P.M.

Whereas Capt Lewis [sic] Commander of the Lay Paste hath proferred to surrender himselfe, men and Ship together with what effects thereunto belongeth provided he may have quarter which I grant him on performance of the same and referr him and his men to the mercy of my Royal Master King William the third whom God preserve.[13]

The terms were accepted and *La Paix* surrendered. The fight had ended.

It was unclear to Nathanael McClanahan at precisely what point *La Paix* surrendered to HMS *Shoreham,* although he and other spectators had watched the deadly battle from the beach at Lynnhaven Bay. Nor could he determine whether it was three or four men who had jumped from the shattered hulk of the pirate ship to swim ashore. When he ran to meet them, however, he discovered that only one man had managed to survive the long swim.

"I took him up," McClanahan later related, "and asked if he could speak English."

"Yes," replied the winded seaman.

"What country man are you?"

"New York."

"Are you one of the pirates?" McClanahan asked excitedly.

"No, I was a prisoner forced," answered the man, producing a paper written in Dutch.

"Why have you come ashore?"

"For a boat," came the reply.

McClanahan noticed that the man's fingers were somewhat swollen.

"I took him for a Rogue and believed he had fought," he stated days afterward, "but he excused himself and said he was forct to hand powder."

Within minutes McClanahan and the New Yorker were surrounded by a group of curious spectators who had gathered to watch the battle, but now vied to see one of the participants in the flesh. The New Yorker appeared frightened, but was even more agitated when he spotted a boat from *Shoreham* making for the beach. Suddenly he shouted, "Make heist from the shore . . . the Pyrates designed to blow up their ship." The crowd disappeared into the nearby wood as quickly as they had appeared, leaving McClanahan and the New Yorker nearly alone. In a second, the New Yorker too had bolted.

"Stop him!" yelled McClanahan, instantly aware that he had been duped by a very clever pirate.

Within minutes, the fugitive had been captured and was soon a prisoner to a shoemaker. The fugitive was John Houghling.

The battle had been costly. Aboard *Shoreham,* which had suffered the least, four men, including Peter Heyman, had been killed and many more wounded. The ship was severely damaged and had lost her mainmast. The pirates suffered far more than the King's ship. Of a company in excess of one hundred fifty men, twenty-five or twenty-six had died in battle; twelve or fourteen more had been seriously wounded, eight of whom would die within two weeks. Passenger took one hundred twenty-four prisoners, who were turned over to the custody of the militia of Elizabeth City County to await shipment to England, where they would face the King's justice. Three of the buccaneers—John Houghling, Cornelious Frank, and Francois Delaunee—had been exempted from the terms of surrender, for none of them had been aboard *La Paix* at the time of her capitulation. Houghling had been taken ashore, and Delaunee and Frank were found aboard *Nicholson,* having slept through the entire battle.

At Elizabeth City Church the body of brave Peter Heyman was laid to rest with full honors at the order of his friend and mentor Governor Francis Nicholson. A large, flat tombstone surmounted with a coat of arms marked the site. Upon the marker was inscribed:

This stone was given by his Excellency Francis Nicholson Esq. Lieutenant General of Virginia in Memory of Peter Heyman esq. Grandson of Sir Peter Heyman of Summerfield in ye county of Kent—he was Collector of the customs in ye lower district of James River and went voluntarily on board the King's Ship Shoreham, in Pursuit of a pyrate who greatly infested this coast—after he had behaved himself 7 hours with undaunted courage, was killed with a small shot, ye 29 day of April 1700. In the engagement he stood next to the Governor upon the Quarter deck and was here honorably interred by his order.[14]

XII

Three Gibbets

Eager to be finished with the *La Paix* affair, Francis Nicholson lost little time in bringing John Houghling, Cornelius Frank, and Francois Delaunee to trial.[1] A Court of Admiralty was ordered to convene at Elizabeth City courthouse on Monday, May 13, 1700. Edward Hill was appointed Judge, and a commission of oyer and terminer [to "inquire, hear, and determine"] was appointed by virtue of an Act of Assembly of April 27, 1699, whereby "all Treasons Pyracys Murthers or Capital Offences committed upon the high Seas or in any River, Haven, Creek or Bay where the Admiral hath Jurisdicōn shall be awarded & done within this his Majesties Colony and Dominion." To that end, fourteen commissioners, five of whom could act, were designated. These included: Edmund Jennings, Charles Scarborough, John Lightfoot, Matthew Page, and Benjamin Harrison, all members of the Council of State; and nine noble gentlemen of the colony, William Wilson, Anthony Armisted, Philip Ludwell, Thomas Barbor, Thomas Ballard, Will Buckner, Humphrey Harwood, William Cary, and William Rascow. Peter Beverly was appointed clerk of arraignment to record all proceedings. Page and Armistead administered the oath of office to Judge Hill, who, in turn, commanded Sheriff Walter Bayliss of Elizabeth City County to empanel a grand jury and a petit jury to attend the court the following morning. It was all very prompt and proper, for the state had already made up its mind as to the verdict; the trial was to serve as a warning to all pirates that Virginia would act with force to halt depredations and with vigor in its courts to prosecute and execute any and all piratical miscreants.

At 9:00 A.M. on May 14 the court sat, the clerk was sworn in, and the grand jury and its foreman, Miles Cary, were administered an oath requiring them to be impartial and to "present things truely as they come to your knowledge according to the best of your understanding."

Then Judge Hill addressed a strong opening statement to the jury. *Gentlemen of the Grand Jury the occasion which calls this Court and you hither is very Extraordinary there being no President [sic] before of a Pyrates being taken within this his Majesties Colony and Dominion of Virginia for which at this time we have great reason to praise God being thereby delivered from many miserys, degradations, Robberys, and perhaps barbarous murthers which otherwise this Country might have smarted under, Pyrates being a Sort of men whose Robberys are generally accompanied with the greatest and most horrid Crueltys and Tortures to the persons of such whose hard fate it is to fall into their hands and very frequently with the most Execrable murder of their Captives in cold blood.*

Hill informed the jury in no uncertain terms where its duty lay. Because the case was setting a precedent, since no similar proceedings had occurred in Virginia under the recent law, he promised to help the jury by being brief, "to remove some Scruples which may arrise and thereby Enable you to better performe what is Expected of you." A foreigner guilty of piracy or robbery upon the high seas and brought to Virginia, he noted, was in no way different from a subject of the King of England liable for the same offenses, and it was the jury's duty to make its findings without respect to the nationality of the defendants.

Eleven witnesses, many of them officers and members of vessels captured by *La Paix*, were sworn in. The grand jury then presented an indictment against John Houghling "for a Pyracy and Robbery comitted upon the Shipp Pennsylvania Merchant." Another indictment was presented against Cornelius Frank and Francois Delaunee for piracy and robbery upon the ship *Nicholson*. The grand jury then withdrew to hear their evidence.

While the grand jury was out, two interpreters, Stephen Fouace and Isaac Jemmart, were sworn in for the benefit of Frank and Delaunee, neither or whom could speak English. Depositions were taken from several persons, and a brief examination of Captain Guittar, "the Grand pyrate," who was to be sent to England under the agreement reached with Nicholson on the sea of battle, was undertaken. The grand jury returned but failed to agree on any bills, though it had interviewed several witnesses provided by the court. The witnesses, it seemed, "did not know the persons Indicted by their names," and therefore the jury asked that the prisoners be brought before the court to see whether or not they were the persons mentioned in the indictment. Houghling, Frank, and Delaunee were brought before the bar and questioned to the satisfaction of the jury.

Again the jury withdrew. Within a short time it had reconvened with bills against the three pirates. Then the court proceeded to the arraignment of John Houghling, and the clerk read the indictment.

On April 24, Houghling, a mariner late of New York, "not having the fear of God before thine Eyes but being moved & seduced by ye instigation of the Devill," stood accused, "Pyratically and feloniously in a Hostile and Warrlike manner with force of Armes of great Gunns small Armes Cutlasses and other weapons of Warr," and in concert with several others, of attacking and capturing the ship *Pennsylvania Merchant,* of eighty tons, belonging to subjects of the King and commanded by Samuel Harrison, mariner. He was also charged with putting Harrison and his crew in fear for their lives and in danger of bodily harm and stealing his ship, as well as tackle, apparel, furniture, and provisions valued at six hundred forty pounds sterling, and her lading of goods and wares valued at three thousand pounds sterling.

"How sayst thou, John Houghling," charged the clerk. "Art thou guilty of the Pyracy and Robbery whereof thou standst indicted or not guilty?"

"Not guilty," murmured the defendant.

"How wilt thou be tryed?"

"By the honorable Court."

"You must say, 'By God and my Country,'" corrected Judge Hill.

"What sayst thou?" said the clerk.

"By God and my Country."

"God send thee a good deliverance," continued the clerk.

The petit jury was then summoned. As each of the jurors stepped up to the Holy Bible to be sworn in, Houghling was permitted the opportunity to challenge them. No challenge was made, and "Twelve good men and true" were sworn in and convened to hear the evidence.

The Attorney General of Virginia Bartholomew Fowler began the trial by presenting a statement to the jury. He outlined to that body that Houghling stood accused of a crime that was "an Act of the worst men and thet he is the worst of that sort if we prove what the indictment speakes." He was certain that the evidence was enough to convict the defendant as well as to show him to be "guilty of many Actions more Barbarous & Villanous." The punishment for such crimes, he reminded the jury, was death.

The first witness, Edmund Ashfield, taken prisoner by the pirates on April 17, provided the court with testimony concerning the capture of the pink *Baltimore,* in which he had sailed. He made note of Houghling's efforts to induce the pink's crew to join the pirates, and of the defendant's participation in the boarding of *Pennsylvania Merchant* several days later. Though a prisoner confined to the hold of *La Paix,* Ashfield stated that Houghling had also been "very active" in the taking of *Indian King.*

"Did you observe any act of cruelty used towards the English prisoners by the Pyrate?" queried the attorney general.

"Some they did strike and one they cutt in the Arme with their Swords and Cutlaces," answered Ashfield.

"Did the Pyrates talk of blowing their Shipp up?"

"Yes they did and went to prayers upon it."

"Did you see me plunder any body?" asked Houghling.

"No," replied Ashfield bluntly, "but I saw you in Armes."

The next witness, Samuel Harrison, testified that he too was a prisoner aboard *La Paix* when *Pennsylvania Merchant* was captured, and had been forced to board her with the pirates after she had been plundered. Staring coldly at the defendant, he stated, "I saw this man the Prisoner at the Barr in the great Cabbin by a fire Stooping downe to the fire with a Chip in his hand which he threw upon it and there was none [other] by it besides, nor no fire but in the Cabbin."

Houghling, having no attorney, challenged the witness, asking whether he had seen him kindle the fire. There was no answer, only silence. The witness was dismissed.

The third witness was Edward Whitaker, master of *Indian King.* He identified Houghling as *La Paix*'s pilot, and noted that the defendant had "rejoyced" at the capture of *Nicholson,* and had later observed him cleaning arms plundered from the ship.

And so it went throughout the day, witness after witness bringing testimony against the defendant, quoting his statements and cataloging his piratical activities throughout the various stages of *La Paix*'s rampage on and near Chesapeake waters. Accounts of his close companionship with Captain Guittar, the murder of the master of *Friendship,* and his participation in the plunder and destruction of *Pennsylvania Merchant* were repeated time after time by nearly a dozen witnesses. There seemed little rebuttal possible, and the attorney general, confident of his presentations and "loath to take up any more of the Court's time," finally rested his case.

Houghling's defense was one frequently offered by pirates in their own behalf: he had been forced and kept against his will. He produced as evidence the "tickett" allegedly given to him months earlier by Captain Cornelius Isaac, master of *La Paix,* when he was first taken by the pirates, attesting to the fact that the defendant had been forced into pirate service.

"It might be," noted Judge Hill, "you was not willing at the first but afterwards might."

"I would have gone home about my business to my family," replied
Houghling, "but the Capt. of the pyrate would not suffer me. He took
his Cane and strook me and when I came upon Deck he took his sword
and Drubbed me," and threatened to maroon him.

"I perceive you agreed with him afterwards," retorted Judge Hill
sarcastically.

When questioned about the accusations of killing the master of
Friendship, Houghling denied it, declaring indignantly: "I shott no
man. God is my witness the will of God be done. What God pleaseth
what I did on board I was forced to do for fear of death."

The attorney general closed with a skillful address to the jury. He
first sought to define the nature of piracy in general, and then as it
particularly related to the company with which Houghling was as-
sociated. Piracy, he stated catagorically, was the worst of crimes, and
pirates the worst of men. Indeed, they degraded themselves below the
rank of men and were little more than beasts of prey. Governed by no
laws, they were merciless, living by rapine and violence. They were
enemies to all mankind and violated all the laws of God and man
without remark or regret. "They love mischief for mischief sake & will
do what mischief they can tho' it brings no advantage to themselves,
they destroy Trade and thereby defraud the King of his Customes."
Piracy at sea was worse than robbery on the land, "for the mischief is
greater and more universall and the benefit less to the Taker." For the
sake of a little rigging, he explained, a pirate would destroy a ship of
£10,000 value.

In regard to the pirates of *La Paix,* the attorney general declared,
they were "the worst sorts of Pyrates and indeed the Prisoner at the
Barr the worst of them." His kind were "Indeed Prodegies of Wickedness & their Vallanyes Exceed beleife." Though testimony suggested
that they had said their prayers, "what God they prayed to I cannot
conceive."

In conclusion, he reiterated the evidence against Houghling. He had
been very busy in the pirate's service, served as their pilot, and was
personally responsible for the burning of *Pennsylvania Merchant.* And
the defendant had fought against a King's ship and was thus guilty of
treason. The attorney general demeaned the defendant's defense. "I
beleive [*sic*] if he was forced it was by the instigation of the Devill and by
his owne Principles." How indeed, he asked, could a forced man serve
as pilot and officer, set a helpless merchantman afire, and fight a king's
ship so vigorously?

The jurors were then instructed to withdraw and deliberate. Upon

their return, the jury foreman, William Lowry, brought in the verdict.
"Guilty."
"Look to the Keeper," ordered the Clerk of the Court, "for he is found guilty of Piracy and Robbery."
The jury was then discharged and the sheriff ordered to empanel another petit jury to attend the court on the following day.

The next morning, Wednesday, May 15, the Court again sat with a new jury, and Cornelius Frank and Francois Delaunee were arraigned for acts of piracy against the ship *Nicholson*. Speaking through interpreters, both men entered pleas of not guilty. Fifteen witnesses were sworn in to testify against the two defendants. Robert Lurtine, commander of *Nicholson,* was the first witness. He provided the court with a detailed account of the capture and plunder of his ship. He readily identified the two defendants as having been among the pirates who boarded his vessel, but he could not say whether they had participated in its plundering. At least one of them, he recalled, had been asleep in his cabin after he was carried off as a prisoner. The second witness testified that they had drunk, "at their pleasure," much of the red wine and beer that had been aboard and had fallen asleep. He also testified that the defendants were among those pirates who had tied up members of the crew, beaten them with cutlasses, and forced them to unload the ship. They had been involved in the torture of the ship's carpenter while trying to secure information concerning the naval defenses of the Chesapeake, and had, after learning of the presence of a large man-of-war in the area, beaten the poor man, telling him not to lie the next time.
"Had they taken his word it would have been better for them," suggested Judge Hill caustically.
John Staples of *Nicholson* was a much more sympathetic witness. He informed the court that Frank and Delaunee had been asleep when *Shoreham* and *La Paix* fought, and while they dozed in a drunken stupor, they had been secured and locked in the cabins by their former prisoners. "When we brought them out upon the quarter deck," Staples testified, "Cornelius ffranc said must I be hanged that can speak all Linguoes." His fellow pirate Delaunee, said the witness, had even cried when the ship's gunner had been whipped, and proclaimed for all to hear that "he never plundered nor toucht a man."
"Is it possible," conceded the attorney general regarding Delaunee's demeanor, "he might not be guilty of so much cruelty as Cornelius ffrank but nevertheless he is guilty of ye same Piracy!"
Staples added, before leaving the stand, that though he had seen

Delaunee in arms, the defendant had exhibited concern for the welfare of the prisoners aboard *Nicholson* by bringing them wine and beer when they were thirsty.

Other witnesses were not so kind, testifying that they had seen the two defendants actively participate in throwing tobacco overboard from *Nicholson,* or at the very least forcing their prisoners to do so. Frank, while guarding the laboring prisoners, had, according to the testimony of one Robert Hatton, threatened to stab anyone who would not work throughout the night. John Lavier stated, "That man that you call Cornelius was the worst of the two, the other struck none of us."

Having examined seven key witnesses, the attorney general rested his case.

In his defense, and through the interpreters, Cornelius Frank, like John Houghling before him, claimed that he had been forced by the pirates to go along with him. He had been taken out of a Dutch ship and had been unwilling to follow the buccaneer's trade, "but when these pyrates had him they would not part with him because he could speak severall languages that the Capt. would not take a hundred pounds for him and told him he should have the same fate with him." He claimed he had been carried against his will onboard *Nicholson* and had borne no arms but had had a cutlass put into his hand. He had been sent onboard after the ship had been taken with directions to put her in the best posture for defense.

Francois Delaunee's story was similar. He informed the court that he had been taken by the pirates while on a voyage to St. Domingo, and had been forced to join them. He had not opposed the pirates "for fear of being put to death" and had always shown his unwillingness to excel in his forced profession by treating prisoners with kindness. He gave pillows and rugs from his own cabin to unfortunate sailors from captured ships which had been burned. When he told the pirates that he would not continue to follow their calling, they threatened to "sett him on shore amongst the Rocks and let him starve." When pressed in battle, he claimed, he had always fired into the air or into the water.

"Has he any Evidence?" queried the attorney general.

"It is natural for all pyrates to say they are forced," chided Judge Hill. "The Capt. of the *La Paix* [himself] saies he was forced."

Delaunee responded, "Whatever he did was to avoid death & that he was resolved to leave ye Trade."

The attorney general then addressed the jury in summation. All the witnesses had brought damning evidence. While under arms, Frank and Delaunee had boarded *Nicholson,* kept her crew prisoner, forced them to labor on pain of being stabbed if they faltered, struck the prisoners with their cutlasses, and committted other outrages. "'Tis true indeed," he stated, "some do say that Delaunee seemed to be more mercifull then the rest and to Comiserate their Sufferings as also that he wept but what of all that I hope you will consider the Evidence given against 'em both is plaine and positive they have made a defence as weak as their cause is wicked. They had pleaded force but have brought no Evidence to prove it."

The attorney general cautioned the jury that, though Delaunee might be an object of mercy, "you are to leave mercy in its proper place" requesting that they determine a verdict based upon the evidence alone.

The jury withdrew to consider the verdict after remarks from the advocate of the Admiralty similar to those of the attorney general, and returned with a decision. Cornelius Frank was found guilty as charged, but Francois Delaunee, to the astonishment and disgust of the court, was found not guilty. The attorney general was mortified.

"Gentlemen of the Jury!" he shouted.

The evidence in my Opinion against ffrancois Delaunee was very full and positive for what he stood indicted plainly proving that he was in Armes with the pyrates that took the shipp Nicholson that he went on board her with them, that he plundered with them & that he was one of those that kept the possession of her. He was not indicted for beating any body or being more Cruell then his Comrades, and therefore you would do well to consider your Evidence.

"We have done according to our Consciences," replied the foreman.

"If your Consciences go contrary to your Evidence I would not have such a Conscience," retorted the attorney general, "if you have plaine Evidence that this man was on board with the rest that took the shipp your Consciences cannot tell you his Intentions were different from his Actions."

The clerk asked if the jury's verdict stood.

"Yes," replied the foreman.

Attorney General Bartholomew Fowler had lost a battle, but not the war. Without missing a beat, he informed the court that he had other charges of piracy to bring against Delaunee, and requested that another jury be empaneled. Again the sheriff was directed to summon both a grand jury and a petit jury for the following day, May 16.

Seventeen men were selected for the grand jury to hear the second trial of Francois Delaunee. Addressing the jury in his opening remarks, Judge Hill caustically noted that the jurymen would perhaps not have "had this Trouble if one of them that has been upon his tryall for a

Piracy and Robbery comitted upon the Shipp Nicholson has been brought in according to the merit of his Offence, and the Expectation of the Court but it seems how guilty soever he is of that ffact there are more to charge him." He directed the court to inquire and present its findings as the indictment related to piracy and other offenses charged.

"Pyrates are the worst part of mankind and there is no offense almost against God or man," stated the judge,

> but what in the course of their lives they become guilty of, and we particularly are Sensible of it and should I am afraid have been much more were it not for the late deliverance before menconed. Therefore I hope you will consider that if such men Escape Justice it will encourage not only them to continue in their wicked practices but others who have no designe that way to joyne with them when they have an apprehension they may do it with Impunity.

The attorney general then presented an indictment against Delaunee for piracy and robbery committed against *Pennsylvania Merchant*. Three witnesses were then sworn in to deliver evidence to the jury. While the jury was out, one John Vriling was sworn in as an interpreter, and the court proceeded to make a list of pirates who had been given quarter aboard *La Paix*. Before the list was completed, however, the jury returned with a *bill vera* of piracy against Delaunee. In view of the previous jury's verdict, and thus unsure whether the grand jury would be needed again, Hill requested that they remain until a final determination against the defendant had been made. The listing of the remainder of the pirates given quarter was then completed, depositions were taken, and Francois Delaunee was again arraigned. A petit jury was then sworn in.

Again, Delaunee pleaded not guilty to the charges. The first witness, Abraham Surtley, a Dutchman, required an interpreter. He had been a prisoner aboard *La Paix* for four months, and had grown to know the defendant well during that time. Delaunee, he testified, had been a maker and cleaner of small arms, and bore the rank of corporal among the pirates. He knew that the defendant had borne arms against *Pennsylvania Merchant* and had shared in the plundering of several of the pirate's prizes.

"Had the prisoner ever refused to bear arms in the pirate ship?"

"I never saw him refuse," replied the witness.

"Here," said the attorney general in obvious relief, "is plaine Evidences that the Prison[e]r at the barr was in Armes . . . or else I know not what is plaine Evidence."

When the interpreters informed Delaunee of Surtley's testimony, the defendant unhappily conceded that he had once borne arms and had taken a share of plunder. He then requested that the witness be asked if he had not, in fact, given that plunder away to the prisoners. Surtley could not answer either way.

"If he did," noted Hill, "it does not lessen the fact."

Delaunee asked the witness if he ever saw him abuse any captives.

"He is not," injected the attorney general indignantly, "indicted for Cruelty but Pyracy." The witness was excused.

The next witness, Thomas Murray, a passenger aboard *Pennsylvania Merchant,* testified that he had not seen Delaunee board the ship but that he had seen him bearing arms and pistols and in possession of some of the plunder, including several items belonging to the witness himself.

Delaunee asked if he had not given him a pair of shoes, an act of mercy for which he was threatened to be beaten by the rest of the crew. Murray did not know about the shoes, but acknowledged that the defendant had given him a blanket.

"This was a piece of humanity only," sneered the judge.

Joseph Wood, the third witness, had been a passenger aboard *Pennsylvania Merchant.* When brought aboard *La Paix,* he had seen Delaunee bearing arms, and had heard him addressed by the nickname of Major. He had once watched him dancing, celebrating their villainies. He too acknowledged that Delaunee had shared in the division of the plunder upon the quarterdeck of the pirate ship, and had served as an armed guard over the prisoners.

Again Delaunee asked if the witness had seen him abuse anyone.

"The prisoner is indicted for Pyracy not for Barbarity," the attorney general reminded the court, and then closed his case.

Called once again to testify in his own behalf, Delaunee repeated to the jury that he had been forced into piracy and had lived under the threat of being marooned. He never killed anyone, and always fired too high or too low, so that "the rest of the pyrates blamed him for not shooting well."

"Pyrates will say any thing to save their lives," responded Judge Hill.

When asked to produce evidence to prove his story, Delaunee stated sadly that he had no witnesses, but had been forced to arms only out of fear of being knocked in the head. Several of the pirates, he assured the court, would speak in his favor to that effect. The court refused to admit any of *La Paix*'s crew to testify in his behalf, for it was believed that "they will clear one another at any rate." Delaunee, thus cut off from any supporting testimony by the court, concluded his futile defense by reiterating that he had fallen in with the pirates against his will and was "very sorry he was ever at that trade."

In summing up, the attorney general requested the jury to reflect
upon the mischief that pirates cause all nations and the consequences
of acquitting the guilty, "Enimyes to all mankind," in such cases. More
than a hundred pirates had been examined, he informed the court,
and they all pretended to have been forced, some even going so far as
to give each other certificates attesting to it.

*I hope Gentlemen you will take care to repaire the Credit of your County
and country which was very much impaired by Yesterdays verdict. . . . I
doubt not but you will discharge the duty you owe to God the Country and all
the world and find the prisoner guilty, if the Evidence prove him so if not,
God forbid but you should acquitt him. So I leave it to you.*

The jury retired, returning with a finding of guilty.

"Gentlemen of the Jury I am very glad you have knowne your
business so well," said a relieved Judge Hill. "You have done very much
to regain the honor of your Country and vindicated the Justice of your
Country." Though the jury empaneled on the preceding day had
failed to find as the judge would have liked, he did not condemn them
for their actions. He was of the opinion that they were not well acquainted with trials of this nature and that they had been mistaken in
their charity. "However Gentlemen by this verdict you set all right and
have my thanks and the Courts for it."

The prisoners were again brought before the bar on the morning of
Friday, May 17. John Houghling, the first to receive sentence, was
addressed thus by Judge Hill:

*The crime you are convicted of is of so deep a Dye that the law for its
punishment assignes not only death but an ignominious One, And the
Judgement which the Law awards is this, that you be taken from hence to the
place whence you came and from thence to the place of Execution and that
there you be hanged by the neck untill you are dead. And may the Lord have
mercy upon your Soul.*

A similar sentence was passed upon both Frank and Delaunee,
though the latter again stated that he had been an unwilling pirate and
had never abused prisoners and always showed them pity and charity.
The attorney general then moved that the prisoners be removed to the
custody of the sheriff of Princess Anne County. Papers were prepared,
signed, and sealed. The warrant for the execution of John Houghling
was written as follows:

*Whereas John Hooghling Marriner at a Sessions of Oyer and Terminer
held at Elizabeth City County Court house the 14th day of this Instant May
hath been arraigned and convicted of a Piracy and Robbery comitted upon
the high Seas and within the Jurisdiction of the Admiralty of England on*

the Ship Pensilvania Merchant for which he hath received Sentence of death.

These are therefore in his Majestys name to require and Command you forthwith to receive the said John Hoogling into your Custody from the Sherriff of Elizabeth City County and him to keep in safe custody. And on ffryday the 24th day of this Instant May you are to cause the said John Hoogling to be carryed to the place of Execution and between the houres of Eleven and One of the same day You are to hang the said John Hoogling upon a Gibbett to be executed by you for that purpose up by the Neck till he be dead dead dead and there to let him remaine and hang and for so doing this shall be your Warrant of which you are to make due Returne to his Majesties Secretarys Office at James City Given under my hand and Seal this 17 day of May 1700 in the twelfe yeare of his Maijesties Reigne.

The warrants for the execution of Frank and Delaunee were identical, except for the dates, which were May 25 and May 29 respectively. The sheriff of Elizabeth City County was ordered to deliver the prisoners to the sheriff of Princess Anne County for execution.

The sheriff was to erect three gibbets of cedar "or other lasting wood," one at "ye Cape One where John Hoogling was taken and one near the place where the pyrate first ingaged his Maijesty's Shipp the Shoram." Delaunee was to be hung at the Cape, Frank near the place of battle, and Houghling at the site of his capture. "You must leave 'em hanging in a good strong Chaine and Rope til they rott and fall away."

Houghling, Frank, and Delaunee, placed in the custody of Sheriff Major John Thorowgood, were soon housed in the Princess Anne County jail. Within days of their sentencing, all three escaped from their confinement and made a desperate flight across the Chesapeake Bay to Accomac, where pirates had almost traditionally found sanctuary. The Nicholson administration, however, imbued many Virginians with a new intolerance for pirates and fear of authority, even in isolated Accomac, where less than two decades earlier they had traded freely and outfitted their expeditions. In Accomac, the fortunes of the three fugitive pirates completely expired; they were apprehended by the local inhabitants. Their captors, after nearly a year's delay, were rewarded by a grateful government for their efforts.[2] Houghling, Frank, and Delaunee were returned immediately to Princess Anne, and there were executed without further delay or reprieve. Their bodies were hung in chains at the designated sites for all would-be pirates to see and contemplate.

The disposition of Captain Lewis Guittar and his crew was high on Governor Nicholson's agenda, for he wished for nothing other than to rid the colony of such a large, dangerous body of miscreants. Though Attorney General Fowler was of the opinion that the pirates should be tried in Virginia like Houghling, Frank, and Delaunee, Nicholson was as good as his word given in the heat of battle: they would be placed at the King's mercy as promised them. There were also the practical aspects to consider, for "there are no Publick Prisons of force in this Colony & Domain." The cost of guarding so many prisoners with the militia was excessive, and those militiamen, mostly farmers, obliged to such duty faced "utter rune & loss of their crops by which only they subsist." Thus, it was resolved at a meeting of the Council of State that the pirates, then in the custody of Lieutenant Colonel William Wilson, Commander of the Elizabeth City County Militia, be sent to England as quickly as possible. Thirty of the "least resolute and dangerous" were to be sent aboard *Essex Prize,* guardship for the next homeward-bound convoy. The rest were to be distributed in smaller parcels among the various ships in the convoy, while Guittar was to be sent separately to prevent any chance of insurrection. For the "better securing them in the Passage it is directed that Irons be procured for their hands, to be kept on at all times, and that in the Night their Leggs be also tyed to prevent any mischeif they might otherwise attempt to committ."[3]

Captain Aldred was permittted personally to select the thirty prisoners who were to be carried aboard his ship, but was directed to take some of the more seriously wounded and their surgeon. No master of any ship selected to carry prisoners would be allowed to refuse, and warrants were issued to that end. Since many of the prisoners were nearly naked, they were to be allowed canvas and old sails taken from *La Paix* as necessary to clothe themselves. In the event of insurrection aboard any ship, every captain was authorized to subdue the insurrectionists and "inflict such Punishment on them . . . as ye nature of ye offence requires."[4] Governor Nicholson himself would accompany the convoy as far as fifty leagues from the Virginia coast in *Shoreham* as double protection against attacks or rescue efforts by other pirates. When the convoy arrived in England, Captain Aldred was to report directly to the Secretary of State and the Lords of the Admiralty the numbers and names of the prisoners, who were to be delivered up immediately.[5] Two key witnesses who had been held prisoner by the pirates, Abraham Surtley, a Dutchman, and William Hunt of New England, were also sent aboard the convoy to give evidence in England against their former captors. As a precaution, no pirates were permitted to be carried aboard the same vessel as the two state's witnesses.[6]

The voyage was uneventful. On November 23, 1700, Captain Lewis Guittar and twenty-three of his companions, having been expeditiously acquainted with the mercy of the King, were tried, convicted, and condemned in London, and hanged. Twenty of their number were buried in Limehouse Beach. Not long afterward, forty more of their mates were ignominiously executed in similar fashion.[7]

La Paix was condemned in Admiralty Court in Virginia on May 23, 1700, and ordered sold, the proceeds to be divided by the captain and crew of HMS *Shoreham*. Governor Nicholson, though a participant in the battle, graciously declined a share. Neither would he claim credit for the victory, but extended that to Captain Passenger. The captain was duly authorized to sell the ship on July 4, but the sale was delayed until July 25 because of inclement weather.[8] *La Paix,* however, was a complete wreck, and though offered for sale on many occasions, she found no takers. Nearly a year later, on May 8, 1701, Passenger reported to the Virginia Council on the ship's deplorable state, noting that "if she stayes here she will be rendered Utterly incapable for any Service." He offered a single, albeit profitable, solution. Considering that a large quantity of tobacco remained in the colony for want of adequate freight (as a result of an embargo imposed by Nicholson owing to the danger of pirate attacks on shipping), the good captain proposed to load her himself and send her to tobacco-starved England in behalf of, and for the profit of, Crown and self. The suggestion proved acceptable to Nicholson and to the Council.[9]

Her last mission agreed upon, the former terror of the high seas and the Chesapeake Bay passed into oblivion.

XIII

No Farther Than Ye Soundings

The capture of Captain Lewis Guittar and his crew of sea rovers had been a heady victory for Governor Francis Nicholson. It had not, unfortunately, entirely alleviated the immediate peril of piratical attacks on tidewater shipping. Though *La Paix* had been taken, her swift little consort, the pink *Baltimore*, and possibly other pirate ships, still skulked about the Virginia Capes preying upon shipping.

On Tuesday, April 30, in fact, the day after the climatic battle, *Baltimore*, without benefit of great guns and armed only with small arms, captured the Bristolman *Wheeler*, which had recently left the York River after unloading a cargo of brandy. The pirates, approximately fifty in number, after conducting the usual robberies, cut down her masts and bowsprit, bored a hole in her bottom, set seven of her crew adrift in a boat, and left her to founder.[1]

Two days later, on the afternoon of May 2, *Baltimore* fell in with another ship, this time a brigantine also out of the Chesapeake, eight or ten miles below Cape Henry. At about 3:00 P.M., while at anchor, the merchantman was boarded and taken. The pirates stripped her of her sails, masts, and provisions, and cut away her rudder. The brigantine's master, for simply speaking to one of the rover's prisoners, was threatened with instant death. By nightfall the work of plundering had been completed, and the pirates abandoned their victim to her fate. Fortunately, the brigantine's crew was eventually able to bring her back to the Capes and safety.

News of *Baltimore*'s depredations did not reach Virginia until the morning of May 3, when the survivors from *Wheeler* hauled their small boat ashore in Princess Anne County and reported their story to Sheriff Thorowgood. Their account was enlarged upon by a witness, one Adam Harris, who had observed the capture of the brigantine from the beach near his home. Thorowgood dashed off immediate communiques to Governor Nicholson and to Captain Passenger. The Governor, having only shortly before returned to Jamestown, received the express on the evening of Friday, May 4. At 11:00 P.M., dismayed by the rebirth of a threat he had thought over, he hastily scribbled orders for Captain Passenger. If *Shoreham* was capable of again putting to sea to pursue the pirates, he wrote, "I would have you do it soon as, God willing, wind and weather permitts." If the ship was not in sailing condition, the good captain was directed to send off his small boats to patrol and take or burn *Baltimore*. More important, he was authorized, for the safety of commerce, to keep all ships from leaving the Capes and order them up to Kecoughtan.[2]

Though the immediate danger to outward-bound shipping was evident, Nicholson's *pro tem* embargo of Friday evening would have to wait for formal action by the Council of State at its regular meeting on Monday, May 6, before becoming official. Then, among the first orders of business scheduled were the instituting of an embargo and instructions to all ships departing the colony that they would be obliged to sail only under convoy of *Essex Prize*, scheduled to depart on May 30. No ships would be permitted to sail before that time or alone. In the meantime, both *Shoreham* and *Essex Prize* were directed to "go out and Cruise in the Bay of Chisapeake, for the safety and defence of all Ships and Vessells coming down the same, to take the opportunity of the said Convoy." Maryland Governor Nathaniel Blackiston was to be informed of the convoy so that he might apprise merchant shipping in his colony of the embargo and the sailing date.[3]

Deeply concerned that pirates might once more venture into the Chesapeake, Nicholson sought to reinforce his sea defenses. He requested Governor Blackiston to order Captain Peter Cood and His Majesty's little advice boat *Messenger* down to Kecoughtan for patrol duty. Considering it "very probable that these Pyrates will attempt to Land, and by robbing such People as live near the Sea Coasts to furnish themselves with Provisions and such other necessaries as they stand in need of, for the better enabling them to continue in that wicked and detestable Course of Pyracy," he reinstated the system of coast watchers on May 7. The militia commanders of the counties of Elizabeth City, Norfolk, Princess Anne, Accomac, and Northampton were directed to provide one or more men each to patrol Point Comfort, between Lynnhaven River and Cape Henry, between Cape Henry and Currituck Inlet, upon Smith's or Mocken Island to the north, and along the seaboard shores of Northampton and Accomac. Each lookout, as before, was to watch for any suspicious ships or landings and report all such activities to the county militia commanders. They in turn were to mobilize their forces when necessary and dispatch the news to both the Governor and Captain Passenger "with the best information and advice . . . of the most probable measures of either taking or destroying such Ship or Vessell suspected of Pyracy."[4]

With *Baltimore,* and possibly other pirates, believed to be lying off Princess Anne, the Governor recommended to the officers and inhabitants of that county that they keep an especially alert watch. Major Thorowgood was specifically directed to hold a boat and hands in continual readiness at a convenient place, to be dispatched at a moment's notice to Captain Passenger at the first sighting of a suspect ship. Nicholson sweetened the pot by offering a ten pound sterling reward for any pirate "apprehended by force or killed in the pursuit on land."[5]

On May 13 Admiralty Court hearings over the adjudication of *La Paix* commenced, and on the following day the trial of Houghling, Frank, and Delaunee began. Coming hot on the heels of the battle and the news of subsequent attacks on Chesapeake shipping, public anxiety over possible pirate invasion began to grow with every revelation brought out during the proceedings. Within days, the justifiably giddy citizenry of Virginia began to grow suspicious of any new face encountered in their midst.

On May 22 the Governor added fuel to growing public fears. He issued a formal proclamation which was to be displayed in all churches, chapels, courthouses, and other public places throughout the colony, in which he declared that "diverse Seamen do daily come on shore pretending to belong to Merchant Ships and wander from place to place under which pretense it may probably happen that several Pirates may come on Shore and escape Justice and the Punishment due by Law . . . or may come as Spies to discover the State of the Country his Majestys Ships of War or the Merchant Ships Lying in this Country." Such were fears of pirates, perhaps of the likes of Houghling, walking the streets among honest citizens, that without compunction or concern for individual rights, Nicholson ordered the outright seizure and arrest of vagabond seamen or anyone even suspected of piracy. Suspects were to be taken before the nearest justice of the peace and jailed unless they could prove without a doubt that they were not pirates and had not aided and abetted pirates. Anyone found harboring or entertaining such suspicious persons were to be "proceeded against with the utmost Vigour & Severity of the Law." In so doing Nicholson made it abundantly clear that Virginia was engaged in nothing less than an all-out war against buccaneering.

Such tactics occasionally had the effect of legitimizing even local rumors regarding piracy. In early September, a minor flurry of activity arose over the gossipy allegations made by one Samuel Alderson of piracies carried out by several inhabitants of Norfolk County. One of the more prominent citizens charged was Captain Samuel Bush, a government naval agent. Several letters and papers, and a report of the charges which intimated Bush's complicity, were laid before the Council of State by Attorney General Fowler. No evidence, however, accompanied the obviously spurious accusations. Bush indignantly issued a complaint against Alderson, who was promptly hauled before Norfolk County Justice of the Peace Mathew Godfry for a hearing. Alderson requested a *dedimus* [to take testimony] for the examination of witnesses in Princess Anne County. The Council of State ruled that though "the same belongs to A Judiciall Process as Law, & is not within their Cognizance, But to End all Just, and Legall means may be used for the detecting and discovery such illegall and dishonest Practices," necessary to bring offenders to punishment. Orders were issued to the magistrates of Norfolk and Princess Anne counties to take depositions and examinations and turn them over to the Council.[6] Ultimately, the charges were found to be baseless, and the affair, an obvious embarrassment to the government, was quickly forgotten except by the querulous individuals involved.

Despite the frenzied efforts of the Nicholson administration to secure the *Baltimore,* the little pink disappeared from the Virginia coast without a trace. The Governor, however, proved tireless in his resolve to maintain a strict vigilance throughout the pirate season. Having personally accompanied Aldred's outward-bound convoy aboard the escort warship *Shoreham,* which was to remain as a guardship in the colony, the Governor had gained valuable personal insight into the practical aspects of the difficulties and limitations of coastal patrol duty. Though *Shoreham* had escorted the convoy eastward from the Capes for barely forty or fifty leagues, it was discovered that "ye strength of ye Current to be such yt . . . they made it above one hundred thirty Leagues inward bound and if they had not had fair Winds might have been two or three weeks before they had recovered ye Capes." Thus, on July 9, when Captain Passenger was ordered to begin regular cruises of the coast at twenty-day intervals, he was specifically directed to go "no farther than ye Soundings," or the Chesapeake might well be left defenseless for weeks on end.[7]

Nicholson also addressed the practical matter of convoy assembly. Vessels coming down the Bay had hitherto been required to muster at

Hampton Roads. To do so, they were obliged to thread the tricky channel between the shallows of the Middle Ground and the Horseshoe Shoals, which extended southward from the James Peninsula. They thus found it necessary to sail southward dangerously close to the exposed mouth of the Chesapeake (where pirates often patrolled with impunity) before turning the Tail of the Horseshoe and returning north into the James. The Governor wisely recommended that the York River, instead of the James, would serve as a more convenient and far superior assemblage point for all traffic coming down from the upper bay.[8]

HMS *Shoreham* continued her cruises throughout most of the summer of 1700, occasionally intercepting illegal traders, but encountering no pirates. The duty was both hot and arduous. In late August a violent Bay storm seriously disabled the guardship, and Passenger was forced to bring her into the Elizabeth River to careen and effect repairs. To make matters worse, more than forty of his crew had become "Dangerously afflicted with Sickness." To prevent the remainder of the ship's company "from being infected by the Noisomness of the Smell," the sick were ordered ashore to convalesce in Hampton.[9] And once again, the Chesapeake stood temporarily defenseless. Fortunately, no piratical incursions were attempted.

By late fall, Passenger had returned to patrol duty, but, like John Aldred before him, found the Chesapeake a most fickle mistress. On November 19, and again on November 30, he dispatched letters to the Governor "wherein he sets forth that by Reason of the sudden & frequent Stormes in the winter Season and Dangerous Sholes and Sands in the bay and the hard and Excessive Frosts he Cannot nor dare not adventure to hazard his Majesties . . . Ship by Cruising in the Bay the winter Season." A small sloop, he suggested, would be a suitable alternative to such duty and might also assist *Shoreham* as a tender.[10]

Holding Captain Passenger in more favorable esteem than they did his predecessor, the Governor and Council informed him that *Shoreham* would be obliged to cruise the Bay only "at all faire and seasonable opportunities" deemed suitable by the captain. In accordance with his suggestions regarding the use of a small tender, the Council directed that a new sloop be purchased off the stocks to serve as an auxiliary. Passenger was ordered personally to examine the vessel, report on her value, outfit her from the King's stores under his command, and employ her in the Bay as a revenue cutter, fire ship, and tender to *Shoreham*. The tiny vessel eventually selected, named *Elizabeth*, was soon employed in keeping the guardship in provisions which in good weather allowed her to maintain a constant vigil of the Capes.[11]

With the spring of 1701 came the resumption of the seasonal threat of pirate attacks. Again Nicholson instituted a coast watch system, though this time he limited it to Princess Anne County. Unhappily, the danger of buccaneering incursions was eclipsed by a newer, more ominous menace: possible war in Europe. In May, letters from England and other parts reached the Chesapeake and produced great concern that "there is, or suddenly will be a vigorous warr on foot." England, Austria, and the Netherlands were squaring off against the mighty Bourbon powers of France and Spain for a contest history would call in America Queen Anne's War and in Europe the War of the Spanish Succession. England could not long refrain from entry. The tidewater braced itself for the coming conflict by laying an embargo on all outward-bound shipping unless sailing under authorized convoy.[12] Again, albeit futilely, Nicholson requested from Maryland Governor Blackiston the services of Captain Peter Cood and the advice boat *Messenger*. He also directed Captain Passenger to dispatch *Elizabeth* to patrol the Bay, stopping any outward-bound vessels and escorting them into the James to await the sailing of the next convoy.

On May 8 Nicholson informed the Council that the Admiralty was dispatching HMS *Southampton* to relieve *Shoreham*, which was to escort the summer convoy home to England. *Southampton*, a fourth-rate man-of-war, was a substantial improvement in firepower over *Shoreham*. Originally commissioned at Southampton in 1693, she had been rebuilt in 1700 at Deptford. Her 122-foot length, 34-foot beam, and 626-ton displacement far exceeded the smaller *Shoreham*. She carried a full 16 guns more than her predecessor on the Virginia Station and a complement of no less than 180 men. A second man-of-war, a 48-gun fourth-rater of 679 tons displacement named *Lincoln* was assigned to temporary duty cruising between Cape Fear and Cape May, but was to station herself whenever possible in Lynnhaven Bay. Her assignment, specifically, was to free the coastal waters of pirates, which she was directed to take, sink, or destroy, and to effectively buttress the naval defenses of the Chesapeake.[13]

In June HMS *Lincoln*, Captain Edward Neville commanding, arrived in the Chesapeake, bringing with her a commission for Governor Nicholson, authorized by Act of Parliament, to try all pirates in the colony. The governor, lieutenant-governor, a member of the Council, and a commander of a Royal Navy ship were now authorized to be included along with others appointed by the Crown and under the Great Seal of England, to form a Court of Admiralty whenever necessary.[14] Possibly because of the cozy friendship exhibited toward pirates by the authorities in the Carolinas, Nicholson's commission permitted him to try pirates not only in Virginia, but in those colony areas and on the high seas as well. And furthermore, he was authorized to take any and all measures necessary to resist all enemies, pirates, and rebels "both at Land and Sea."[15]

Francis Nicholson was for the first time buoyant and confident, despite the degenerating state of affairs elsewhere in the world. He and Virginia had weathered one of the worst pirate attacks in colony history. The threat of further pirate invasions had failed to materialize. And now, he had both the legal and naval strength to meet such perils head-on, for there would continue to be, for the foreseeable future, a strong Royal Navy commitment to defend the Chesapeake.

"I thank God," he wrote from the deck of *Shoreham* on June 24 during an inspection tour as she lay anchored near Cape Henry, "that this Colony is in peace and quietness." The colony revenues from tobacco and quitrents were up, and there was every appearance of a bountiful year ahead.

"And if any enemy should come to disturb us, I hope to God we shall be too hard for him."[16]

XIV

The Guardships

On June 10, 1701, the Governor of Virginia laid before the Council of State the King's royal letter of February 2 containing directives relating to the trials of pirates in Virginia and the Carolinas pursuant to Parliament's "Act for the more effectual Supression of Pyracy."[1] With the rampant rumors of impending war in Europe and the need to provide continuing protection for the tobacco fleet, however, both Nicholson and the Council were now more concerned over the danger of attacks by French privateers than by buccaneers. Captain Passenger informed the dismayed Governor that he could not undertake to convoy the tobacco fleet home without being officially relieved from the Virginia Station by the Admiralty. Nor was his ship in any condition to do so had he been ordered. Nicholson anxiously turned to Captain Neville, whom he requested to convoy the fleet at least as far as twenty leagues beyond the Virginia Capes. Neville, whose orders from the Admiralty were more flexible than Passenger's, agreed. Planning went forward to organize the convoy. Captain Edward Whitaker of *Indian King,* whose experience with French rovers was certainly firsthand, was appointed commodore and commander in chief of the convoy beyond soundings. Having attended to getting the fleet ready, Nicholson next turned to the colony's defenses. Wishing to inform the Crown of Virginia's status in the event war were to break out, he proposed to the House of Burgesses to send all the journals of the Council and the Assembly along with the fleet. The Council, no doubt with the capture of state records in 1699 by the *Providence Galley* still fresh in its memory, was adamantly opposed to the idea "because the whole state and condition of the whole country in general may be thereby discovered" should the data fall into the wrong hands en route.[2] Nicholson wisely permitted the issue to rest in order that he might resurrect it at a later time.

By September 17 *Shoreham*'s replacement, HMS *Southampton*, Captain James Moody commanding, had finally arrived. Moody brought, among other things, word of the impending arrival of a small vessel, HM advice boat *Eagle*, Captain Nathaniel Bostock commanding, to relieve Captain Cood's *Messenger*, then cruising Maryland waters. But more important, he related the latest intelligence of the state of affairs in Europe. Although hostilities had not yet commenced, he offered a studied opinion "that open war is by this time proclaimed." Disturbed by the captain's views, the Governor and the Council immediately sought the House of Burgesses's opinion as to whether all three warships on the Virginia Station—*Southampton*, *Lincoln*, and *Shoreham*—ought to be employed as a convoy for the fall shipping to England, and whether or not it was proper to lay an embargo on all outward-bound ships to force them to join the convoy. The House responded that *Lincoln* and *Shoreham* should accompany the fleet, in compliance with prior Admiralty orders, and that an embargo must be laid. It would be necessary to retain *Southampton* for the defense of the colony.[3]

Pressed by the degenerating situation in Europe, Virginia was forced to take a pragmatic look at its own vulnerability. On September 25 the House of Burgesses, in a realistic analysis, resolved that a naval force was the best way to secure the country from an enemy attack by water, but that the charge of maintaining such a force would be altogether insupportable by the colony.[4] Nicholson and the Council were in full accord with the House over the issue, but were also acutely aware of the need to secure additional defensive capabilities and to assess the state of readiness of the colony to fend off French privateers or invaders. Hence the Governor suggested that a request be sent to the Crown "to send in two fire Masters with all materialls of fire workes and fire Ships and some hand morters & Granadoes suitable and fitt for them," as well as grenadiers and dragoons arms, pistols, powder, and bullets.[5] *Lincoln* and the ships sailing with her were directed to tarry until October 21 and *Shoreham* and her convoy to remain until November 4 to permit the government to inventory the militia and the colony's defenses and to prepare a report for the Privy Council.[6] Owing to delays in completing the inventory, *Shoreham*'s departure was ultimately postponed until November 28.

Unlike the friendly relations between Passenger and the colony government, the relationship between his replacement, Captain Moody, and the Executive Council was strained. With the impending departure of *Shoreham*, her tender, the sloop *Elizabeth*, had been assigned to serve as a consort to *Southampton*. Moody was not pleased with the little sloop and requested that another vessel of fifty or sixty tons be provided to attend his ship on all occasions. The captain even offered to build one if the Governor would give the order. He further requested orders to careen when and where it would be most convenient, credit to provide for necessary stores while on station, and colony care for his sick and injured. Not entirely happy with the anchorage at Kecoughtan ("the rapid Tydes & Other dangers being attendant" there), he asked for permission to ride at a more convenient place.

The Council replied promptly to Moody's requests. *Elizabeth*, they told him, would have to suffice throughout the winter, as no instructions from the Admiralty to build a new sloop had been received (nor could the colony coffers afford one). Because of the navy's unpaid bills run up by Captain Aldred while on the Virginia Station—bills which eventually had to be paid out of the Governor's own pocket to avoid embarrassment to the Crown—neither could credit be extended; nor would the colony cover the cost of maintaining the navy's sick and injured. Moody was, however, permitted to careen "when & as often as he thinks Proper & [at the] most Convenient Place." Finally, the captain was authorized to anchor wherever he considered it suitable, as long as he did not fail to "Cruise in yᵉ Bay at all faire and Seasonable Oppertunities" for the King's service "in discovering Illegal Traders & yᵉ Countries Security in detecting & Beating off Pyrates or Sea Rovers."[7]

The growing fear that the Bay might be seriously imperiled in the event of war was reinforced by the arrival of a royal communique from England. In late November, Nicholson was informed by the Crown that a French squadron under the command of Monsieur de Coetlogon had been sent to the West Indies. If war broke out, the French might well have the Chesapeake on their list of targets. The Governor was therefore directed to be on his guard.[8]

Though war clouds continued to loom on the horizon, merchant shipping from England to the Chesapeake continued unabated. The pressure from the London mercantile community to secure additional Royal Navy protection for the trade, however, was great. By the end of January 1702 more than two hundred ships had sailed or were ready to sail for the Bay country. Most, it was expected, would be ready to return home by the end of May or early June. Noting that the fleet would pay "a considerable Sume to his Majesty for Customes," the merchants of London petitioned the Privy Council that one fourth-rate and one fifth-rate man-of-war be sent to Virginia by mid-May. With revenues from tobacco duties providing the King's treasury with an average of three hundred thousand pounds sterling annually, the Board of Trade was not out of line in assuring the Lord High Admiral that the Chesapeake trade deserved "a most particular regard." On January 29 the King agreed and gave the Admiralty orders to dispatch the two ships.[9]

In the meantime, Governor Nicholson worked tirelessly to improve the colony's defenses, personally traveling from county to county to review the drilling and training of the militia. By March 1702 both horse dragoons and foot troops had been "put into as good a posture of defence, as it is capable of." It was not enough. The colony militia, estimated at eight thousand strong, was "so undisciplined and unskillful and in such great want of arms and ammunition proper and fit for action" that barely a fourth of the force was fit to oppose any enemy pirate or invader. There were no magazines or "stores of war" in the country, and powder supplies consisted of those suitable for cannons but not pistols.

On March 17 Colonel Quary addressed a memorial to the Lords Commissioners of Trade and Plantations reviewing the colony's vulnerable state and begging for arms and powder. Despite the shabby defensive posture, he took the opportunity to air his dim view of the establishment of a system of fortifications, as had been done in earlier years.

As to the land Fortifications, we have not any, what have heretofore are demolished, neither indeed can they be to the benefit, but rather disadvantage of the country, for land Fortifications cannot be made sufficient to defend this country from the danger of enemies, privateers, or pirates.

Because the coastal regions were generally low and sparsely settled, landings, he pointed out, could be made almost anywhere and forts were thereby vulnerable to attack from the rear. Fortifications, in fact, were quite useless to prevent insurrections from within. They could never, Quary felt, be secured from concerted attempts by an enemy, nor could illegal trading be prevented by their presence. The rivers of the tidewater were so broad that the guns of the forts could not command the channels, and "the only places fitt for such fortifications are only Point Comfort and the mouth of James River and Tindals Point on York River." To build and maintain such a defense system, he argued, would pose a greater expense than the country could bear. Finally, Quary noted, Virginia was adjacent to the route of all fleets coming from the West Indies. Any enemy coming upon the coast that way might easily land an amphibious force of seven hundred or eight hundred men and destroy or ruin both riverfront and Bayfront plantations on both sides of the Chesapeake. Since most single plantations were widely dispersed and lay on large necks of land, an amphibious attack on any one, by pirates or by regular military forces, might expose militia units drawn down to their defense to being cut off from the rear.[10]

The Privy Council, on reading Quary's analysis, was in full agreement. "Virginia and Maryland being huge Territorys and lying open by Great Rivers," they noted, "cannot be Secured by Fortifications and are therefore no ways able to Defend themselves against an Attempt of any Enemy by Sea" unless a sufficient naval squadron were provided to cruise the Bay area during the periods of greatest danger, from April to the end of October. The Privy Council dutifully referred the matter to the Lord High Admiral, who promptly shelved it.[11]

While the government debated the modes of defending the Chesapeake in the coming war, *Southampton* had degenerated into such a poor state that by February she was unable to cruise. Captain Moody was obliged to impress carpenters from Nansemond and Elizabeth City counties to assist in careening the ship.[12] Several months later, additional repairs were necessary, and "a very Convenient Place at Point Comfort" was fitted out for another careening. By May the ship was finally deemed fit to patrol between Point Comfort and the Capes. Governor Nicholson requested the Governor of Maryland to order the advice boat *Eagle* to cruise with her to assist in "defending this Colony and Ships trading here from yᵉ Attempts of Pirates and Sea Rovers who are found frequently to Infest those Coasts at this Season of yᵉ Year," as well as from other enemies.[13]

Yet it was not the danger of pirate attacks but the shadow of war that remained foremost in everyone's mind. Harking back thirty-five years to an Act of Assembly instituted during the Second Anglo-Dutch War, the government, in an effort to prevent surprise attacks, instructed all shipping to ride only in specified anchorages.[14]

Unfortunately, when solidarity among the English colonies of America was paramount, intercolonial disputes frequently threatened to scuttle efforts to produce a cooperative defense. On the Chesapeake, Maryland and Virginia argued incessantly over the stationing of the advice boat *Eagle*. By early October the long-awaited declaration of war against France and Spain had finally reached the Bay country.[15] Had enemy raiders attacked they would have found the poisonous bickering between the two colonies still going on. For the defense of the lower Bay, Nicholson repeatedly sought the services of *Eagle*, which was stationed at Turkey Point, in Maryland, almost as frequently as he had requested the use of *Messenger*. The Maryland government, jealous of its more favored neighbor and eager to retain the services of the advice boat as a revenue cutter to enforce the Acts of Trade and Navigation as well as customs, just as frequently refused.[16]

There were other disagreements that also got in the way of maximizing the defense effort. The merchants of London and the English outports could not agree upon a standard time for the sailing of convoys to the Chesapeake, and the government was obliged to step in. On December 23, 1702, the Lord High Admiral, after consulting with the Board of Trade on the issue, laid before the Privy Council a proposal for a resolution to the problem. Two fourth-rate warships would be dispatched by the end of January 1703 to escort all trade from England to the Chesapeake. These were to rendezvous with two others detached from Vice Admiral Benbow's West Indian Squadron. The combined force would then escort the homeward-bound fleet, which would be scheduled to depart the Chesapeake between July 1 and July 10. In the meantime, the warships could serve as guardships for the Bay during the early period of greatest peril. Two more fourth-rate warships, meanwhile, would convoy another fleet to the Chesapeake by the end of August 1703 and depart for England by April 1704, thereby protecting the Bay during the latter period of danger. These last two warships, during their stay, however, had their range of patrol extended to protect the trade of the Leeward Islands in the West Indies. Finally, the plan called for the governors of Maryland and Virginia to be instructed "to take Care that noe Ships Sayle out of the Capes" without benefit of convoy.[17]

The plan was complicated during its promulgation by a variety of difficulties, not the least of them outright opposition by many London merchants as well as colonial officials. One of the loudest opponents, in fact, was Colonel Quary, who wrote in May 1704 that "Noe Trade belonging to England is worse managed than the tobacco trade." Quary proposed not two but one convoy a year, to arrive in the Bay before November and depart before April or May, taking advantage of the weather.[18] Others claimed that a guardship was necessary not only during the "pirate season" of April through October, but all year long.[19] Despite the difficulties, a regulated guardship-convoy system, flawed as it was, proved to be a superior deterrent against both pirate and privateer attacks on Chesapeake shipping as well raids on the country proper.

There were, however, occasional invasion scares that would have strained the best of systems.

In early May 1705 a letter from Philadelphia, dated April 16, reached Governor Nicholson with alarming intelligence from Antigua.

It was reported, and later verified by both the governors of Maryland and Pennsylvania, that no less than twenty-seven French privateers were fitting out at Martinique, at least three of which (including a large and powerful brigantine) were to cruise between Virginia and New England. From Maryland came more alarming news: an Indian attack against Maryland and Virginia from the north was also expected.[20] The Chesapeake country, it appeared, was to be threatened from both land and sea.

The Virginia government moved to streamline its ability to mobilize the colony defenses. The Assembly passed an act for the security and defense of the country, authorizing the Governor to call out the militia in case of invasion or insurrection. He was also empowered to impress supplies, vehicles, and vessels necessary for the transport of the militia. All males of military age—except servants, slaves, millers, overseers of more than four slaves, and government officials—were deemed subject to military duty.[21]

The Virginia Council of State's first inclination regarding coastal defense was to permit the guardship then on station, HMS *Strombulo*, Captain Matthew Teate commanding, to pursue standing orders to cruise "as far as shal find it for her Majestys Service." Problems with this course of action immediately cropped up. With *Strombulo* sailing wherever seemed most appropriate to her commander, the Chesapeake would be defended only by the tiny sloop *Elizabeth*. Unfortunately, worm-eaten *Elizabeth* had recently been surveyed, and it was advised that she be sold.[22] *Strombulo* was scheduled to return to England on June 10, and with *Elizabeth* no longer available, the colony and the Bay would "be left defenceless towards the Sea, and the Privateers may not only easily land & burn & plunder the Plantations but also attack the Ships in the very River & Ports." Virginia merchants, becoming skittish, petitioned the Governor that their ships be permitted to sail under convoy of *Strombulo* even though it was before the newly established departure date.[23]

The Governor and Council, on May 31, resolved to request Captain Teate to delay his departure for a month to discourage the expected privateer raids. The militia was placed on alert, and lookouts on the coast were ordered to be particularly attentive.[24] Nicholson personally visited Teate at Kecoughtan to request a delay in departure, and encouraged his decision by producing funds from the colony treasury for victualling while *Strombulo* remained in the Bay. The Governor was buoyed by the captain's willingness to stay, and even more so by news that two men-of-war were at that moment en route from England to convoy the fleet home. Untimately, *Strombulo* remained on station until

August 1.[25]

A year later, during the spring of 1706, a similar emergency tested
the viability of the Chesapeake defenses. On May 7 Captain Robert
Thomson, commander of HMS *Woolwich,* then guardship on the Virginia Station, informed the Governor and Council that from a vessel
recently arrived at Kecoughtan from the West Indies he had learned
that eight French 70-gun warships, twelve frigates, upwards of forty
privateers, and four thousand soldiers had captured the islands of St.
Christophers and Nevis. The Council was thoroughly intimidated and
assumed "that y[e] Fleet and land forces may probably make an attempt
on this Colony," where one of the larger merchant fleets in colony
history was assembling.[26]

The following day the government moved swiftly into action. All of
the arms and ammunition lying at Jamestown, except those allowed for
the use of the various counties, were removed inland to Williamsburg.
Powder supplies allotted for the frontier counties to the west were
reduced by half, and a battery for the defense of the shipping at
Jamestown was authorized. The coast watch was again established, and
a general embargo "for preventing any intelligence being given to the
enemy" as much as for the preservation of trade and shipping was laid
down. All vessels were once more forbidden to sail unless in armed
convoys. Collections and naval officers of the York River and James
River districts were directed to give notice to all masters of vessels in
their jurisdictions to meet with the Governor and Council on May 14 to
receive instructions on what was necessary for their defense and preservation in case of a French attack. All firing of guns was strictly
forbidden to prevent false alarms. All owners or masters of small
watercraft were directed, upon word of the enemy's approach, to carry
their vessels as far up the colony's waterways as possible; and all pilots
were ordered either to board *Woolwich* or to retire into the country to
prevent being captured and made use of by the enemy. Militia commanders were instructed to hold their units in readiness to march.
Persons living near the ocean, Bay, or rivers "where the greatest danger is" were required to have their stocks, corn, and other provisions
ready to move into the country and out of reach of the enemy at a
moment's notice. *Woolwich* was instructed to patrol between the Capes,
and her commander was requested to send for HMS *Advice,* then in
Maryland waters, to come down to assist in the defense of the lower
Bay.[27]

On meeting with the masters of the ships riding in the James and
York, Governor Edward Nott, the colony's new chief executive, who
had replaced the able Francis Nicholson upon the latter's recall by

Queen Anne, requested their collective opinions as to the best way of securing their shipping. At least eight ships lay in the James and another twenty-one in the York, and both groups of mariners presented their suggestions to the Governor and Council the following day. Accordingly, after some deliberation and contradictory instructions, it was decided that if good fortifications and batteries were established on the river side of Jamestown, which was situated "amongst marshes and being almost entirely encompassed with water," the shipping riding off the town in the James would be quite safe. The York River contingent was advised that they might seek security by retiring upriver to West Point, a peninsula also encompassed by marshes and the Mattapony and Pamunkey rivers. A battery on the point could easily defend the entrance to the Mattapony River and disturb any enemy ship that might try for the Pamunkey River, where all of the larger merchant ships might also ride in safety. Not far from the mouth of the Pamunkey there was a small bight where the channel was very narrow. A modest fort here, Nott suggested, would effectively close off that river to enemy access.[28]

Fortunately for Virginia, on May 15, the exercise became moot when it was learned that the French had other plans for their fleet. The enemy squadron, it seemed, was actually intended to convoy the rich treasure galleons of their allies, the Spanish, back to Spain. Despite such welcome news, the colony government did not entirely release its grip or lift the embargo, "contrary to the inclinations of the Masters lest if any accident should happen to them, it might be charged as a fault of this Government."[29]

While the Virginia government wrestled with the frequent alarms of French invasions, pirates of the homegrown variety occasionally cropped up in the more poorly patrolled waters of Maryland. In the late summer of 1705 five men outlawed in Maryland on charges of high treason seized the West River sloop *Little Hannah* and were "suspected to be going on a Pyratical design." The villains included one Thomas Sparrow; a Philadelphia mariner named John Staples; John Taylor, described as a tall, thin brown man; and a flaxen-haired youth of middle stature and clean complexion called Sterritt. The leader of the band was a notorious desperado named Richard Clark from the South River region of Anne Arundel County. "A thick well Sett man, neare forty years old, short darke haire, a flat Nose, & [whose] under jaws overjetts his upper Lipp," Clark had been involved in an assortment of criminal activities before turning to piracy. In 1704 he was wanted in Maryland for forgery and for "uncasing and altering the Quality of

Tobacco." Arrested and thrown in the Annapolis jail, he and several accomplices, including an Indian jailed for murder, escaped when a file was smuggled in. It was then charged that he and his accomplices were contriving "to draw down the Indians upon the Inhabitants of this Province and to Levy War again^t her Majestys Governour & Government." Clark and one of his fellow fugitives, Benjamin Celie, proceeded to initiate a veritable crime wave, roaming about the region, robbing homes, and threatening death to anyone getting in their way. The government issued a ten-pound reward for their apprehension. Celie was eventually captured but Clark escaped.[30]

Governor Seymour of Maryland, suspecting that the brigands had fled south, dispatched an urgent express to Governor Nott to inform him of the danger. On September 6 Nott issued a proclamation requiring all masters of ships, naval district officers and collectors, civil and military officers, and citizens of the colony to assist in apprehending the would-be pirates. Harboring, concealing, or entertaining them was forbidden, and anyone even remotely suspect was to be brought before a justice of the peace and examined.[31]

Clark managed to elude authorities, apparently continuing to conduct his nefarious undertakings amid the shoally coves of the Chesapeake. Among the illicit activities he indulged in during this time was counterfeiting. He and his men had become quite expert in manufacturing fake Spanish pieces of eight out of "pewter glass and other mixt Mettall." Bits and pieces of his trail tantalized authorities. In April 1707 a report reached Annapolis that three white men, two black men, and a woman had been spotted on a small bight in Hooper's Strait. One of the men fit the description of Clark. Not long afterwards, the sloop *Margaretts Industry,* commanded by one Captain John Spry, came into South River in Maryland and anchored off Beard Creek. Spry had come at Clark's order to collect some of the pirate's personal belongings. Word soon reached government officials and Spry and his mate were immediately taken into custody and brought by the sheriff of Anne Arundel County before Governor Seymour. It was soon learned that Clark, using an alias, Robert Garrett, maneuvered about in Virginia with ease, frequenting Cartwright's Rose and Crown Tavern in Norfolk and consorting with two other villains, Richard Shipley and John Smith. But most important, Spry revealed that he was lying at the captain's place on the little Wicomico River in Northumberland County, plotting revenge against Maryland. The Maryland government was stunned by the magnitude of Clark's planned revenge.

Richard Clarke with his Gange of Runaway Rogues had concerted to Seize on our Magazine, and burn this Town and Port of Annapolis, & then

Steal a Vessell and turne pyrates, where they thought it most Feasable.

Despite Clark's notoriety, the Marylanders had in the past been unable to catch him on his occasional returns to the colony because "he has So many near Relations that Wee find it very difficult to discover his haunts." With Captain Spry's news about his whereabouts, however, Governor Seymour was encouraged that with Governor Nott's help, Clark might be ensnared. The Governor and Council of Maryland, expecting his apprehension, issued a warrant for his hanging.[32]

On April 15 Seymour dispatched Major John Freeman to call upon the Virginia Governor with a letter again requesting his assistance in apprehending the pirate, and cautioning him that Clark "is a notorious Villain and has made many Escapes from the Sheriffs, and others who have had him in Custody." Not wishing to permit him to escape to yet another colony, he directed a small vessel with ten men to proceed to North Carolina with a letter to the Governor demanding that Clark and his accomplices (should they flee there) be turned over to Maryland. The reward was upped to twenty pounds.[33] It was apparently not enough, for Richard Clark was never heard from again.

Rumors of piracy continued to plague the nervous Chesapeake tidewater. It was implied that some sea rovers were sailing with French commissions in their pockets and had found refuge in sparsely populated North Carolina, from where they planned to launch plundering raids into the Chesapeake.[34] Wild stories continued to shade the truth, and after the invasion scares of 1705 and 1706, many people were willing to believe almost any accusation.

In June 1706, one victim of the pirate fever that gripped the tidewater, Captain Thomas Pitton, commander of the privateer ship *Factor* of Biddeford, Massachusetts (now Maine), was taken into custody by Captain Thomas Lowin of HMS *Advice* on charges of piracy and robbery on the high seas. Pitton, whose ship had been brought into Kecoughtan, stood accused of taking several casks of wine and brandy from a neutral Danish hoy. Though the purported act was petty in nature, the Governor and Council of Virginia were duly informed by Lowin's superior, Captain Thomson. They turned the case over to the Attorney General of Virginia, who studiously reviewed the pertinent letters and depositions. He found the charges baseless and the evidence questionable. Pitton, who had posted bond in London to insure his good conduct at sea, claimed that after stopping the hoy, her captain had boarded *Factor,* but before he could return, a sudden squall came up, jeopardizing the transfer. When the transfer was finally made, Pitton claimed that he had been given some wine and molasses as a reward for his efforts. When Captain Lowin heard the story, he read it as an act of piracy. On June 22 the government dropped the whole case.[35]

In 1707, for the first time since the beginning of the war, the Chesapeake Bay was, by an oversight of the Admiralty, without a guardship. As a consequence, the first privateer scare of the year sent colonial authorities in Maryland and Virginia into a virtual panic. In early June a single 18-gun privateer captured six ships—one each from Lynn, Plymouth, Whitehaven, and Bristol, and two from New England— while cruising barely six leagues off the Virginia Capes. One of the New England vessels was ransomed and sent into the Chesapeake with the companies of three of the other captives. Fearing that the lone rover could easily pick off vessels sailing alone, the government ordered all outgoing Virginia ships to assemble in Hampton Roads by July 1, where they would be joined by the shipping from Maryland. From there they would proceed en masse to discourage the sagacious rover. An express was sent to Maryland's Governor Seymour informing him of the danger. Both Seymour and the President of the Executive Council of Virginia Edmund Jennings (acting governor after the untimely death of Nott), dispatched letters to Governor Lord Cornbury of New York requesting that one of the Royal Navy ships on that station be sent to cruise in search of the privateer and convoy the July merchant fleet a safe distance from the coast. Colonel Jennings warned that the privateer's continued success would only encourage others to visit Virginia waters, and two such vessels might well intercept all trade, both incoming and outgoing. A single guardship, even a small one, would put an end to such dangers. Two days after receiving the news, Cornbury dispatched HMS *Triton's Prize,* a sixth-rate man-of-war. The warship, though not successful in capturing the privateer, at least retook one of her prizes some seventy miles off the Virginia Capes and intimidated the rover into leaving.[36]

The June privateer incursion had been most illustrative of the need for a guardship to be continuously on the Virginia Station. Both Maryland and Virginia appealed to the Crown, the Secretary of State, the Lords Commissioners of Trade, and the Lord High Admiral for a ship.[37] Finally relenting, the Admiralty dispatched HMS *Garland.*

In February 1708, when *Garland,* having unfortunately sprung a mast en route, reached the Virginia Station, she was in such a fouled condition as to be "incapable of doing . . . service against Privateers." Her commander, Captain Charles Stewart, sought permission to careen, clean, and caulk her, and also to secure the use of a purchased or hired sloop to serve as a tender.[38] On April 15 the Executive Council, aware that "the Enemys Privateers being most numerous about this time of year . . . will have great Oppourtunitys of intercepting our inward bound Ships that are now daily expected," denied Stewart's request to careen. They suggested he delay such operations until the arrival of the London fleet, the convoys of which might serve as guard-ships while *Garland* was cleaned and fitted. In the meantime, they agreed to launch an immediate effort to secure a tender.[39]

The very next day, Virginia's temporary naval impotence was high-lighted when word came in that a four-gun, seventy-man French privateer from Martinique had taken two vessels near Cape Henry. One of the victims was a Liverpool ship bound for Virginia, and the other a New York sloop bound home from the West Indies. With *Garland* in no condition to sail—despite the directives of the Council—there was little alternative but to authorize Stewart to impress any vessel convenient and to direct her to take or destroy the marauder. The captain was authorized, with the aid of Major Samuel Bush, now Sheriff of Norfolk County, to impress men to flesh out his manpower needs from the crew of the Liverpool ship who had been set ashore by the privateers. Within days, Stewart had also impressed into service the sloop *Roanoke Merchant* for a period of one month, at a rate of thirty pounds sterling. Unhappily, the efforts came too late and the raider escaped. The Council then moved to prohibit outward-bound vessels from sailing unless convoyed, and appointed new lookouts for the coast.[40]

Much to the sorrow of Virginia, despite her poor showing against the privateers, a few months after the guardship's arrival on the Virginia Station, Stewart received Admiralty orders to escort the summer to-bacco fleet home. Again the Chesapeake was left to the mercy of enemy raiders. The problem was soon to be compounded, for with an increase of Royal Navy dominance in West Indian waters, French privateers were being driven in increasing numbers toward the poorly defended coast of America. And for the unguarded Chesapeake, the conse-quences appeared particularly bleak. After *Garland*'s departure, French privateers advanced "to the very mouth of James River & York in the sight of her Majestys Ships of war," vessels belonging to Commo-dore Huntington's squadron which had briefly stopped in the Chesa-peake to take on water. Brazenly, the raiders pursued a merchantman from her anchorage at the mouth of the York, and then when chal-lenged retired to shoal water where the deep-draft warships could not pursue. Soon almost every small vessel arriving in or departing from the Bay was being snapped up with impunity.[41]

The situation degenerated from bad to worse. In early February

1709 word of a planned privateer invasion of Virginia reached the colony. Two French privateer commanders, Captains Crapeau and Pasquerreau, and others, it was learned, were preparing a concerted plundering raid on the colony to obtain "good booty" in the form of slaves, plate, and sundry other goods. They had offered considerable rewards to various prisoners to pilot them into the James, York, and Rappahannock rivers. Two Englishmen who had taken up arms in the enemy's behalf, one Hendrix, an inhabitant of North Carolina who had traded on the Bay, and a servant of one Edward Thruston, were both well acquainted with the channels. Both were expected to be employed as pilots during the invasion.[42]

The Virginia Council's first reaction to the news was to alert the militia and reappoint lookouts for the coast. A small quantity of powder, shot, muskets, and swords was dispatched to Yorktown, in the event the enemy made an attempt against that exposed town. Acting Governor Edmund Jennings, hoping to secure assistance from New York as before, immediately wrote to Lord Governor Lovelace to request that a man-of-war be sent to cruise southward as far as the Virginia Capes. So important was the dispatch that two copies were sent to avoid the chances of interception, one overland via Pennsylvania and the other by ship. When no reply was forthcoming, the Council dispatched a third copy overland with directions for the messenger to bring back an answer that could be depended upon.[43] Little came of the request.

On March 1 the Council met to discuss a more comprehensive approach to the crisis. In view of the enemy's successes of the previous year, it was "feared they will be earlyer and bolder in their attempts this Spring and may prosecute them with greater security now when the Country is defenceless by Sea," and the arrival of a guardship was uncertain at best. With knowledgeable pilots in the enemy's employ, the Council feared deep penetration of the Bay region and moved to establish lookouts not only in the usual coastal areas, but at Point Comfort, New Point Comfort, Gwynn's Island, on the south point of the Rappahannock River, on Windmill Point, and on Damerons Point on the Wicomico. This time, two lookouts were appointed for each site instead of one to insure that a constant vigil be maintained. Cannons were stationed at strategic points along the coasts to sound the alarm, and all vessels in the colony were strictly forbidden to fire any guns to avoid false alarms. County militia commanders were placed on full alert and empowered to impress any sloops, boats, or flats necessary for the transport of troops. There was also an overriding need for a small vessel to warn of landings, particularly at night when privateersmen might "come ashore & burn & plunder the Inhabitants about the mouths of the Rivers." Accordingly, the Council, though ever concerned about the expense but forced by public pressure to act, unwillingly ordered that a vessel of eight or ten guns and eighty men be fitted out. Colonel William Rhett was selected to charter his brigantine *Seaflower* to the colony for such service for ten weeks at a rate of 50 pounds per month, and was guaranteed an indemnity of 400 pounds should the vessel be damaged or lost. The vessel was specifically employed to cruise the Bay to annoy the enemy and to serve as a lookout for French raiders. Finally, to prohibit the rovers' easy ascent up the Chesapeake waterways, pilots were strictly forbidden to board any ship until completely assured the vessel did not belong to the enemy.

Such measures were not without cost. The frequent emergencies were causing a drain on the treasury that was extremely irritating to the cost-conscious Council. The colony's customs, "by the loss of labour of a great many poor people who liveing in continual fears & being unactive in their Employments," were suffering terribly. Mobilization, it seemed, was becoming a very expensive undertaking, and the colony coffers were drained by this single alert and by the concerted effort to put Virginia on a defensive footing of more than eight hundred pounds.[44]

Having addressed every avenue of defense possible on the home front, the Virginia Council petitioned the Admiralty for a deterrent that would subvert future enemy attentions, a fourth-rate frigate to cruise the Chesapeake and an eight- or ten-gun sloop or brigantine to pursue small privateers into shoally waters. The Admiralty, hard pressed on many fronts, once again dispatched *Garland* to serve as guardship. It also authorized the purchase of a sloop from New England to serve as her tender.[45]

With the arrival of *Garland* in early July with a twenty-ship convoy, Virginia's frantic efforts had not gone in vain. Enemy attacks on colony shipping declined rapidly, as the hated French privateers turned their attentions southward to the poorly defended Carolina coast and northward to the Delaware. A delay in the arrival of the promised sloop from New England induced some concern in Virginia, for there was still a danger from the smaller, lightly armed privateers which could not be pursued into shoal waters by the deep-draft man-of-war. Fortunately, though their presence was a nuisance, their impact was negligible. The outlook for the Chesapeake trade had brightened considerably.[46]

Then, on November 29, 1709, disaster struck. While cruising off the Outer Banks of the Carolinas, where the enemy had been marauding, the warship *Garland* was tragically wrecked on the south side of Currituck Inlet. All of her officers and crew but fifteen were fortunately saved and managed to reach Kecoughtan, albeit in a decrepit state. Despite efforts to save the ship's rigging and stores, salvage operations were closed down by the weather, and HMS *Garland* became a total loss.[47] The Chesapeake Bay was again open to attack.

Upon learning of the calamity, Edmund Jennings immediately dispatched an urgent request to the Secretary of State and the Lord High Admiral for another guardship, as well as a small sloop of ten or twelve guns. Not long afterwards, HMS *Enterprize* arrived on the Virginia Station from New England, but being in such poor condition as to be useless, she was obliged to retire to New York to refit. In a belated response to Jennings' plea, the Admiralty ordered *Triton's Prize* to the Chesapeake in April 1710, but ignored the long-awaited sloop. In the meantime, before the guardship's arrival, the tidewater was bereft of naval protection, and the consequences were terrible.

In May reports of enemy penetration of the Bay and raids against Virginia shores poured in. One account told of a small privateer coming to anchor in Lynnhaven Roads. A landing was made on the nearby beach. Several houses were plundered, and one inhabitant and several slaves were carried off. The following day the same rovers attacked the ship *James* of Plymouth and took her after a two-hour battle. Another privateer seized two more ships, *Lark* of Falmouth and *William and Mary* of London. After plundering the Falmouth ship, they set her afire and departed on their merry way. A third privateer took several North Carolina sloops and a Bermuda sloop bound for the Bay. Reports from coast watchers noted the sighting of two more ships burned at sea. And worse yet, a 30-gun privateer from Martinique was reportedly en route specifically to cruise off the Bay.[49]

On June 20 a vigorous new Governor of Virginia, Alexander Spotswood, arrived in the Chesapeake, accompanied by his surgeon and fifteen servants, aboard HMS *Deptford,* in company with the man-of-war *Bedford Galley* and a merchant fleet of twenty ships. At thirty-four years of age, the aristocratic Lieutenant Colonel Spotswood was already a hardened veteran of Marlborough's campaigns in Europe, and had fought at Blenheim and Oudernarde. The imperious young chief executive arrived ready to govern Virginia as it had not been governed since the days of Berkeley. The arrival of the new governor and the warships that had brought him could not have come at a better time, for the maritime counties of the colony had been in an almost continual state of alarm since the departure of *Enterprize.* Fortunately, both Captain Tancred Robinson, commander of the 50-gun *Deptford,* and Captain Lee of *Bedford Galley,* had been instructed to remain in the Chesapeake for at least ninety days, to cruise between Lynnhaven and the Capes "to prevent any Attempts that may be made by the Privateers of the Enemy." The Admiralty, to discourage Robinson and Lee from simply lying at anchor during their stay, forbade the captains from remaining in any river "longer than may be absolutely necessary to furnish their Ships with what they may really want." Robinson, being the senior officer, was commanded to remain on the station until further orders arrived directing him to convoy the fall fleet home to England. Within days of their arrival, both warships were actively patrolling the Bay and Capes.[50]

Spotswood moved with resolution to strengthen Virginia's coastal defenses. He quickly resurrected the time-worn old idea that a small fort at Point Comfort would serve as a defense against pirates and privateers. He suggested to the Board of Trade that an agent victualler be appointed for Virginia and a permanent facility for careening and refitting be established at Point Comfort, where guardships might repair beneath the protection of the proposed fort's guns. A petition from Elizabeth City County reinforced the Governor's proposal, but the petition was rejected by the Virginia Assembly, which had no wish to assume the expenses involved in maintaining a garrison. Spotswood suggested that a company of invalids be employed in the garrison duty. Their physical handicaps would prevent them from deserting to the merchant marine or becoming planters, and the expense to the colony government would be no more than their cost at the invalid veteran's facility at Greenwich Hospital in England. If attack threatened, the garrison would be reinforced by the colony militia who, he assured them, would perform better in the company of experienced soldiers (invalided or not) and behind walls than they would if standing alone and exposed. Neither the Assembly nor the Board of Trade thought much of the plan. The only thing agreed to was the Governor's request for a powerful man-of-war and a revenue cutter or customs sloop to strangle a growing illicit trade between the islands of St. Thomas and Curacao, and the lower James River district.[51]

Spotswood wisely delayed the homeward-bound convoy of *Deptford* and *Bedford Galley* until late September, near the end of the "pirate season," and by the spring of 1711 HMS *Enterprize* was back on the Virginia Station. *Enterprize*'s presence proved of immediate benefit when she took a French privateer off the Capes. The privateer's crew of eighty-eight men was kept in Virginia for nearly two months before being sent to England. The Governor said he was unwilling to send the prisoners under a flag of truce to the West Indies primarily to avoid all suspicion of illegally trading with the enemy. He may have had other motivations. Having once been a prisoner of the French himself, he felt that by sending them to England he might initiate an equal exchange of prisoners with the enemy (and also permit the commissioners for sick and wounded in England rather than the colony to bear the expenses for keeping the prisoners).[52]

The summer of 1711 was a harried one for Virginia's new Governor. A massive, concerted attack by land and sea was being planned by the British military for the reduction of French Canada. Concerned that her colonies, stripped of their military strength needed to mount the allied offensive, would be subject to a counterattack by the French fleet to force a withdrawal of the expedition, Queen Anne directed the colonial militia establishment in America to be kept under arms. Though Virginia provided no ships, funds, or supplies (save for seven hundred barrels of pork) for the expedition, the colony stood, as did the rest of the Atlantic seaboard, in general fear of attack. In August word that a French squadron was actually being fitted out for America forced the Virginia government to again go through the expensive motions of putting the colony in a posture of defense.[53]

The militia was reorganized, mustered, and drilled. An armed sloop, *Fanny and Mary,* with fifty men under the command of Captain Joseph Brinston, was hired and fitted out to cruise at the Capes and provide early warning of an enemy approach. Signal beacons and cannons were set up at various plantations on the rivers and Bay to relay the message. A battery of 15 guns was erected at Point Comfort and a defense line cast up between the Bay and Mill Creek. Other batteries were established at Tindall's Point and Yorktown, the first of fifteen guns and the second of ten. Sixteen more guns were mounted at Jamestown and a defense line established from the James River to Back Creek. A major secondary defense line was measured out across the entire peninsula, running from the James to the York, protecting Williamsburg and providing the people of the lower neck with a refuge in the event that the enemy passed the works at Point Comfort. A mobile unit of ten guns was mounted on field carriages for land service as necessity dictated. The necessary artificers and laborers were impressed, and lookouts established at the usual coastal locations.[54]

Spotswood received less than total cooperation from the rest of the government and much of the citizenry of Virginia. He complained of opposition from the Quaker community, who outright refused to work or permit their servants to work on the forts. The colony was destitute of guns, ammunition, and powder. He wrote to England for help. When the munitions finally arrived, not at colony expense but as a gift from Queen Anne, he cajoled the Assembly into authorizing the erection of a magazine at Williamsburg to house them. A vigilant watch was kept on the Capes by *Fanny and Mary,* which sailed out every morning and returned every evening to Point Comfort. And through it all, Alexander Spotswood eventually bullied and blustered the defenses of Virginia into shape.[55]

When the Virginia Assembly convened in the fall, the Governor indignantly castigated many of its less-than-militant members.

"I cannot but wonder," he said,

at the Supine notions of many people here who argue that either their poverty will discourage or their wilderness⁵ frustrate an Invasion—Surely they do not consider that a fleet which happens to want Sustenance and Refreshment will long more for the Stocks and Plantations of Virg^a than for the Mines of Peru.[56]

He had pulled off one of the most massive mobilization efforts in colony history, which the increasingly independent-minded Assembly was legally committed to meet the expenses for by the acts for security and defense. And many, though admiring the feat, were not quite sure of what to make of their new governor, for the attack never came and the defenses were never tested.

By the winter of 1711 the war had reached a virtual standoff between the contending powers. The emergency on the Chesapeake had diminished to the point that Spotswood was able to permit *Enterprize* to leave the Bay to convoy a fleet of merchant ships to Barbados, and then to join for a time the navy's West Indian Squadron. Though the privateer menace still existed, and a powerful French navy ship of one hundred eighty men, which had menaced the mouth of the Chesapeake, was taken by HMS *Severn* while convoying the Virginia fleet in the spring of 1712, the war was nearing its end.[57] Peace talks had begun in earnest in January, and on April 11, 1713, after nearly fifteen months of negotiations, Great Britain signed the Treaty of Utrecht with France. The Chesapeake tidewater received the joyous news when a 20-gun frigate arrived with a royal proclamation calling for an end to hostilities. The long privateering seige was over.

The Golden Age of Piracy was about to begin.

XV

We Plunder the Rich

Throughout the War of the Spanish Succession the Chesapeake Bay, though constantly harassed by enemy privateers, had, with the exception of a few brigands such as Richard Clark, been largely free of major pirate activity. Governor Spotswood, confident in the ability of the lone guardship on the Virginia Station to protect the Chesapeake trade, concerned over the cost of maintaining a large force, and impressed by the paucity of pirate activity in the region, dismissed in late December 1713 a petition by worried planters and merchants for an additional man-of-war to protect the Bay. It had been generally assumed that if there was to be a resurgence of buccaneering, as was normal after the cessation of hostilities following every war, it would focus on the Caribbean. There the rich treasure galleons of Spanish America (which had not sailed as a result of the war since 1708), and the sugar, cocoa, and mahogany-laden ships of France, Holland, and England would provide much more inviting targets than the tobacco fleets of the Chesapeake. The concern of British merchants trading with Maryland and Virginia, however, whose fears could not be assuaged, was far stronger. As a consequence of their petitions to the Privy Council, a new guardship, HMS *Valeur,* of 24 guns and 321 tons, was assigned to the Virginia Station and entered the Bay in June 1715 for a tour of duty.[1]

That the Caribbean was likely soon to be infested by pirates again was a fact given birth by one of the very mechanisms that helped make global war at sea possible in the seventeenth and eighteenth centuries—privateering. Although such modes of warfare had been well known and practiced since the days of Sir Francis Drake, in 1708 privateering was given a new dimension. In that year Parliament, in order to encourage privateering in the colonies, had enacted legislation that provided the owners of privateers and their crews the right to any and all prizes and plunder taken, whereafter the Crown voluntarily gave up its one-fifth share of the proceeds. Thus privateering as a profession became more firmly entrenched than ever before as a way of life for English seafarers.[2] With the signing of the Treaty of Utrecht, however, after more than a decade of war, thousands of British mariners engaged in privateering suddenly found themselves unemployed. It is not surprising that many, whose skills at sea-roving had been honed in their quasi-service to the Crown, were driven by their poverty into the not-unrelated activity of buccaneering. So many, in fact, chose the calling that within a few years of the war's end, the West Indian trade was virtually paralyzed.

The resurgence of piracy in the West Indies, to proportions never before experienced, happened almost overnight, and the Bahama Islands, on the eastern lip of that major nautical highway of America, the Bahama Channel, became the pirates' lair. These strategic, if unproductive, islands, continually sacked and plundered by French and Spanish expeditions during the war years, were owned by six Lord Proprietors (all Lord Proprietors of Carolina) and two others, but had, for all intents and purposes, been abandoned by the English government after the war. In the vacuum created by the lack of governmental administration and the initial failings of the Royal Navy in the West Indies to maintain order, the islands and their settlements, especially the town of Nassau on New Providence Island, became major rendezvous sites for "loose disorderly People from the Bay of Campeache, Jamaica and other parts." Nassau was soon termed by Spotswood a "Nest of Pirates" in which buccaneer democracy was in undisputed control.[3]

On July 30, 1715, a Spanish treasure flota, en route from Havana to Spain, consisting of twelve or thirteen ships commanded by Captain-General Don Juan Esteban de Ubilla, and carrying nearly 6,500,000 pesos in registered gold and silver in bars, coins, and gold dust, as well as precious consignments of pearls, silverware, Chinese porcelains, indigo, cochineal, drugs, hides, brazilwood, copper, and ceramics, was wrecked by a hurricane. Ten or eleven of the vessels were lost on the Florida coast near present-day Cape Kennedy. Spanish salvage operations commenced almost immediately, and were, for the times, highly successful in recovering nearly 5,250,000 pesos in silver specie and bars. Yet a fortune in sunken treasure still remained unrecovered.[4]

News of the disaster spread rapidly about the West Indies and

eventually to Virginia. Governor Spotswood first received intelligence
of the treasure fleet loss the following summer, along with word "that a
number of profligate fellows have posssess'd themselves of the Island
of [New] Providence" in the Bahamas. The two intelligence items were
neatly interwined, for it was also reported that crews of several vessels
fitted out at Jamaica to fish for the treasure upon the Spanish wrecks
had begun committing piracies against both Spanish and French vessels in the same waters. The pirates had even succeeded in looting the
treasure wrecks of twenty thousand pieces of eight, antagonizing the
fragile peace between England and Spain. The Englishmen, afraid to
return home, had decided to settle at New Providence and there to
strengthen themselves against "any power that shall attack them."[5]

Spotswood was deeply disturbed by the aggressiveness of the freebooters and their ever-increasing force. They had, he noted on July 3,
1716, taken a French ship of thirty-two guns in March and manned her
with a company of desperadoes, giving out that their intention was to
capture all French and Spanish ships that happened to sail across their
path. Though the pirates had purportedly claimed that they would
spare all English vessels, the "Gang at Providence" had already taken
and plundered vessels belonging to New England and Bermuda, and
were exacting tribute from ships traversing the Bahama Channel. One
ship's master, Captain Alexander Stockdale, a merchant of Barbados,
was forced to pay twenty pounds in gold as a tribute or suffer a severe
flogging. It was soon reported that the pirate Thomas Barrow had
taken control of New Providence and had established a virtual reign of
terror, and he was but one among many.[6] It appeared to Spotswood to
be only a matter of time before the pirates gained full control of the
Bahama Channel and the shipping that passed through from Jamaica,
since the channel was "almost in sight of the harbour they have possess'd themselves of." Indeed, he feared that "the whole Trade of this
Continent may be endangered if timely measure be not taken to suppress this growing evil." Thus, backtracking on his earlier refutation on
the need of an additional guardship, he requested of the Lords of
Admiralty that another man-of-war

> be speedily sent hither to Cruise on this Coast for ye protection of our
> Merchantmen; And if it shall be found practicable, in Conjunction with the
> Shoreham, to attack these pyrates in their Quarters before they grow too
> formidable.[7]

In June 1716, Spotswood's interest in the Florida treasure wrecks
was whetted when four freebooters were picked up in Virginia. Their
tale only corroborated others of the great sunken treasure that lay
beneath the warm Florida waters, but the involvement of pirates in its

salvage worried the Governor. Among the four buccaneers taken was one Captain Josiah Forbes, formerly master of *John and Mary.* Forbes' first story, given out upon his arrival in the colony, was that he and his men had been cast away at Cape Hatteras but had somehow survived and made their way to Virginia. Both the captain and his men, their tongues perhaps loosened by tidewater tavern conviviality, were soon boasting that they "had been concern'd in beating the Spaniards from their Batterys erected on the Coast of Florida for guarding the Wrecks" (although Forbes later claimed it had been in self-defense). Soon it was discovered that they had been involved in the taking of a 32-gun French ship. Upon learning of their self-proclaimed complicity in the piracy of the French ship, Spotswood immediately caused Forbes to be arrested and jailed until he could post bond.[8]

Though Forbes escaped almost immediately after his arrest, the information he brought worried the Governor. He began to fear that the treasure wrecks would draw pirates to the mainland. Piracy on the North American coast might well migrate northward, perhaps even to the Chesapeake. The Jamaica trade with the Bay was already in jeopardy, and buccaneering loosed upon the Atlantic coast itself might well endanger such important commerce as the Virginia salt trade, as well as Chesapeake shipping itself.

Though little accusation was made against the Royal Navy for its failure to cope with the cancerous crisis in the West Indies, the Navy did in fact bear some of the blame. Aged ships, undermanned by desertion, sickness, and death, were, of course, constantly obliged to repair and refit after cruising warm, tropical, shipworm-infested waters. Yet motivation among Royal Navy officers at sea to suppress piracy was at best limited, since Navy men themselves frequently profited from the menace. Naval commanders, under Admiralty law, were permitted to charge a fee of 12½ percent of the total value of the cargo of a ship under convoy. It was not uncommon for illegal bargains to be struck between merchants and corrupt naval commanders, the latter offering to transport cargoes in their own vessels at less than the going rate in commercial freight haulers. And since pirates infrequently attacked convoys escorted by Royal Navy warships, the Navy seldom bothered pirates (the cause for the convoys in the first place), no matter what orders said.[9] It simply wasn't worth the risk, for, unlike privateersmen, pirates, faced with a noose if captured, would fight to the death.

Spotswood, aware that his commission, which entrusted him to make appointments to the Admiralty Court in the Bahamas, also gave him some jurisdictional say in Bahamian affairs, resolved to act where others failed to do so. He was eager for any information he could get. Thus, when one Harry Beverly, a Virginia militia officer, surveyor, lawyer, and would-be adventurer, determined to take his new sloop, *Virgin of Virginia,* to Florida waters to hire her out to the Spanish treasure salvors, or perhaps to fish the wrecks himself, Spotswood's interest was titillated. When Beverly revealed that should his treasure-hunting fail, he intended to sail to the West Indies to sell his cargo of provisions, the Governor saw an opportunity he could not let pass. He would utilize Beverly as a quasi-official government agent to gather data not only about the Spanish operations on the Florida wrecks, but about the pirates of New Providence as well. The captain sought permission from the Governor to man his vessel with forty or fifty armed men, for which a bond was posted as security to insure their honest and peaceable deportment. Though a number of the crew were pressed men, indentured servants, and Indian slaves, (and perhaps of questionable value), permission was granted to make the voyage, with the proviso that Beverly not antagonize any Spanish vessels that might be encountered in the vicinity of the treasure wrecks. The captain was instructed to assist the Spanish in every way to recover that which was rightfully theirs, and to content himself with what the Law of Nations allowed for reasonable salvage. Under no circumstances was he to jeopardize the fragile peace between England and Spain by conducting any hostile acts. If he should encounter HMS *Shoreham,* then detached on a mission to St. Augustine for the colony of South Carolina, he was to assist fully her new commander, Captain Thomas Baker, in every way possible. Beverly's principal mission, however, was to ascertain the number, strength, and objectives of the buccaneers at New Providence. If attacked by the freebooters, he was authorized to "repel by force, and do your best endeavor to sink, burn & destroy all such pirates or Sea Rovers as you shall meet with. . . . "[10]

On June 23, 1716, *Virgin of Virginia* sailed for the coast of Florida. Beverly's voyage provided more hardship than the good captain and his crew had expected. Several days after clearing the Virginia Capes, his ship was ensnared in an Atlantic gale that drove her to Bermuda. Then, on July 5 *Virgin* was stopped by three shots fired by the Spanish man-of-war *St. Juan Baptista,* Don Rocher de la Peña commanding, and a consort sloop. Though Beverly was flying English colors, the suspicious Spaniard refused to even look at his papers, and belligerently demanded to know where he was from. When several of *Virgin*'s crew, the indentured servants and Indian slaves, perhaps out of revenge for some unrecorded act, swore she was en route to join English buccaneers from Jamaica, the ship was instantly seized and plundered, and her company beaten, stripped, and hauled naked aboard the warship to perform menial tasks.[11]

The Spaniard then sailed for Puerto Rico and on to St. Domingo. Beverly demanded a trial, and that proper authorities be notified of his situation, but in vain. Held incommunicado, he was informed he would soon be receiving his just desserts when *Baptista* reached Vera Cruz. A dismal future in the mines of Mexico loomed large for Beverly and his men. There was to be no trial. *Virgin*'s plundered goods were sold at Puerto Rico, and the vessel itself disposed of at Vera Cruz without legal proceedings of any kind. The first news of Beverly's predicament reached Spotswood on August 14, when a hastily scrawled message smuggled from the warship by the unfortunate Virginian was delivered. At Vera Cruz, the captain and his company were apparently given freedom to roam the city but, denied subsistence, were soon reduced to begging on the streets for handouts. Several of their number died of starvation. The crew was eventually permitted to go to Cuba, but Beverly remained a prisoner at Vera Cruz. Finally, after seven months of captivity, the captain managed to escape and returned to Virginia in August 1717. He brought with him the intelligence that a veritable horde of seaborne brigands was descending on the Bahamas to take up the trade of freebooting.[12]

For the Chesapeake tidewater, the news that Harry Beverly had so painfully acquired arrived too late. The vermin of the sea, crawling up from the Bahamas, had already infested Virginia waters.

Captains Samuel Bellamy and Paul (or Palgrave) Williams were not atypical of the New Providence breed of pirates that came to haunt Chesapeake waters in 1717. Bellamy, it was said, came from Dorset County or Essex County, England. Others claimed he was a native of Plymouth, London, Bristol, Liverpool, or Canterbury. Unfortunately, all that could be said for certain was that he had a wife and family living near Canterbury; the remainder of his early life remains a mystery. The record of his friend and accomplice, Paul Williams, is only slightly better defined. A dark-complexioned man given to wearing perukes, Williams was the son of a reputable merchant and Attorney General of Rhode Island whose properties included holdings at Block Island, Newport, and Boston. Stricken with gold fever, both men had been drawn away from home and family by the lure of the Florida Spanish treasure wrecks.[13] Like others who had ventured to the inhospitable, mosquito-infested coast of Florida, they had found only the leavings of the Spanish salvors, "and not finding their expectation answered," resolved, perhaps at the suggestion of several New Providence pirates also working the wrecks, to go upon the account.[14]

Both Bellamy and Williams, having joined a company of buccaneers commanded by Captain Benjamin Hornigold, soon found themselves in Nassau. Bellamy was apparently a charismatic man who quickly began to gather about him a following among Hornigold's crew, as he accompanied his chief on piratical cruises around the Carribbean. In June 1716 Bellamy was voted into command of Hornigold's ship when the captain vowed to attack only Spanish and French vessels—a policy his crew refused to accept—and was deposed. Then, Bellamy and his cohort and quartermaster, Paul Williams, commenced caroming about the West Indies in an orgy of plundering.[15]

In February 1717 the two pirates, in command of a pair of vessels, encountered and took up pursuit of a merchant ship of force called *Whidah Galley,* a ship of three hundred tons and eighteen guns and manned by a crew of fifty under the command of Captain Lawrence Prince. Bound from Jamaica to London, Bellamy's prey was laden with a rich cargo of gold, silver, elephant ivory, sugar, indigo, and resins for varnish. After a vigorous three-day chase which carried predator and victim from the Windward Passage to Long Island in the Bahamas, *Whidah* finally surrendered.[16]

Overjoyed at the capture of the exquisitely designed and maneuverable galley and its rich cargo, Bellamy graciously exchanged his own ship, *Sultana,* with Captain Prince and released him and his crew. The pirates soon increased *Whidah*'s force to twenty-eight guns and two hundred men. Her crew was a motley one, the majority of whom were natives of Great Britain and Ireland, although there was a sprinkling of colonials, Indians and other nationalities, and about twenty-five blacks taken from a Guinea slave ship. Working in close concert with the galley, Captain Williams commanded a yellow-and-blue 8-gun sloop with worn, patched sails, manned by eighty seamen.[17]

Bellamy's intolerance of the stratified, and frequently unjust, society from which he had fled, and his unswerving support of the democratic brotherhood of pirates of which he had become a member was once exhibited in a speech delivered to one of his victims, a certain Captain Beers. It was undoubtedly illustrative of the feelings and philosophy of many Brethren of the Coast. After capturing and plundering Beers's ship, both Williams and Bellamy had been of a mind to return the vessel to the unfortunate mariner, but their crews were opposed and sank the vessel. Before marooning Beers, Bellamy took the opportunity to deliver a tirade that offered a peculiar insight into the thinking of his kind. "D—n my b—d," said the pirate,

I am sorry they won't let you have your sloop again, for I scorn to do any

mischief, when it is not for my advantage; damn the sloop we must sink her, and she might be of use to you. Though damn ye, you are a sneaking puppy, and so are all those who will submit to be governed by Laws which rich men have made for their own security, for the cowardly whelps have not the courage otherwise to defend what they get by their knavery. But damn ye altogether. Damn them for a pack of crazy rascals, and you, who serve them, for a parcel of hen-hearted numskulls. They vilify us, the scoundrels do, when there is only this difference, they rob the poor under the cover of Law, forsooth, and we plunder the rich under the protection of our own courage. Had you not better make of us, than sneak after the a-s of those villains for Employment?

Captain Beers replied that his conscience would not allow him to break the laws of God and man.

"You are a devillish conscientious rascal, d—n ye," retorted Bellamy. *I am a free prince, and I have as much authority to make war on the whole world as he who has a hundred sail of ships at sea, and an army of 100,000 men in the field, and this my conscience tells me. But there is no arguing with such snivelling puppies, who allow superiors to kick them about deck at pleasure and pin their faith upon a pimp of a parson, a squab, who neither practices nor believes what he puts upon the chucklehead fools he preaches to.* [18]

Shortly after making *Whidah* his flagship, Bellamy fell in with and plundered *Tanner Frigate* and then turned his bow toward the Virginia Capes, "which coast they very much infested, taking several vessels." The two pirates arrived about the beginning of April and wisely ignored ships outward bound from the Chesapeake during their brief stay, well aware that their cargoes usually consisted of heavy hogsheads of tobacco difficult to get rid of in the Americas, and too bulky for the speedy vessels they commanded. Instead, they waited for rich inbound cargo ships from Europe and the West Indies heavily laden with marketable merchandise. They did not have to wait for long. Their first prize, taken five leagues off the mouth of the Bay at about 8:00 A.M. on April 7, was the ship *Agnes* of Glasgow, Captain Tarbett, bound for Virginia from Bermuda with rum, sugar, molasses, and miscellaneous European goods. Not much later on the same day, the snow *Anne Galley* of Glasgow, Alexander Montgomery master, and the pink *Endeavour* of Brighton, John Scott master, were taken. Two days later, after removing the crew and passengers from *Agnes* and plundering her of her cargo, Bellamy ordered her masts cut away, and the ship sunk. The following day, April 10, the pirate captured a vessel commanded by a Captain Young, from Leith, Scotland, bound for Virginia. After the usual robbery, the buccaneers persuaded six of Young's crew and two servants to sign the pirate articles and join the complement of *Whidah*. The rover's captives were now placed aboard *Endeavour* and the Leith ship and permitted to sail away. At least one of the vessels made directly for the Chesapeake. Bellamy was apparently unconcerned, for he did not release *Anne Galley* or her crew, but obliged them to accompany him to assist in careening his ship.[20]

Captain Williams, cruising some distance from Bellamy, was also successful—at first. In his shallow-draft sloop he had found the maze of inlets and islets festooning the mouth of the Chesapeake, a superb place from which to monitor maritime traffic entering the Bay. In the early morning light of April 9, he spotted a sail standing into the Capes. Darting from his lair, he fell upon his surprised prey with an efficiency born of experience. The victim offered no resistance. She proved to be *Tryal* of Brighton, commanded by Captain John Lucas. Looting of the prize began immediately and continued well into the late afternoon, until a strange sail was sighted steering directly for the two vessels. Bidding Captain Lucas to follow in his wake, the pirate moved to flee. When a favorable breeze sprang up, however, Lucas stood off and escaped into the Chesapeake.[21]

Bellamy and Williams were soon thereafter reunited. *Whidah* was in desperate need of cleaning. Thus, escorted by *Anne Galley*, the two pirates entered the Cheapeake in search of an isolated, suitable place to careen. By this time Bellamy had apparently become skittish over the possible presence of a guardship. He was entirely unaware that HMS *Shoreham* was away on detached duty in South Carolina, and that the Bay was wide open and vulnerable. He sighted a large ship in Lynnhaven Bay and, fearing the vessel might be a man-of-war, he ordered his flotilla to come about and bear away to the north. Neither Sam Bellamy nor Paul Williams, who parted company off the Virginia Capes, would see each other again. Nor would they ever return to terrorize the Chesapeake, for on April 26, *Whidah* would wreck on the shoals of Cape Cod, drowning 130 of her crew and prisoners in the process. The notorious Sam Bellamy and seven of his company would eventually be captured, tried, and convicted of piracy, and would swing from the gibbet.[22]

None of this, of course, could be foreseen. On April 17 Captain Tarbett and the supercargo of the ill-fated *Agnes*, having made their way into the Chesapeake, reported to Governor Spotswood on the pirates' cruise at the mouth of the Bay. They informed him, having overheard the conversation of several rovers, that Bellamy's declared intention was to cruise for ten days off the Delaware Capes and another ten days off Long Island to intercept Philadelphia and New York vessels bound for the West Indies with provisions, and then to careen their vessels at Green Island, near Cape Sable, Newfoundland. The Governor was undoubtedly disturbed to learn of the damage the pirates had done, but was more distraught to discover "that they Expected Several others to follow them in a Small time," and that at least ten sail of pirates were cruising the West Indies and the American coast at that very moment. Spotswood, with the advice of the Council of Virginia, could do little but dispatch warning to the governors of New York and New England to order out their own guardships to try to intercept Bellamy and Williams.[23]

In exasperation, he wrote to Secretary of State Paul Methuen on May 30 of the colony's plight.

It is now near a twelve month ago since I communicated to his Ma'ty's Ministers, particularly to the Board of Trade and the Lords Comm'rs of the Admiralty, the apprehensions I had of the growth of Pyrates in these parts, with my humble opinion that some additional Strength of Men of War would be absolutely necessary to be sent to these Plantations for the Security of the Trade. Experience has shew'd how just my fears were. Our Capes have been for these six Weeks pass'd in a manner blocked up by those Pyrates, and diverse Ships, inward bound, taken and plundered by them. Their Strength increases daily by the addition of new men from these Ships that fall in their way, though they give out that they will force no man into their Service, being resolved that none who join them shall have any hopes of mercy on that account.[24]

Spotswood sought to neutralize the festering sore that endangered the Chesapeake trade. HMS *Shoreham*, which had finally returned to the Virginia Station, had received Admiralty orders to proceed to England. But the ship was in desperate need of careening and repairs, and was in no condition to either make the Atlantic crossing or to undertake any long cruises in pursuit of pirates. The Governor therefore seized the opportunity to prevail upon Captain Barker to remain in the colony until relieved by another ship. *Shoreham*, in the meantime, might be employed to convoy both the Virginia and Maryland trade beyond the soundings and the danger of pirate attack. He was quick to point out to the Lords Commissioners for Trade and Plantations and the Secretary of State, in explaining his actions, the consequences of the failure to maintain *Shoreham* on station. If she were to return to England, she "would leave a great part of the Trade of these two Plantations at the Mercy of the Pyrates, and even give them an easy access into our Bay and Rivers to plunder the Inhabitants." He begged for reinforcements to protect the Chesapeake trade, and for a major effort to dislodge the pirates from their Bahamian base, either by force "or by an offer of pardon upon their Submission." Of the two options, he urged the former be employed, as many pirates would accept pardons, but few would reform, and most would quickly return to their old ways.[25] Yet with the departure of the *Whidah Galley* and her consort, the Chesapeake was given a welcome break from pirate attacks on its shipping, a break that would soon be extended beyond Spotswood's hopes.

About August 7, 1717, the Governor's prayers for another guardship were finally answered with the arrival of the 32-gun, 384-ton Royal Navy man-of-war *Lyme,* under the command of Captain Ellis Brand. The Governor was delighted. "We have had for some time," he happily confessed to the British Secretary of State soon after the warship's arrival, "a Respite from the Insults of the Pyrates which infested this Coast and doubt not the Guard Ship now sent to this Station will free us from their Depredations for the future."[26] By then, however, even more reinforcements were on the way. On October 6, a second well-armed man-of-war, HMS *Pearl,* of 42 guns and 559 tons burthen, commanded by Captain George Gordon, came to anchor in Lynnhaven Bay to replace the debilitated *Shoreham* and begin guard duty. Throughout the following winter and spring *Lyme* and *Pearl* would be constantly employed either on patrol off the Capes and in the Bay or on convoy duty, shepherding Chesapeake merchantmen to Bermuda, Barbados, and New York, or escorting vessels en route to Europe safely beyond soundings.[27]

For the first time since the end of the late war, though pirates continued their depredations elsewhere with impunity, the Chesapeake tidewater seemed safe from attack.

In England, the impact of the tidal wave of piracy in the Americas was finally being felt. The British government, moved by a sea of complaints from governors and merchant syndicates alike, finally began to act along the two lines suggested by Spotswood and a host of others. The first move was to reestablish law and order in the very seat of piracy itself, in the Bahamas. To accomplish this task, one of the most accomplished mariners of the age, Captain Woodes Rogers, was appointed Governor of the Bahamas and given a small naval escort and a band of soldiers and orders to put an end to the plague of piracy. No more capable man could have been chosen. Rogers was himself a former privateersman who had not only circumnavigated the globe, but sacked the city of Guayaquil in South America, captured the fabled Manila galleon, and returned home to tell about it with a treasure valued at £800,000 to boot. Among the most important weapons in Rogers's arsenal to combat buccaneering was a royal proclamation promising pardon for all piracies commited prior to January 5, 1718, if offenders surrendered before September 5 of that same year. The proclamation stipulated that those persons guilty of piracy could surrender directly to any governor or lieutenant governor in the colonies. And furthermore, any murders committed upon the high seas prior to the January 5 cutoff date would be forgiven. Goods unlawfully seized during acts of piracy could be retained.[28]

The proclamation was received without fanfare in Virginia on January 3, 1718, and though it was accompanied with great joy by some and dismay, and even outright opposition, by others in the Bahamas, it appeared to be a step in the right direction. It was also an expedient with fatal flaws made in total desperation, as future events would soon illustrate. Gradually, pirates began to drift into the Chesapeake Tidewater to surrender to the King's Proclamation. The consequences of such elements in the authoritarian society of colonial Virginia were predictable, and there were bound to be backsliders, as Governor Spotswood had foreseen.

One band of seven pirates, mostly Englishmen mixed with a few colonials, arrived from New Providence in April 1718, having detached themselves from a complement of 142 pirates. Securing a pardon, the seven—Richard Tucker, Edward Wells, John Jackson, James Carr, Barthena Leed, Edward Lee, and Peter Oliver—lasted barely a month. Soon after their surrender, they had purchased a boat, allegedly to transport themselves to Pennsylvania. According to a complaint sworn out against them by Captain Richard Smith, master of the Maryland sloop *Anne,* the ex-buccaneers had seduced his mate, Edward Limbry, into joining them. It was not so much the loss of his mate that upset Captain Smith, but the apprehension that "they have a design to Seize his said Sloop, they having in their discourse threatnd the same." Whether or not the ex-pirates actually intended to go aroving again is unknown. The Executive Council of Virginia, however, took no chances and immediately issued warrants to the sheriffs of York, Warwick, and Elizabeth City County for their arrest. They were to be seized, brought before the Council to answer the charges against them, and to post security for their good behavior in the future.[29]

Such was the mindset of the Virginia government on the eve of the greatest pirate fright in colony history, caused by the most notorious buccaneer of the age—Blackbeard.

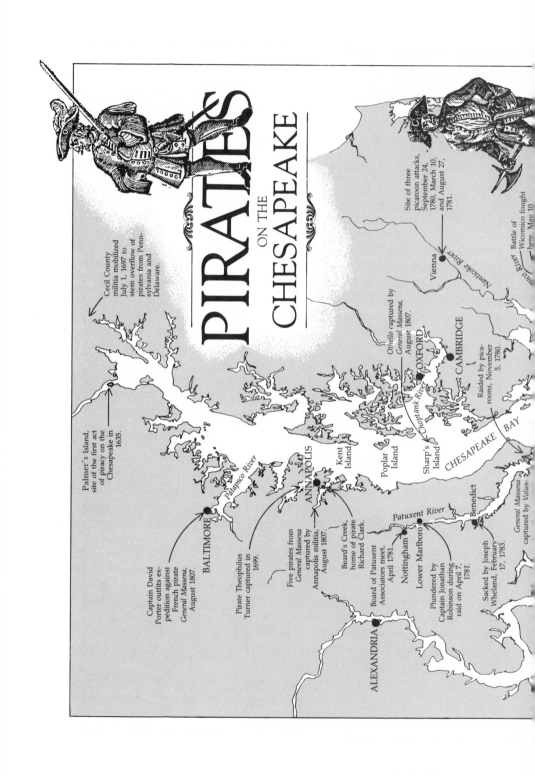

PIRATES
ON THE
CHESAPEAKE

Cecil County militia mobilized July 1, 1697 to stem overflow of pirates from Pennsylvania and Delaware.

Palmer's Island, site of the first act of piracy on the Chesapeake in 1635.

Captain David Porter outfits expedition against French pirate *General Massena*, August 1807.

BALTIMORE

Pirate Theophilus Turner captured in 1699.

Patapsco River

Five pirates from *General Massena* captured by Annapolis militia, August 1807.

ANNAPOLIS

Kent Island

Poplar Island

Sharp's Island

Choptank River

Othello captured by *General Massena*, August 1807.

OXFORD

CAMBRIDGE

Raided by picaroons, November 5, 1780.

Vienna

Site of three picaroon attacks, September 24, 1780, March 10, and August 27, 1781.

Nanticoke River

...co River

Battle of Wicomico fought here, May 10

CHESAPEAKE BAY

Beard's Creek, home of pirate Richard Clark.

ALEXANDRIA

Board of Patuxent Associators meet, April 1781.

Nottingham

Plundered by Captain Jonathan Robinson during raid on April 7, 1781.

Lower Marlboro

Patuxent River

Benedict

Sacked by Joseph Wheland, February 17, 1783.

General Massena captured by Volun-

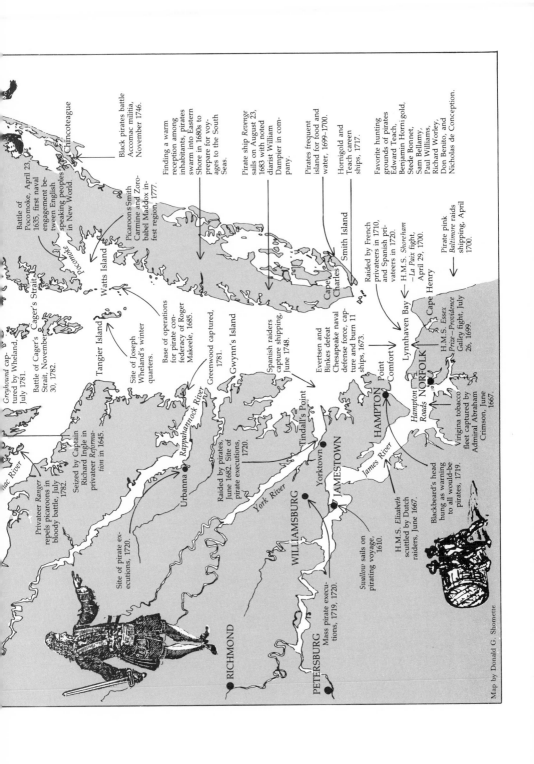

Black pirates battle Accomac militia, November 1746.

Chincoteague

Battle of Pocomoke, April 23, 1635, first naval engagement between English speaking peoples in New World.

Finding a warm reception among inhabitants, pirates swarm into Eastern Shore in 1680s to prepare for voyages to the South Seas.

Picaroons Smith Carmine and Zorobabel Maddox infest region, 1777.

Watts Island

Pirate ship *Revenge* sails on August 23, 1683 with noted diarist William Dampier in company.

Pirates frequent island for food and water, 1699–1700.

Hornigold and Teach careen ships, 1717.

Smith Island

Favorite hunting grounds of pirates Edward Teach, Benjamin Hornigold, Stede Bonnet, Sam Bellamy, Paul Williams, Richard Worley, Don Benito, and Nicholas de Conception.

Greyhound captured by Wheland, July 1781.

Battle of Cager's Strait, November 30, 1782.

Cager's Strait

Site of Joseph Wheland's winter quarters.

Tangier Island

Base of operations for pirate confederacy of Roger Makeele, 1685.

Cape Charles

Raided by French privateers in 1710, and Spanish privateers in 1720.

Lynnhaven Bay

H.M.S. *Shoreham* – *La Paix* fight, April 29, 1700.

Cape Henry

Pirate pink *Baltimore* raids shipping, April 1700.

H.M.S. *Essex* Prize – *Providence Galley* fight, July 26, 1699.

Privateer *Ranger* repels picaroons in bloody battle, July 1782.

Seized by Captain Richard Ingle in privateer *Reformation* in 1645.

Greenwood captured, 1781.

Gwynn's Island

Spanish raiders capture shipping, June 1748.

Evertsen and Binkes defeat Chesapeake naval defense force, capture and burn 11 ships, 1673.

Point Comfort

Hampton Roads

NORFOLK

Virigina tobacco fleet captured by Admiral Abraham Crimson, June 1667.

Rappahannock River

Urbanna

Raided by pirates, June 1682. Site of pirate executions, 1720.

Tindall's Point

Yorktown

HAMPTON

Site of pirate executions, 1720.

York River

WILLIAMSBURG

JAMESTOWN

H.M.S. *Elizabeth* scuttled by Dutch raiders, June 1667.

Blackbeard's head hung as warning to all would-be pirates, 1719.

Swallow sails on pirating voyage, 1610.

James River

RICHMOND

PETERSBURG

Mass pirate executions, 1719, 1720.

Map by Donald G. Shomette

XVI

A Fury from Hell

"In the commonwealth of Pirates," wrote the immortal Daniel Defoe, under the nom de plume Captain Charles Johnson, in 1724, "who goes the greatest length for wickedness is looked upon with a kind of envy amongst them, as a person of a more extraordinary gallantry, and is thereby entitled to be distinguished by some post. And if such a one has but courage, he must certainly be a great man."[1]

Such a man was Captain Edward Teach, the most feared and legendary buccaneer in the history of piracy.

Some said his name was Tash, Tatch, Tack, Tache, or Thatch; the last of these names would not have been unfitting, for it was also a nickname for the devil. A few stated that he had been born Edward Drummond in Bristol, England, while others claimed he was a son of Accomac County, Virginia.[2] Yet it was by the name of Blackbeard that he was to become famous—a name which caused honest seamen to quake, and with which children were threatened before bedtime. His visage was certainly one which induced fear among his victims and foes, and respect and obedience among his company. Blackbeard's trademark, his coal-black beard, was long, beginning close beneath his eyes and extending almost to his waist, and was festooned with ribbons twisted in small tails, and turned about his ears. His eyes, hooded by bushy, black brows, were penetrating. In battle he wore a sling over his shoulder, with three brace of pistols dangling in holsters like bandoliers. Adding to his fierce appearance, he wore loosely-twisted hemp cord matches, dipped in saltpetre and lime water, lit and slowly burning, hanging from under his hat on either side of his face, which "made him altogether such a figure that imagination cannot form an idea of a Fury from Hell to look more frightful."[3]

Teach was a man of enormous personal courage who sought to capitalize on a reputation for wickedness by making his men believe him to be a "devil incarnate." His stamina and great strength encompassed drink, pain, and the very elements themselves. One day at sea, flushed with rum, he challenged several of his crew to a contest. "Come," he dared, "let us make a hell of our own and try how long we can bear it." With two or three willing to accept the trial, he went into the hold, closed the hatches, and filled several pots with brimstone and other combustibles. The materials were then set afire, filling the hold with suffocating smoke. The crewmen, holding out as long as possible, cried out for air and threw back the hatches to escape. Teach, having held out the longest and bested his men, was the last to emerge.[4]

Many of Blackbeard's superstitious crew believed their commander to be in league with the devil, if not himself a devil. They recalled that on one cruise, a mysterious man was discovered aboard who was not a member of the ship's company. No one could give an account of the stranger, who disappeared from the ship almost as surreptitiously as he had appeared. Indeed, "they verily believed it was the Devil" himself.[5]

Though little is known about Edward Teach's early years, or even his age, it is believed that he began his life at sea shipping out of Bristol as a merchant seaman, and had embraced the career of a privateersman during Queen Anne's War, sailing out of Jamaica.[6] Though never elevated to command during the war, he had readily distinguished himself by his "uncommon boldness and personal courage."[7] With the peace, Teach found himself drawn to New Providence, in the Bahamas, a lawless island upon which unemployed privateersmen, seamen, and the very dregs of the high seas had begun to assemble in increasing numbers. Indeed, the island was evolving, as already noted, in the wake of peace, into a veritable spawning ground of piracy in the West Indies. By 1718 New Providence had become a buccaneer stronghold from which sorties against shipping of all nations were launched. Debauchery, pain, and cruelty reigned supreme among a robber society of low-lifes and misfits.

Teach, whose thirst for action was enhanced by his brutal but capable fighting abilities fit in well, and had soon joined the company of Captain Benjamin Hornigold, reputed to be the fiercest and ablest pirate leader in the Bahamas. He rose quickly under Hornigold and by 1716 had been placed in command of a sloop taken in combat. The following year Hornigold, in command of the brigantine *Ranger*, with Teach commanding his consort sloop, set out to cruise off the mainland of America. En route, the two pirates took and plundered with little effort a sloop from Havana laden with 120 barrels of flour, another from Bermuda with a cargo of wine, and a ship bound from Madeira for Charleston, South Carolina, with a cargo of great value.[8]

Arriving off the Virginia Capes in the late summer or early fall of 1717, the two pirates found it necessary to clean the fouled hulls of their ships. Selecting an isolated backwater of the Eastern Shore of Virginia, the vessels were careened and again made ready for sea.[9] On September 29 they fell in with, attacked, and captured the Virginia sloop *Betty* near Cape Charles. Laden with pipes of Madeira wine and other goods and merchandise, the vessel was quickly plundered and scuttled.[10] Hornigold and Teach then turned their attentions northward. On October 22, in Delaware Bay, they seized and plundered the sloop *Robert* of Philadelphia and the ship *Good Intent* of Dublin, both bound for Philadelphia with goods and merchandise.[11]

After continuing their successful cruise of the American coast for several more months, the pirates returned to the West Indies, bloated with plunder. In December, near north latitude 24 degrees off the coast of St. Vincents, they sighted a large Dutch-built French Guineaman bound for Martinique. The vessel was *Concord* of St. Malo, commanded by Captain D'Ocier. After a few broadsides, the pirate's quarry surrendered. She proved to be an extremely rich prize, for she was laden not only with a valuable cargo of slaves, but also with gold dust, money, plate, and jewels. Having borne up well under the attackers' broadsides, *Concord* was a vessel of strength and sailing qualities which drew Teach's admiration. Soon after her capture, he requested her from Hornigold, who, having grown wealthy from his sea roving, had begun contemplating retirement from piracy and readily consented. The prize was soon armed with forty guns, manned by a crew of nearly three hundred, and renamed *Queen Anne's Revenge*.[12]

Thus commenced the story of Edward Teach's infamous career, a saga that moved forward with heady swiftness. As a pirate cheftain his first victim was the ship *Great Allen*, a rich prize. His reputation for daring and courage among the "Brethren of the Coast," however, was firmly cemented afterwards when he sagaciously engaged the 30-gun Royal Navy man-of-war *Scarborough*, forcing her to retire to Barbados after a several-hours-long engagement. Teach now turned his attention to Spanish America, setting sail for the Bay of Honduras. There he fell in with another pirate ship, a sloop of ten guns, commanded by Major Stede Bonnet, one of the most unlikely pirates to grace the pages of buccaneering history.[13]

Major Bonnet, once a "gentleman of good reputation in the island of Barbadoes," had literally been driven to piracy "by some disaffections he found in a marital state." He knew little or nothing of the sea, it seemed, and having entered the piratical profession, soon found himself, when confronting the cunning Blackbeard and his crew, to be a sheep among wolves. Unlike most who entered the nefarious profession, Bonnet had armed and fitted out his sloop, dubbed *Revenge*, at his own expense (instead of seizing one, as was the custom), and *hired* a crew to go pirating. His first hunting grounds were to be the Virginia Capes. For a man of so little experience, Bonnet's successes at the Capes were considerable. There, he readily snapped up several ships and plundered them of provisions, clothes, money, and munitions. The first to succumb had been *Anne*, Captain Montgomery, from Glasgow, followed by *Turbet* from Barbados, which was plundered and burned. Then came *Endeavour*, Captain Scot, from Bristol, and *Young*, from Leith. From the Capes, Bonnet sailed north to New York, then returned south to the Carolinas, and finally to the Carribbean and to the Bay of Honduras, taking and occasionally destroying honest merchantmen as he went.[14]

Although Bonnet had experienced great success, he was still no sailor and as a consequence was constantly obliged to acquiesce to the demands of his more knowledgeable company, who had little faith in his abilities. Thus, when they fell in with *Queen Anne's Revenge*, the consequences were inevitable. Bonnet's ability to assert leadership and command amid the often chaotic democracy aboard a pirate ship stood in stark contrast to the demagogic authority of Edward Teach. It was with ease that Bonnet's *Revenge* was taken on as a consort by Blackbeard, who convinced her naive commander

that as he had not been used to the fatigues and care of such a post, it would be better for him to decline it and live easy, at his pleasure, in such a ship as his [Teach's], where he should not be obliged to perform duty, but follow his own inclination.[15]

With the consent of his own men, Teach appointed one Richards as commander of *Revenge* and removed the befuddled Bonnet, who realized his error too late, to the *Queen Anne's Revenge*.[16]

Then commenced a piratical rampage, ranging from the Bay of Honduras to the Bahamas, in which approximately sixteen vessels were captured and plundered and several were destroyed.[17] While on their campaign of terror and robbery, the pirates took on two of their prizes as consorts. Blackbeard now commanded a veritable pirate flotilla of four ships, carrying over sixty guns and manned by a complement of almost seven hundred men.[18]

Flushed with success, Edward Teach chose as his next target no less an objective than the total blockade of the busiest, most important port in the southern colonies of English America, the city of Charleston, South Carolina. Near the end of May, having assumed the title of Commodore of the pirate fleet, he came to anchor off Charleston Bar and proceeded to stop all inward- and outward-bound traffic. Within less than a week, no less than eight or nine vessels were captured and plundered, and their crews and passengers taken prisoner, interrogated, and cruelly imprisoned in the hold of the pirate flagship. The city was panic-stricken, for with no man-of-war within several hundred miles, there was neither the capability to defend the port from direct attack nor, as so many of its citizens were being held hostage, the ability to resist any ransom demands. Maritime traffic came to a halt and eight or nine more ships lay at the wharves awaiting the denouement. Incredibly, Teach did not demand gold or money, but proceeded to ransom the lives of his hostages for a simple chest of medical supplies, which, after considerable delay (much to the uneasiness of the hostages), was finally delivered. At last, after looting his captives and his prizes of £1,500 in gold and silver, provisions, and other supplies, he released the prisoners, many of whom had been stripped, and set them ashore. The prizes, too, were freed. Then, "for pure mischief sake and to keep their hands in," the rovers seized two innocent inward-bound vessels and wantonly destroyed their provisions and cargo. Tiring of such amusements, the flotilla of corsairs upped anchor and sailed for North Carolina. Teach now had in his hold the accumulated loot of the richest cruise in his life and had accomplished a feat few professional military commanders could achieve in a lifetime—the reduction to complete submission and humiliation of an entire city without firing a shot or causing one life to be lost.[19]

While blockading Charleston, Teach had learned from the crews of inward- and outward-bound ships the latest intelligence from Europe and America. He discovered, among other things, the startling news that the British government had dispatched Captain Woodes Rogers, an ex-privateersman himself, with a squadron of warships to Nassau to clear out the nest of pirates and to purge the West Indies of the buccaneering scourge. At New Providence, Teach's old mentor Captain Hornigold waited to accept a promised pardon offered to all pirates who surrendered before a specific date.[20]

Teach now began to think of breaking up his own company and of securing the money and choicest portion of the booty for himself and his closest companions and to cheat the rest of their share. As some historians have suggested, it is highly likely that some members of his crew may have been entertaining similar ideas themselves, which would have been a not uncommon spur for the pirate chief to act first.

Around June 1718 Blackbeard nosed *Queen Anne's Revenge* into Topsail (now Beaufort) Inlet, North Carolina, on the pretense of cleaning her hull. As if by accident, he grounded the ship on a sandbar and then bellowed for his trusted lieutenant, Israel Hands, commander of one of the consort sloops, to come to his assistance and warp the flagship off the bar. As planned, and also as if by accident Hands ran his own vessel aground. Both vessels, stuck fast in the Carolina sands, were damaged beyond repair.[21]

Informing his unhappy guest, Captain Bonnet, of his intention to accept the King's pardon, extended to all pirates who surrendered before September 5, Blackbeard, in what seemed a magnanimous gesture, turned over *Revenge* to its former master, suggesting that he too accept the pardon and then secure a privateer commission to sail against the Spanish, with whom fighting had again broken out in Europe. He then boarded the remaining tender sloop, the *Adventure*, with forty hands and left, even as Bonnet scurried off to Bath, North Carolina, to seek a pardon. This being done, Teach proceeded to maroon approximate twenty-five members of his crew "upon a small sandy island, about a league from the Main, where there was neither bird, beast, or herb for their subsistence, and where they must have perished if Major Bonnet had not two days after taken them off."[22] When Bonnet returned to Topsail Inlet, pardon in hand, he found *Revenge* as promised, but stripped of all booty, small arms, and effects of value, and *Adventure* nowhere to be seen.

Though initially intending to go to the island of St. Thomas in the West Indies to secure a Dutch privateering commission, Bonnet learned from a bum boat selling apples and cider to *Revenge*'s crew that Teach lay at Ocracoke Inlet, North Carolina, with barely eighteen or twenty hands. Enraged at the deception against him, he set off in pursuit, but was never to see his cunning nemesis again. After cruising fruitlessly for four days, he steered a course for Virginia.[23]

In July *Revenge* hove to off the Virginia Capes. There she encountered a pink laden with a stock of provisions. Seizing the vessel, the pirates took out of her ten or twelve barrels of pork and four hundredweight of bread. But having accepted the King's pardon, and not wishing to have the taking of the pork and bread "set down to the account of Piracy," they surrendered the pink back to its hapless master and gave him eight or ten casks of rice and an old cable in exchange. Their ability to refrain from their old ways, however, was severely limited by their lack of money and supplies. Two days later they took up pursuit of a 60-ton sloop, overtaking her two leagues off Cape Henry. The *Revenge*'s company was elated to discover the sloop to be laden with a supply of liquor, and handily removed two hogsheads of rum and two of molasses. With no money to pay for the goods, or ability to post security, Bonnet and his crew returned to piracy. Eight men were sent aboard the prize. It is not surprising, considering their disdain for their captain's leadership, that the prize crew took the first opportunity to sail away and was never heard from again.[24]

Bonnet cast off all restraint and "relapsed in good earnest into his old vocation" assuming the alias of Captain Thomas, and commenced pirating with renewed enthusiasm, capturing and plundering every vessel he met. At the Virginia Capes hunting was bountiful, if not particularly lucrative. Off Cape Henry he seized two Glasgow-bound ships from Virginia, one of which had little aboard but a paltry hundredweight of tobacco. The following day he captured a Bermuda-bound sloop from Virginia with twenty barrels of pork and some bacon, for which he gave in return several barrels of rice and a hogshead of molasses. Two of the sloop's crew enlisted aboard *Revenge*. The third day, he took another Virginiaman bound for Glasgow, but the pickings were slim and consisted of only a few casks of combs, pins, and needles, for which he gave a barrel of pork and two barrels of bread.[25]

Stede Bonnet's luck as a pirate was as dismal as his leadership and sailing abilities. Frustrated by the poor catch off the Virginia Capes, he turned north to the Delaware, taking a few ships with an equally poor lading in booty. At the end of July, he departed the Delaware for the Cape Fear River in the Carolinas. There the gentleman pirate was to meet his end. Bonnet was captured in a running battle in the river with the enraged citizens of Charleston. Seven of his men were killed and, after one of the largest mass pirate trials in American history, he and forty-nine others were hung at White Point, Charleston, and their bodies buried in the nearby mudflats.[26]

Edward Teach's day was also fast approaching.

With twenty of his men, Teach sailed into Pamlico Sound bound for Bath, some fifty miles from the sea, to surrender according to the terms of His Majesty's proclamation and to receive certificates to that effect from North Carolina Governor Charles Eden. The arrival in the little town of the blackest pirate on the Atlantic coast must have been as traumatic to the Governor as it was a cause for great excitement to the general populace. Undoubtedly intimidated from the very outset, Eden readily drew up pardons for all of the buccaneers, as he had for Stede Bonnet several days earlier. Blackbeard, with his band of brigands and an armed vessel to back him up, immediately "cultivated a very good understanding" with the Governor, and decided to settle in the town. Establishing his base on an idyllic elevation on the east bank of Bath Creek called Plum Point, directly opposite the Governor's home, the pirate chief quickly became something of a celebrity, courted by planters who relished an association with the famed buccaneer, and began living the life of a wealthy gentleman of leisure.[27]

Having thus comfortably ensconced himself at Bath, Teach proceeded to wed a girl of sixteen, a daughter of a Bath County planter. The ceremony was performed by Governor Eden himself. Unhappily for the young bride, who had unwittingly become the pirate's fourteenth wife (twelve of them were still living, one with child, in London; none of them had benefit of a divorce), her marriage would prove less than pleasant. Blackbeard's appetites were bestial. On one occasion, while his sloop lay in Ocracoke Inlet, he was ashore at a plantation where his wife lived, with whom he had spent the night. To amuse himself, he invited five or six of his brutal companions to come ashore and forced his bride to prostitute herself to them all, one after another, while he watched.[28]

Such was the life of "gentleman" Edward Teach.

Having received immunity, a number of Blackbeard's men quickly became bored and restless. They yearned for a return to the sea. It came as no surprise that some soon slipped away from Bath to resume their former trade. Some struck out for New York and Philadelphia, while others, such as Teach's quartermaster, William Howard, went to Virginia. Those who remained became more and more boisterous. It was obvious from the start to Charles Eden, who lacked every defense against the intimidating Blackbeard and in whose awe he stood, that the pirates had sought a pardon not "from any reformation of manners, but only to wait a more favourable opportunity to play the game again."[29]

Teach played rough, and began to lord it over the town. When his men became rowdy he threatened Bath with fire and sword if any injury were afforded him or his companions. On one occasion, suspecting that a plan was afoot to seize him, he drew up his sloop against the town and went ashore to the Governor's house, well-armed, leaving orders with his men that should he not return in an hour, they were "to batter the house about their ears," even with him in it.[30]

Having thus effectively bullied and intimidated the highest authority in North Carolina, Blackbeard proceeded to settle the status of the sloop he had taken while cruising in *Queen Anne's Revenge*. Though *Adventure* was clearly an English merchantman, a Vice Admiralty Court convened by Eden condemned the prize as "taken from the Spaniard," and relegated clear title to Blackbeard.[31]

Blackbeard the Pirate.

*Major Stede Bonnet,
the "gentleman" pirate.*

The execution of Major Stede Bonnet.

Captain Charles Vane.

*The epic battle between Blackbeard the
Pirate and Lieutenant Robert Maynard at Ocracoke Inlet.*

In late June, bored with the life of Bath and armed with a pardon and clear title to his sloop, Teach again put to sea, ostensibly on a trading voyage to St. Thomas. Instead, he headed for Philadelphia, once a port of convenience to pirates, but discovered Pennsylvania far from his liking. A warrant for his arrest had been issued there by Governor William Keith, and an expedition of two sloops was eventually fitted out for his capture.[32] Teach set a course for the warmer climes of Bermuda. En route he fell in with several English vessels, taking from them provisions, stores, and necessaries.[33]

Managing a crew of cutthroats on the open sea was occasionally a tricky business even for Blackbeard the Pirate, but certainly one at which he was adept. In his journal, which was discovered aboard his ship in November after the Battle of Ocracoke, lay a clue to his management techniques. "Such a day," it read,

> rum all out!—Our company somewhat sober:—A damn'd confusion amongst us!—Rogues a-plotting:—Great talk of separation—so I looked sharp for a prize: Such a day took one, with a great deal of liquor on board, so kept the company hot, damned hot; then all things went well again.[34]

Off Bermuda, about the last of August, *Adventure,* mounting eight guns, fell in with and took two French ships, one laden with sugar and cocoa, and the other light, bound for Martinique. Transferring the crew from the heavily laden vessel to the empty one, Blackbeard released the latter and carried the former back with him to North Carolina. Arriving at Bath, the pirate chief and four of his crew called upon Governor Eden and made out an affidavit stating that they had found the French ship at sea without a soul on board. Eden, in his office as Governor and Admiral of North Carolina, immediately convened a Vice Admiralty Court at Bath which promptly judged the vessel a derelict at sea. Under the system of admiralty law which ruled in such cases, sixty hogsheads of sugar were awarded to Eden, twenty to the Chief Justice and Secretary of the Colony, Tobias Knight (who was also the Collector of Customs and a member of the Vice Admiralty Court), and the remainder to Teach and his crew.[35]

After the booty had been divided, and fearing that some mariner might "discover the roguery," Teach contrived to destroy the evidence. Under the pretense that the ship was leaky and might sink in and stop up the mouth of the inlet or cove where she lay,

> he obtained an order from the Governor to bring her out into the river, and set her on fire, which was accordingly executed, and she was burned to the waters edge, her bottom sunk, and with it, their fears of ever rising in judgement against her.[36]

For the next several months, Blackbeard passed the time in the North Carolina sounds, sometimes lying idle at anchor in various coves, and at others sailing from one inlet to another, trading with sloops that he might occasion to meet, for the plunder he had taken in exchange for stores and provisions ("that is when he happened to be in a giving humour"). At other times he simply took what he wanted, "knowing well they dared not send him a bill for the payment." Occasionally he would venture ashore to visit the planters, where he revelled for days on end, making presents of rum and sugar to his hosts and taking liberties with their wives and daughters that they dared not contest. On occasion he would demand contributions from them, and carried on in a lordly manner. He continued to bully the Governor, who, lacking any military or naval force, had little alternative but to acquiesce.[37]

Teach toyed with brutality almost as an avocation. One night, while drinking in his cabin with his pilot, Israel Hands, and another crewman, he quietly drew out a small pair of pistols, without provocation, and cocked them under the table. Hands was unaware of the move, but the other man, seeing the pistols and knowing of Teach's malicious bent, removed himself to the deck, leaving the pilot and the captain alone. When the pistols were ready, the captain blew out the candle and, crossing his hands, discharged them at his companion. Hands was shot through the knee and crippled for life. When asked why he had done it, Blackbeard damned his inquisitors, saying "that if he did not now and then kill one of them, they would forget who he was."[38]

As time passed, the presence of the evil Blackbeard and his uncouth, brutal crew became a burden upon the entire population of the Carolina coast. Sloops trading up and down the rivers were so frequently pillaged by the pirates that they consulted with the traders and some of the best planters as to what course to take. It was obvious that any application to the Governor of North Carolina would be in vain, though that would have been the proper form of seeking redress. In desperation, they sought assistance from another quarter, a quarter wherein lay the heart of a true pirate fighter—Governor Alexander Spotswood of Virginia.[39]

There was every reason in the world for Alexander Spotswood to be concerned about the activities of Edward Teach and to receive the pleas of help from the North Carolina "Trading People" with sympathy. Between August 1717 and May 1718 the Virginia coast had been relatively devoid of piratical activities, owing as much to the presence of several powerful Royal Navy guardships as to the season

(when pirates traditionally sought warmer climes).[40] The effects of the
King's proclamation had resulted, in fact, in a number of pirates
coming in to surrender, obtain their pardons, and spend their booty
much to the delight of Virginia merchants, whose favor they courted.
Spotswood had sought to control the former pirates to prevent them
from taking "themselves again to their old Trade" by issuing a proclamation on July 10 which directed them to present themselves, immediately upon their arrival in the colony, to a justice of the peace or
militia officer, to turn in their arms, and not to travel or gather in a
company of greater than three persons.[41]

Yet there was an undercurrent of danger which seemed to grow as
more and more pirates came in, some from as far away as New Providence. Worse, by 1718 it was reported that at least a score of pirate
ships were operating between Virginia and South Carolina, some of
them undoubtedly fugitives from the breakup of the pirate enclave on
New Providence by Woodes Rogers.[42] Fortunately, most were held at
arm's length from the Chesapeake by the guardships *Lyme* and *Pearl*. In
September, Blackbeard had encountered one of these "Brethren of the
Coast" at Ocracoke, the notorious Captain Charles Vane, one of the
few who had refused to accept the King's pardon. Blackbeard and
Vane had saluted each other with great guns upon their meeting, and

*The meeting between Blackbeard and Captain Charles Vane at Ocracoke Inlet
helped to stimulate fears of the establishment of a pirate stronghold on the North
American mainland similar to that once erected at New Providence.*

had passed several days together. News of this chance meeting, resulting in the largest conclave of pirates ever held in North America, reached Spotswood soon afterward in a very garbled version which suggested that the combined pirate forces of Blackbeard and Vane were scheming to build a fortress at Ocracoke Inlet and convert Ocracoke Island into a veritable pirate stronghold of the likes of New Providence or the buccaneer enclave on the island of Madagascar.[43]

The news was disconcerting to Spotswood, to say the least, but he could do little without hard evidence against a pirate who had made the entire coast of North Carolina his dominion and the Governor and officers of that colony, such as Tobias Knight, his servants. The pirates had accepted the King's pardon, and to venture into the jurisdiction of a neighboring colonial government to capture them would be viewed as a direct affront to the Crown and a virtual usurpation of Governor Eden's authority over his own colony's affairs.[44] Spotswood desperately needed information—and an excuse. He was to be provided with the former by a tangible, physical link to Blackbeard and his nefarious company, in the person of William Howard, former quartermaster of *Queen Anne's Revenge.*

Howard, a previous resident of Virginia, had returned to the colony with two black boys, slaves, one of whom had been taken from a French ship and the other from an English brigantine, to surrender and obtain the King's pardon.[45] Having achieved that objective, he began to draw considerable attention to himself by continually defying the law and living in a disorderly, raucous manner. Despite the Governor's prohibitions concerning assembly, he and several former members of Blackbeard's crew had frequently gathered together and, it was charged, cajoled sailors from merchant vessels calling in the Chesapeake to form a company, seize a ship, and "go on the account."[46]

Spotwood saw in Howard his opportunity to extract information about Blackbeard, and possibly an excuse for action against the pirate. He directed a justice of the peace to seize Howard and his two slaves. On September 16, 1718, the ex-pirate was arrested, fifty pounds in his possession confiscated, and, on the grounds that he had been insolent and unable to prove he had any lawful business, was hauled aboard the warship *Pearl* as a vagrant seaman. There he was forced to serve as a member of the crew.[47] The charges were spurious at best, and there was even a question as to the jurisdiction of the courts to try him as a pirate. On September 29, however, it was found that he had been a participant in the capture, plunder, and sinking of *Betty* of Virginia off the Capes, as well as the capture of *Robert* of Philadelphia, *Good Intent* of Dublin, and *Concord* of St. Malo.[48]

Howard refused to submit without a fight. He retained one John Holloway, an attorney of the Marshalsea Court of London who had emigrated to the Virginia colony, and a close friend of Governor Eden, for a fee of three ounces of gold dust. Holloway, a member of the local vice admiralty court, and later to become the first Mayor of Williamsburg, was one "of the chief lawyers" of Virginia.[49] He immediately instituted a civil suit in the common law court of Virginia against Captain George Gordon and Lieutenant Robert Maynard of *Pearl*, on which Howard was detained, and the justice who had signed the warrant for his client's arrest, alleging false imprisonment, and seeking damages of £500.[50]

Spotswood retaliated by instituting criminal proceedings against Howard. "This extraordinary behaviour," wrote the Governor to the Council of Trade and Plantations,

> *of a pirate well known to have been very active in plundering divers vessells on this coast but the year before, occasioned a more strict inquiry into his course of life after his departure from hence, and at last it came to be discovered that, tho he and the rest of Tache's crew, pretended to surrender and to claim the benefits of H. M. Proclamation, they had nevertheless been guilty of divers piracys after the fifth of January for which they were not entitled to H. M. pardon. I therefore thought fitt to have him brought to tryal, but found a strong opposition from some of the Council agt. trying him by vertue of the Commission under the great Seal pursuant to the Act of the 11th and 12th of King Wm. tho I produced the King's Instruction directing the tryal; but having at length overcome their scruples, I had this person tryed. . . .*[51]

Howard protested that he had surrendered in good faith to the King's Act of Grace and should therefore be its beneficiary. Spotswood, having thoroughly investigated the ex-pirate's background, was no less determined to see him tried for participating in no fewer than a dozen piracies. Howard was brought from *Pearl* and lodged in the Williamsburg jail to await trial. The indictment against him, in five parts, was extensive. He was specifically accused, among other things, of: joining with Edward Teach and "other Wicked and desolute Persons" in fitting out the sloop *Revenge* to engage in piracy upon the high seas; participating in the capture, plunder, and sinking of *Betty* of Virginia; the seizure and plunder of *Robert, Good Intent, Concord*, a Spanish sloop near Cuba, and a London brigantine.[52]

On October 29 Spotswood met with the Council of State. Though the majority of the members present were of the opinion that Howard be given a jury trial pursuant to an oft cited Statute of Henry VIII, as had been done in the trials of the three pirates from *La Paix* in 1700, the

Governor convinced them that the defendant should be tried without benefit of jury under Statutes 11 and 12 of William III.

Captains Ellis Brand of HMS *Lyme* and George Gordon of the *Pearl* were among the commissioners who were to sit as judges at the General Court to try the case of William Howard. When the day of trial arrived, the two captains were surprised to discover that they were to sit as judges in the company of John Holloway. Incensed, they objected to the attorney's presiding at the trial of a man whose fees had been accepted in the related lawsuit against Gordon and Maynard. The officers notified Spotswood that they would not serve on the court under such conditions and requested Holloway's removal. The Governor, who had little stomach for Holloway (who was one of his critics and a political foe) confessed to the fact that he was not displeased with the opportunity to replace the attorney with an "honester man." He thus sent a civil message to Holloway, requesting that he not preside at the trial of his former client. Holloway, fuming over the affront to his integrity, refused to sit on any vice admiralty cases. The Governor quickly filled the position with John Clayton, the Attorney General of Virginia. [53]

With two naval officers, commanders of guardships whose specific mission was the abortion of piracy in Virginia, and the Governor's handpicked man serving as judges, the outcome of the trial was never in doubt. William Howard was convicted of taking no less than twelve vessels after January 5, long after the utterance of the King's Act of Grace. Remanded to the Williamsburg jail, he would there await his execution—death by hanging.[54] To the combative ex-pirate quartermaster, fate was kind. On the night before his execution, a ship arrived in the James bearing an extension of the King's mercy for all acts of piracy committed before July 23, 1718. William Howard was thus saved from the gibbet.[55]

Although Howard was freed soon afterwards, his arrest, the subsequent investigation, and the trial had served Alexander Spotswood well. Not only did it establish the fact that Edward Teach and his brutal coterie had violated the provisions of their pardon, but "like Dogs to their Vomits they have returned to their old detestable way of living. . . ."[56] Enormously valuable information had been gleaned regarding Blackbeard's strength, his hideouts in the Carolina sounds, his relationship with Governor Eden and Tobias Knight, and, undoubtedly, insight into the very mental workings of the "fiend incarnate" himself. It was information that would soon lead to the defeat and death of Blackbeard the Pirate.

XVII

Cut Them to Pieces

The flag which flew over the little 6-gun sloop that had come to cruise the Virginia Capes was designed to strike fear in the hearts of all who saw it. Black, with a white death's-head in the middle of it, the ensign fluttered defiantly in the offshore breeze. It was the flag of Captain Richard Worley, a buccaneer new to the trade, but one no less vicious than his contemporaries. Worley had become a pirate noviitiate in September 1718 and rose to the high priesthood of buccaneering with amazing rapidity by his wanton acts on the Atlantic seaboard and in the Bahamas.[1]

His cruise off the entrance to the Chesapeake was conducted with impunity and apparent disregard for the Royal Navy warships that were usually within. Taking at least one prize, the ship *Eagle,* bound from London for Virginia with upwards of one hundred men and thirty women aboard, convicts bound for labor in the colonies, his cruise was short, as would be his career. Yet the brief presence at the Capes of Worley, and of others whose acts were equally piratical, served to fuel Alexander Spotswood's zeal to destroy Edward Teach. For now, every pirate act committed off the Virginia shore, and, indeed, every strange sail sighted, was soon being attributed to Blackbeard.[2] Edward Teach's villainous image had outstripped the man himself. And since Charles Eden did not act against him, the Governor of Virginia would.

Spotswood resolved to put an end to the infamous Blackbeard and his evil minions, who were believed to be gathering in North Carolina's waters, for they threatened to engulf the Virginia trade and the very shores of the Chesapeake itself. He would invade North Carolina and conduct a surgical extraction, removing the cancer of piracy before it could grow and spread to the shores of his colony. Employing the greatest secrecy, and fearing that the least breach of intelligence would permit his prey to escape, he began to plan his strategy. Consulting only those persons indispensable to his operation, he forged ahead. Not even the Assembly or Council were informed since certain factions therein possessed "an unaccountable inclination to favour pyrates." The slightest rumor, in fact, could prove disastrous.[3]

Spotswood quietly sent for pilots from North Carolina, familiar with the shoally waters indigenous to that colony. He dispatched spies southward to gather intelligence. Confiding only in Captains Gordon and Brand, he discussed the best way "to extirpate this nest of pyrates." The officers informed the Governor that the employment of either *Lyme* or *Pearl,* both deep-draft vessels, would be impractical owing to the shallow waters and the convoluted channels of the Outer Banks and the sounds and rivers behind them. Though they could provide the manpower necessary to conduct the operation, they refused to pay for the hiring of necessary small craft (preferably sloops) without orders from the Admiralty. And they were certainly not about to pay for the vessels out of their own pockets.[4]

Undeterred, Spotswood hired two sloops and put pilots aboard at his own expense. Gordon and Brand agreed to supply fifty-five men to man the vessels, and a naval officer, Lieutenant Robert Maynard, a seasoned veteran and the oldest navy lieutenant in America, to command them.[5] Captain Brand was given overall command of the expedition and was to travel with an armed force overland to Bath, while Maynard was to approach by water. Gordon would remain in charge of the two guardships in the James.[6]

Aware that Royal Navy sailors were likely to be somewhat reluctant to risk their lives against the likes of a pirate such as Blackbeard (who had fought a mighty Royal Navy frigate to a standstill), and a few of whom might even consider going over to him, unless there were an incentive not to do so, the Governor promised a bonus from the Virginia Assembly over and above the reward they would receive under the King's proclamation.[7]

Spotswood now revealed his intentions and stimulated assertive action by the government. On November 13 he and the Council urged the House of Burgesses to post rewards for the capture of the pirates. Referring to intelligence gleaned at the Howard trial, he noted that there was advice that the pirates "threaten to revenge on the Shipping of this Country the taking up of the above mentioned Quarter Master." It was, stated the Governor and Council, absolutely imperative that the "Knott of Robbers" be speedily and effectively broken up.[8]

On November 24, as a consequence of these efforts, an "Act to Encourage the Apprehending and Destroying of Pirates" was passed and signed by the Governor and duly enrolled. By this act, it was directed that for one year from the date of November 14, 1718,

all and every person or persons . . . [who] shall take any Pirate or Pirates, on the sea or land, or in case of resistance, shall kill any such Pirate or Pirates, between the degree of thirty four and thirty nine Northern latitude, and within one hundred leagues of the Continent of Virginia, or within the Province of Virginia, or North Carolina, upon the conviction or making due proof of the killing of all, and every such Pirate, and Pirates, before the Governor and Council, shall be entitled to have, and receive out of the public money . . . the several rewards . . . [9]

For death or capture of Edward Teach, a reward of £100 was offered; for the captains of any of his vessels, £40; for every lieutenant, quartermaster, boatswain, or carpenter, £20; for every inferior officer, £15; and for every private or common seaman, £10.[10] On the day the statute was enacted, Alexander Spotswood issued a proclamation announcing the reward and publicly revealing for the first time his intentions to capture or kill Blackbeard. Such an announcement could now be made openly, for the invasion of North Carolina had already begun. Indeed, unknown to all, a climactic battle with the pirates at Ocracoke Inlet had already been fought two days before the passage of the act.

At 3:00 P.M. on November 17, four days after Spotswood urged the House to authorize a bounty for the capture of Blackbeard, Lieutenant Maynard set sail from Kecoughtan with two small, shallow-draft sloops, *Jane,* which he commanded, and *Ranger,* commanded by Midshipman Baker of *Lyme.*Each vessel carried thirty-two men from *Lyme* and *Pearl,* nine more than volunteered by Captains Brand and Gordon. Though neither vessel carried cannon, each was well-equipped with small arms and accoutrements.[11]

The same day, Brand set out overland for Bath with a force of men, where he hoped to arrest Teach should he be found ashore. By November 21 he had marched to within fifty miles of the town, and the following day, assisted by two North Carolina officers, Colonels Edward Moseley and Maurice Moore, crossed Pamlico Sound. By 10:00 P.M., November 23, Brand's invasion force had come to within three miles of Bath. The Royal Navy officer promptly halted and directed Colonel Moore to slip into town to see if Teach was there. Soon after, Moore reported back that the pirate was not there but was momentarily expected, whereupon Brand marched up to Governor Eden's house and informed the startled chief executive that he was in search of the villainous Blackbeard. Apparently, even the Governor was unaware of his whereabouts, or refused to relate any pertinent intelligence, for Brand failed to uncover any information relative to either Teach or Maynard. Resolving to find out where one or both were, he dispatched two canoes to Pamlico Sound the following day, November 24, to gather intelligence. They returned with stunning news. Maynard had already engaged Blackbeard in deadly battle at Ocracoke Inlet on November 22.[12]

Lieutenant Robert Maynard had pressed southward with great caution, stopping and questioning vessels as he proceeded. On the afternoon of November 20 he had entered the narrows of the Roanoke and had spoken with a sloop, the master of which reported Blackbeard's *Adventure* aground on Brant's Shoals and another sloop attempting to haul her off. Proceeding to the shoals, Maynard found nothing. As he continued to probe, he was careful to insure the utmost secrecy by "stopping all boats and vessels he met in the river from going up" and preventing word of his presence from reaching Teach.[13]

On the morning of November 21 Maynard hove off Ocracoke Inlet. In the forenoon he began to work over the bar. It was then that the oldest Royal Navy lieutenant in America discovered the most infamous pirate of all time anchored snugly within a sheltered cove in the inlet. Edward Teach welcomed his guests with a round of cannonfire. Maynard's efforts at surprise had all been for naught.[14]

The question as to whether or not Blackbeard had been warned of the Virginia expedition by North Carolina Secretary of State Tobias Knight has been debated for more than two centuries. On November 17 Knight had dispatched a letter from Bath with several of Blackbeard's crew urging him "to make the best of your way up as soon as possible . . . I have something more to say to you than at present I can write," and told him to question the bearer for the important details.[15] Some, including Daniel Defoe, have suggested that Knight was intimating that the Governor of Virginia was up to something and for Blackbeard to be on his guard.[16] The pirate had, however, already heard several reports of expeditions against him, all of which had proven unfounded, and thus gave little credence to Knight's alleged warnings. Yet he was apparently ready to receive Maynard, for as the King's men moved to cross the bar, Teach did not stir from his anchorage but "kept firing great gunns at our sloops who anch[ore]d by him & they kept firing at her."[17]

Maynard found the inlet shoally and the channel intricate, and as the day progressed into twilight, he found it too dangerous to attempt getting into the cove (now known as Teach's Hole) where the pirate lay, and was thus forced to come to anchor. With the evening, the firing stopped and both sides, sheltered by the dark of night, prepared for the battle that awaited the dawn. Blackbeard had little fear of the life-and-death contest that lay ahead, and sat up the entire night drinking with some of his men and the master of a merchantman anchored nearby "who 'twas thought had more business with Teach than he should have had." When one of his men asked him, in case anything should happen to him in the coming fight, whether his wife knew where he had buried his money, the pirate blustered in characteristic fashion that "nobody but himself and the Devil knew where it was, and the longest liver should take all."[18]

With the early dawn of Friday, November 22, *Jane* and *Ranger* weighed anchor and, at about 9:00 o'clock, began to pick their way through the shoals behind a small boat sent out ahead to take soundings, for they required at least a fathom or more of water to maneuver if they were to close with Teach.[19] There was little wind and the weather was fair.[20] It was indeed a fit day for a fight. As the small boats cautiously closed to within range of the anchored pirate, a shot from *Adventure*, which mounted eight guns and was now manned by approximately twenty-five seamen, sent them scurrying back to the protection of their sloops.[21] Maynard, aboard *Jane*, the larger of the two Virginia sloops, now hoisted the King's colors and ordered the smaller *Ranger* to bear directly down on the pirate "with the best way his sails and oars could make." His own sloop would follow in *Ranger*'s path. Blackbeard, eager for battle, cut his cable and endeavored to make a running fight of it by keeping a continual fire on his enemies with his heavy cannon. Not having artillery, Maynard was obliged to close to within several hundred yards to return the fire with his small arms.[22]

As the three ships maneuvered, *Adventure* ran aground. *Jane*, drawing even more water than the pirate, however, could not come near and anchored within a half-gunshot from the enemy. In order to lighten his vessel that he might reach the pirate and board, Maynard ordered all ballast cast over the side and all water casks aboard staved in. He then directed *Ranger* to block the channel to prevent *Adventure*'s escape, and then weighed his own vessel and stood directly in for the pirate across the shoals.

"Damn you for villains! Who are you? And from whence come you?" bellowed Blackbeard.

"You may see by our colors," replied Maynard, "we are no pirates!"

"Send your boat on board that I might see who you are!"

"I cannot spare my boat," retorted *Jane*'s commander, "but I will come aboard of you as soon as I can, with my sloop."

With that, Blackbeard took a glass of liquor, and, toasting his adversary, drank it down. "Damnation seize my soul," he roared, "if I give you quarter or take any from you!"

Maynard ended the conversation with the reply that he expected no quarter nor would he give any.[23]

As *Adventure* began to float, Blackbeard ran his evil black ensign with death's-head up, but found his way to the channel blocked by Midshipman Baker's sloop. Obliged to swim across the shoals and up the channel under oars, Maynard's small vessel, barely a foot high at the waist, offered little in the way of protection for his crew. As they approached the pirate, that vulnerability was to prove disastrous. Blackbeard was well aware of his attacker's weakness and swung *Adventure*, which now lay directly between the two King's ships, around and delivered a blistering pair of broadsides from both port and starboard guns, charged with all manner of small shot. The results were devastating. Aboard *Ranger* nine men were killed and wounded. Midshipman Baker, as well as his second and third in command and several others, died instantly. Aboard *Jane*, which had been approaching across the shoals from the opposite direction, twenty men fell dead and injured. Command of *Ranger* evolved to Thomas Tucker, master's mate, but with his ship's foremast and jib shot away, and his vessel beginning to drift helplessly, there was little he could do but keep up a desultory fire from a distance and try to effect repairs.[24]

Maynard, finding his own vessel still had way, yet fearing that another broadside might conclude the fight, ordered his own crew below decks but gallantly remained for some time topside along with the helmsman, "whom he directed to lie down snug." In the meantime, he ordered the men in the hold to ready their swords and pistols and come up at his command. Two ladders were placed in the hatchways to facilitate an expeditious surge to the deck. He then went to his cabin, ordering his pilot, William Butler, to inform him of anything that happened. He would not have to wait long.[25]

Blackbeard watched as Maynard's sloop pressed relentlessly forward. As *Jane* closed, the pirates began to throw a particularly deadly type of grenade, devised by Blackbeard himself, aboard the oncoming vessel. These were square case gin bottles filled with small shot, slugs, and pieces of lead or iron, with a quick match at one end. The consequence of the blast was usually death, destruction, smoke, and pandemonium.[26]

Through the heavy smoke caused by the grenade explosions aboard *Jane*, Teach could make out only a few men on her deck, unaware that

Maynard had hidden most of his company below. Setting a course for the King's ship, Blackbeard boldly rallied his crew for the final push to victory.

"They were all knocked on the head except three or four," he shouted. "Let's jump on board and cut them to pieces." Then, hidden by the smoke of a grenade or two, *Adventure* bumped against *Jane,* grappling irons were tossed aboard, and the pirates, with Teach in the lead, with a rope in hand to bind the two vessels together, prepared to board the sloop by the bow. Followed by ten to fourteen of his men, screaming and yelling, Teach climbed aboard. At that moment, Butler passed the word to Maynard, and the lieutenant signaled his men to attack. Pouring out of the hold, they assaulted the startled pirates "with as much bravery as ever was done upon such an occasion." Then, suddenly, as the smoke cleared, Blackbeard and Maynard were face to face. At point-blank range they fired their pistols almost simultaneously at each other. Blackbeard's shot missed. The lieutenant's ball struck squarely home, but the massive pirate barely winced. Both men drew their cutlasses and engaged in a brutal hand-to-hand fight, until a mighty blow from the pirate snapped the lieutenant's sword in half near the hilt. Instantly, Maynard dropped back to cock his pistol, and in the same moment the pirate lunged forward for the kill with his raised cutlass. In a heartbeat, as Blackbeard's weapon descended, one of the King's men stepped up from behind and "gave him a terrific wound on the neck and throat." The blow caused the downward force of Blackbeard's own swing to swerve. Maynard escaped an otherwise fatal blow with but a small cut on his fingers.[27]

The contest upon the bloody deck, already littered with a score of dead and wounded from the fatal broadside, was Homeric, with Maynard's dozen against Blackbeard and his minions. The focal point of the attack of the King's men, however, was the pirate chief himself. Time after time he was struck, spewing blood and roaring imprecations as he "stood his ground and fought with great fury." One mighty arm swung his cutlass like a deadly windmill, while the other fired shot after shot from the brace of pistols in his bandolier. The sea about the sloop became literally "tinctured with blood." Then, suddenly, while cocking his pistol, Blackbeard the Pirate fell down dead, having suffered twenty-five cut wounds and five pistol shots.[28]

"Here," remarked one contemporary, "was an end of that courageous brute, who might have passed in the world for a hero had he been employed in a good cause."[39]

The battle continued but a short time longer, for those of Blackbeard's crew who remained alive, seeing their leader and five or six of their comrades dead, began to jump overboard, calling for quarter and mercy. Some were "destroyed" in the water, some drowned, but most were fished out and taken prisoner. By the end of the action, which lasted no longer than ten minutes, *Ranger* had returned to the battle and come up to attack the pirates remaining aboard *Adventure*. After boarding the notorious sloop, one of *Ranger*'s crew was himself mistaken for a buccaneer and shot dead by another of the King's men. His death would be the last in the Battle of Ocracoke Inlet.[30]

It had been fortunate for Maynard that the hand-to-hand engagement had occurred aboard *Jane*, for Teach had prepared a reception for the lieutenant in the event that *Adventure* should be taken. He had taken the precaution to post "a resolute fellow, a negro whom he had bred up," with a lighted match in the powder room with direction to blow the ship up when ordered, or as soon as the King's men came aboard. When the black discovered how the battle fared, however, it was only through the persuasion of two prisoners in the hold that he refrained from carrying out his deadly assignment.[31]

The Battle of Ocracoke Inlet, though only minutes in duration, was, for its size and the number of men involved, one of the bloodiest on record. Though accounts differ, casualties were extremely high on both sides. As many as twenty-nine of Maynard's sixty-four men were killed and wounded, while Blackbeard and eight of the fourteen crewmen that had boarded *Jane* were killed and nearly as many more wounded. One pirate prisoner, who had signed on with Blackbeard only the night before the battle, Samuel Odell, had received no fewer than seventy wounds during the engagement but survived to stand trial.[32]

Hardly had the smoke from the battle cleared, and with the moans of the wounded and dying still heavy in the air, than those who remained jubilantly severed Blackbeard's head from his body and hung it from the bowsprit of *Jane*.[33]

Maynard sailed first to Bath to secure medical attention for the wounded. En route he rummaged through Blackbeard's cabin and discovered evidence of correspondence among the buccaneer, Governor Eden, and Secretary Knight, and several New York traders. It was incriminating data that would eventually generate unending controversy between Virginia and North Carolina, but Maynard was more interested in completing his job. Upon arriving at Bath, he promptly arrested several members of Blackbeard's crew, including the crippled Israel Hands. He seized from Governor Eden's storehouse the sixty hogsheads of sugar, and from Secretary Knight's the twenty hogsheads of sugar acquired from the condemnation of Blackbeard's French

prize. Following the recovery of most of his wounded men, he sailed
back to Virginia with fifteen prisoners in Blackbeard's sloop, a quantity
of captured goods, and the pirate's head firmly affixed to the bowsprit.[34]

On January 1, 1719, *Ranger* arrived in Hampton Roads and her
master informed Gordon "of the destruction of . . . Thatch & most of
his men and the seizure of their Effects." The following day 5,540
pounds of cocoa, 2 bags of cotton, and a quantity of sugar were taken
from her hold.[35] On January 3 Maynard arrived in *Adventure*, bringing
with him "Thach's head, hanging under his bowsprit in order to
present it to the Colony of Virginia." As he passed HMS *Pearl*, lying at
anchor, he saluted her with 9 guns and was returned a like number by
Captain Gordon. A 9-gun salute was a most singular honor extended to
the victor of Ocracoke, for Gordon had always made a point, as a rule,
of returning fewer guns than he received. Soon after *Adventure*'s arrival, sloop *Jane* also came in, and longboats began to unload the prize
goods. Some 732 pounds of bread were taken from her, and 4,487
pounds of cocoa were unloaded from *Adventure*.[36] In all, the goods
seized aboard the pirate ship, and at Bath, totalled 25 hogsheads of
sugar, 11 tierces and 145 bags of cocoa, a barrel of indigo, and a bale of
cotton.[37]

The fifteen prisoners were lodged in the Williamsburg public jail,
where a Court of Admiralty was held in March. The prisoners were
indicted and tried for piracy. Thirteen of Blackbeard's crew were
found guilty and sentenced to die. Among those who were spared was
Israel Hands, who was in fact convicted, but who managed to escape
the gallows. He would eventually die begging in the streets of London.
Samuel Odell, who was able to prove he had been taken out of a trading
sloop the night before the battle and forced to become a member of
Blackbeard's crew, was acquitted. The thirteen condemned prisoners
were hung from gibbets or trees on Capitol Landing Road in Williamsburg.[38] Apparently not all of the pirates were tried in the same court, as
the log of HMS *Pearl* notes that on January 28, at 9:30 A.M., two
condemned pirates who had been held aboard ship were sent ashore to
Hampton and hung.[39]

Blackbeard's head, it was said, was eventually transferred from the
bowsprit of *Adventure* and raised upon a pole at the mouth of Hampton
River, near Kecoughtan, where it would dangle for many years as a
warning to mariners. The skull was later fashioned into an enormous
drinking cup that is said to be yet in existence—a most fitting end to the
blackest of buccaneers. He would, no doubt, have liked it that way.[40]

XVIII

Golden Luggage

The bloody defeat of Edward Teach brought to the tidewater a temporary respite from piracy. Yet the piratical plague was still a very real menace to the Chesapeake region and to the entire Atlantic seaboard. Less than a year after the Battle of Ocracoke, more than seventy pirate crews were still actively plundering shipping off the North American coast, and Spanish privateers were constantly playing havoc with English colonial trade. "These Rogues," observed the venerable Virginia patrician William Byrd II in a masterpiece of understatement, "swarm in this part of the World."[1]

Somehow, there had been an evolution in the attitudes and objectives of the loosely knit pirate community. One modern historian noted that the greatest change in freebooting was that the buccaneers seemed to have declared open war on all honest men, and that more often than not they were "bent on revenge for those colleagues who had fallen victims to the forces of law and order."[2] Many more, especially those still flush with the ill-gotten fruits of their successes, occasionally seemed eager to take their loot and retire before their necks stretched a noose on some colonial backwater. Many who did retire lacked the ability or good sense to mask their free-spending ways and were easily spotted by the authorities ashore. For Governor Alexander Spotswood, these changes in style and objective fueled an obsession to continue the crusade to bring anyone even remotely tainted by piracy to justice and the gibbet. In the early months of 1720, Virginia would once again have the opportunity to mete out punishment to another raucous band of sea rovers. These brigands were one-time members of a company commanded by one of the most notoriously successful buccaneers of the era, Captain Bartholomew Roberts. This time justice would be served through the resourceful self-control of a most unlikely individual, a peace-loving, gun-hating Quaker sea captain named Luke Knott.

Captain Bartholomew Roberts—occasionally referred to as the Crimson Pirate for his fanciful attire, but more frequently as Black Bart— was one of history's most colorful and audacious buccaneers. Capturing literally scores of ships during his brief career, he was certainly one of the most accomplished at his trade, and definitely one of the most feared. Roberts, like many freebooters, began as an honest seaman. In 1719, while serving as second officer aboard the London slave trader *Princess,* he had the misfortune to be captured by the notorious rover Captain Howell Davis. With the rest of *Princess*'s crew, Roberts was pressed into service aboard Davis' ship, *Royal Rover,* and after the pirate chieftain's death in battle, found himself elected to command in Davis's place.[3]

Roberts's cruise aboard *Rover* became the fabric of pirate legend when he sailed alone into Bahia de Todos Santos, Brazil, and into the midst of a great Portuguese armada of forty-two ships. The fleet was guarded by two 72-gun men-of-war, which did not deter the pirates in the least. Carefully, they singled out the richest vessel, attacked her, and compelled her to surrender. A fabulous treasure of 40,000 moidores valued at more than £50,000 sterling, beautiful jewels, chains, trinkets, sugar, tobacco, and hides fell into the buccaneers' laps with relative ease. Among the elegant trinkets—valuables meant for Portuguese nobility—was discovered a beautiful cross set with diamonds which had been designed for no less a figure than the King of Portugal, John V.[4]

With his prize and booty in hand, Bartholomew Roberts managed to escape to Devil's Island, "a sleazy Spanish colony off Guiana" in the Surinam River. Here, the pirates secured their welcome from the governor and his subordinates by presenting them with the diamond-studded cross as a bribe. For weeks the sea rovers lingered at Devil's Island, pouring their booty into gambling, rum, women, and self-indulgences of every kind.[5] Roberts, unlike his comrades, was a tea drinker, and while permitting his men to debauch themselves, kept a wary eye open for any opportunity that might present itself.[6] When a Rhode Island sloop commanded by a good-natured chap named Cane fell into his hands, Roberts learned of the imminent approach of a rich, provision-laden ship from Rhode Island, and set off with a small, sober company of forty men to take her. He unfortunately made the mistake of leaving behind him *Rover* and the Portuguese prize under the

Captain Bartholomew Roberts, the Crimson Pirate.

command of his lieutenant, one Walter Kennedy, "a bold daring fellow but very wicked and profligate."[7] When Bartholomew Roberts and his forty thieves returned to Devil's Island, after a most miserable, nearly fatal pursuit which ended in their being empty-handed, they discovered that Kennedy and the rest of the company had vanished. And with them had gone *Rover*, the rich Portuguese prize, and all of the treasure.[8]

"This," wrote one chronicler of the adventure a few years afterwards, "was mortification with a vengeance, and you may imagine they did not depart without some hard speeches from those that were left and had suffered by their treachery."[9]

Walter Kennedy seemed to the mutineers a logical choice for the captaincy of *Rover*, for he was a brave man, proven in combat against the Portuguese at Todos Santos and elsewhere. Whatever other vices or virtures he may have had counted little, for he was readily elected commander of the ship on the basis of his courage at Todos Santos. Popularity and courage in battle, however, did not necessarily make a leader, for, try as he might, Kennedy could not bring his company to a resolution as to their next objectives. Some were for continuing their nefarious employment, but the majority, undoubtedly bolstered by the great treasure in their possession, were for dividing their booty and getting home the best way they could. It was finally agreed that they would break up, every man shifting for himself.[10]

Their first problem was how to dispose of the great Portuguese prize, still partially laden with tobacco, sugar, and hides. This they graciously turned over to Captain Cane, master of the sloop taken in the Surinam River, along with several Negroes and his own crew.[11] The reasoning behind this unusual move may seem strange in the twentieth century, but it was not out of the ordinary for pirates, men of the sea themselves, to follow such a course of action. Cane had proved to be a somewhat engaging toady to his buccaneer captors, and had become the object of their affection and friendship. And as it was "a common practice among the Pirats to make presents to Masters of Ships and Seamen of such Commoditys they have less use of, in lieu of what they take away," the decision to turn the prize ship over to Cane was not unusual.[12] The elated New Englander soon made his way to Antigua, where he found a profitable market for the commodities in his new ship.[13]

Captain Kennedy then set *Rover* on a course for the West Indies and the island of Barbados. The voyage was not uneventful; several English vessels crossing *Rover*'s path were easily snapped up, stripped of provisions, and released.[14] One of these unfortunates, the New York snow

Sea Nimph, Captain Bloodsworth commanding, bound from New York for Surinam, was plundered of whatever goods the pirates "had Occasion for" and taken into temporary service as a consort to *Rover.*[15]

Kennedy's meanderings about the West Indies had drawn attention in the colonial newspapers, one of which noted "the Pirates are very rife about that Island [of Barbados] and other parts of the West Indies, and do a great deal of Damage, taking several Vessels . . . some they plunder, and others they carry away."[16]

At the beginning of January 1720, some two hundred leagues from the Virginia Capes and near Barbados, Kennedy fell in with "a very peaceable ship belonging to Virginia" called *West River Merchant.* The 150-ton merchantman was manned by a crew of twelve and bound from London to Virginia, apparently via the West Indies. She was commanded by an unlikely sort, a devout, peace-loving Quaker named Luke Knott. Unlike most merchant captains sailing troubled seas, Knott strictly forbade any type of arms aboard his ship—no pistols, swords, or cutlasses. Now, faced with the threat of assault by a heavily armed and heavily manned pirate (32 guns, 27 swivels, and a company of 148 men)[17] and her consort, Captain Knott had little alternative but to surrender.

After boarding *West River Merchant,* the pirates began rummaging about the hold, but took little more than a few provisions and some merchandise. Captain Knott's passive cooperation, however, impressed Kennedy and his men. Several among their number saw an opportunity finally to take their share of the booty and, using the Quaker's ship, slip unnoticed back into society. The pirates offered Knott compensation for the provisions and merchandise which they had removed. Ten chests of sugar, ten rolls of Brazilian tobacco, and thirty moidores and some gold dust, in all valued at £250, were presented to the captain as recompense. Gifts of a similar nature were also given to each member of his crew. In return, Kennedy (who presented himself under the assumed name of "Callifax," presumably to foil attempts to link him to recent events) "Obliged Knot to take 8 of his Men on board his Ship, and made him give an Obligation under his Hand, that he Ship'd them as Passengers from London, to Virginia." Knott wisely acquiesced without objection.[18] He had, in fact, little choice in the matter.

The eight pirates—William Williams, Tobias Butler, William Farrow, Daniel Degat, William Pomeroy, Thomas Hall, William Lake, and Peter Minshal[19]—took with them as part of their booty three Negro men and a boy, a sizable quantity of gold dust, and a large sum of money.[20] Kennedy also provided his departing comrades with a boat, which Knott was directed to make available to them "when they required it, to help go from his Ship." In addition, two Portuguese, taken prisoner at Todos Santos, and two Jews were placed on board to be set ashore in Virginia.[21]

West River Merchant was then released and made all sail for the Chesapeake. The erstwhile pirates aboard "lived a jovial life all the while they were upon their voyage," but for the pacific Captain Knott the remainder of the trip was sheer terror. The only possibility of overcoming his unwelcome passengers was to surprise them when they were either asleep or drunk, for when they were awake they wore their weapons constantly. Knott was aware that the pirates could murder the crew and seize the ship if they so desired. Yet he would probably not have accepted the opportunity to expel them by force had he the means to do so. He was a man of honest Quaker principle whose iron will, cunning, and dedication to his men and God would see him through until justice might be done.[22]

About February 7 *West River Merchant* arrived within the Virginia Capes, but before she reached Hampton Roads, the wind turned westerly and obliged her to come to anchor. Taking advantage of the temporary respite, four of the pirates went to the Quaker captain and required leave to hoist their boat out, a demand with which Knott instantly complied. The boat shoved off with the four pirates merrily pulling at the oars, bound for Maryland. Muscle did not match zeal, however, and when a sudden, frosty Bay storm struck, they were forced into Back River, "an obscure place at the mouth of York River."[23]

"As soon as they came ashore," it was later reported,

their first care was to find a Tavern, where they might ease themselves of their Golden Luggage. They soon found a place to their mind, where for some time they lived very profusely treating all that came into their Company, and there being in the House English Women Servants, who had the good fortune by some Hidden Charms, to appear pleasing to these Picaroons, they set them [the women] Free, giving their Master 30 Pounds, the price he demanded for their time.[24]

The pirates spent liberally at the public houses, and with their new "wives" in tow, indulged in all forms of merriment. They had, in so doing, committed the unpardonable sin of living *too* extravagantly. The local authorities soon discerned that they were not simple immigrants from London, but were in all likelihood a party of free-spending buccaneers. Thus, within a few days of their arrival, they found themselves prisoners in the county jail, incarcerated on suspicion of piracy.[25]

Not far away, their four companions, intent on traveling overland to the pirate haven of North Carolina, remained with Captain Knott until he sailed into the James River. They were landed, along with the two Portuguese, at Hampton. These pirates also launched into riotous debauch.[26] Soon afterward, Captain Knott went ashore and hastened to call upon Governor Spotswood to tell him "what kind of passengers he had been obliged to bring with him." For the revelling pirates, their delay for the purpose of making merry proved fatal. The Governor reacted instantly by directing the immediate apprehension of the suspected villains. His orders were carried out with great zeal, and the eight retired sea rovers were soon behind the same bars.[27]

The trial for piracy was held in the Virginia Vice Admiralty Court in late 1720. The government's principal witnesses were the two Portuguese. Unable to speak English, and having been set ashore at Hampton with the pirates, they had been obliged to fend for themselves without resources in a foreign land. Fortunately, they encountered the kindly master of an English vessel who spoke Portuguese. To him they first related their sad odyssey, from the time they were taken prisoners at Todos Santos in the Vice Admiral of the Brazilian Fleet, to their setting foot in Hampton. The eight men in the local jail, they explained, were members of the crew that had captured them. The master and the two Portuguese immediately called upon Governor Spotswood. Under oath, the two foreigners reiterated their tale of woe to the Governor, with the master serving as an interpreter. It was upon this information that the pirates were brought to trial for the taking and plundering of the Portuguese Vice Admiral.[28]

As the trial progressed, the eight defendants readily admitted that they had been aboard *Royal Rover* as alleged. And, as expected, they also claimed that they had been forced into pirate service, being themselves the unfortunate victims of buccaneers on the Guinea coast. With the master acting as sworn interpreter again, the two Portuguese were asked whether the prisoners appeared to act "by constraint" with the pirates. The replied "that they appeared as forward in Action, and were busy in Plundering as any of the Crew, and that one of the Prisoners at the Bar, took in a Particular Gold Ring from the Wife of one of the two Portuguese."[29]

The court was informed that one of the prisoners understood the Portuguese language, whereupon he was asked if he had any objections against the interpretation. He had none, for "the Master Interpreted very Faithfully between them."[30]

Additional damning evidence was presented by the Jew, Aaron Levy, and a sailor named Job Newman, as well as by Captain Knott, five of his crew, and a certain Hannah Miles (possibly one if the innkeepers visited by the pirates).[31] Some testimony in the course of the trial was not particularly civil. Six of the defendants appeared to Governor Spotswood to be "the most profligate Wretches I ever heard of, for, as they behaved themselves w'th the greatest impudence at the Bar, they were no sooner taken from it than they vented their imprecations on their judges and all concerned in their prosecution, and vow'd if they were again at liberty they would spare none alive that should fall into their hands."[32]

The verdict was a foregone conclusion; the eight defendants were found guilty of piracy. Four of their number, who had served as officers of the pirate company and who had acted in the most outrageous manner during the trial, "for the greater Terrour" of others who might consider entering the employment of buccaneering, were sentenced to be executed and their bodies to be hung in chains, two at Tindall's Point on the York River and two at Urbanna, on the Rappahannock.[33] Two more were to be executed a week later, presumably at Williamsburg, but, while the bodies of their mates would hang until they rotted, the latter two would be granted the "liberty to be buried."[34]

As for William Lake and Peter Minshal, both of whom "shew'd a just Abhorrence of their past Crimes" and behaved during the trial with civility, the Governor's Council recommended a pardon. With the concurrence of Spotswood, the two defendants were sentenced to serve onboard one of the guardships on the Virginia Station, presumably *Pearl* or *Lyme*.[35]

The six condemned prisoners died as they lived, showing no signs of remorse or repentance. When they came to their respective places of execution, one of them called for a bottle of wine, and, taking a glass of it, drank a final toast, to which the rest pledged: "Damnation to the Governor and Confusion to the Colony."[37]

Though the executions and impressments put an end to the eight pirates, the government still had several tangled residual issues with which to contend. The pirates had brought ashore with them a small fortune in gold specie and dust.[37] But "as they were some days travelling in the Country before they were taken, they had found means to lodge part of their Effects in ye hands of some of the Inhabitants," planters with whom they had become acquainted and friendly.[38] On February 22, Spotswood, with the approval of the Council, was obliged to issue a proclamation notifying the citizenry of Virginia that anyone who knowingly concealed the buccaneers' booty and refused to surrender it voluntarily would be considered an accessory to piracy.[39] Few of the planters acquiesced, and it was not until "a great deal of Search and trouble" had been undertaken that some of the loot, between £1,500 and £2,000 sterling in gold and silver, was recovered by the government. Yet four months later, the Governor was still unable to produce a complete tally of the treasure, or even of the state's expenses incurred in the prosecution of the pirates (which was to be charged against the booty).[40]

Governor Spotswood's problems were not confined to locating and recovering the booty. He had to keep tabs on what he had already secured. Henry Irwin, a customs collector at Hampton, was granted power of attorney to receive the "considerable sums of money being the effects of William Farrow, William Williams, Toby Butler, Daniel I'gotta [Degat] and Thomas Hall, pirates." Spotswood, given the likelihood of accusations of misdeeds should anything go amiss with the treasure, noted that it was his practice in all cases such as this to deliver the recovered effects to the court, "to have them decreed into my hands for his Maj'ty's use," as well as to produce a complete accounting of all particulars. Somehow, Irwin, a man whose integrity had been challenged on several previous occasions, failed to hold onto the loot. On February 12, 1721, being held personally accountable to the Crown for the sum of £450 "current money of Virginia," Irwin was obliged to convey a deed for a half-acre lot in Hampton and other property to the government as compensation.[41] It would appear from these proceedings that not all of the pirates in Virginia were of the seagoing sort.

In contrast to the Virginia planters and the government agent, Luke Knott drew only praise from the Governor. The Quaker's prudent conduct had probably saved not only his ship, but the lives of his crew and the witnesses whose testimony would eventually convict the pirates as well. Had it not, in fact, been "for the good management of the Captain," wrote Spotswood in a fulsome letter, "it is not supposed the Pyrats would have left any of them to Witness against them." Though Knott had been plundered of some of his stores, liquor, and English money, as well as a quantity of merchandise paid for out of his own pocket, for which the pirates had given him sugar, tobacco, gold dust, and moidores "as a Recompence," he was still a man of principle. He saw the goods and money given to him (far more valuable than the items taken from him) as stolen property, tainted by evil men. Thus, he not only willingly turned over to Governor Spotswood every item presented to him by the pirates, but he obliged his men to do the same. Spotswood actively solicited from the King reparations for Knott out of the pirate booty turned over by the captain to the government.[42] It was the least he could do for a man of such forthright courage and honesty.

In March a second ship entered the Virginia Capes and soon reported an adventure similar in many respects to Knott's travails. This vessel, a Bristol slaver named *Callabar,* was commanded by one Thomas Kennedy,[43] and had been taken by the pirate Edward England while sailing off the Guinea coast of Africa during the spring of 1719. The pirates, who sailed aboard the ship *Royal James,* had stripped *Callabar* of her cargo of beads, copper bars, assorted trade goods, guns, and powder. But the most serious loss had been the 160 slaves onboard.[44] The freebooters confiscated them, treating several of the misfortunates so poorly that they died. As for Kennedy and company, the treatment was equally harsh. For nine months they were imprisoned, brutalized, beaten, and abused—and they were among the more fortunate victims of England's crew. Though England himself was usually averse to the ill usage of prisoners, the pirate community was a democracy and the captain was usually overruled in such matters by his often barbarous crew. Thus, by proxy, Edward England had quickly become a pirate renowned for his cruelty.

One barbarity stood out among all others. At Sierra Leone, England captured a Bristol snow called *Cadogan.* As soon as the merchantman's master, one Captain Skinner, had come aboard the pirate, he found himself face-to-face with a former crewman, with whom he had once had a long-standing feud. Overjoyed at finding his antagonist in his grasp, the crewman, now a boatswain on the pirate ship, directed that Skinner be strapped to the windlass. The buccaneers then pelted the helpless captain mercilessly with broken bottles, cutting him terribly. Then, as he bled, "they whipped him about the deck till they were weary, being deaf to all prayers and entreaties." Finally, because he had been a good master to his men, "they said he should have an easy death, and so shot him in the head."[45] An honest first mate of *Cadogan,* who steadfastly refused to sign England's pirate articles, even in the face of such torture, was, ironically, Howell Davis, who soon afterwards was to become a pirate chieftain himself, and the mentor of Bartholomew Roberts.[46]

Kennedy and his crew survived their long captivity, and even engendered in Captain England's breast a liking for them. Ultimately, Kennedy and *Callabar* were permitted to continue their voyage to Virginia. In "recompense," the pirates presented Kennedy with a gift of twenty-two Negroes, two iron guns, and a small hawser. Having taken some English coins from him, the pirates bestowed upon him an additional present of Portuguese moidores of much greater value.[47]

As soon as Kennedy reached Virginia, he, like Knott before him, delivered up his gifts, the Negroes, to Spotswood. The Governor was

Torture of the unfortunate Captain Skinner, commander of the Bristol snow Cadogan, *was typical of many pirates during the so-called Golden Age of Piracy.*

again very impressed. "When Masters of Ships are so honest as to discover and Yield up what is thus given them in lieu of their own private losses, I cannot but recommend them to his Maj'ty's favour that some consideration may be had of their sufferings and damage."[48] Sobered by the problems encountered in recovering the loot spread about the countryside by the pirates brought in by Knott, the Governor now believed he had stumbled upon a solution to such difficulties. Honesty, for a change, just might pay. Would it not, he reasoned, be appropriate to offer a reward to those who faithfully recovered or discovered "Piratical effects" and turned them over to the Crown out of the said booty if the proper owners were not likely to submit a claim? If a proclamation were made to that end, the Governor suggested,

> *I am persuaded it would be a means to discover abundance of Piratical Effects, w'ch otherwise may be concealed and converted to private use, many men being rather willing to run all risques in keeping what they have*

*gott than to put themselves to the trouble of a discovery, when they have
nothing to expect.*[49]

Unfortunately, for all their honesty, neither Knott, Kennedy, nor
the owners of *Callabar* would receive much by way of compensation,
despite Spotswood's support for such actions. The Governor accepted,
in behalf of the Crown, the Negroes, but since they were slaves and not
considered "strictly within the meaning of goods perishable," and since
the pirates could not legally transfer property as they had in the case of
poor Captain Kennedy, the issue of compensation was dragged
through a sea of legal red tape. In good faith, the Governor allowed a
valuation of £126 for the slaves, but the owners of *Callabar* argued that
the slaves were worth four times that amount. The ship's owners
petitioned the government that they be granted an award of £1,200 for
damages to the ship and cargo, or the return of the slaves. Finally, the
government acquiesced, and the slaves were returned,[50] though such
reparations were undoubtedly small consolation to Kennedy and his
men, or to the poor black slaves who had absolutely no say in their
dismal future.

Captain Knott fared the worst of all. The honest Quaker was obliged
to relinquish forever his career as a sea captain "on account of the
Pirates [most notably Roberts] threatening to Torture him to Death if
he ever falls into their hands."[51]

The executions of the six pirates, unfortunately, set in motion an
even more serious concern for Governor Spotswood than he could
have anticipated. When Bartholomew Roberts was told of the hangings, he vowed revenge against the Virginia authorities. Off Bermuda,
he stopped the ship *Jeremiah,* bound from the Isle of Man for Hampton, and learning of her destination, charged her master, Captain
Turner, to convey the message that he would be paying Virginia a visit
with his flotilla to avenge the death of his men. Upon Turner's arrival,
he informed Captain Thomas Whorwood, commander of HMS *Rye,*
then anchored off Hampton, of Roberts' threat. He also provided
further information about the pirates' force, noting that their flagship
carried 36 carriage guns, 12 swivels, and a crew of 140 men. Accompanying the flagship was a consort brigantine of 18 guns and
equally well manned. Roberts, by last account, was in expectation of
being joined by another ship of 46 guns with a sizeable crew.[52]

Whorwood quickly relayed the intelligence to the governor, declaring that it would be impossible for his own ship to resist such a great
force should it descend on the colony. Spotswood and the Council,
nearing panic, immediately ordered the country better armed. He had
only to review recent history to know that Roberts was certainly capable

of carrying out his threats. Indeed, in June 1720 the pirate had bra-zenly sailed a 10-gun sloop, manned with sixty men, into Trepassy in Newfoundland "with their black Colours flying, Drums beating, and Trumpets sounding," capturing twenty-two ships lying at anchor—all but one of which he sank.[53]

Spotswood ordered the construction of batteries mounting fifty-four guns at the mouths of the Rappahannock, York, and James rivers. One was erected at Point Comfort, the second at Tindall's Point, and the third at an undisclosed place on the Rappahannock, but probably near Urbanna. Powder was distributed from the magazine at Williamsburg. Two lookouts were stationed in Princess Anne County, at Cape Henry and farther south. Another coast watch base was established in North-ampton County at Cape Charles. Beacons, for instant relay of signals, were erected at all three places. The Governor dispatched letters to the governors of New York, New England, and South Carolina, informing them of the pirates' force and intentions, and requesting that any Royal Navy ships on their stations be sent to reinforce *Rye,* the guardship. He requested additional aid in seeking out and destroying the buccaneers.[54]

Governor Alexander Spotswood's anxiety intensified when word arrived informing him that Roberts had captured a French warship with the governor of the island of Martinique aboard. It was said the rovers had proceeded to hang the unfortunate Frenchman from the yardarm. Others aboard had their ears sliced off or were tied to the yardarm and used for target practice.[55]

Fortunately for Virginia and her vigorous antipirate Governor, Cap-tain Bartholomew Roberts would not make good his threat. In Febru-ary 1722, during his fortieth year, the notorious pirate captain was killed in a heated battle with HMS *Swallow,* Captain Chaloner Ogle commanding, and would never again pose a problem for the colony of Virginia. His mark, however, upon the colony's governor was indelible. Spotswood's fear of pirates would remain with him throughout his life. Two years after being relieved of his post, he was still in Virginia, refusing to produce an account of his administration in England be-cause he would have to put to sea to reach there. Such fears were because "of the Vigorous part I've acted to Suppress Pirates: and if those

barbarous Wretches can be moved to cut off the Nose & Ears of a Master for but correcting his own Sailors, what inhuman Treatment must I expect, should I fall within their power, who have been markt as the principal Object of their Vengeance, for cutting off their arch Pirate Thatch, with all his grand Designs, & making so many of their Fraternity to swing in the open air of Virginia.[56]

XIX

Toes Tied Together

It was not surprising, as the cancer of piracy continued to infest the Americas, that the activities of so many miscreant Englishmen led to friction between British and Spanish authorities. Not only had many English buccaneers declared outright that their intentions were to attack only French and Spanish vessels, but they had interceded in such Spanish affairs as the salvage of the 1715 treasure fleet by illegally fishing the wrecks themselves, raiding salvage operations, and even attacking Spanish installations erected to protect the wrecks. Equally disturbing to Spanish authorities charged with maintaining the commercial monopoly of trade within their colonies was the violation of trade restrictions by English interlopers. Response to such actions, whether condoned by the British government or not, was frequently harsh, and, as the case of Captain Harry Beverly so adequately exhibited, even English vessels employed on legitimate business often met with rough usage.[1]

Relations with Spain, which were never very good, degenerated to the breaking point. Since the Treaty of Utrecht a desultory, undeclared war had been gradually flickering to life. On February 1, 1720, British Secretary of State Cragg dispatched word to Governor Spotswood that a cessation of hostilities between Spain and England had been achieved. Yet with Spanish hostilities nurtured by antagonisms caused by the English sea rovers, the quasi-war would soon begin to heat up in America. And once again Spanish privateers would invade Chesapeake waters.

Near the end of April 1720, the beginning of the "pirate season," the first Spanish privateers bearing letters of marque from the Governor of St. Augustine, Florida, began to cruise off the Virginia Capes.

Their successes came quickly. On April 28 a privateer sloop of four guns and seventy men, from St. Augustine, seized the first victim off Virginia, a ship bound from London for South Carolina. On May 4 the same raider, while cruising seven leagues off the Bay, fell in with a small sloop from Woodbridge, New Jersey, bound for North Carolina. The Spaniards placed three of their crew, all Frenchmen, onboard, leaving only the prize's mate and another crewman aboard to assist in navigating the vessel (none of the privateersmen, it seemed, being competent at navigation). The sloop was directed to follow the privateer to St. Augustine, but during the night the two vessels parted company. The two Englishmen were ordered by the prize crew to steer the prize directly for St. Augustine, but the mate sought to bring her into a friendly port. Upon the inevitable discovery of the scheme, fighting broke out, both sides suffering wounds, but with the Frenchmen prevailing. Knowing they could not navigate the vessel themselves, they gave the Englishmen "good quarter and were very Civil to them." On the day following the fight, hard, contrary weather forced the sloop northward, though the prize crew wanted to go south. With provisions and water undoubtedly running low, and seeing their chances of ever reaching St. Augustine rapidly evaporating in the contrary winds, the nervous Frenchmen agreed to put into New York. Upon landing, they were interrogated, and informed authorities that at least three more privateers were fitting out at Havana to cruise the American coast.[2]

Almost overnight word of Spanish privateering attacks up and down the Atlantic seaboard began to filter into the seaports of English America. Off the Carolinas a 2-gun sloop with fifty men from Havana fell in with and captured an 8-gun London ship, and then a sloop from Glasgow.[3] A Philadelphia schooner, commanded by Captain Thorpe, bound from Barbados for Virginia with a cargo of rum, was snapped up on May 15 within the Capes before anyone even suspected a privateer was in the vicinity.[4]

On May 16 a Spanish privateer of 10 small guns and 36 men slipped unnoticed into the Chesapeake and surprised an outward-bound London ship at anchor in Lynnhaven Bay and laden with 630 hogsheads of tobacco. The ship, commanded by Captain John Lowbridge, surrendered instantly and was immediately boarded and manned by a prize crew. Spanish colors were raised over the prize, which was promptly sent in pursuit of another outward-bound ship, commanded by Captain Cobb, with which she had been sailing. Discovering his predicament, Cobb skillfully came about and fled back toward the James, easily outdistancing the Spanish prize, but not the sloop, which pursued him doggedly under oars. Many merchant vessels which had been gathering in the roads scattered before the advancing Spaniards, who had, fortunately, set their sights only on Cobb. As the raiders began to close in for the kill, Cobb entered the James and eventually beat off the small attacker.[5]

Though the privateer had failed to take Cobb's ship, penetration of the Bay (again temporarily devoid of a guardship) had been carried out successfully and without loss. In June, it was reported in Philadelphia, no fewer than five Spanish privateers were patrolling the coast, and several had on one occasion actually sailed eight leagues up the Chesapeake itself.[6] So tight had the blockade become that anyone attempting to run in or out of either the Chesapeake or the Delaware, which was also closely watched, did so at great risk of capture. On June 21, when Captain Bartholomew Radford, in a sloop from Surinam, attempted to run out of the Chesapeake, he was obliged to sail at night to avoid a privateer brigantine then cruising in sight of the Capes. After successfully evading the Spaniard, he made for the Delaware. A mile off Cape Henlopen he encountered two privateer sloops which raised Spanish colors, began firing at him, and took up hot pursuit. Finally, "with much difficulty he got clear of them" and entered the Delaware. His was the last vessel to enter that river for a week.[7]

Predictably, the Chesapeake trade once again began to suffer from interdiction by seaborne raiders, and the toll began to mount. The Spanish privateersmen were no less savage than the English pirates they were supplanting. Occasionally, they were humane and civilized, but just as frequently they seemed to be governed by the laws of neither God nor man and acted barbarically. In July, they set seventy English prisoners ashore in Virginia; they eventually arrived safely on the York River. Two Virginia sea captains, Potter and Langford, had recently been released under a flag of truce at St. Thomas in the Virgin Islands, and it appeared at first that the conflict would be conducted with some regard for human life. Then eighteen bodies were washed ashore on the Virginia Capes, "some of them tied back to back, and one a Gentleman by his Cloaths which he still had on, was found with his hands tied behind him, and his two great toes tied together."[8]

Not all Spanish raiders on the Chesapeake operated under legal commissions from St. Augustine or Havana. Some, following in the footsteps of their English counterparts, simply forged their authorizations or didn't bother with them at all. In late September, one such well-armed Spanish brigantine, manned by 140 seamen from St. Augustine, both Spaniards "and others of diverse Nations," and commanded by Captain Nicholas de Conseption, a Spanish mulatto, began

cruising within the Virginia Capes, occasionally darting up the Chesapeake to pursue potential victims. Although a guardship, HMS *Rye*,
Captain Whorwood commanding, had been assigned to the Bay as a
replacement for *Lyme* and *Pearl*, she was of little value, for soon after
her arrival she was laid up in the Elizabeth to clean. For the privateersmen the hunting was good, and numerous vessels fell into their hands.
Their first victim proved to be *Mary*, a Philadelphia sloop laden with
bread and flour and commanded by one Captain Jacobs, which was
promptly fitted out by the Spaniards as a privateer and consort to the
brigantine. Soon afterwards a vessel commanded by Captain Sipkin
was taken and dispatched to St. Augustine with a prize crew aboard. On
September 23 a pink en route from Barbados to Virginia and commanded by Captain Spicer was taken in Chesapeake Bay. As with
Sipkin's vessel, a prize crew was placed aboard and the pink sent off to
St. Augustine.[9]

Shortly afterwards, the Spaniard's new consort sloop fell in with and
captured a sloop from New York bound for Virginia laden with bread
and flour and commanded by one Captain Seymour. This vessel was
also promptly dispatched to St. Augustine. En route, on September 28,
the prize encountered a sloop owned by Captain John Martin of
Virginia, and armed with four carriage guns, four swivels, and small
arms and ammunition "fit for Engagement." Though the sloop was
equal, in weapons and men, to the Spanish prize, her crew declined to
fight and struck immediately. Andrew Bradford, printer of the *American Weekly Mercury* of Philadelphia, sought to excuse the failure to
engage. "The Reason of this Cowardice in the English, frequently
found in our Merchant Vessels of Force," he wrote,

> is not to be attributed to their Want of Spirit, but the Inhospitality they meet
> with from us; having no Retaliation made for their Loss of Limbs or
> Wounds sustained, and a certain Knowledge that their being taken can not
> equalize the Loss of Leg or Arm. Whereas in the King's Service in Men of
> War, in the Casualties of Fight, Men are sure of some Recompence and
> Smart-Money [payment for the loss of limbs, eyes, or ears] which some way
> gratefully makes up the Damage sustained by those who escape with Life,
> encourages to fight for Plunder and Pension, and at least keeps them from
> Misery. It would be well if our Merchants would have a Thought of this,
> and make some Provision as a Gratuity for those who are maimed and lose
> Limbs in their Service, venturing their Lives to preserve Ship and Cargo ...[10]

The privateer brigantine continued to cruise the Capes and lower Bay
for several more days, capturing at least one or more additional prizes
before turning her bow southward. When belated word of the raider's

presence reached the James, the masters of a number of merchantmen lying in the river, along with the lieutenant from HMS *Rye,* angered over the temerity of the invader, immediately set out in two sloops with the intention of surprising the privateer and rescuing the prizes. They succeeded in retaking only one, the ship *Planter* of Liverpool, manned by a prize crew of eight Spaniards, a Frenchman, and an Irishman. While perusing the belongings of their prisoners, they discovered a copy of a commission from the Governor of St. Augustine dated long after the cessation of hostilities between England and Spain. At first blush, it appeared to Governor Spotswood and his Council, who were apparently apprised of the rescue attempt after the fact, that by the granting of such commissions "the Spaniards pay no regard to said Cessation."[11]

Spotswood was undoubtedly upset over the raids into the Bay, and summoned Captain Whorwood of *Rye* to ask him why the Navy had failed to act. Whorwood calmly explained that his ship was in the Elizabeth River to be cleaned, "and that before She could be ready to put to Sea, it was probable the Privateer, having already taken as many Prizes as his Crew could mann, would be gone off of the Coast."[12]

Whorwood, who had failed to lift a finger, save for dispatching a lieutenant with the rescue sloops, was definitely not of the same cut as a Passenger or a Maynard.

The Governor found better counsel among the Virginia merchant captains. John Martin, who had already suffered the loss of one vessel to the privateer, proposed to fit out another of his sloops to go to St. Augustine with a flag of truce and demand restitution and the return of the vessels. Failing in that, he proposed to attempt to retake them by force if the Governor would provide him with men, arms, and ammunition. Spotswood liked his fighting spirit as well as his suggestions. On October 7 he presented the proposition to the Council. The Council summoned Captain Whorwood to ask what condition his ship was in for the protection of trade. Whorwood replied that the ship was being prepared to heave down and clean and would not be ready for two or three weeks. He could, however, furnish fifty or sixty men for Martin's proposed mission to St. Augustine.

The Council quickly approved of Martin's plan and authorized him to take command of the sloop *Ranger,* which was to be hired by the Virginia government, and proceed with a flag of truce to St. Augustine. He was empowered to act offensively against all pirates and defensively against all other enemies (namely the Spanish) that might attack him en route. At St. Augustine he was to inform the Governor of the repeated infractions of the cessation of hostilities and demand restitution for the captured ships. He was to be furnished with a copy of the proclamation announcing the cessation of arms and a letter from Governor Spotswood. *Ranger*, valued at £200 pounds, would be indemnified in case of loss, and Martin and two of his crewmen were to receive pay according to rates usual in such instances. The sloop would be manned by sixty seamen from *Rye*. But the Council, ever wary of the colony's naval weaknesses, ordered that should the Virginia coast be molested by pirates or privateers during their absence, a bounty of ten shillings over and above normal navy pay would be awarded seamen and landsmen to flesh out *Rye*'s complement during the emergency. Failing in this, the justices of the peace of Elizabeth City and Norfolk were authorized to impress men for service.[13]

While Captain Martin hastened to outfit *Ranger* for the mission, the Spanish privateer scudded homeward, fat with plunder. As she neared Florida waters, she encountered Captain Spicer's pink, taken earlier in the Chesapeake and manned by a Spanish prize crew. Not recognizing her prize and thinking her to be another Englishman, the privateer drove down on the vessel and forced her ashore on the bar at the mouth of the St. John's River, barely twelve leagues north of St. Augustine. The pink was totally wrecked, and though all of her men and part of the cargo were saved, the ship's boy was lost.[14]

Among the Spaniard's prizes, Spicer's vessel was not to be the last lost through such accidents. Captain Sipkin's ship had also been wrecked on the bar at Matanzas Inlet, leading into St. Augustine. Though no record has been found concerning the event, it was later speculated that Captain Seymour's ship was also run aground and lost "from the Unskilfulness of the Spaniards."[15]

When Martin arrived at St. Augustine in November, he discovered the privateer brigantine at anchor with three brigs which had fallen into her hands. The remainder of her prizes had been dispatched to Havana or wrecked entering Matanzas Inlet or elsewhere. Martin forcefully pressed his case with the Spanish Governor. The Governor denied having issued commissions for privateers to cruise the coast of Virginia. Aware of the implications of failing to abide by the terms of cessation, he sought a compromise with the captain. A London ship called *Recovery*, taken in ballast, and Captain Jacobs' sloop, taken in Virginia waters, would be released. The Governor, however, imperiously requisitioned the bread and flour from the sloop, offering as payment 2,098 pieces of eight, claiming that it was of no value to the owners, "seeing they dare not send to demand it at any place where their Vessels are lyable to be Seized upon the most trifling pretences." The release of a third prize, a London ship taken en route to Virginia with a cargo of slaves, was not approved, as the Governor claimed that it had redwood boards onboard, "the Growth of the Spanish Plantations," and had thus probably been involved in illicit trade in Spanish territory. Martin was unsuccessful in securing reparations for prizes which had been wrecked or dispatched to other Spanish ports. The consequences for the privateer captain who had made the captures in the first place, and who was directly responsible for the Governor's embarrassment, were far more serious. It was later reported in the Philadelphia press that he was eventually arrested, imprisoned, and "condemned to die for counterfeiting a Commission from the Governor."[16]

By late November the sloop of Captain Jacobs and the London ship had been returned and cleared for departure with *Ranger*. On November 26, with a strong westerly wind blowing, the three vessels prepared to sail, with *Ranger* the first to weigh anchor. A small boat moved out ahead, tossed a tow rope to the sloop, and prepared to assist in keeping her head to the wind. Suddenly a great wave dashed the little craft against *Ranger*, and three men, including the captain of the London ship, were lost. Another small boat nearby, with four men aboard, set off to offer assistance, but was also upset in the surf and two of her party were immediately drowned. The remaining two men clawed desperately over the hull of the overturned boat to the keel, even as they were being driven over the bar. Suddenly, another wave righted the craft, and the two men clambered aboard and were eventually saved. *Ranger* was not so fortunate. Having no wind or boat to keep her head, she was driven in an instant onto the bar, wrecked, and totally lost, although her crew was saved.[17]

Neither Captain Jacobs's sloop nor the English ship beside her ventured forth that day. On the following morning, however, the sloop was towed out of the harbor and across the bar by her anchor line. Misfortune followed in her wake. An hour and a half after putting to sea, she lost her mast. Unwilling to return to the lair of the hated Spaniards, Jacobs resolved to jury-rig a sail upon the mast stump and press on. Fifteen days later, on December 12, "by God's Providence they brought the Sloop safe into Hawkins' Hole in Virginia."[18]

Governor Spotswood and the Council were grateful for the costly, almost futile, efforts expended by Captain Martin and his men, and proposed that he be compensated for the sloop and its fitting out and rewarded for his suffering. The House of Burgesses voted £200 for the captain and a similar sum for other victims of the episode, but stingily refused to make good for the loss of *Ranger* or defray the charges incurred for outfitting her. In 1723 the captain was finally paid £30 as wages for his trip to St. Augustine.[19]

Though restitution for the losses incurred was only partial, Captain John Martin, with the backing of Governor Spotswood, had almost single-handedly secured a cessation of Spanish molestation of the Virginia trade, for the privateers ceased to roam the Capes at will. It was to be but a temporary respite.

XX

I Never Intended to Go A Pirating

Alexander Spotswood did not relent in his quest to secure the Chesapeake and its trade from pirate or privateer attack. In May 1721 he informed the Board of Trade that in his opinion there were no ships of war in all of America that were individually strong enough to take on a pirate force of the likes or strength of a Bartholomew Roberts. Nor was it an easy matter to bring two guardships together from different colonies to suppress any great force of pirates. Indeed, for the Chesapeake trade it had become an absolute necessity to have no less than a 40- or 50-gun warship to convoy merchant ships beyond soundings. But it was, he noted, equally important to have in hand a sloop or brigantine "to pursue little puckeroons in Shoal Water where a great Ship cannot come at them." Such a vessel, he hinted, would be very serviceable in driving pirates from the Virginia coast "where they frequently resort to furnish themselves w'th provisions as well as to wait for good Ships when their own is grown out of Repair." Had there been two men-of-war in the Bay in 1720, he pointed out, one on patrol duty while the other was cleaning, the colony's losses to the Spanish privateers might have been prevented!

Not long after the Governor addressed his suggestions to the Board of Trade, the guardship *Rye* was replaced on station by HMS *Enterprize*, of 44 guns and 700 tons burthen, Captain Yeo commanding. A second guardship was not sent, despite the Governor's pleas. The Lords of Admiralty and the Board of Trade no longer shared Spotswood's zeal. Perhaps their reluctance to dispatch additional vessels was founded not only in the costly fiscal realities of such undertakings, but in a growing sense that the threat of piracy to the Chesapeake was at last on the wane. The buccaneer stronghold of New Providence was now firmly under British control, and though a few predators continued to roam aimlessly about the sea-lanes, the great rogues of the age—Blackbeard, Bonnet, Vane, Roberts, Kennedy, Hornigold, and others—were either dead or in the King's service.

Yet in every era of transition, those in its midst are frequently among the least likely to recognize it. As a consequence, Virginia under the Spotswood administration did not relax from its vigil. When it was learned during the summer of 1721 that three ships had arrived in the colony from the pirate stronghold of Madagascar on the east coast of Africa and had traded with the rovers ensconced at that place for guns and stores of war, warrants were immediately issued for the arrest of the ship captains. The masters of these ships, Richard Herbert of *Henrietta* of London, Chalonce Williams of *Gascoign Galley* of Bristol, and Joseph Stratton of *Prince Eugene,* also of Bristol, were immediately interrogated and evidence against them assembled. The evidence against Stratton as having been an accessory to piracy by trading with the freebooters was the strongest, and he was quickly hauled aboard *Rye,* which was then preparing to sail, and sent to England to face trial.[2]

Others suspected of piracy and believed to be going upon the account were occasionally picked up in Virginia and jailed. One party of seamen, belonging to the sloop *Endeavour,* and led by one George McDowell, were committed to the York jail on suspicion when it was touted that they were preparing to run away with the sloop to go pirating off Africa.[3]

Yet such incidents were becoming less frequent as the Atlantic seaboard was gradually purged of English freebooters. It was not to be so with the Spanish.

In 1724 a brief resurgence of Spanish privateering again struck the Chesapeake trade when, in June, a Guardia de la Costa ship, *St. Francis de la Vega,* which had been armed, outfitted, and commissioned by the Governor of Cuba, began to cruise the Virginia Capes. Commanded by a self-proclaimed Spanish knight known as Don Benito and manned by a mélange of nationalities including Spaniards, Frenchmen, Irishmen, and even Englishmen, the privateer warily patrolled just beyond the horizon line and out of sight of the guardship *Enterprize.*[4]

Don Benito's first victim was *John and Mary,* Captain John James commanding. As James approached the Virginia coast, he had been put at ease by falling in with *Enterprize,* which assured him that there were no rovers in the vicinity. Thus, he continued on his way, innocent of what lay ahead. About sunrise the following day he encountered a ship wearing British colors. As he drew near, the stranger hailed out, "God damn you, Strike, you English doggs, Strike!" James surrendered immediately to *St. Francis de la Vega*. Laden with a cargo of 175 blacks from Africa, the *John and Mary* was quickly stripped of 76 slaves, some gold dust, and clothing.[5]

Not long afterwards, the privateer, with *John and Mary* in company, encountered the newly built brigantine *Prudent Hannah* two leagues off Cape Charles, en route from Boston for Virginia with rum, molasses, hops, and dry goods. Valued at £500, the vessel was commanded by Captain Thomas Moussell and owned by Moussell, Thomas Jenner, and Daniel Oliver of Boston. Snapped up with little difficulty, the brigantine was outfitted by Don Benito as a consort. On the following day, June 6, the Spaniards fell in with and captured *Godolphin*, en route to the Rappahannock.[6]

Don Benito held the masters of all three prizes prisoner aboard his own ship until menaced by the approach of *Enterprize*. Not wishing to engage the man-of-war, he transferred his captives to *John and Mary* and released her, then turned eastward with the remaining two prizes. As the little squadron sailed away, one of the pressed men aboard *Prudent Hannah,* an Italian named Mark Legaur, standing watch at the helm, steered his vessel away from the privateer in the dark of night. Having separated from the Spaniard, he then fell upon the prize master and in a desperate fight killed him, and forced the other four members of the prize crew to surrender. Legaur and two of his fellow crewmen then sailed *Prudent Hannah* to New York. There, three of the pirates were executed, while the fourth was acquitted on the grounds that he had not participated in the fight with the crewmen.[7]

In 1727 Virginia was to engage in its last significant confrontation with pirates, but this time it would be in the courts, and the pirates belonged to neighboring North Carolina. The freebooters in question belonged to a gang of petty robbers headed by one John Vidal, an Irish protestant "of Desperate fortune." Vidal and his little gang had set out across the Carolina sounds in a small open boat to seize and rob vessels entering Ocracoke Inlet. Yet word of their amateurishness preceded them, and within a short time he and two of his crewmen, along with one Martha Farlee, who had been forced to join the gang, were captured. North Carolina lacked the appropriate authority to try pirates, and for awhile it seemed that the four would be tried in the general court as common felons. Finally, it was directed by Governor Sir Richard Everard of North Carolina, with the compliance of Virginia, that the pirates would be sent to Williamsburg for trial before the Vice

Admiralty Court. Five witnesses were dispatched to testify against them. Vidal and his two accomplices were found guilty and condemned to die. Martha Farlee, who had been forced, was acquitted and given money to return home.[8]

The execution date for John Vidal was set for October 6, 1727,[9] but apparently, through influential connections, including Richard Fitzwilliam, one of the men retained by the pirate William Howard for his own defense nearly a decade earlier, a move to secure a pardon was initiated. Vidal's efforts were well timed, for the militant antipirate administration of Alexander Spotswood was being replaced by the untested William Gooch and was in a state of transition, presided over by Robert Carter, President of the Council and Acting Governor. On August 31, from his prison cell in Williamsburg, Vidal addressed a letter, rich in florid rhetoric and repentance, to the Acting Governor. "The Dolefull and most miserable state that I am under," he wrote,

makes me with a very heavy heart write to your Hon^r in this lamentable case which must overwhelm my poor parents and friends with greif, when they shall hear of my being brought to so an untimely end. The many misfortunes which happened to me and tenderness of youth in being overtaken by the temptations of the world together with the late loss I sustained by the master of my vessel, who run away with her from Potomack in Maryland, with her load of Tobacco put me quite out of ever seeing my Dear parents, which threw me in dispair and mellancholly—this is well known by Severall Gentlemen in Maryland, likewise by Mr Fitzwilliams Surveyor Generall—this finishing stroke of my misfortunes almost bereaved me of my senses, which God forgive me for it, but I never intended to go a pirating, which was declared by Edward Coleman in his Dying minute—Yo^r Hon^r will be so good to me, as to give me longer time of Repentance than the Rest, which God bless you and yours for; but however Dear S^r with a weeping heart, I crave, and for the love of God, I beg your hon^r will be so good as to give me such a time longer of Repentence as your hon^r in your Discretion shall judge proper—this will be a grate benefit to my poor soul which must answer before the great tribunal of heaven, for all my Sins Done in the Body— What a comfortable thing it is for a Dying man to have a little time to make his peace with God—in hopes whereof that the Almighty God may Reward you and yours at the last Day shall be the prayers of a poor miserable and unhappy wretch.[10]

Vidal's address fell upon sympathetic ears, and though his two associates had already been executed (one of them Edward Coleman), Vidal was reprieved until the arrival of Governor Gooch, who read his commission to the Council on September 11.[11] One of the new governor's first topics on the agenda of state was the case of John Vidal.

Gooch queried the Council about whether or not the pirate was a fit object for the King's mercy. After some debate, the Council voiced its opinion that "in Respect of His Majests [George II] Succession to the Throne, and the arrival of the Governor it is very fit to begin His Administration with an Act of Mercy," and advised that the rover be pardoned. On October 27 John Vidal was ordered released from jail.[12]

Governor Gooch found himself, like all of his predecessors, quickly immersed in the quagmire of Virginia's naval defense problems. On September 21, as he placed pen to paper to inform the British government of the Vidal case, he was informed that within the last ten days no fewer than seven ships and sloops had been taken by two Havana privateers within forty leagues of the Virginia coast. The Spaniards, it seemed, were at it again. Yet with the end of the "pirate season" at hand, and the probability that the raiders would soon depart until the following spring, the Governor did not pursue the problem other than to order an inquiry.[13]

In April 1728 a new guardship, HMS *Biddiford,* of 20 guns and 371 tons burthen, Captain Covel Mayne commanding, arrived on the Virginia Station to replace her predecessor. Mayne brought with him disturbing intelligence received at sea from one James Seymour, master of the sloop *Fanny* from Antigua, "that divers vessels are fitting out by the Spaniards at St Domingo and other ports in the West Indies to cruize on this coast, and may be speedily expected." The Governor and Council immediately imposed an embargo on all outward-bound vessels until May 6, at which time the shipping was to rendezvous in the mouth of the James and sail under convoy of *Biddiford.* The embargo would then be reimposed until notice of the next convoy was published.[14]

As Virginia moved to place itself on yet another wartime footing, however, and Gooch began to assess the now-dilapidated condition of the defense works of the colony, forces of peace were already in motion in Europe. On June 1, 1728, the King of Spain ordered a cessation of arms at Cartagena, effectively halting the quasi-war at sea. Less than two years later, in 1730, the Treaty of Seville was signed, ending the tired conflict that had for so long afflicted the tidewater trade. As for piracy, its golden era had passed, although for the Chesapeake there lay more than three quarters of a century more of attacks by seaborne raiders, privateers, and picaroons.

XXI

Pests of Trade

In 1730 the Treaty of Seville effectively terminated the nasty little war between England and Spain and provided the Chesapeake country with its first respite from seaborne attackers of any kind in nearly a century. The pacific decade which followed was one of consolidation and growth. The tobacco fleets could now sail brazenly across the Atlantic without fear of assault or need of convoy. The Bay itself no longer required the services of a permanent Royal Navy guardship, and both Maryland and Virginia enjoyed an era of tranquility, prosperity, and maritime expansion of unprecedented proportions. Thus, when peace came to an end, as it inevitably does, the contrast was all the more disconcerting.

Unhappily, as before, the tidal wave of events in Europe washed American shores with devastating effect. In 1740 the War of the Austrian Succession broke out in Europe, and Great Britain found herself pitted against her ancient enemies, Spain, and later, France. By the spring of 1741 Spanish privateers again began to converge upon the Virginia coast, harassing merchant shipping and imposing serious losses on tidewater trade.[1]

Without regular guardships, the Virginia Council was forced to make do as it had in so many similar emergencies in the past. A three-man commission was appointed to impress and fit out a pair of privateer sloops to patrol the coast for a period of three months. Each vessel was to carry a complement of sixty to seventy men. Mariners signing aboard would be paid a bountiful salary of forty shillings per month and have a share of every prize taken. Shot, powder, and small arms would be provided from the colony's magazine at Williamsburg. The owners of the vessels were to be paid a fee of fourteen shillings per

ton a month hire, and they would be indemnified by the government
for any damages incurred while their vessels were in service.² For the
owners it was a no-lose proposition. For the Chesapeake, it was a
makeshift operation at best.

After the usual delays in getting underway, the two state privateers
set sail under the command of one Thomas Goodman, captain of the
armed sloop *Ranger*. Not long after putting out to sea, the two sloops
encountered a Spanish privateer which was permitted to escape under
embarrassing conditions for Captain Goodman, and the Virginians
were obliged to settle for a Plymouth ship recaptured from the all-too-
swift Spaniard. Upon his return to the Chesapeake, Goodman's alleged
negligence and cowardice were censured by the Virginia Council as "a
lasting mark of Infamy."³

The almost pitiful effort, of course, failed to discourage the Spanish
privateers that ventured into Virginia waters. In the spring of 1742 a
single Havana letter of marque cruising the Virginia Capes captured
no less than seven prizes in a three-week period.⁴ Governor Gooch
responded by issuing a letter of marque to the two-hundred-ton ship
Happy. Mounting ten carriage guns and six swivels, the privateer,
carrying a small crew of twenty-five men, was authorized only to attack
Spanish vessels, since France and Great Britain, though teetering on
the brink, were not yet officially at war.⁵

Finally, the Chesapeake's naval defense system was reinforced by the
arrival of HMS *Hector*, an ancient fifth-rate, 44-gun man-of-war, commissioned thirty-nine years earlier.⁶ *Hector* proved to be of marginal
value. The failings of her commander, Sir Yelverton Peyton, Bart., in
fact, were of such magnitude that in June 1742 he was court-martialed
and dismissed from the Royal Navy for being "negligent in the Execution of the Orders he was under while he was Stationed in Virginia."⁷

Governor Gooch placed little faith in things naval, preferring to
plant his own feet, and those of Virginia's defenses, firmly in Virginia
soil. Like Spotswood before him, he felt that the colony's interests were
best protected by strategically situated batteries at the mouths of the
colony's rivers. Yet, unlike several of his predecessors, the Governor
was of the opinion that the linchpin of the system was at Point Comfort
at the mouth of the James. Thus, he sought not only to rehabilitate the
ancient river batteries of earlier times, but also to construct a new brick
fortification at the point. The work at Point Comfort was dubbed Fort
George and mounted twenty-two cannons. It was never to fire a shot in
battle or in its defense during the entire war.⁸

In late 1742 *Hector* returned to England and was replaced by HMS

Hastings, another fifth-rate, 44-gun man-of-war, commanded by Lord Banff. *Hastings'* arrival on the Chesapeake Station caused a stir of excitement, for en route she had fallen in with and captured the ship *Pallarcha,* a vessel of French registry freighted by the King of Spain. *Pallarcha* had been bound from Vera Cruz, Mexico, to Spain with a precious cargo of 180,000 pieces of eight, cochineal, vanilla, indigo, drugs, and hides. The prize was estimated to be worth £36,000 sterling and was readily condemned, despite her French registry, by the Virginia Court of Vice Admiralty. Banff, unlike his predecessor, was not recalcitrant in patrolling the coast. Soon after his arrival, he took an 80-ton Spanish privateer of seventy men, ten carriage guns, and twenty-four swivels while cruising off the Capes.[9]

When Great Britain finally declared war on Spain's ally, France, in 1744, beginning a conflict known thereafter in America as King George's War, the danger to colony shipping intensified. England was hard pressed on all fronts, and for the first time, the convoy system which had seen Chesapeake shipping through hard times in earlier years completely broke down. Defense of the English Channel was paramount, and both Maryland and Virginia shipping interests took a back seat. The Royal Navy was needed in European and West Indian waters, and few vessels could be spared for the defense of the middle Atlantic coast of America. Seeking to reinforce Great Britain's seaborne strength at the least cost, King George I issued a declaration for the encouragement of privateering. Within a very short time, as throughout English America, Virginia was swept up in a frenzy to convert any and all available merchantmen into privateers. Such was the extent of the effort to field vessels that the colony's rich Bristol trade languished for want of shipping. There was money to be made and an abundance of enemy ships to be captured. Success stories of instantaneous riches from such seaborne adventures abounded. Typical of such accounts was that of the little Virginia-built brig *Sea Horse,* purchased by a tidewater concern in Bristol for a mere four hundred guineas. The little vessel was readily converted into a privateer, renamed *Ranger,* and during a single month's cruise captured prizes valued at £10,000 to £12,000.[10] Virginia privateers, such as Captain Walter Codd's *Virginia,* began to chalk up a remarkable record of successes in the West Indies that encouraged others to try their hand in the game. Unfortunately, such adventurism served only to redirect resources away from the defenses of the Chesapeake itself.[11]

With the French now in the fight, the British demand for ships of war increased commensurately, and *Hastings,* too, was recalled from the

Chesapeake. Bereft of its naval defense, the tidewater was swept by invasion jitters reminiscent of those during Queen Anne's War. On May 23, 1745, an electrifying report from Commodore Knowles arrived via New York from St. Christophers. The commodore reported that seven French men-of-war had recently arrived at Martinique from Calais, along with twenty-eight transports and upwards of three thousand soldiers. By another vessel recently arrived at Norfolk from Barbados, it was learned that the French buildup was accompanied by an inordinate increase of French privateers in the West Indies. The danger to English shipping was so great that an embargo had to be laid to prevent serious damage to the British merchant marine. But worse, it was "uncertain where the Fury of the French," who were growing stronger in the Americas with every passing week, would fall. One thing was certain: no English colony was strong enough to hurl back the attack of such a mighty force, and the entire Atlantic seaboard, including the Chesapeake region, trembled in fear of invasion.[12]

In Virginia, Governor Gooch did his best to improve the colony's paltry defenses. The militia was put into a state of readiness, and lookouts were posted once again along the seacoast. The government also advised "the driving away of the Cattle, from those Parts, in case of an Invasion" to deny the enemy provisions. Seeking to provide the barren coastline with at least a rudimentary form of naval protection, the Governor and Council ordered a vessel to be hired and fitted out to guard the coast. Accordingly, a fine Bermuda-built sloop, reportedly a good sailer belonging to a Colonel Mackenzie, was acquired and prepared for duty.[13]

Fortunately for the Chesapeake, French attentions were turned elsewhere, and the feared invasion never materialized. Neither French nor Spanish privateers, however, veered from their growing lust for Chesapeake shipping. Reports of enemy privateering captures, some verified and others only rumored, filtered in throughout the spring of 1745. "We have had several reports," one typical article in the *Virginia Gazette* noted, "That Capt. Friend, and some other Ships that sail'd with him, were taken, soon after they got out to Sea, by a Spanish Privateer," but the story was unverified for months.[14] Another more solid account, gleaned from a Scottish ship which had arrived in the Rappahannock, reported "an English ship taken by a Frenchman in 14 Fathom Water near the Capes."[15]

Despite the harassment of Virginia shipping, English merchantmen frequently gave excellent accounts of themselves, occasionally against overwhelming odds. One such ship was *Cunliffe,* Captain John Pritchard commanding, a vessel of only thirty-eight crewmen, which fell in with a French privateer while en route from Maryland to England. The foe, "strong, fleet, and greedy of spoil" was a vessel mounting twenty carriage guns and numerous swivels, and manned by two hundred men. After being pursued and engaged by the Frenchman in a near-day-long affair, in which Captain Pritchard and others of his crew were killed or injured, in a battle where "Shot flew about as thick as Hail," *Cunliffe* successfully beat off the attacker. Upon reaching Liverpool, the battered merchantman and her crew were lionized in the press. "By this we may judge," wrote one proud crewman, "that French Superiority in Number is in no wise adequate to true English Courage."[16]

Virginia-bound merchantmen occasionally got lucky on their own accord. On June 14 the London ship *Banstead,* Captain Robert Whitney; *Neptune,* Captain Archibald Crawford; and *Expedition,* Captain Robert Robertson, arrived in the York River from London with the recently captured French prize ship *Elizabeth. Elizabeth* had struck to *Banstead,* which had fired several shots into her after meeting her at sea, but *Neptune,* in close company, was first to board. Having physically taken the ship and secured the French captain's papers, Crawford was able to lay claim to a portion of the prize. And a rich one she was. Laden with 282 hogsheads of sugar, 4,000 or 5,000 weight of indigo, and a parcel of mahogany planks, the prize was condemned in Virginia Admiralty Court on June 20. Ship and cargo were placed on sale on July 4, with the shares of the proceeds to be divided among Captains Whitney, Crawford, and Robertson, who apparently played some small part in the action.[17]

In most cases English pluck and luck, despite such occasional strokes of fortune, were no substitute for ships of force. By the summer of 1745 the coastline between the Chesapeake and the Delaware was crawling with French and Spanish privateers. In June it was learned at Annapolis that the enemy had boldly sailed up the Delaware River as far as Reedy Island and had taken numerous vessels as prizes. Three of their victims, bound from Massachusetts to Maryland, had been chased into the river, where they were subsequently captured. The situation was so alarming at Philadelphia that an express was sent to Williamsburg "to get a Man of War to cruise off the Capes of Delaware for the Privateers which infest these Parts."[18] It was, unfortunately, a wasted journey for the express rider, for the Virginia Station was as devoid of protection as the Delaware.

The Delaware incursions proved an ill omen for the Chesapeake, for a month later the enemy ventured into the Bay itself for the first time. On July 26, it was reported, the masters of two vessels belonging to

Norfolk, who had been taken sometime before, had returned home. They brought with them the news that no less than five privateers were cruising off the Capes, one of them mounting thirty-six guns and commanded by a Spaniard named Don Pedro. Don Pedro had already captured several Maryland ships, including those commanded by Captains Russel and Anter. Soon afterward, the privateers penetrated the Bay and took a Scottish ship or snow. The consequent alarm was so great that Governor Gooch was forced to institute an embargo against the exportation of provisions lest they fall into enemy hands.[19]

On August 10 more news reached Annapolis. A score of merchant-men under convoy of two men-of-war, "many of them bound into this Bay," had all but one been taken on June 12 off the English Channel by the French Brest squadron of nineteen warships. Simultaneously, it was learned that two Maryland-bound ships, commanded by Captains Hopkins and Kinney, had been captured by enemy privateers and carried into St. Malo and St. Sebastian, France.[20]

Happily, as summer began its lazy swing into fall, the enemy priva-teer siege of the Chesapeake began to dissipate, much as the pirate threats of years before. On September 10 Gooch lifted the embargo, and both Maryland and Virginia breathed a little easier. It was a time for some reflection, painful as it was. The Chesapeake trade had been severely bludgeoned during the year. No fewer than sixteen ships were listed by the *Gentlemen's Magazine* as having been captured by Spanish and French privateers, the most notorious of them said to be *Sultana* and *Hermoine*, and the toll of undocumented losses was unquestionably higher.[21]

Now when merchantmen such as Captain Philip Thomlinson's *Pel-ham* ventured to sail from the Bay unescorted, they were usually armed to the teeth or they would not sail at all. Advertising that *Pelham* would take on tobacco on freight to James Buchanan of London at £13 per ton and would sail in October, Captain Thomlinson made special note that his ship was protected by twenty-two cannons.[22]

Virginians had not lost their lust for privateering, despite the de-moralizing casualties among the merchant trade, and advertisements for seamen frequently appeared in newspapers. "This is to give Notice, to all Seamen and Others," read one such advertisement in the *Virginia Gazette,*

> that the Privateer **Raleigh**, *now lying at Norfolk Town, Capt. Mason Miller, Commander, Capt. Morgan, first Lieut. will sail on a Cruize by the 10th of October next, at farthest: Therefore all Persons that have a Mind to go on a Cruise, must take Care to apply by that Time; for they intend to have their Men together by the 5th of the Month.*[23]

The voyage of *Raleigh* proved eventful, for it was her fate to fall in with and take several prizes, most notably a large French ship which was brought into Providence, Rhode Island, in the spring of 1746. The ship was "said to be the richest Prize carried into that Port this War." Soon afterward, rumors began to circulate that Captain Miller and his lieutenants "gain'd away a considerable Sum of Money" at St. Kitts, the produce of two other prizes taken by *Raleigh*. The rumor, which implied embezzlement of the owner of *Raleigh's* share of prize money, "scandalously and maliciously reported, by some ill designing People," so incensed Miller and his two senior officers that they advertised a reward of fifty pounds to anyone who discovered the persons responsible so that they might be prosecuted for slander.[24]

The privateer war occasionally caused unforeseen calamities for the inhabitants living in remote coastal areas. One particularly vicious incident began on November 1, 1746 when five blacks, who claimed to belong to the crew of the Spanish privateersman Don Pedro, but supposed by authorities "to be the Property of some Persons in Pennsylvania" visited Sinepuxent Inlet, on Maryland's Atlantic shores. They arrived in a small rowboat, carrying with them a sheep, and no arms whatsoever except an old broken scythe fixed into a wooden handle. A lone sloop which was lying at that time in the inlet was promptly boarded by the blacks. One of the two men aboard the vessel, hearing a noise, came up from the cabin to the deck. Stunned at encountering the ragged band of Negroes, he immediately demanded to know what they wanted. The blacks replied by splitting the poor sailor's head open in two places with the scythe, mangling his body, and throwing him into the hold where he died. The second crewman, who had been cleaning a fowl in the forecastle, then appeared and asked the blacks what was the matter. They answered him "in good English, that if he was not easy, they would serve him the same Sauce" and then slashed his cheek to prove their point.[25]

Without further ado, the Negroes took possession of the sloop and set sail. Apparently being unfamiliar with sailing or the area, they promptly ran aground. Unable to get the sloop off, they plundered her, changed boats, and left. The following morning, the wounded crewman of the sloop, who was still aboard with his dead companion, signalled to the shore for help. Eventually a party of men rowed out to his assistance. Having related the story of the murder of his comrade to the authorities, the injured crewman had the satisfaction of seeing the high sheriff of Worcester County raise a posse and set off in hot pursuit. An express was dispatched overland to the Virginia side of the border notifying authorities there of the fugitives coming their way. The blacks managed to elude the sheriff's posse, but only by the narrowest margin. Behind them they left a trail of plundered vessels. Between Sinepuxent and Chincoteague they captured a North Carolina boat bound for Philadelphia laden with potatoes. After robbing her, they let her go and entered Chincoteague Inlet and promptly captured a sloop belonging to one Captain Taylor. Aboard they found Taylor, his only son, and three slaves, all of whom were seized. While in possession of this vessel, they boarded a New Englander and took out two hands from her. In this vessel they prepared to put out to sea, but the wind being out of the east, they were frustrated in their objective. When "the Pyrate Negroes proposed going out to Sea," it was later reported,

> One of the New England Men, and a Negroe of Capt. Taylor's, seemingly approv'd of the Design; and representing to the five Negroes that they were in want of a good Quantity of fresh Water for such an Enterprize, themselves were deputed to go on shore in the Boat and fetch it. Being got safe ashore, they alarmed the Country . . .

A number of periaugers were quickly manned by the local inhabitants, armed, and set off after the rovers. Finally cornered, the blacks put up a stout defense with arms captured aboard their prizes. During the fight, one of their company was shot through the cheek, but all continued to resist capture. Finally, with their ammunition expended, and boarding imminent, they threw themselves overboard, endeavoring to escape. Three were soon picked up by the periaugers while a fourth was overtaken and secured ashore. The wounded pirate drowned. The four survivors were then carted off to the Accomac County jail to face the inevitable trial and execution.[26]

The war continued to have wide ranging and disastrous effects upon Chesapeake trade. As early as the spring of 1745 marine insurance rates had risen from a peacetime norm of three or four percent to nearly twenty-five percent for outward-bound passage from the Bay. By the fall of that year London brokers refused to insure Chesapeake-bound shipping, while Bristol brokers spoke of rates of forty and fifty percent. Freight rates nearly doubled.[27] Commodity prices in the Tidewater increased commensurately. And worse was to come.

The most trying time of the war for the Chesapeake was 1748, a period likened to that of the Dutch raids of Binkes and Evertsen nearly eight decades earlier. The year got off to a bad start when it was reported in January that the ships *York*, Captain Saunders, and *Gooch*, Captain Churchman, laden with tobacco and bound from Virginia to

Bristol, were taken off the Virginia coast by a Spanish privateer. While
being carried into St. Augustine, Florida, *York* struck on the bar and
was stove to pieces, though all on board were saved. In May the
Maryland Gazette reported the capture of the ship *Lydia,* Captain William Tissin, taken while en route home by a French privateer. *Lydia* was
fortunately recaptured by a Dutch warship, an ally, and carried into
Plymouth. Not so lucky was Captain John Fearon's ship *Marshal*, which
had loaded in the South River, Maryland, only to be taken on the last
leg of her homeward-bound trek near or in the Downs.[28]

In a belated effort to stem the attacks on Chesapeake shipping and to
protect the Bay, the British Admiralty finally dispatched two warships,
HMS *Looe,* Captain Norbury, and *Hector,* Captain Masterman, to the
Virginia Station. *Looe* was a relatively new fifth-rate, 44-gun warship of
716 tons displacement. Her consort, *Hector,* was of equal strength and
the second man-of-war of that name to serve on the Virginia Station
(the first having been broken up in late 1742).[29]

The presence of the Royal Navy guardships was of immediate benefit. In May 1748 *Looe* set out on a patrol of the Bay and the Capes, and
on Tuesday the 30th, returned to port with two Spanish privateers as
prizes. One of the ships was a Havana snow of 14 carriage guns, 15
swivels, and 144 men which had been at sea only 20 days. The other was
a sloop out of St. Augustine, armed with 2 carriage guns, 25 small arms,
and 42 men. From the crew of the snow it was learned that a veritable
swarm of Spanish privateers, at least 10 in number, under the command of Don Pedro, were fitting out at Havana specifically to cruise the
Virginia coast.[30]

Havoc, it seemed, was finally about to visit the Chesapeake itself, and
the Royal Navy would be hard pressed to turn the tide.

On the evening of June 13, the sloop *Sarah,* Captain James Goodridge
commanding, lay quietly at anchor off the mouth of the York River,
north of Horseshoe Shoals, and not far from a merchant snow also at
anchor. Goodridge had recently been up the Bay where he had taken
on a cargo for Boston, and, perhaps unaware of the recent news from
the Caribbean, was entirely unprepared for an attack by Spanish privateers. After all, they had ventured into the Bay itself only once so far,
and he was anchored miles up from the vulnerable mouth. The details
of the events that followed are sketchy, but one can imagine the
sequence: a dark, unidentified shape closing in from the east after
twilight, a booming voice with a Spanish accent ordering surrender,
the roar of a cannon to accentuate the demand, followed by a boatload
of cutlass- and pistol-wielding Spaniards swarming aboard *Sarah* and

the nearby snow. *Sarah* was taken easily, stripped and manned by a prize crew. Goodridge and the ship's boy were later set ashore on Cape Henry.[31]

The following day a schooner commanded by Captain Ingraham, belonging to Durham Hall of Norfolk, was taken by a 14-gun privateer brigantine near Point Comfort. Nearby Fort George graphically demonstrated the utter uselessness of Gooch's land fortifications in protecting shipping as her guns remained both silent and impotent. It was later learned that the brazen privateer had recently arrived from the Delaware, where she had raided as high up as New Castle and captured nineteen vessels. Ingram's vessel was plundered of four blacks, four hundred pounds, sails, rigging, and everything else that could be carried off, and then released. Within sight of the first capture, the privateer seized another vessel, the snow *Pearl*, Captain Jefferd, recently arrived from Glasgow and bound for the Rappahannock with bale goods. The Chesapeake, it appeared, was ripe for the plucking, for a third privateer was roaming about farther up the Bay, and had "done considerable damage, by taking and rifling several small Vessels."[32]

At the same time, Spanish privateers were infesting the waters between the Capes of the Chesapeake and the Delaware in increasing numbers, and tragedy often followed in their wakes. One unfortunate victim, the ship *Rose,* laden with £30,000 worth of goods, was taken near the Virginia Capes. Her captors permitted 14 or 15 of her crew to put off for land in a small boat, but the boat capsized, and all but one person were drowned. Yet some privateer victims were more fortunate. One ship, bound for the Chesapeake in ballast, was taken by a raider off the Capes and released only to be captured within the Bay by a second, but was again released because she had no goods to plunder. A few days later another large ship, with a "considerable Cargo," was taken and held. Occasionally, numbers and a determined resistance saved the day. On June 28, the ship *Peggy,* Captain Mouatt, and two other vessels from Maryland and Whitehaven, were attacked off the Capes. They were able to beat off their assailant and return to the Chesapeake to tell about it.[33]

Looe and *Hector* maintained an almost constant patrol of the Bay and Capes in a desperate effort to stifle the Spaniards. Short of support craft, Captain Norbury manned several of the privateers he had captured in May and took them to sea with him.[34] The Virginia government, seeking to reinforce the Navy's valiant efforts to secure the Chesapeake from "these Pests of Trade, that swarm to a greater Degree than has ever been known in these parts," authorized the fitting out and arming of a small vessel. Encouraged by the move, Captain Masterman generously offered his assistance in manning the vessel.[35]

Results of the concerted efforts of the Royal Navy were telling. Captain Norbury had soon taken a Spanish privateer and sent her into the Bay with one hundred fifty prisoners. Not long afterwards, *Looe* and one of her tenders brought in a Spanish privateer sloop and forty-seven more prisoners, taken near the Capes. On July 17 *Hector* and the sloop *Otter*, Captain Ballet, arrived in Hampton Roads with six more prizes. The account given was that *Otter* had taken two French vessels while they were illegally trading under a flag of truce. As she was bringing the two ships in, a Spanish privateer schooner, her tender, and two of her prizes were spotted riding at anchor within the Capes. *Otter* presented the privateer with a broadside, upon which the Spaniard weighed and put to sea. After securing the tender and the two prizes, Captain Ballet set off in chase of the enemy. Meeting *Hector* at sea and to the windward of the fleeing raiders, *Otter* and the man-of-war were soon able to secure the surrender of the privateer. It was later learned that her two prizes were heavily laden with rum from the West Indies and consigned to Captain Hutchings of Norfolk.[36]

The guardships continued to cruise successfully and gradually succeeded in blunting, and then in appreciably stemming, privateer attacks on the coast and in the Bay. Such was their success, in fact, that before the end of summer so many Spanish and French privateersmen had been taken in Virginia waters that Governor Gooch was obliged to hire a cartel ship, *Mermaid,* then at Yorktown, to take them to Havana to be exchanged for English prisoners of war.[37]

Though the Royal Navy had finally put a damper on Spanish privateering on the Virginia coast and in the Bay, there were occasional recurrences. On August 10 the joyous news of a cessation of hostilities was announced in the pages of the *Maryland Gazette.* Unfortunately, the announcement was preceded by the last privateering act of the war on the Virginia coast, when a French ship took the snow *Dunlop,* Captain Alexander, off the Capes while en route from Annapolis to Scotland. The unfortunate Alexander was taken to France as a prisoner of war. Though of small consolation to the unhappy captain, his ship was recaptured immediately afterward by a Rhode Island privateer and carried into Newport.[38]

The long war had not been as injurious to the Chesapeake as it had to other regions of the Americas, but it had certainly been devastating to many shipping interests. Once again the vulnerability of the tidewater and the absolute necessity of strong naval protection during times of

crisis were graphically illustrated. The convoy system, which had operated with relative, albeit flawed, success in earlier years, had dramatically broken down, with disastrous results. The reliance upon land
fortifications alone to protect shipping had once again proven an
ineffective and expensive expedient. In 1749 a violent storm deci-
mated Fort George. The guns of the fort were dismounted and were
soon so honeycombed and pitted by oxidization as to be useless. By
1755 sea and wind had eradicated all traces of the works, and the
remaining river batteries of Virginia were so out of repair, and their
guns so rusted, that they too were unfit for use.[39]

The defenses of the Chesapeake were left to degenerate. Despite
fears of invasion and the lack of guardships on the Bay (with one brief
exception), the tidewater remained relatively free from attack during
the French and Indian Wars (1756-1763). Only once before the onset
of the American Revolution would the Bay be penetrated by a hostile
privateer. In August 1761 a French privateer captured the schooner
Peggy of Hampton, Virginia, and plundered her of eight carriage guns
and twelve swivel guns as she was en route from Oxford, Maryland.[40] It
was to be the last time that either the French or Spanish "Pests of
Trade" would cause the Chesapeake to grimace in despair.

XXII

Tory Villains

Not long after the opening volleys of the American Revolution were fired upon the field of Lexington Green in April 1775, the Maryland and Virginia tidewater far to the south was swept into the midst of a conflict more destructive than any hitherto visited upon that region. For nearly eight terrible years the towns, plantations, and peoples clustered along the shores of its intricate complex of rivers, creeks, marshes, islands, and embayments would suffer repeated invasions and raids by both land and sea. Neither was the war discriminatory. There would be no sanctuary for either patriot or Tory anywhere along the thousands of miles of shoreline, or on the waters of the Bay itself.

The unbridled depredations of the last Royal Governor of Virginia, John Murray, Earl of Dunmore, in 1775-1776, resulting in the total destruction of Norfolk, was but a beginning. In 1777 the invasion fleet of Admiral Howe, bound up the Bay to the Head of Elk with an army intent on the capture of Philadelphia, watered the seeds of loyalist disaffection on the Eastern Shore in its wake. The massive naval incursion by Admiral Sir George Collier in 1779 saw the burning of Portsmouth, the plunder of Suffolk, and the sinking or destruction of scores of ships in the Elizabeth River. A bold thrust into Virginia by the traitorous general Benedict Arnold in 1780-1781 resulted not only in the capture of Richmond and Petersburg but the destruction of the core of the Virginia State Navy as well. At last, with the arrival of General Charles Cornwallis and a strong army of seasoned British and Hessian veterans at Yorktown, Virginia, in the late summer of 1781, the War for American Independence reached its climactic phase. After the epic naval Battle of the Virginia Capes and the surrender of the

besieged Cornwallis to American and French forces commanded by
General George Washington and the Marquis de Rochambeau, America's struggled for nationhood appeared to be finally resolved.

That the war, which would officially last for another eighteen
months, was nearly over was a beguiling and cruelly premature mis-
conception in the Chesapeake tidewater. For here, from the very
outset, the conflict was fought on two planes: one between the forces of
the major combatant armies and navies and the other a nasty guerrilla
war waged principally on Chesapeake waters by loyalists against the
populace and merchant marine of both Maryland and Virginia. It was
a conflict whose principal weapons were the barge, whale boat, row
galley, and schooner. There was no strategy, and tactics consisted of
little more than brutal, lightning raids launched from remote islands,
no-holds-barred skirmishes, and the wanton plunder of innocent civilians. In short, it was for the loyalists a reign of seaborne terrorism
without rules or objectives that would continue until word of peace
reached Chesapeake shores. For the patriots it proved a hopeless
vortex into which men, money, and resources were poured without
effect.

One of the most notorious and feared Tory raiders of the Revolution
was Joseph Wheland, Jr., whose career commenced with the ascent of
Lord Dunmore's fleet up the Chesapeake in 1776, and concluded only
after the signing of the Treaty of Paris in 1783. Wheland was a "tall,
slim, gallows looking fellow"[1] whose first efforts in behalf of the Crown
began in early 1776 when he sought to trade with Dunmore's fleet
while carrying goods up to the Potomac River for a Somerset County
merchant named Geahagan.[2] By June, after Dunmore's forces had
retired up the Bay from the Elizabeth River to Gwynn's Island, at the
mouth of the Piankatank, Wheland had joined the King's men and was
in command of a loyalist squadron of tenders charged with foraging
and raiding on the Eastern Shore.

On June 25 Wheland's career as a Tory sea raider, or "picaroon,"
began in earnest. In command of a small fleet which included two
10-gun sloops, an armed schooner, a pilot boat, and possibly a fifth
vessel, he entered Hooper's Strait. Landing unopposed on Hopkins
Island, Wheland's picaroons handily carried off upwards of sixty cattle, two young men, and "every thing else that was valuable." The
raiders then launched a strike against the mainland of Somerset County, a hotbed of loyalist activity, and cast local patriot forces into total
confusion. The Tories were never gentle in conducting their depredations, and frequently personal grudges, not military necessity, served
to guide their actions. William Roberts, a wealthy farmer living near

the water at Dames Quarter, who had somehow incurred the enmity of one of Wheland's associates named Wallace, served as a typical example. Landing at night, Wallace and his crew dragged the unfortunate farmer from his bed, tied his hands and feet, and hustled him off as a prisoner along with a number of slaves and much of his property. On June 30, the raiders, with Wheland as their pilot, carried out another vendetta, landing on Nanticoke Point and burning the home of Samuel McChester.[3]

Such picaroon depredations became a nightmare for patriot militia commanders, who scarcely knew where to turn to meet the next landings. Even worse, local Tories in strongholds of loyalist affections in the county, such as at Merumsco and Perrihawken, gained moral support from the raider's successes and began to assemble in "a disorderly and tumultuous manner" to act whenever possible in concert with Dunmore's forces. The desperate chairman of the Somerset Committee of Safety, Thomas Haywood, dispatched urgent calls for assistance from as near as Worcester County and as far north as Sussex County, Delaware, even as Somerset's own militia gathered to meet the emergency. But it was already too late, for the picaroons departed down the Bay with their plunder as swiftly as they had arrived.[4]

For several days, the central Bay region was a loyalist lake, with raiders frequenting or blockading shipping in the nearby waterways. Picaroons seemed to be everywhere, in Honga River, in Fishing Bay, and in the mouth of the Nanticoke. Wheland himself lingered about the Nanticoke, where he fell in with and seized a sloop belonging to one John White. He immediately launched a plan to outfit his new prize with four 4-pounders and twelve swivel guns "to guard the Islands and keep the Shirt Men [Virginia militiamen] from going on to abuse the inhabitants."[5]

On July 11, while Wheland was cruising about the Nanticoke, Lord Dunmore was dislodged from his base on Gwynn's Island by the concerted attacks of Virginia forces led by General Andrew Lewis. The Royal Governor's fleet fled northward to the Potomac, where they attempted to seize tiny St. George's Island as a new base of operations.[6] Wheland, apparently unaware of the retreat, continued with his own private war against the Eastern Shore patriots.

Four days after Dunmore's withdrawal, the Tory captain began cruising off Smith's Island. There he almost immediately encountered a vessel anchored under the lee of the island. The boat, laden with tar and planks, had been en route to the Potomac, but on seeing Dunmore's fleet spread across the Chesapeake, had scurried back down the Bay and anchored under the island, only to be spotted by the picaroons. Upon boarding the merchantman, Wheland interrogated her master to determine where his loyalties lay. Had he seen Dunmore's fleet? Where had he come from and where was he bound?

Captain Yell, master of the vessel, attempted to remain neutral by deftly asserting that "he had not a Design to kill any Person, but was a Friend to his Country."

"Who was right," queried the picaroon pointedly, "King or Shirt-men?"

"The Americans," Yell replied, whereupon Wheland revealed that he "was for the Fleet and had Orders from Lord Dunmore to take any Vessel belonging to the Rebels and destroy such as he thought proper and carry the rest to the fleet." The picaroons then ordered the mas-ter's papers, a pocketbook, forty shillings, and all of his clothes except what was on his back seized. When Yell protested, he was carried aboard the tender as a prisoner and threatened with being thrown in irons in the ship's hold. Wheland immediately set about removing the mast from his new prize and placing it in White's sloop, which had lost her own when driven ashore in a recent storm.

Captain Yell remained a prisoner aboard the Tory ship, under the guard of one Marmaduke Mister. In the course of the evening, Mister also questioned his charge as to his loyalties. The prisoner answered diplomatically that "he was a Friend to every person that behav'd well."

"In the King's name," commanded Mister, "tell the Truth."

"I was born in this country and have a right to defend liberty."

"What these damned rebels call liberty," sneered the guard, "I call slavery, and so the people will find it."[7]

Not long after Captain Yell's capture, Wheland, then lying near Vien-na, on the Nanticoke, received an express from Lord Dunmore order-ing him to come up to the Potomac as quickly as possible to assist him in getting fresh water as orders had arrived for part of the fleet to sail to Martinique and part to New York or Halifax. Wheland im-mediately abandoned the refitting of White's sloop, set both her and another prize recently taken afire, released his prisoners, and sailed to join his master.[8]

Whether Joseph Wheland participated in Dunmore's ascent up the Potomac River for water is unknown. But by late July, he and three of his men were back in the Hooper's Strait area aboard a small schooner. While anchored in a creek which ran into Holland Straits, the pica-roons were surprised by a detachment of thirty patriots commanded by Major Daniel Fallin. Wheland and two of his company "were just out of the small Pox" and in no condition to flee or resist. Thus, they and their vessel, along with a hogshead and a half of rum, thirty bushels of salt, sails, and rigging for a sloop, a large quantity of iron, and a few guns, swords, and cartridge boxes, were soon in patriot hands.[9]

The captured picaroons faced charges of trading with Dunmore's forces and piratically burning John White's sloop. Testimony brought against Wheland before the Dorchester County Committee of Observation was damning. It was charged that his actions had been prompted not only by a strong allegiance to the Crown but by a complete dislike of the local patriots and a lust for profit from plunder.[10]

Wheland was sentenced by the Maryland Convention to be confined in a log jail in Frederick County, far from the Bay, until full restitution was made to John White for the destruction of his sloop and a bond for good conduct in the future was paid. John Evans, Robert Howith, and John Price, the three men taken with Wheland, were ordered to post bonds ranging from twenty pounds to fifty pounds each and to be confined in Anne Arundel County jail until they did so. Considering his actions, Joseph Wheland's sentence was lenient for the times. Yet, he persisted in his efforts to secure a quick trial and release, both of which had been denied him. While temporarily lodged in the Annapolis jail, he petitioned the Maryland Council of Safety. He admitted to carrying on a commerce with Dunmore's forces, but claimed that he had been unjustly accused of burning White's boat at Vienna. There were, he claimed, witnesses then in town who would attest to the fact that it was Dunmore's fleet that burned the sloop, and not himself.[11] His efforts, however, at least for the next five years, would prove in vain. But when he was finally released, he would return to his picaroon ways with such a thirst for revenge, the entire tidewater would be held in thrall.

For the most part, after Wheland's capture, Tory activity on the Bay was largely limited to New York privateering raids, often in concert with Royal Navy operations. Sporadically, Toryism on the Eastern Shore flared up into open insurrection ashore, but few picaroons would again roam the Chesapeake (thanks to the Maryland and Virginia State Navies) until the spring of 1779. Those that did were little more than waterborne highwaymen willing to take whatever crumbs fell their way.

One incident typical of such activities occurred in early July 1777, when Captain Alexander Gordon ran his ship aground near the Pocomoke River. Loyalists from the Eastern Shore, including two locally known "Tory Vilains," Smith Carmine and Zorobabel Maddox, descended upon the helpless ship and plundered her of a hogshead of molasses and ten barrels of salt. It was little more than petty robbery, but Gordon indignantly petitioned Governor Thomas Johnson of Maryland for a warrant to "cause those people who infest the Bay to be Apprehended."[12]

Another such incident occurred about midnight, March 30, 1779, when a local Tangier Sound schooner lying off Dames Quarter was boarded by four armed men, two whites and two blacks, commanded by a Captain Roache. At gunpoint, the schooner's operators, Charles Hamilton and Athanatius Jarboe, were forced to surrender their arms while one of the picaroons, a Lieutenant Morris, with a lighted candle, searched the hold. A bag of corn and a keg and ten gallons of brandy were seized. When the Tories spotted a Continental flag they threatened to burn the ship, noting that one of their colleagues, Captain Gutridge at Fox Island, wanted all such ships destroyed. Roache permitted a stay of execution after extracting a solemn promise from Jarboe never again to raise arms against the King.[13]

Jarboe and Hamilton proceeded to report to Colonel George Dashiell of Somerset County "regarding an act of piracy." On April 3 Dashiell wrote to Governor Johnson, enclosing depositions from both men. He noted bitterly that it was not the first time such acts had been committed, and that only the day before a group of citizens had "applied for measures to stop the pirates." The colonel was unsure of his authority to call out the militia in such cases, but informed the Governor that several had volunteered their services, at their own risk and expense, if they could be permitted to try to catch the pirates. A force of militia, properly commanded, the colonel suggested, "would speedily help this affair." He concluded with a request for a number of armed vessels to assist in catching the scoundrels.[14]

Roache was not the only seaborne scoundrel operating out of Somerset County. One of the more notorious of the lot and leader of a resurgence of picaroon activity was Stephen Mister, nephew to Marmaduke Mister of Smith Island and former accomplice to Joseph Wheland, Jr. Mister began to operate an armed barge out of a base on the Annemessex River in the spring of 1779. Reportedly favoring the waters about the mouth of the Nanticoke, he soon gained a reputation as one of the most active picaroons on the lower Bay. In a single week's raiding, he plundered a plantation on an island near Hooper's Strait, captured more than half a dozen vessels in Tangier Sound, and effectively instituted a total blockade of the Nanticoke. Captured vessels were regularly dispatched to Smith's Island, where his uncle either kept them or gave them to the British.[15]

On April 4, 1779, the Maryland Navy schooners *Dolphin* and *Plater*, in response to a growing cry of outrage from Bay mariners, arrived in

Tangier Sound with orders to find and capture Stephen Mister and Smith Carmine and to put an end to their depredations once and for all. A detachment of the Dorchester County Militia under Captain Smoot had already chased the marauders from the lower Tangier Islands. A few days later they learned that the picaroons had sailed up the Pocomoke to secrete their boats. Colonel Dashiell, in concert with the Maryland Navy schooners, moved quickly to seal off the area. A temporary blockade was soon established in Tangier Sound to prevent "the villains" from trading with the inhabitants of the island, where they might be sequestered. Dashiell then called a special meeting of the field officers of the Somerset County Militia, at which he decided "to secure a person well versed in [the] area where the men were hiding." Unfortunately, though such a man was found, the boats searched the islands for twelve days without success. The picaroons had skillfully eluded their frustrated pursuers amid the myriad waterways, marshes, and islands of the region.[16]

Undismayed (if somewhat hamstrung by the departure of the Maryland schooners on other business), Dashiell proposed to Colonel Henry Hooper of the Dorchester County Militia another plan to drive Mister and Carmine into a part of the country where they could be found. He suggested that the lieutenants of Accomac, Worcester, Dorchester, and Somerset counties send small, mobile search parties throughout the region and inspect every boat passing through Hooper's Strait. A dragnet of this kind might flush the rovers from their hiding place or snare them trying to escape. Dashiell acknowledged, however, that there was a good possibility that Mister had fled up the isolated Honga River to his father's home. With the recent arrival of several British warships in the area, belonging to Sir George Collier's fleet bound for an attack on Portsmouth, there was the distinct danger that "those pirates" would escape to the Royal Navy.[17]

Despite the best efforts of Colonels Dashiell and Hooper, Mister did escape, and would continue to evade capture until August 1780, when he finally fell into patriot hands in Virginia. Nothing more was heard from Smith Carmine. There would be others to take their places.

The summer of 1780 was permeated with misfortune for patriot mariners plying Chesapeake waters. Enemy privateers seemed to be everywhere, raiding and robbing at will from Tangier Sound to the Patuxent River. In early July it was reported that more than twenty-five enemy sail were in the Bay, the James River was entirely blocked up, and more than a score of vessels had fallen into enemy hands. A fleet of more than twenty merchantmen, banded together for mutual protection,

had sailed down the Bay only to meet the enemy near Smith's Point on
the Potomac. They were forced to seek protection by fleeing into the
Patuxent. By August many waterways were "so infested by the Enemy"
that shipment of goods by sea was simply considered too risky to
consider.[18] And worse, the picaroons had returned in force to add their
own vindictive ingredients to the stew. The situation degenerated
rapidly.

The raiders, both privateers and picaroons, took to attacking the
inhabitants along the shores of the Bay between the Potomac and
Patuxent. On September 4, the harried citizens of St. Mary's County
sent an urgent request for protection to Governor Thomas Sim Lee
and his Council. The Maryland government was ill-equipped to meet
the emergency. A little more than two weeks later, Governor Lee
received reports that a force of boats and small sloops was conducting
daily depredations in the Potomac region. Major Ignatius Taylor's
house on Wicomico was plundered of everything and the balance of his
property destroyed. Robert Armstrong's plantation at Point Lookout
was likewise hit, not once but twice, on August 23 and again on September 16, almost ruining the estate and his fortunes. Up and down the
Potomac coast, on both Maryland and Virginia shores, the raiders
landed time and again, carrying off slaves and livestock.[19]

"In short," remarked Colonel Richard Barnes of St. Mary's in total
frustration,

> *they are a pack of the most abandoned Fellows that ever hath molested us.*
> *They are now in Potomack and its more than probable will do considerable*
> *damage before they leave us. There force from the best information I can*
> *collect is but trifling and in my opinion reflects disgrace on this State to let*
> *them pass unmolested.*[20]

Unfortunately, events were moving too swiftly for the tidewater
governments to concentrate on just one set of marauders. They now
seemed to proliferate with each new day, and every urban settlement
or plantation on the water lived in dread of their approach.

Near the end of September, the New York Tory privateers and local
picaroons were in virtual control of the central Bay region. They began
to focus their attention on the Eastern Shore. The residents of Vienna,
Maryland, at the head of the Nanticoke, where several large patriot
ships were anchored or on the stocks abuilding, petitioned the Governor to assist them. Attack by the enemy was in the offing, and the good
citizens of the town reminded the Governor that Worcester, Somerset,
and lower Dorchester counties were equally imperiled. A half dozen
cannons, they suggested, would be a welcome addition to the town's
defenses.[21]

The appeal came too late. On September 29 Colonel Joseph Dashiell of Snow Hill dispatched a report to the Governor bearing dreadful news. Raiders had penetrated some twenty miles up the rivers of Somerset and Worcester counties, burned a brigantine belonging to Captain Robert Dashiell of the Maryland State Navy and Colonel John Henry, and plundered the goods of a number of local inhabitants. Colonel Henry alone had suffered nearly £30,000 in damage, and several vessels loaded with corn and pork for the Continental Army were locked up tight and unable to escape. Local people, he reported indignantly, had had a hand in the raid, the local militia refused to turn out, and there was a distinct danger the inhabitants would rebel if the depredations were not stopped.[22]

Soon afterward, Colonel George Dashiell fired off his own report of the affair to Lee, informing him that it was on the evening of September 24, a Sunday, that two or three barges ascended the Nanticoke as far as Vienna and burned several vessels there. The Tories and privateers were invading and looting both Somerset and Worcester counties at will, and the militia seemed helpless to prevent them from doing so, particularly at places contiguous to the water. A number of armed boats were cruising in the Pocomoke River, and several privateers were reportedly patroling Tangier Sound in search of prizes.[23]

More reports were forthcoming in the wake of the invasion. Several local Tories had gone aboard the enemy privateers, and at least a score of slaves had run off to join the foe. The vessels destroyed at Vienna included those belonging not only to Robert Dashiell, but also to James Shaw, and one under construction on the stocks belonging to Prichet Willeis. The raiders overlooked a sloop belonging to a Mr. Hopkins, but, returning downriver, had totally devastated Colonel Henry's plantation. They had returned unchallenged and triumphant to Dames Quarter, where they were received "with open arms." Colonel Joseph Dashiell had desperately sought to raise a militia force to protect several ships lying in the river laden with corn and pork for the army, but local support was so poor he could barely maintain a guard of thirty men, and then only with the greatest difficulty. Few of the militiamen would accept the government's worthless money, and the collectors of taxes "have not paid a farthing toward the governor's orders." The public coffers were bare. Even the public arms, which had been loaned to Captain Robert Dashiell of the Maryland State Navy on his last trip to Annapolis, had been captured by the raiders. The direst news, however, was that the Tories had casually remarked that "there is a large embarkation at New York bound for the bay."[24]

It seemed the worst was yet to come.

XXIII

Fangs of the Same Vulture

"We anchored in Chesapeake, after a most favorable passage, and the next day proceeded up as high as Lynnhaven." Thus wrote British General Alexander Leslie of his arrival in Bay waters with 2,500 soldiers aboard a strong Royal Navy task force on October 20, 1780.[1] Leslie's orders were to destroy rebel munitions supplies at Richmond and Petersburg and to establish a permanent post on the Elizabeth River. For the picaroons of the tidewater, the presence of the British, especially the naval squadron commanded by Captain George Gayton, rekindled flickering loyalties to the Crown. Within days of Gayton's arrival, the lower and central Bay region, particularly in the vicinity of Tory hotbeds along the Eastern Shore, literally swarmed with the predatory barges, galleys, and privateers of the enemy. Some began to probe as high as the Patuxent on the western shore, while others contented themselves with penetration raids, plundering, and foraging into the heart of the defenseless Delmarva Peninsula.

For Maryland the enemy's return to the Bay came at a most inopportune time, for the state's naval defenses had practically ceased to exist. Never very large, by early 1780 the state navy force, with the exception of the little schooners *Dolphin* and *Plater,* had all been auctioned off. Virginia, against which the main thrust of the enemy was directed, was in near chaos as far as defense capabilities for the lower Bay. Now, suddenly, the Chesapeake was being subjected not only to the assault of powerful regular land and sea forces of the British, but also to the "numberless Depredations committed with Impunity by Picaroons."[2]

One of the first targets on the revitalized picaroons' map was the Patuxent River, one of Maryland's most important and commercial waterways. Of its 110 miles, nearly 50 were accessible to seagoing ships of up to 300 tons burthen, and it sliced directly through the very heart of the western shore's richest, most productive tobacco-growing regions. The little towns dotting its banks, such as St. Leonard, Benedict, Huntingtown, Nottingham, Upper and Lower Marlboro, Pig Point, and Queen Anne's, were easily among the more prosperous in the central tidewater. Its waters were deep, its plantations numerous, and best of all for the picaroons, it was practically defenseless.

On November 5, 1780, the enemy finally entered the mouth of the Patuxent, probing only as high as Point Patience, a narrow finger of sand projecting into the river from the Calvert County peninsula. The raiders landed without warning on the point, burned the home of a local planter, John Parran, and seized two vessels laden with eighty hogsheads of tobacco. Retiring downriver, they sought provisions from Colonel William Fitzhugh's estate, Rousby Hall. Denied, they battered Fitzhugh's manor house to pieces with cannon fire, then burned what was left.[3]

With the assistance of local Tory pilots from both St. Mary's and Calvert counties, the raiders hovered about the mouth of the Patuxent and Potomac for weeks on end, pouncing on any unsuspecting prey that sailed their way. The *ad hoc* blockade was so effective that on January 3, 1781, Joseph Ford, Maryland Commissary of Purchases for St. Mary's County, complained to Annapolis that the "enemies Barges so closely watch Patuxent and Potomac Rivers, [that it] is too dangerous to send forward supplies . . ."[4]

Among those Tories who had taken heart from the resurgence of Royal Navy power on the Bay was Joseph Wheland, Jr., who had, after nearly five years of confinement, finally secured his freedom when a £10,000 bond was posted in his behalf at Baltimore by Samuel Covington and Thomas Holbrook.[5] Wheland superficially appeared willing to reconcile his loyalist leanings, for in December he met with Colonel George Dashiell of Somerset County and sought to explain away his former actions. He had, he lied, indeed been concerned in attacks on patriot shipping, but it was only because he had been a British captive, in irons, and locked up below decks during actual fighting. He had been released and his boat was returned to him soon afterward. Now he chose to come up the Wicomico with his family to remove them from exposure to the picaroons. To prove his supposedly newfound loyalty, he told Dashiell he would even serve against the Tories and contribute to the expense of building a barge to be used against them![6]

George Dashiell was completely taken in by Wheland's story, and sent a letter to Governor Lee exculpating the crafty picaroon. Immediately afterward, he received an urgent express from Colonel Henry Hooper, commander of Dorchester County, requesting him to arrest Wheland, enclosing with the letter an affidavit from one Captain Valentine Peyton of Stafford County, Virginia. Peyton, it seemed, had been captured by Wheland on August 31 off Poplar Island. Soon afterward, Captain Oakley Haddaway's vessel had also been snapped up, as was one belonging to William Barnes.[7] It seemed that the old picaroon had returned to his nefarious activities without batting an eye, in command of a white-bottomed pilot boat fitted with a jib, and a small crew of veteran Tories. Others of his kind followed suit. Among these was John Botsworth, a onetime ship's carpenter from Annapolis who had piloted British raiders up the Annemessex. Once, when a vessel Botsworth was piloting had gone into action against an American vessel, he had himself placed in chains so that in the event of capture he could claim he had been pressed into service. There were active loyalists from Holland and Tangier islands such as Thomas Prior and a desperado known only to authorities as Jack. Wheland was soon working frequently in close concert with the roaming armed barges of the Brtitish, passing secret signals of recognition when occasion demanded: three successive hoistings and lowerings of the mainsail, and then an English Jack raised at the masthead.[8] He would soon become the undisputed king of the picaroons and gather about him a loyal following. Within a short time he had assembled a small but deadly flotilla of four barges, each of them commanded by himself or one of his trusted lieutenants, Shadrack Horseman or the brothers Michael Timmons and William Timmons, Jr., of Hooper's Strait.[9]

Wheland's activities caused injury to friend and foe alike, even before he turned to outright piracy. On December 11, Samuel Covington and Thomas Holbrook were obliged to acknowledge themselves to be indebted to the State of Maryland for £5,000 each if the picaroon captain did not appear before Governor Lee and his Council "to answer a charge of high treason." Wheland, of course, failed to appear, and the bond was presumably forfeited.[10]

By late fall 1780 there seemed to be no sanctuary for patriot shipping anywhcre on the Chesapeake. "Several of the enemy's small armed vessels have recently," reported the *Pennsylvania Gazette,*

visited Oxford and other places on the Eastern Shore, Poplar Island in the Chesapeake and the Mouth of the Patuxent, on the Western Shore of this State, at all of which places their crews committed the greatest outrages. Not content with plundering the inhabitants of their Negroes, cattle and other property, they savagely laid several of their inhabitants in ashes.[11]

On January 11, 1781, the Maryland Council learned that the notorious
traitor Benedict Arnold, taking up where Alexander Leslie left off, was
at the head of an army said to be nearly three thousand strong. He had
taken Richmond and had sent a sizable force to capture Petersburg.
The state of Virginia was, of course, panic-stricken. Towns on the
Rappahannock and the Potomac, such as Fredericksburg and Alexandria, feared imminent attack. Maryland warned its county commanders that invasion of the state was expected. Relay systems were set
up along the Potomac to warn of the enemy's approach. And the
enemy did approach.

On January 22 a British frigate drove three Maryland State chartered vessels ashore, two of which were destroyed, at Cedar Point, near
the mouth of the Patuxent.[12] Raids were carried out on plantations at
Point Lookout and Smith Creek, on the Potomac. A schooner was
seized and burned several days later on the St. Mary's River. More raids
were carried out in St. Mary's County.[13]

The spate of plundering and foraging attacks continued unre-
strained on the Eastern Shore as well as on the western shores of the
Bay, and Joseph Wheland seemed to be in the thick of it. Colonel
Joseph Dashiell of Worcester County, apparently aware of the Tory's
release on bond, was more than a little upset over his inauspicious
reappearance. On March 4, Dashiell wrote in irritation to Governor
Lee:

*Joseph Whalland that old offender is down in Somerset plundering Again
and we have reason to believe that the Gaoler in Baltimore is alone to blame
as Wheland's Father informed one of our Neighbours that he let him go at
large sum time before he Came away if this practice is followed no one will
venture to take any of them up and send them forward as they will be there to
suffer for it. If I had Directions to go into Somerset, I think I could
apprehend him, as he has lately robed a certain Thomas Reuker who I think
would assist me to Trap him.[14]*

Dashiell was equally distraught over the nest of Tories on the islands
in Tangier Sound. Citing the recent robbery of a local citizen, one
Plannor Williams, by a band of nine picaroons from the sound, he
volunteered to the Governor that

*whenever your Excellency & Council propose to Remove the people and
stock of the Islands I should be Glad to assist with all my heart as I consider
them at this time the most Dangerous Enemy we have to watch the Motions
off—and am Certain if they Can do us no other Damage they will rob &
Plunder all they Can before they are removed.[15]*

Neighboring Somerset County was being constantly savaged by hit-
and-run raids, for which Dashiell repeatedly blamed British cruisers,

and more often than not, the picaroons from the larger islands in the sound.[16] On Saturday morning, March 10, he was right on both counts, when a joint privateer-picaroon expedition once again assaulted the town of Vienna.

The invaders approached the town by water, coming up the Nanticoke in a brig and two sloops, one of them newly built and armed with fourteen 18-pounders. They began their attack with a heavy bombardment of the town, firing both round and grapeshot. A few resolute militiamen, commanded by Colonel John Dickinson and Captain William Smoot, gathered along the riverbank to stand their ground. When an enemy barge loaded with men rowed toward the shore, the defenders opened up with a brisk fire on them. Three times the enemy attempted to land, and three times they were beaten back. Finally, the intense fire from the shipping drove the militiamen back, and the barge reached the shore, though not without loss on both sides. Three of the attackers were wounded and one was killed, while the defenders suffered one killed. Soon after the enemy drew up on the shore, a flag of truce was forwarded to the militiamen. The attackers said they wanted nothing more than the grain stored in the town. If the militiamen would give it up, the invaders would leave a part of it for the inhabitants and would plunder nothing more. They promised to pay the market price for the grain, but if the defenders refused to agree to the deal and resumed hostilities, the town would be burned to the ground and everything in it destroyed. Colonel Henry Hooper, who had apparently arrived on the scene just before the landing, reasoned that as his force "could defend nothing, the Town and Grain lying under the command of their Vessels we agreed to their Terms."[17]

The raiders carried off between 900 and 1,000 bushels of Indian corn before the eyes of the militiamen. While the flotilla lay at anchor, Hooper learned that another privateer brig guarded the mouth of the river, preventing possible relief or rescue by water. Speaking to several of the enemy, he discovered that they were actually foraging for Benedict Arnold's forces in Virginia. The invaders expressed disappointment that there had not been more grain stored in the town. They hinted broadly that they might next try the Choptank or Wicomico rivers for additional grain supplies. Since there was also a serious need for planks to complete the construction of some forty flat-bottomed boats being built at Portsmouth, they were also in the market for lumber boats. In fact, much to Hooper's chagrin, they had already captured two or three during their short visit to the Nanticoke! On Monday morning the invaders, having honored their word, and to Hooper's great relief, departed.[18]

Colonel Joseph Dashiell, whose hands were quite full resisting landings from the raiding cruisers and barges on Worcester County shores, was deeply angered over the surrender of Vienna and blamed Hooper for the militia's retreat under fire. The "Lieutenant of that County arrived and ordered the Militia to retreat as I am told, & has made a Capitulation that in my Oppinion will Disgrace us, & be attended with the worst Consequences."[19]

British depredations continued without letup in the Bay. The port of Annapolis was blockaded by enemy warships. The Elk River area was threatened. Landings were carried out on Poole's Island and in Harford County, and the Maryland state government rushed to mobilize. Scenes of chaos and disorder were repeated throughout the central and upper Bay region—a schooner run ashore by Tory barges here, a refugee with all his belongings forced to flee before the marauders there, and everywhere looting, homes burned, and waterborne commerce throttled by picaroons, privateers, and the Royal Navy.[20]

By early April Maryland's two principal waterways, the Potomac and Patuxent, were being brutally hit almost simultaneously. On Saturday, April 7, a picaroon barge, manned principally by blacks but commanded by Captain Jonathan Robinson, a white man, probed far up the Patuxent, causing the local population along the banks no end of despair. Within a short time of the alarm, riverfront homes from Swanson's Creek northward to Upper Marlboro were totally abandoned in an atmosphere of panic. The picaroons proceeded as high up as Lower Marlboro, where they landed unopposed and promptly plundered the town. The home of Captain John David, former commander of the Maryland State galley *Conqueror,* along with an unsuspecting traveler sleeping inside, was burned to the ground. Colonel Peregrine Fitzhugh and William Allein, a local merchant, were taken prisoner but later released. All of the vessels lying before the town, including one fully laden with provisions, were captured. The tobacco stores in the local warehouse were entirely plundered. On Sunday morning, the raiders, satiated by their robberies, set off down the river, with a strong northwest wind behind them and a large band of slaves belonging to Colonel Fitzhugh, now freed from their bondage.[21]

"Every hours experience," wrote Stephen West, a leader and civic bulwark of the Patuxent mercantile community, "shows the necessity of having some Armed Vessels in the great Rivers especially the Patuxent and Potowmack." His prognosis was underscored almost immediately, for the barge escaped unscathed and on the day following the raid rendezvoused with two ships and a brig at the river's mouth. That evening, the barge landed a few miles to the south at Cedar Point on the Bay, and its occupants ruthlessly burned the home of Nicholas Sewell, an ardent patriot of St. Mary's County.[22]

Similar depredations were carried out by enemy privateers on the Potomac. Probes were carried out as far upriver as Alexandria, followed by a series of landings at various places along both shores of the river. Homes and plantations were plundered and burned, slaves stolen, and innocent civilians carted off as prisoners. At Young's Ferry, Hooe's Ferry, Robert Washington's plantation, and Port Tobacco they came ashore and conducted their nefarious activities. Estates such as Walter Hanson's, the "Elegant Seat" of George Dent, and others fell victim. Local militia units seemed powerless to stem the assaults. At Alexandria the militia mustered, and the foe turned his attentions to the Maryland shore. There too, opposition congealed only to fall away under heavy attack.

Finally, about the latter part of April, the raiders withdrew, the holds of their ships and barges filled with plunder. It had been a miserable experience for Maryland and Virginia, both of which had been entirely unprepared to meet the emergency. "I expect we shall have frequent visits from these plundering Banditts," wrote Thomas Stone of Maryland after the raiders' departure. "I hope we will so well prepare as to repel their attacks that they will find the business as unprofitable as it is disgraceful."[23]

It was a vain hope.

Despite the best intentions of the nearly impotent Maryland government to blunt the amphibious depredations of picaroons and privateers, it was becoming painfully evident that the burden of naval defense—until the State Navy might be revitalized and operational—would have to fall on regional self-defense efforts. The Eastern Shore, isolated from the center of state government and frequently cut off from outside help, was particularly vulnerable. "Local circumstances render it Difficult," wrote two Dorchester County leaders, Robert Goldsborough and Gustavus Scott, "for the Inhabitants of this Shore, exposed as they are to the utmost Calamities of War & Piracies to expect assistance from our more powerfull neighbours of the western shore." Dorchester County, with 1,700 effective fighting men (of which only 150 were armed), reflected the deadly vulnerability to attack of all the Eastern Shore counties without naval protection.[24]

One of the first major efforts to address the issue of regional defense in the absence of a state navy force was in Somerset County. On March 21, 1781, twenty-six of the county's leading citizens, stirred to action by the mounting attacks against their region by picaroons and privateers, proposed to the Maryland Council a scheme fathered by Captain Zedekiah Walley. Walley's plan was to build a barge of 50-foot keel length capable of carrying 60 men and a 24-pound bow gun to protect county waters. Such a vessel might be built for less than £150 hard money, and Walley himself volunteered to superintend the construction.[25] Though the state was sympathetic to the proposal, there was virtually no money in the treasury. Somerset Countians, therefore, went ahead on their own with the project. Built at Snow Hill, the barge was dubbed *Protector*. She was destined to sail with great success, on one occasion even driving the picaroon raiders from the Pocomoke region and capturing several prizes. Soon, taking heart from Somerset's self-reliant stance, Queen Anne's and Talbot counties offered to support and maintain a barge called *Experiment,* and to build a number of boats for their own protection. These vessels would be stationed in Eastern Bay and would cruise occasionally between Kent Point and Tilghman Island. Dorchester County followed suit with the construction of the barge *Defence.* Eventually, more barges, either captured from the enemy or finally constructed for the state government, began to appear in Bay waters, vessels with names like *Intrepid, Terrible,* and *Fearnaught.*[26]

On the western shore, the first area to consider a local naval defense force and a policy of its own were the counties bordering on the Patuxent River, but principally Prince George's and Calvert counties. It had been apparent, even before the Lower Marlboro raid, that the Patuxent needed a standing defense system to counter picaroon incursions. Driven, like their counterparts on the Eastern Shore, to desperation, twenty-three merchants and gentlemen of Calvert and Prince George's counties convened a meeting at the river port of Nottingham on April 21. There, they set in motion a plan to raise their own naval defense force. Calling themselves the Board of Patuxent Associators and led by Colonel William Fitzhugh, the body was soon able to secure authority from the Governor of Maryland to manage their own regional defenses, impress vessels, move equipment, and protect the Patuxent.[27]

Yet even as the Board of Patuxent Associators sought to improve the river's defenses against the picaroons, the battle raged on. On April 25, off the mouth of the river two American privateer schooners, *Antelope,* Captain Frederick Folger, and *Felicity,* Captain Cole, fell in with a New York privateer called *Jack-a-Lanthorn,* Captain Mangen, of six guns and thirty-six men, and a small prize sloop. The two American privateers had already captured a British ship called *Resolution* in the lower Bay, and when they encountered and took the New Yorker, they not only relieved the Patuxent region of a potential attacker, but promised to enrich the coffers of their owners through the sale of their new prizes.[28]

The Board of Patuxent Associators was frustrated by lack of funds, state support, and a paucity of armament, supplies, and vessels. Yet the members pressed ahead. Artillery was mounted at strategic positions on the river. Beacons were erected at appropriate locations to provide early warning of intruders. And a move was set afoot to secure a row galley, a 40-foot-long armed barge, and a whaleboat to serve as lookout. A committee was sent to Baltimore to examine the recently captured *Jack-a-Lanthorn* for possible purchase, but the price was too high. On May 10, the Board's agents, Samuel Maynard and Renaldo Johnson, purchased a ship, a battered schooner called *Nautilus,* salvaged from the shoals of Cedar Point, where she had been run aground by a British warship in January. This vessel, of eighty-five tons burthen, was armed with eight 3-pounders and lay at Fells Point. The price was right, and an agreement was struck with her owners, Dorsey Wheeler and Company and Thomas Worthington. The ship was sold for 357,000-pound weight of tobacco.[29] Captain John David of Lower Marlboro was charged with command of the vessel and with getting her down the picaroon-infested Bay to the Patuxent. Apparently, though, no one bothered to consult with David before assigning him the task, for he had already engaged to serve in another vessel. By the end of May *Nautilus* was still lying at Fells Point, Baltimore. A barge and a whaleboat had yet to be procured. When *Nautilus* finally did reach the Patuxent, her suitability as a guardship was apparently questionable, for on August 11 she was put up for sale at Nottingham by the Board.[30] With the sale of *Nautilus,* the intended fulcrum of the Patuxent naval defense, the efforts of the short-lived Board of Associators to protect their river ended in abject failure.

The fear of an invasion of Maryland lingered like a dull headache throughout the early summer of 1781. County militia units were held in readiness to march at a moment's notice, and commissaries were directed to purchase or seize all stocks in the event of attack to prevent them from falling into enemy hands. Enemy warships appeared in the Potomac again in early June, dispatching armed barges on occasion to conduct foraging raids or simply to plunder and terrorize the civilian population. By mid-June the enemy had disappeared from the river, but the picaroons, hovering like birds of prey, frequently flew in to pick up the leavings.

In July, Joseph Wheland struck again. This time the victim was *Greyhound,* "a beautiful boat laden with Salt, Peas, Pork, Bacon and some Dry Goods." Captured in Hooper's Strait, the skipper and his crew were detained for twenty-four hours aboard Wheland's barge, during which time one of the passengers, a Mr. Furnival, was robbed of his money and watch "and indeed every Thing that the Thieves could lay their Hands on." The captain of the schooner and his men were set ashore at Dames Quarter. Before he was released, Furnival later reported, he "saw several other Bay craft fall into the Fangs of the same Vultures."[31]

As the picaroon attacks continued unabated, pressure increased for the Maryland government to act. The region between the mouth of the Patuxent south to Tangier Sound had become a virtual no-man's-land through which shipping ventured to pass at its own great risk. In early July Samuel Smith of Baltimore informed Governor Lee that two of his vessels, commanded by James Rouse and Martin Trout (apparently chartered to the state to carry tobacco), had been taken. "This is a heavy loss to my business," he complained, as "they were taken just coming out of Patuxent by three Barges full of Men one of which went down & the other two up to burn Capt. [Jeremiah] Yellet's Brig."[32]

From Salisbury, Joseph Dashiell informed the Governor that "there is four privatars and as many Barges in our sound they have plundered the Houses of Leven Gale & Levin Dashiell & Burned all the Houses of the Latter yesterday morning."[33] Such reports flowed daily through the Maryland chief executive's office. Not only were picaroons becoming bolder, but the occasional barbarity of their actions seemed to be increasing as well. In mid-July Captain Gale of the Somerset County Militia was literally hauled from his bed by a protégé of Joseph Wheland, one Captain John McMullen, commander of the picaroon barge *Restoration*, accompanied by four white men and nine black men. The unfortunate militiaman was hauled off to Clay Island, "where he was most inhumanly whipt six lashes" and then hung until they believed him dead. Soon after he was cut down, he revived. McMullen attempted to persuade his crew to hang their victim again, but they refused. He proposed drowning the poor man, but again they refused. Finally, Gale was released after taking an oath not to bear arms against the King.[34]

Wheland, McMullen, and Robinson frequently acted in concert now, occasionally rendezvousing at Courtney's Island before setting out upon a cruise. Wheland and his chief lieutenant, William Timmons, Jr., occasionally preferred the mobility of a small whaleboat to the larger barge, and visited the Wicomico or any other place along the Eastern Shore to their liking, defended or not, with relative impunity.

They did not discriminate in the selection of their men, and frequently employed black slaves whom they had freed during their attacks as crewmen. Indeed, the black picaroons proved to be so ferocious in battle as to intimidate their white opponents, a trait that frequently played in Wheland's favor. Neither were the picaroons particular in the selection of their victims, be it a helpless widow or a patriot militia officer of local political or economic stature.[35] Eventually, for Joseph Wheland, it wouldn't even matter whether his prey was patriot or Tory.

At last, in response to the picaroon and privateering depredations of the foe, Maryland fielded its first barge flotilla to cruise since the reduction of its Navy in 1778-1779. The flotilla's first expedition, initiated on July 28, 1781, was designed specifically to rid the Bay of the picaroons. Commodore George Grason of the Maryland Navy was given command. The flotilla was to be composed of the barges *Intrepid,* Captain Levin Speeden, *Terrible,* Captain Robert Dashiell, and Grason's own flagship *Revenge.* Two days after sailing, on July 30, the little squadron engaged two picaroon barges, a whaleboat, and two smaller vessels. By chance they had fallen in with the leading pirates on the Bay, Wheland, Robinson, and McMullen. The barge *Restoration,* with McMullen, and two boats were taken. Robinson in the second barge, and Wheland in the whaleboat, were put to flight. Euphoria over this victory was contagious on the Eastern Shore. "The event has given general joy," wrote one Matthew Tilghman on August 3, "and if we cannot flatter ourselves with peace, we begin to think we have a chance of remaining safe from the plunderers that have late infested us."[36]

The picaroons were not intimidated in the least and did not refrain from their attacks. In late August they again visited the Patuxent, leaving the river only after capturing three vessels laden with tobacco. On August 27 two barges pushed up the Nanticoke to Vienna, plundered the inhabitants of the town, and captured two or three fully laden vessels lying in the river there. One of the barges proceeded up beyond the town and captured two more vessels, even as her sister barge retired downriver with her prizes. Belatedly alerted, Colonel Henry Hooper collected a party of militia as quickly as possible and retook three of the vessels. Then, posting some men on each side of the river, he effectively cut off the retreat of one of the barges, forcing the enemy to run her ashore and make their escape on foot. Three picaroons were captured and sent to Annapolis on August 31. After securing the barge, Hooper dispatched a party of light horse down the river, but the second barge and her prizes had disappeared. Upon receiving a report from the party of light horse that the enemy's barge was not to be seen in the river, the colonel discharged the militia.[37]

At one o'clock the following morning, Hooper received an urgent express that the barge had returned in the night and made the inhabitants of Vienna prisoners. Orders were issued for the militia to reassemble and march to the town. But it was already too late, for the elusive enemy had escaped once again.[38]

Farther south on the Chesapeake, Tory and privateer raids were conducted with equally unvarnished bravado, though they were increasingly motivated, as the war dragged on, by a desire for the fruits of plunder rather than by patriotic devotion to the King and England. Occasionally, but with accelerating frequency, picaroon raids were conducted without discrimination against both sides. By the late summer of 1781 Gwynn's Island at the mouth of the Piankatank River was frequently being used as a picaroon base for barge operations—which were increasingly directed against fellow Tories as well as patriots. A number of picaroons had, in essence, degenerated from seaborne guerrillas to little more than out-and-out pirates, who plundered at will, when and whom they pleased. In mid-June, General George Weedon of Virginia wrote that some "of their vessels are continually in the mouth of the river and I am convinced from many circumstances hold a correspondence with . . . inhabitants of Gwyn's Island and Middlesex . . . " The loyalists of the region, as far away as Urbanna on the Rappahannock, a place patriots called a "sink" of Tory disaffection, were rapidly becoming disenchanted with their so-called waterborne allies. On June 19, it was reported that such notable and influential loyalists as Ralph Wormley of Rosegill, John Randolph Grymes, Beverly Robinson, and the inhabitants of Urbanna themselves had been plundered by Tory picaroons. When Wormley and Robinson assembled a band of loyalists at Robinson's estate, "to consult a plan of recovery," the picaroons struck again "and plundered them a second time, without landing at any other house . . . "[39]

The depredations of the pirate picaroons and privateers had by now disgusted the leaders of both sides. Even Lord Cornwallis, who had recently arrived at Portsmouth, Virginia, with his veteran army, was shocked by their vindictive activities and commented in a letter to Sir Henry Clinton, British Commander in Chief in North America, that the "horrid enormity of our privateers in the Chesapeake Bay" was quite "prejudicial to his Majesty's service." Indeed, it was driving some loyalists away from the Crown and hardening the resolve of the American cause.[40]

Cornwallis, however, had more important matters to occupy his time than the dirty little guerrilla war on the Bay. He had an army to move, and a town to fortify—a little place on the York River called Yorktown. Tory picaroons, such as the likes of Joseph Wheland, Jr., were Maryland's and Virginia's problem.

XXIV

A Set of Gallows-Marked Rascals

By the summer of 1781 the accumulated stories of the adventures and exploits of young Captain John Greenwood, master and part owner of a small Bay trading schooner, would have filled a volume had the selective eye of history been upon him. At the tender age of fifteen he had joined the ragtag American Army encamped before his native town of Boston. As a fife-major for the fifteenth Massachusetts Regiment, he had served from Bunker Hill to the Battle of Trenton. Leaving the army, he went to sea, sailing under such redoubtable mariners as Commodore John Manly and Captain David Porter. Once captured, he suffered five months of hell in a Barbadian prison, and then returned to sea as second mate of a Boston letter of marque. In August 1781, his ship arrived at Baltimore, and twenty-one-year-old John Greenwood decided to become his own master.[1]

"As I did not like," he wrote years later,

to sail with a captain, who was afraid of his own shadow, and as from the voyage having been altered to return to the West Indies, I was at liberty to go with him or not, [and] as I pleased, I quitted him.[2]

With a pocket full of money, presumably his share of the proceeds from the privateering venture, Greenwood proposed to the privateer's first mate, a man named Myrik, that, since neither of them liked the captain, they purchase between them a small vessel to haul freight on the Chesapeake Bay. With the mouth of the Bay again crawling with British cruisers and Tory barges, and Lord Cornwallis's army firmly ensconced at Yorktown, Chesapeake commerce was sorely depressed, and a schooner of forty tons burthen was procured with little difficulty. Neither Greenwood, who owned two-thirds share, nor Myrik, who owned the remainder, seemed the least bit worried. Since ownership was entirely between the two men, they "were then both Captains." A crewman was hired, and the first freight, a load of Indian corn for Elkridge Landing on the Patapsco, was taken aboard at Baltimore. After their first voyage and a great deal of disagreement, a stranding or two, and other tribulations, Myrik proclaimed "he would rather make a West Indian voyage than take another such trip" on the Chesapeake. His share in the schooner was sold to a Fells Point mariner, and John Greenwood found himself with a new partner.[3]

Greenwood assumed total command and took on freight consisting of rigging and other articles for his second voyage, this time consigned to interests on the Piankatank River. That the Piankatank was perilously close to the entrenched army and fleet of Cornwallis, a score of miles to the south, or that the river lay in the heart of picaroon territory, did not dampen the young captain's resolve. Despite the danger, he arrived safely, discharged his cargo, and took on a load of oats bound for Baltimore and seven passengers, sutlers or rum sellers to Washington's army, who carried "considerable money with them."[4]

The little schooner made sail out of the Piankatank late on a Sunday afternoon, but, wind and tide being adverse, Greenwood decided to drop anchor. "My passengers, and partners likewise," he later recalled, "being nearly drunk, all went down in the cabin to sleep and left the man we hired and myself on deck to take care of the vessel." With the tide, the anchor was hauled, and all sail made for the mouth of the river. The schooner passed the shoals of Stingray Point and stood into the Bay. Since the wind was ahead, Greenwood was obliged to bring his ship about and tack for pine-covered Windmill Point at the mouth of the Rappahannock.

As he neared the entrance to the river, he casually noted another schooner at anchor close under the point. Thinking everything in order, and growing sleepy, he called for his partner to take the helm. With his greatcoat wrapped about him, Greenwood crawled down into the hold and fell fast asleep on the cargo of oats. A few minutes had passed when he was jolted into consciousness by a loud noise on deck and the clatter of swords and cutlasses. Thinking it nothing more than some of the passengers playing, he gruffly barked out for them to be quiet. Suddenly, through the open hatchway, "a fellow leapt down into the hold, gave me a stroke or two with his sword and bade me jump up on deck." The first person the captain saw on coming out of the hold was a man he knew as well as his own brother.[5]

"Why, Montgomery," exclaimed Greenwood, "are you among these pirates?"

Before the man could reply, a tall, gaunt-looking fellow in his shirt sleeves, wearing a gold-laced jacket that "he had robbed from some old trooper on the eastern shore," stepped up. With a hasty glance, Greenwood noted with dismay that the schooner he had spied near the point had shielded from view two row galleys, one with thirty-two oars and more than sixty men aboard, the other with twelve to fourteen oars and twenty-five or thirty men.[6]

"Sir," said the fellow with the gold lace, obviously the commander of the large galley, incensed at the charge of piracy, "I will let you know that I have as good a commission as any seventy-four in his Britannic Majesty's service."

The man with the gold lace proved to be none other than the notorious Joseph Wheland, Jr. Greenwood quickly attempted to make amends, noting that he had mistaken them for one of Maryland's own fleet from Annapolis, "who would at times board and plunder even our own vessels." The young captain sighed at the sad fortunes of war which had permitted him to fall into enemy hands and beseeched the infamous Tory to let him keep his clothes at least. Wheland consented.[7]

With half an hour's daylight left, Greenwood's still-groggy passengers were transferred to the large galley, and his partner, "having abused the Captain," was placed in irons in the stern of the small galley under the guard of a black man. Greenwood and an Irish passenger were permitted to remain aboard the schooner, which was manned by a prize crew consisting of the captain of the small galley and nine crewmen, including Montgomery. The Tory prize captain was a six-foot-tall former slave named George, whose late master had been Colonel Fitzhugh of Virginia. Captain George's galley was effectively fastened by her grappling to the schooner's stern sheets for towing.[8]

As evening fell, Wheland prepared for a descent upon the loyalist estate of Mr. Gwynn, on Gwynn's Island, where Greenwood had just deposited freight and a hogshead of rum. Orders were given for Captain George to follow, and come to anchor off the island. There he was to await Wheland's return. With muffled oars, the Tory raiders set off to perform another robbery, this time on their own people.[9]

The wind shifted and blew fair from the north. As Captain George, "in beating about to fetch Gwynn's Island," struck upon the sands of Stingray Point, he decided to come to anchor to await morning and the tide. At daylight, a tobacco drougher was spotted, fully laden, standing along shore. Captain George ordered the anchor raised and set off in hot pursuit. As the drougher passed by within gunshot range, the Tories began firing their muskets. With the small galley in tow behind, however, George found it impossible to overtake his quarry. Ordering another man into the galley and transferring Greenwood's partner back to the schooner, the black captain left her at anchor and renewed the chase. About this time, Wheland's galley reappeared and also took up the chase, firing a 6-pound cannon in her bow, without effect. As Wheland passed, Captain George gave over the chase, hauled wind, and prepared to take the small galley back in tow. Afterwards, he ordered three more of his men back aboard, thus making five in all. They were set to work cleaning several of their muskets, which had misfired at the drougher.[10]

Eventually, Captain George ordered the schooner to stand off to join Wheland's galley, which was about six miles distant and running in for Gwynn's Island. Though each of the four Tories remaining aboard the schooner was armed with a pair of pistols, a sword, and a gun, and the small galley was close by under tow, Greenwood and his partner boldly decided to attempt to retake their ship.[11]

> Our plan was to persuade the captain that there was money hidden in the cabin, this was done forthwith and down he went in search of it. There now remained on deck Montgomery, a person at the helm steering and a man by the fore-mast. As I stood by the cabin door I called Montgomery to me and, as he came near, seized him by the collar, tripped him up with my foot, and pitched him into the cabin, at the same time my partner caught up the cutlass, which the man at the helm had carelessly left on the stern-sheets, and running forward struck down the man there.[12]

Terrified, the helmsman cried out, "Heim! heim!"

In desperation, he hauled out the tiller and made a swing at Greenwood with it but missed. The tiller dropped to the deck. In an instant, Greenwood's partner was aft with his cutlass raised, ready to strike the Tory's head. The helmsman, frightened by the sudden attack, jumped over the side. Unable to swim, he struggled to stay afloat. Greenwood and his partner, however, had their hands too full to attend to a rescue, for the galleymen in the schooner's wake now began to fire at the two mariners as fast as they could load their muskets.[13]

"Our schooner was then all in the wind," recalled Greenwood,

> in sight of the large galley and dropping astern and afoul of the smaller one. I told my partner to run forward and bear off the jib to wear or fetch the schooner round, so that we might put her head towards Baltimore; this he did while I was casting off the main-sheet which was close hauled. At the time the galley in tow was so near that I could have jumped on board her, and the fire of the muskets almost burned my hair, but they were such bad marksmen that they did not hit either of us.[14]

Greenwood, at the suggestion of his partner, quickly seized the grapnel in the stern sheets and threw it overboard.

"There, my boys," he said, "you have got your galley all to yourselves."

"Fire at that fellow with the great coat on," shouted the galleymen futilely. But it was already too late, for Greenwood and his partner had made good their escape. Wheland, however, doggedly refused to give up the chase.[15]

The schooner pressed northward before a fair wind. It was quickly decided to let Montgomery, who was locked in the cabin with Captain George, come on deck and dress the wounds of his mate at the foremast, who had been struck with the cutlass across the shoulder bone. When Montgomery emerged, he trembled uncontrollably, "for he was a great coward, and I presume," remarked Greenwood later, "never fired a gun in war during his life time." He then ordered Captain George topside.

"Master, I hope you will not kill me," George pleaded.[16]

Greenwood sternly informed the ex-slave that he would be safe as long as he behaved in a proper manner, but if he made so much as a wry face, he would be put to death instantly. The black man was so terrified that his obedience was total. With Wheland's galley closing the distance between the two vessels, Greenwood ordered George to take the helm, but with a reminder "that, if, either through accident or design, he jibed the vessel, I would that instant kill him."[17]

The pursuer and his quarry were soon "wing and wing" before the wind, but the schooner proved the better sailer, and after a desperate chase, the galley gave up. Wheland returned to Gwynn's Island, declaring in no uncertain terms that had he overtaken his former captives, he would have massacred them all.[18]

Greenwood also had a few choice remarks about the predatory picaroons who had captured him. They were, in general, he said,

a set of gallows-marked rascals, fit for nothing but thieves; hellhounds and plunderers from inoffensive, unarmed people, they seemed to be without any kind of principle and I really believe that ten honest, religious, determined men could intimidate or drive a hundred such villains. Their whole object was plunder and they paid no manner or regard to the vessel they despoiled, be it loyal or otherwise; gain was all they sought, and to acquire from others what they were through mere laziness unable to obtain for themselves . . . Capt. Whalen appeared to me to be as great a villain as ever was unhung, and all such characters the British seemed to encourage in their employ . . .[19]

Having escaped, Greenwood now discovered that there was neither food nor water aboard, since the picaroons had devoured and drank everything. Thirsty and hungry, the mariners' tribulations were far from over. After running aground several times among the islands of Tangier Sound and on Smith's Point, "we were again attacked by another pirate, as I call them; the Chesapeake Bay being at that time . . . infested by innumerable pickaroons, barges, gallies and small privateers."[20]

Somehow, Greenwood and his partner reached Baltimore safely. When the news of his capture and escape circulated about the waterfront, a mob gathered and came aboard the schooner, carried the prisoners to the nearest blacksmith shop, and put them in irons. Captain Greenwood, despising the courage of the mob against helpless prisoners of war almost as much as he despised the likes of a Wheland, remonstrated against them. It was pointless to place them in irons, he said, for they had already received their punishment by being made prisoners. The mob instantly turned hostile, accusing the incredulous captain of being a Tory himself![21]

Deeming discretion the better part of valor, Greenwood left the prisoners to the untender mercy of the mob, undoubtedly asking himself who was worse, the thieving picaroons or the Baltimore mob. His own career as a Bay captain, however, was over. "Thinking it imprudent to trust myself again down the bay trading," he wrote with some bitterness, "I was obliged to sell my part of the schooner, for if that rascal Whalen could have taken me I should have been killed without mercy."[22]

XXV

Signal Acts of Valour

The surrender of Lord Cornwallis at Yorktown on October 19, 1781, and the assertion of control of the Chesapeake Bay by the French Navy provided the tidewater with a brief but much-longed-for respite in the war against the picaroons. It was a brief period of euphoria in which many Marylanders began to assume that the worst was over. As a portion of the French fleet wintered blissfully on the York, the Maryland Navy barge flotilla was laid up and its seamen discharged. Joseph Wheland, Jr., and his trusty lieutenant Michael Timmons had fled to North Carolina where they were finally captured. All seemed well, but there were a few discouraging setbacks. When the Governor's Council, in hopes of extraditing the two villains, offered to send a party to bring them back, the crafty picaroons somehow managed to slip through the fingers of the Carolina authorities and escaped.[1]

Despite a temporary decline in raiding during the days following Yorktown, the Chesapeake tidewater was destined to suffer through nearly eighteen more months of ruthless attacks—not by regular British naval forces, but by Royal Navy deserters, marauding privateers, and diehard picaroons from the Eastern Shore. As early as November 1781, barely a month after Cornwallis's surrender, two enemy vessels were pursued, and a third, a schooner, was captured by the Maryland privateer *Porpoise.* John Stewart, writing from *Porpoise* in Hooper's Strait, sent back to Annapolis the disheartening news that other enemy privateers from New York were again entering the Bay in numbers.[2]

Thus, as the war began to wind down in other quarters and peace talks sputtered to life, the picaroons and privateers on the Chesapeake began to reassert themselves. By the end of the winter of 1781-1782 the Maryland government would be faced once more with contending with

incursions in every quarter. On March 12, 1782, the Governor's Council was informed that a Tory sloop or schooner and a consort of two or
three picaroon whaleboats "have done considerable Mischief about the
Mouth of Potowmack, and have taken several Craft higher up, as well
as lower down the Bay." Commodore George Grason was ordered to
proceed to the Miles River, where the state flotilla was laid up. There he
was to fit out the barges as necessary and recruit a sufficient number of
men to man the fleet and cruise against the raiders. Forty men belonging to Smallwood's Regiment of the Continental Army stationed in
Annapolis were to join the force, providing additional manpower.[3]

Four days later, the emergency intensified, as the picaroons were
reported raiding as high up the Bay as Sharps Island, some distance
above the mouth of the Patuxent, where they made more captures.[4]

Grason could neither raise enough men nor prepare the flotilla to
sail in the short time the government demanded. On March 19 the
embarrassed Council dispatched a letter to the Count De Kergaiou
Loemaria, acting commander of the French naval squadron on the
Chesapeake, "in flattering Expectation that it will be in your Power . . .
to take effectual Measures to strip this contemptible Enemy of their
Plunder, and punish them for their Temerity."[5]

In actuality, the French had been quite busy for more than a month
chasing enemy vessels about Virginia waters. The ships *La Suzanne* and
Tarleton, a prize vessel, were stationed in the Bay to maintain a vigil, and
on March 28 Loemaria, from aboard the warship *La Sybille* in York
River, reported the capture of at least one "pirate craft," which was
promptly taken into service and armed. Four French corvettes of six
and fourteen guns, it was promised, would be sent to Maryland's aid as
soon as possible. The French, however, were hamstrung by a scarcity of
shallow-draft vessels. Their frigates were better suited to defend the
entrance to the Bay than to probe up shoally creeks and rivers in which
the picaroons hid. That, the French politely suggested to the Maryland
government, was the business of the state's galleys and armed boats.[6]

On March 29 Commodore Grason informed the Governor's Council
that the barges were almost ready for service. Again he was ordered to
man them, engaging crews for terms not to exceed nine months.[7] And
again Grason had to report that he could not fill out the necessary
manpower quota, though Tory attacks continued unabated, primarily
from bases in the Tangier Island region. On April 13 the Council
presented Grason with a new set of sailing directions.

*That you may not be subject to the Inconveniences resulting from too
particular, or too confined Instructions, we will inform you generally that,
to afford Security to the Bay Trade, Safety to the Inhabitants on the Shores,*

*by taking, destroying, or driving off the vessels of the Enemy, and to
depopulate the Tangier Islands, within the Limits of this State, are the
Objects of your Cruize, and we leave it to your Judgement and Experience
to execute them in the speediest and most effectual Manner in your Power . .*

It was the Council's opinion that there was considerable evidence to
support the conclusion that the people of the Tangier Islands were
among the principal perpetrators of the recent depredations in Maryland waters. Nothing less than a total depopulation of the islands, by
force, would suffice to eliminate the problem. Grason, therefore, was
directed to seize every inhabitant of the islands, within the jurisdiction
of Maryland, below Hooper's Strait, and between the Sound and the
Bay, along with all of their vessels, boats, canoes, and property. Having
done this, he was to turn them over to the militia commanders of the
counties in which they respectively resided, who would then "dispose
of them agreeable to Law." Any of those men taken prisoner that were
willing to serve aboard the flotilla could, if Grason thought proper, be
enlisted. A proper account of the number and names of the people
delivered up, and of their property confiscated, was to be kept. The
commanders of Worcester, Dorchester, and Somerset counties were
directed to keep an accurate list of the inhabitants and their effects
being removed. "The old Men, Women and Children must be disposed
of as the Law directs."[8]

The Council's sailing orders, aside from the preposterous enormity
of their intent, were totally unrealistic in considering the means with
which they were to be carried out. Grason was experiencing extreme
difficulties in even recruiting enough men to sail the tiny flotilla. How
he would fare in rounding up the entire population of the Tangier
region, hearty loyalists who had defeated every effort to bring them to
heel throughout the war, was a question the Council conveniently
overlooked.

The French, it seemed, even with their deep-draft ships, were having
more success in the war with the picaroons than their American counterparts. But they too had their setbacks. On April 25 a French 16-gun
brig chased an 8-gun New York loyalist privateer sloop up the Bay but
lost sight of her in the dark. It was uncertain whether the sloop had
continued her course, run into Eastern Bay on the Eastern Shore, or
tacked back down the Chesapeake. A prize taken by the sloop was
recaptured and the people aboard informed the authorities that their
vessel had been brought into the Chesapeake in the company of two
Tory barges which had then gone raiding up the Potomac.[9]

Dismayed by the news, the Council, again changing its instructions to

Grason, abandoned the idea of depopulating Tangier and directed him to sail without delay to the mouth of the Potomac and capture the enemy marauders. Thirty soldiers under the command of Captain Basque of Smallwood's regiment were assigned to Grason's command. Yet even this failed to flesh out the manpower needs. Owing to "some unaccountable Mismanagement" Basque's men were delayed in linking up with the commodore, and the squadron failed to sail as planned.[10] Grason, now under great pressure from the Council but still unable to fill his squadron's complement, could wait no longer. He boldly resolved to sally out alone in his little flagship *Revenge*. A brief account of his expedition in the *Maryland Journal and Baltimore Advertiser* on May 14 is all that exists to tell the tale of what followed:

> A number of small Privateers, 5 of which are said to be armed Barges, manned principally by desperate Refugees, now infest our Bay and greatly annoy its Commerce. Three of the latter lately captured an armed Boat from Annapolis under Captain Grason's command, near the Tangier Islands, after a sharp Contest in which the brave Captain and several of his Men lost their Lives after performing Signal Acts of Valour.[11]

The Maryland Assembly, humiliated and saddened over the defeat of the Grason expedition, reacted forcefully. On May 22 a new Act for the Protection of the Bay Trade was passed, and a commission to fit, arm, and man four barges and one galley (or other vessel of force) was appointed. This squadron was to cooperate with both Virginia and French naval forces stationed on the York to rid the Bay of the picaroon menace forever. The singular difference between the Act of May 22 and those of earlier times was that for the first time, the Assembly made funds from the sale of confiscated British property available to pay for the barges and the personnel to man them.[12]

In unison with the Maryland Assembly's positive steps, the Chevalier de Villebrune, now acting commander of the French forces on the York, informed Governor Lee on May 24 that French naval forces, including an armed barge, would be available to act in concert with the American barge flotilla on the Bay. If a rendezvous time might be fixed for the two forces, Villebrune volunteered to throw in a sloop for the protection of the combined fleet.[13]

A sense of urgency pervaded the tidewater, even as the Maryland forces were being readied. In early July two enemy barges hovering off the mouth of the Potomac entered the river and attacked an American vessel off St. George's Island. The picaroons were completely unintimidated, even by the patriot ship of force which they had selected as their victim, the Massachusetts privateer brigantine *Ranger*. Though small, carrying only seven guns and twenty men under the command of Captain Thomas Simmons, *Ranger* had sailed down the Potomac from Alexandria bound for Boston unafraid. At 1:00 A.M. on Friday, July 5, off St. George's, she was surprised by the two barges which were commanded by a Royal Navy deserter named John Anderson and a certain Barret (or Barry). Anderson was an experienced brigand who had participated in several raids on the Patuxent, including the plunder of Lower Marlboro with the crew of John Robinson. He had been an occasional accomplice of Joseph Wheland, and was thus well versed in the destructive arts of the picaroon.[14]

The "refugee" barges were crewed by thirty men each and outnumbered *Ranger*'s complement by three to one. Though outgunned, in the dead of night "the barges could not be discovered until they were nearly along side, which gave the [*Ranger*'s crew] but a moment's warning." The picaroons exhibited considerable confidence as they waded into the fray against the surprised but determined privateersmen. The battle lasted for three bloody hours as the barges repeatedly attempted to board. Captain Simmons and his men offered an equally brave defense, repelling boarders with pikes until all but three of their weapons were mere splinters. Then the tide of battle shifted, and the defenders began to play upon their attackers with cold shot. As the gray fingers of dawn reached across the Potomac, the extent of the carnage was revealed for the first time. The bargemen had suffered terribly, one report stating that as many as twenty-seven men had been killed. Another account claimed that fifteen bargemen had died and thirty-four more were wounded, and a third claimed seven dead. *Ranger*'s losses were put at one dead and several severely wounded. Captain Simmons suffered a ball through the leg, and his second lieutenant was badly injured in both arms. The barges, with as many as one quarter of their complement killed, retired from the fight with "the mangled crew." Two of their dead were buried on St. George's, and two others, mortally wounded, were left behind to be taken and treated by the local militia. One black bargeman was captured by *Ranger*. Having no surgeon on board, the privateer was obliged to return to Alexandria on July 8 to obtain medical assistance. Word of the engagement and the brazenness of the picaroons spread about the region with amazing rapidity. Reports were soon circulating that the barges had been commanded by no less a brigand than Joseph Wheland himself, and that he had been badly wounded.[15]

Stunned by the picaroons' bravado and delayed in fielding her own force, Maryland made no secret of her wish that the French would act in her behalf and punish the rovers. Yet no less a warrior than Washington himself opined that the picaroons could not be brought to heel "by any other force but barges of their size which can follow them wherever they make their retreat and where a French sloop cannot pursue them." Indeed, the French already had their hands full patrolling the Capes against the recurrent flurry of Tory privateer incursions. Maryland, it seemed, despite French promises, was likely to be on her own.[16]

XXVI

A Shower of Musket Balls

By the end of July four Maryland barges were finally ready to sail under the command of Grason's replacement, Commodore Zedekiah Walley, builder of the barge *Protector* and a brave officer "well acquainted with the Bay, and the Places where the Piccaroons of the Enemy usually resort." On July 31 Walley was directed by the Council to proceed to the York River to join forces with a few armed vessels of the French. There he was to hold himself subject to the command of Villebrune or his appointed officer. Walley was ordered to contain flotilla activities entirely within the borders of the Bay, unless in hot pursuit of a vessel whose capture seemed likely. It was further proposed that the barges remain on patrol until January, and, to permit deployment so late in the season, William Paca was authorized by the Council to establish a flotilla supply depot at Snow Hill for the occasional provisioning of the fleet.[1] But the inevitable delays soon cropped up, primarily caused by manpower and money shortages, and the flotilla languished in port.

From Middlesex County, Virginia, came word of fresh enemy incursions. The Rappahannock, Piankatank, and Potomac "are daily and nightly exposed to the Robberies of the Privateers," wrote one distraught gentleman. "Sir, the business of horrid nightly Depredations proceeds now, as before, in the same relentless and cruel Manner . . ."[2]

From beleaguered Worcester County came word from Colonel Joseph Dashiell that picaroon barges were again plundering along the county shores.[3] What was even worse news was that Joseph Wheland, Jr., had returned to the Bay and his old games. Dashiell suggested that the militia be called up, but the Council, with the state coffers nearly empty, hedged over such a potentially expensive expedient.

We lament exceedingly, the Distress of the People of your County, and wish it was in our Power to relieve them, by preventing the Depredations of the Enemy. We know of no other Expedient, under present Circumstances, than keeping up a sufficient Guard to protect yourselves. Being on the Spot, you will be better able to judge than we, when it will be necessary to order out the Militia; and as you are well aware of the Expense, as well as the Inconvenience to the People, we rely on your Prudence, that they will not be ordered, nor kept longer on Duty, than Occasion may require.[4]

After weeks of delay, the Maryland State Navy flotilla finally sailed, albeit without benefit of the long-hoped-for linkup with the French. Apparently, the scheme failed to materialize because of the delays and the resulting inability to coordinate time schedules. Nevertheless, Walley was an officer of merit who carried out his mission with noteworthy competence. In September he arrived in Baltimore with four Bay craft recaptured from the picaroons, putting a small crimp in the enemy's depredations.[5]

No sooner had Walley returned, secured back pay for his men, and begun to resupply his squadron than word reached Annapolis that the picaroons were at it again. Their force was small, yet they had ventured as high up as the Patuxent and driven a vessel ashore. As a consequence of the attack, the Council instructed Walley on September 24 to leave Baltimore immediately, to bring his barges to the capital, and to prepare to sail against the enemy the following day. Though ordered to bring provisions, the commodore arrived ill-prepared for another cruise on such short notice. On September 26 the Council, anxious for the flotilla to sail and ignorant of the myriad assortment of details necessary to accomplish such a thing, sternly reiterated its orders to Walley to "proceed down the Bay with the Barges under your Command, and do every Thing which Prudence will dictate, to put a Stop to their Depredations and to protect the Citizens on the Shore and the Bay Trade."[6]

Two days later, Walley was still in port, patiently awaiting, apparently, the arrival of the barge *Fearnaught*. Again the Governor and Council ordered the Commodore to sail immediately, without the late arrival. Adding incentive to the order, they indicated that a French sloop was waiting off the harbor to join the flotilla—a patent falsehood.[7]

Finally *Fearnaught*, commanded by Captain Levin Speeden, arrived. Walley undoubtedly inspected his small force before departure and had every reason to believe it equal to whatever the picaroons might deploy. The barge *Defence* was commanded by Captain Solomon Frazier, one of the finest seamen the Eastern Shore could produce, sailing a vessel built by Eastern Shoremen for their own defense and recently turned over to the government. Captain Robert Dashiell commanded the barge *Terrible*. The armed schooner *Flying Fish,* supply tender to the flotilla, was to be commanded by Captain Daniel Bryan. Walley himself commanded the flagship *Protector,* a vessel heavily armed with 18-pounders. All of the barges were capable of being rowed and sailed, and, though open boats exposed to the weather, they were superb for skimming across the shoally waters of the Chesapeake and its tributaries.

By October Walley had taken up station at Cherrystone, near Cape Charles, where he could watch the comings and goings of Bay traffic with ease. En route down, however, he had apparently overlooked several picaroon hiding places, for soon afterward, he was informed by the Council via Captain Bryan that a number of small enemy vessels were causing damage as high up as Janes Island. Thus the flotilla was brought back up as far as Onancock Creek to monitor activities in the Tangier Sound region.[8]

On November 12 Walley's squadron still lay in Onancock Creek, immediately south of Tangier Sound, when intelligence arrived that five enemy barges were off the Atlantic coast of the Delmarva Peninsula and standing southward. Their objective was clearly the Chesapeake Bay. Suspecting that Gwynn's Island was to be their rendezvous, the commodore immediately moved to intercept them and arrived at the island two days later. His hunch proved correct, for on the evening of the fourteenth two enemy barges hove to under the east side of the island. Discovered the following morning by the Marylanders about a league away, the enemy immediately fled, and a general chase ensued. At 11:00 A.M. the sternmost barge, called *Jolly Tar,* was brought to by Captain Frazier in *Defence,* and eighteen men (including their commander, Captain Daniel I. Brooks) were taken prisoner.[9]

Walley had netted a fine kettle of picaroons. One of the prisoners, Jacob Extine, had been a lieutenant with Wheland. Another, Samuel Outter, had been captain of a picaroon barge on the Delaware, was captured, sent to Dover jail, and escaped to resume his Tory practices. Three of the crewmen were former prisoners who had violated their paroles by sailing on *Jolly Tar.* There were two lieutenants of the picaroon barges *Jackall* and *Victory,* recently routed from Smith's Island by the Virginians. One of these officers was Peter Frank, a Portuguese, who was "notoriously known to be at and Privie to almost every House burnt in this State and on the Eastern Shore of Virginia." Five of the crewmen were black.[10]

The flotilla continued in hot pursuit of the second enemy vessel without letup for nearly fifty miles to the mouth of the Chesapeake. As Walley rounded Cape Charles, he flushed out two more barges lying under Smith's Island. These, too, immediately fled. By 6:00 P.M., the Marylanders, having turned up the Atlantic coast and pursued their quarry out of Wreck Inlet approximately four leagues above Cape Charles and into the open ocean, finally retired and headed back to the Bay.[11]

Satisfied with driving the foe out of the Chesapeake, Walley sailed to the Pocomoke to resume his vigil. There he learned that the enemy barges had rendezvoused at Chincoteague, barely twenty miles from him across the Eastern Shore peninsula on the Atlantic coast, but one hundred ninety miles by sea, and were said to be waiting for the Maryland barges to come up. Later, intelligence arrived that the enemy force had been joined by a powerful galley. The mission of the flotilla, however, was clearly to protect Bay waters and not the Atlantic coast, and Walley remained ensconced at Pocomoke. On November 22 the commodore notified Governor Paca that he would stay in the lower Chesapeake as long as possible, having "not the least doubt of frustrating any attempt they may make on this Bay."[12]

Commodore Walley soon afterward moved the flotilla into the sheltered waters of Onancock Creek, where he could more comfortably keep a close watch on the entrance to Tangier Sound. Unfortunately, adverse winds from the south prohibited him from reconnoitering down the Bay as he would have liked. Finally, at 1:00 P.M., Wednesday, November 27, the flotilla emerged from Onancock to investigate reports of a small privateer said to be lying off the north side of Watts Island with four prizes. Immediately after clearing Onancock Bar, the Marylanders discovered seven sail, six of them barge rigged and the seventh appearing to be a galley, bearing south-southwest. Captain Daniel Bryan in the supply boat *Flying Fish*, "making much better weather than us stood near them." On his return he informed the commodore that one of the vessels was quite likely a galley, and the fleet was on a course for the Tangier Islands.[13] The picaroons, it seemed, had returned to the Bay in full force.

The consensus aboard the flagship *Protector* was that a push should be made after the enemy to the coast of the Tangiers. Upon determining that it would be impossible to intercept the enemy before dark, Walley was convinced by some of his officers to refrain from making a night attack. Instead it was decided to make for Watts Island Harbor, three leagues from the enemy's suspected rendezvous point. The Marylanders arrived at 7:00 P.M., in the midst of a veritable gale, and came to anchor.[14]

It was Walley's intention to reconnoiter the enemy the next day to assess their forces accurately. If a galley was among them, he would not engage; but if there were only the six barges, "which we had gained every Information of that was necessary, and being convinced they were not able to stand our force," his intention was to order an attack. Morale was high, and some officers thought an assault should be made even if there were a galley. None of the officers doubted the Marylanders' ability to drub the enemy, even with seven-to-four odds.[15]

Early the next morning several enemy vessels could be seen at anchor under the southernmost of the Tangier Islands, but the wind blowing strong out of the northwest made a closer reconnaissance impossible. Walley summoned a council of war. It was decided that since the picaroons' numbers were greater than those of the state barge fleet, an express should be sent to the commander of Accomac County, Colonel John Cropper, to fit out a barge then lying at Onancock and to raise volunteers to man her along with another which had been recently captured. By evening the messenger had not returned, and, anxious to speed things up, Walley gave the order to get under way and run into Onancock Creek. Upon arriving, he was pleased to learn that the Onancock barge, a former picaroon vessel called *Victory* which had been taken by Virginians at Smith's Island, would be ready to sail by the following morning. About twenty-five volunteers were ready to man her along with another smaller eight-man barge called *Langodoc*.[16]

Determined to secure as much information as possible before making his next move, Walley dispatched Captain Frazier and forty picked men from the fleet to proceed in *Defence* to Tangier Island and reconnoiter the enemy. The weather was moderate, and Frazier arrived at the island without incident, only to find a barren sea. There was not a sail in sight. Undismayed, he raised English colors to fool the local loyalists and landed at one Crockett's on Tangier. There, masquerading as a Tory, he cleverly made inquiry about the American barges, hoping to dupe the islander into revealing information about the foe as well. Crockett, it turned out, knew nothing about the Americans other than that he had seen them lying off Watts Island the preceding day. Then, taken in by Frazier's ruse, he added "that 6 Barges had Left his House early that morning [the 29th] and stood up for Fox Island up Tanger Sound." But, more important for Frazier, the bargemen had informed Crockett that they would lay over at Cager's (Kedges) Strait that night. After being apprised of the enemy's number and force, Frazier rejoined Walley between 3:00 and 4:00 P.M. in the reach between Watts Island and Onancock. The remainder of the flotilla anxiously awaited the two vessels outside Onancock Bar.[17]

Frazier assured the commodore that there were only six enemy barges. The seventh vessel, believed to be a row galley, was actually a prize, and the enemy was at that moment underway up Tangier Sound. Upon rejoining the flotilla at Onancock Bar, Walley summoned another council of war. His officers were still confident of victory. After "receiving the strongest assurances from the Commanders of the other Barges to stand by and support him to the last," Commodore Zedekiah Walley moved to press a vigorous attack against the enemy.[18]

Colonel Cropper, a veteran of Washington's army, had arrived at Onancock the evening before with twenty-five additional volunteers from the Accomac County Militia, most of whom were embarked at 10:00 A.M. aboard *Flying Fish*. Two or three others shipped aboard *Fearnaught* and *Defence*. Cropper and six of his men, including several "Gentlemen" volunteers, boarded Walley's flagship *Protector*. Samuel Handy, a second lieutenant of marines on *Protector*, was directed to assume command of *Langodoc*. Finally, at 4:00 P.M. the flotilla sailed to overtake the enemy. It was soon evident that *Victory* could not keep up the pace, and after transferring all personnel except a crew to take her back to port, she left the squadron. Walley pressed on.[19]

Between 9:00 and 10:00 P.M. the Maryland Navy came to anchor off Fox Island. Again Walley sought information. He dispatched Lieutenant Handy in *Langodoc* ashore to find out whether the enemy had stopped there on their way up the sound. The local inhabitants told Handy that the enemy had indeed visited the island and had left at 2:00 P.M. that day bound for Cager's Strait. Walley wasted little time. He weighed anchor and stood up the sound for another six hours. At 4:00 A.M. on November 30, the squadron came to anchor off the north end of Jane's Island, with Cager's Strait bearing west and somewhat northerly. The commodore permitted his cold and weary seamen a brief rest and rations. At daylight he learned from a small schooner also lying off Jane's that the enemy barges were in the strait approximately ten miles west of the Marylanders. The schooner had seen their lights at daybreak. Two hours after coming to anchor, even as rations were being drawn from *Flying Fish*, five sail were spotted in the entrance to the strait. Orders were given "to make sail and give chase" as soon as rations were distributed.[20]

Meeting with his officers, Walley outlined his battle plan. The picaroons, he felt, would not attempt to engage the entire Maryland flotilla at once, "but if they shou'd and form a line he wou'd wish to form the same way the Enemy did." The commodore felt that the enemy would probably bear down on him as he intended to push against the strongest enemy barge. He directed all of his commanders to support him, "which they all positively declared they would do or all sink together."[21]

Between 7:00 and 8:00 A.M. the flotilla again resumed the chase, with

Defence and *Terrible* leading the van half a mile ahead of *Fearnaught.* *Protector* was in the center, followed by *Langodoc,* and *Flying Fish* some distance astern and bringing up the rear. Ahead, the picaroon fleet appeared to be under easy sail standing through the straits. At 8:00 A.M. the enemy was seen to take in their sails, form a line of five barges abreast, reverse direction, and begin to "row a light stroke" toward the Maryland van. The sixth enemy barge rowed off to the right, apparently intending to refrain from combat. Soon the two fleets were separated by less than a mile of water.[22]

As the Marylanders sought to form their own line of battle, the two flotillas quickly closed to within two hundred yards of each other. Now the picaroons hoisted their colors, still keeeping line, and pushed forward under oars with vigor. Frazier, in *Defence,* preparing for the melee, lowered his sails and hoisted his own colors. At 9:00 A.M. two of the Tory barges opened fire, concentrating on *Defence.* Captain Frazier replied in kind. Then a staccato of cannonfire erupted as the entire picaroon line chimed in. From aboard *Protector,* Walley and his men saluted *Defence* with three rousing cheers of support as the Maryland center moved forward. Dashiell, in *Terrible,* who later claimed to have received prior orders from the commodore to fall in behind *Protector* and ahead of *Langodoc* to guard the weak rear, peeled off to his allegedly assigned position. Frazier sheered off to starboard, while Speeden in *Fearnaught* moved up to assume a position on the left. Walley plunged ahead to fill the center.[23]

On the left, even as Walley was coming up, *Fearnaught* opened fire with her 6-pound bow gun. The piece burst with her first fire. Desperately, Speeden ordered the gun reloaded to try firing with what was left. Twice the gun was fired, and twice it was found insufficient. Two of *Fearnaught*'s 12-pound guns were run out on the starboard side to bring them to bear where the enemy was thickest, but by this time *Protector* had come up to fill the gap and obstructed the field of fire. Speeden hailed the commodore, informing him of the loss of his bow gun and of his inability to engage unless it was with his side to the enemy. Walley's orders were simply "to keep close to him."[24]

With his forward momentum already up, Walley not only came up with his line, but surged well ahead of it, firing his 18-pound bow gun as he came, with telling effect upon the picaroon fleet. His field of fire now cleared, Speeden joined in with his two 12-pounders, two four-pound howitzers, a swivel, and muskets. Dashiell, too, was now attempting to row up again to form in the line with *Fearnaught* and *Defence.*[25] The enemy's resolve was nearly shattered by the quick, bold thrust of Walley's forces, as the threshold of panic and unbridled retreat loomed ever nearer. Then, as has been repeated in countless battles throughout history, a chance accident altered the entire course of the fight.

Well forward of his line and within fifty yards of the enemy, *Protector* quickly became the target for the concentrated, almost point-blank, fire of the entire picaroon fleet. The consequences were devastating. During the heat of battle an 18-pound cartridge broke as the gunner handed it out of the chest, and spilled out aboard *Protector*'s deck. Walley ordered the spilled powder wetted, but it was not dampened enough to prevent it from taking fire from the flash of a gun. The fire spread along the line of powder to the ammunition chest amidships, and the chest blew up.

Aboard *Defence,* Captain Frazier was informed that a second fire had just broken out on the commodore's barge. There was another explosion. The blasts incinerated two or three crewmen instantly and set five or six others afire. Human torches leaped into Chesapeake waters from the stern sheets, as others, panicked by the disaster, abandoned ship, and swam for their lives. The entire barge was thrown into pandemonium. The short 18-pound guns on the sides were useless, and the picaroons, whose resolve had been nearly broken only moments before, took new spirit and pushed forward with redoubled fury against the helpless drifting Maryland barge.[26] Eager to profit from the accidents, two enemy barges began to bear down on *Protector* to board. Frazier's ship was now subjected to the intense redirected fire of the remaining three enemy vessels, toward which all were directly rowing. At that critical moment, he was informed by his first lieutenant, Levin Frazier, that *Terrible, Langodoc,* and *Flying Fish* had turned about and were retreating as fast as they could. Desperately, he "Rowed round," looking in vain for a signal from *Protector* to continue the fight or retreat, but Walley was engaged in a life-or-death struggle of his own and could not signal.[27]

With Speeden off his larboard quarter and Frazier on his right occupied by three enemy vessels, Walley and his remaining crewmen, outnumbered and alone, opposed the oncoming enemy with daring resolve. The foe would not be given easy access to *Protector.* As the two enemy barges bumped against the Marylander's larboard and starboard bows, desperate hand-to-hand fighting erupted. Walley, standing near the 18-pound bow gun, was fatally hit by a musket bullet but stubbornly refused to haul down his colors. Close beside him his first lieutenant, Joseph Handy, also fell, "nobly fighting though he had lost an arm some time before." Captain of the Marines Levin Handy, though wounded in the head by a cutlass and in six other places, acted with exemplary courage, as did every member of the crew. The fighting aboard the confined little barge was nothing less than a vicious imitation of hell. Cries for quarter were shouted by some defenders but refused by the black picaroons who charged aboard. It was later claimed that many of the defenders "were most cruelly murdered and thrown over board by the negroes." There was, as a severely wounded Colonel Cropper later reported,

> a continual shower of musket bullets, pikes, cold shot, cutlasses, and iron stantials for eight or ten minutes, till greatly overpowered by numbers, and having all the officers of the barge killed and wounded we surrendered, after having wounded their Commodore, killed one Captain, wounded another, killed and wounded several inferior officers, and killed and wounded eighteen of the barge's crew that first boarded us.[28]

Protector had lost not only Walley and Lieutenant Handy, but one of the gallant Accomac County volunteers, Captain George Christian, and a total of twenty-five crewmen. Colonel Cropper and twenty-nine others were wounded, four of them mortally. The casualties aboard the Maryland barge proved to be the highest of any naval engagement involving Maryland State Navy forces during the American Revolution.[29]

When Captain Speeden saw the two enemy barges close on Walley's bow to board, he instantly gave orders to his own men to close with and board the enemy barge nearest him, "but my men was much confused and would not row alongside the Barge," he later reported. Then, seeing *Terrible, Langodoc,* and *Flying Fish* in full flight, and two enemy barges attempting to board *Defence,* he too ordered retreat. Frazier had little alternative but to follow suit. The battle had lasted less than half an hour.[30]

Defence, with two enemy barges hanging doggedly on her stern, was now the sole vessel within reach of the enemy, though not far behind *Fearnaught.* Captain Speeden, seeing Frazier's predicament, ran out a 12-pound gun on his larboard quarter and fired a round of grape at the pursuers, then brought his stern chaser to bear and gave them another dose of grapeshot. Soon Frazier had come alongside, and the two barges fled northward together, far behind the wake of *Terrible.* The picaroons did not relent. The entire Tory fleet pressed ahead, nipping at the Marylanders' heels. *Langodoc* and *Flying Fish,* lesser prey, had retreated eastward into the Annemessex for shelter and were not pursued. By 2:00 P.M. Frazier and Speeden had lost visual contact with both vessels, but not with the enemy, who were pulling up on the slower *Fearnaught.* Frazier ordered his mainsail lowered to drop back and gallantly informed his fellow captain that he would not leave him behind. Finally, at 4:00 P.M., after a chase of nearly thirty miles, the enemy gave up at the upper entrance to Hooper's Strait.[31]

Speeden and Frazier joined Dashiell soon afterward, and together they stood in for the Choptank River. The three barges were in terrible condition, their provisions having been exhausted and many of their men, having been exposed to the open winter chill, were sick and poorly clothed. And over all was the pall of defeat. That night the flotilla came to anchor at Cooke's Point in the mouth of the Choptank. The following morning, perhaps suffering from the pangs of guilt or cowardice, Dashiell separated *Terrible* from the flotilla and arrived at Annapolis on December 2 to be the first to tell his story to a mortified Governor Paca. Frazier and Speeden, detained by winter winds and weather, remained in the Choptank until December 3.

Far to the south, aboard the captured *Protector,* a seriously wounded Colonel Cropper fumed in rage over what he deemed to be a sheer act of cowardice by everyone save the officers and crew of *Protector.* "There was never before on a like occasion so much cowardice exhibited," he later wrote to Governor Paca in his report of the battle. Yet Cropper remained calm enough to negotiate a parole for himself and his men with his captors, for the enemy had suffered also. The picaroon fleet, he learned, was manned by Tory "refugees" and escaped slaves and was allegedly commanded by a Virginia loyalist named John Kidd. For months Kidd's raids along the Eastern Shore had caused unending worry to patriot forces, but the Tory had finally met his strongest opponent in Captain Walley. Kidd had been wounded aboard his barge *Kidnapper* in the battle, and one of his officers, Captain Allen, commander of the barge *Ranger,* had been killed. More than twenty-two men had been killed or wounded aboard *Kidnapper* alone, and many needed immediate medical attention. Thus, when Colonel Cropper offered to take the Tory wounded ashore (or at least those willing to go) and to take care of them at his own expense on the condition that he and his men be paroled, Kidd readily agreed. It was certainly not much to ask for, since only eight of *Protector*'s crew had escaped death or injury in the battle.[33]

Among those who went ashore with Cropper were the bodies of the brave Walley and Lieutenant Handy, the only dead not tossed overboard by the black picaroons during the capture. Both men were interred with a military funeral near Scott Hall. Cropper and his men, who finally returned ashore at Onancock, were received as heroes.[34]

Scathing letters to Governor Paca attacking the characters and conduct of Speeden, Frazier, and Dashiell were not slow in coming, particularly from Colonel Cropper, Captain Levin Handy, and Colonel George Dashiell of Somerset County. On their arrival at Annapolis, both Speeden and Frazier requested an inquiry. Both men were absolved of blame and ultimately reinstated. Frazier was even promoted to the command of the barge flotilla.[35] On December 26 Robert Dashiell, commander of *Terrible,* and Zadock Botfield, lieutenant of *Fearnaught,* were charged with "highly unbecoming and improper Conduct in the late Action with the Enemy" and suspended. Two days later, after a hearing, Botfield was reinstated, but Dashiell was cashiered.[36]

Repercussions resulting from the defeat of the Maryland barge flotilla were immediately felt in Annapolis. On December 5 Colonel Henry Dennis of Worcester County wrote that as a consequence of the picaroon victory "the situation in this and Somerset Counties is truly distressing, for the Enemy are now able to continue their depredations in any part of them, and in the County there is neither Arms or Ammunition were the Militia disposed to make use of them (very few of which are, had they them) . . ."[37]

Governor Paca, stung by the defeat, in a pitiful plea for naval assistance from the French, informed the Chevalier de Villebrune that if the enemy barges remained in the Bay, not only would commerce be destroyed, but every waterfront farm and plantation would be exposed to plunder and desolation. "As the Enemy are now in the Bay," he wrote, "every Hour they are suffered to remain must be productive of some Calamity and Distress to our Citizens."[38] Getting down to specifics, Paca requested the loan of a 14-gun armed vessel called the *Pole Cat.*[39]

Sadly, the Governor's energetic effort to have the Maryland barge flotilla immediately refitted and deployed again was thwarted by the not-too-surprising refusal of their crews to engage in service beyond the January 1 expiration date of their enlistments. The severity of the winter, low morale, and the government's tardiness in paying crews served to thwart the enlistment of new volunteers. Paca again beseeched the French for assistance, if only to station *Pole Cat* or an armed cutter at Annapolis, perhaps to cruise on occasion in the Bay, or to "make a Sortie at the Enemy's Privateers, now in the Chesapeake."[40]

Though as late as early January privateers were reported as high up as the Potomac, enemy depredations declined. Ironically, it was the weather and not French or state navy forces that had stymied their operations.[41] Joseph Wheland, who, it was later learned, had actually been in overall command of the barge force that had defeated Walley, had boldly established winter quarters and built barracks for his sizable forces at Cager's Strait.[42] But the picaroons' respite, like that of their victims, was short-lived.

By February the beast had awakened from his short slumber, and picaroon vessels resumed operations with devastating results. Again reports of depredations flowed into the various centers of county and state governments. Maryland cringed. An attack on a state warship being constructed at Stephen Steward's shipyard on West River was feared, and the Governor was obliged to order troops in from as far away as Frederick to protect the yard. Three barges, manned by an "abandoned Set of Men," were sighted near Young's Ferry on the Potomac, and on their way downriver had landed at one of their favorite stopovers, St. George's Island. Again slaves were kidnapped and plantations were plundered. From Cedar Point on the Bay, Nicholas Sewell sighted three privateers, two sloops and a schooner, which had captured a Bay craft and then moved into the Patuxent. His report had been delayed in reaching the local militia headquarters owing to his haste in moving his own property to safety.[43]

The little flotilla entering the Patuxent was commanded by Joseph Wheland, Jr., aboard the sloop *Rover*. Pushing into the river with his four vessels, Wheland's ultimate destination was the town of Benedict, a thriving tobacco port lying nearly twenty-five miles up from the Bay. Arriving on February 17, the picaroons landed without opposition and marched directly to a warehouse belonging to one Phillip Ferguson. Nearby, in his home, Ferguson and several friends, Joseph Anderson and John Senior, watched in fear as the raiders entered the warehouse. Senior had prior experience with such raids, having once before fallen victim to Wheland's unholy band. Soon, Senior was again a picaroon prisoner, forced to search for hams for his captors. Within a short time 12,000 pounds of salted pork had been stolen, along with £40 worth of articles, including clothing and furniture, belonging to Ferguson. Roaming about the town, the picaroons stopped at the store of Henry Tubman, whom they caught in the act of removing his stocks to safety. The raiders carried off half of Tubman's goods and a slave named Pompey. Another citizen, Henry Greenfield, also lost a slave, named Luke, who stole a canoe to join the raiders. One party of Wheland's men crossed the Patuxent to Hallowing Point, immediately opposite the town, and burned the home of Benjamin Mackall and destroyed his furniture, tobacco, and movable property.[44]

As the marauders rummaged about indiscriminately plundering Benedict, John Senior confronted the gaunt picaroon chieftain. Wasn't he the notorious Wheland, the same man who had made Senior a prisoner the summer before? Wheland laughed and asked the man "if he had used him ill." Walking over to Ferguson's house, the picaroon wrote in bold red letters across the wall: "Joseph Wayland Commander of the Sloop Rover."[45]

Having completed the plunder of Benedict, the raiders reembarked and pushed off downriver. En route, almost as an afterthought, they landed at the estate of Colonel George Plater and plundered him of some of his blacks.[46] The Patuxent raid proved to be the last major raid directly attributable to Joseph Wheland before the war's end—but not the last depredation of the hated picaroons of the Chesapeake.

The Chesapeake situation was again reaching a critical point. On February 21 Governor Paca wrote in exasperation to General Washington describing the dismal state of affairs. The picaroons, he reported, by the most recent count, numbered eleven barges, one sloop, and two schooners operating on the Bay. These, he noted, "proceed in detached Parties, not only capturing our Vessels, but landing on our Shores, and wasting and plundering the Property of the People of this State." Not only had Benedict been ravaged, but two days later, on February 19, another party, consisting of two barges and a sloop, had come up the Bay as high as Kent Point, opposite Annapolis, and sagaciously cruised about in Eastern Bay and off Poplar Island. The worst part of it all was that with peace talks underway, and from letters lately passed between Washington and the British commander in chief in America, Sir Guy Carleton, "there is some Reason to think that Orders have been given by the British Crown, prohibiting offensive Operations on the Continent." If such orders had been given, Paca felt, the Tories were operating in violation of them. He asked the General to do whatever was possible to urge the British authorities to put an end to the depredations.[47]

It was, of course, quite impossible for General Carleton, in far-off New York, to end the rampant plundering on the Chesapeake by picaroons such as Wheland, many of whom had lost allegiance to any cause. Some were refugee deserters from the Royal Navy, while many were blacks who had little to gain by mending their ways but a return to slavery and possibly the end of a rope. Others had simply become out-and-out pirates. In any event, the Maryland State Navy, as several historians have suggested, torn by recriminations over the blame for the defeat at Cager's Strait, was practically impotent.[48]

Governor Paca turned for help to the merchants of Baltimore, who, savaged by losses to the picaroons, had already decided among themselves not to send out any shipping until the results of the peace negotiations, now in their final stage, were known. He begged for the use of three armed sloops and schooners of eight or ten guns and upwards, completely manned, and an additional 150 men to man the

state barges for one month. He proposed that the force be commanded
by officers of the merchants' choosing. With the addition of *Pole Cat,*
which he said was expected from the French at any time (but which he
privately believed was unlikely to come), he enthusiastically declared
that the picaroons might be driven from the Bay. If Villebrune did not
send *Pole Cat,* an additional sloop or schooner would be necessary from
the Baltimoreans. The government would pay the crews at the end of
the voyage and prizes would be divided by them as tradition dictated.
The government would pay for the sloops and schooners by the month
and would cover their costs in the event of loss.[49] To help flesh out the
manpower needs of the barge force, Paca directed the commanders of
Queen Anne's, Talbot, and Dorchester counties to send crewmen still
on the state navy rolls, belonging to *Fearnaught* and *Defence,* who had
returned home after Cager's Strait. Yet secretly the Governor himself
had little hope that his efforts would come to any good. He warned the
Colonels Joseph and George Dashiell, whose counties were the most
imperiled, that "it is possible we may be disappointed . . . you
ought not rely too confidently upon this Assistance but attempt every
Thing which Prudence will permit, for your own Security."[50]

Paca was faced with difficulties at every turn. Because of a bureau-
cratic dispute between the two branches of the legislature, the militia
law had been dropped, and no legal method could be employed to raise
militia troops, leaving the state virtually defenseless on land. The
Governor could do little more than recommend that county commanders attempt to form local defense "Associations" and "hope the Spirit
and Patriotism of the People . . . will supply the Place of a Law."[51]

And still the picaroons ravaged the Bay country.

In early March an enemy sloop and schooner, both very small, with
only twenty-seven men, "had the Audacity to run up the Bay twenty
Miles above Patapsco, where they captured two or three Bay Vessels,
and six or eight, a few Miles below this [Annapolis] and returned again
without being discovered." Governor Paca again urged Villebrune to
send *Pole Cat* immediately to join two of the state barges, which were
now armed and equipped, to recapture some of the enemy's prizes.[52]
Paca's plea was in vain.

Soon afterward, an enemy privateer raided into Fishing Creek,
below Herring Bay, and set fire to a schooner belonging to Captain
Traviss of Baltimore, while two other privateers lay offshore. Fortunately, people ashore were able to extinguish the flames before the
hull was consumed.[53]

Not until March 21 was the state of Maryland finally able to mount
another expedition to attack the picaroon lair in the Tangiers region.

The specific objective of the expedition was to be Devil's (now Deal's) Island, immediately east of the Tangier group and west of the mouth of Manokin Creek. The island was believed to be a favorite rendezvous point where the picaroons had collected their plunder, "and there is every Reason to believe," Paca informed the expedition leader, Captain John Lynn of the Army, "that they think any Precaution for their Security, unnecessary." The enemy was thought to have been extremely weakened owing to the number of men required to bring away the many prizes recently taken to New York. A surprise attack, it was hoped, might just catch them with their guard down.[54]

The strike force was to be composed of: the little schooner *Venus*, carrying three 3-pound guns, and "commanded by a French Gentleman, Capt[n] [Olanyer] Delisle, a Man of great Bravery"; the barge *Fearnaught*, now under Captain Frazier; and the barge *Defense*, under Captain David Bryan. Distributed among the three vessels were sixty sailors and fifteen to twenty soldiers, to whom Lynn was permitted to add as many more as he thought necessary. Paca recommended to the commander that he take passage in *Venus* for the sake of better accommodations, but when nearing the scene of action, he should transfer to Frazier's barge, "as he is a Man of Sense and Bravery, on whom I think you may rely for such Advice as, from your Inexperience in Naval Matters it will be necessary for you to receive."[55]

Indeed, in terms of all naval matters, both en route down and back, Solomon Frazier was in charge, seconded by Captain Bryan, and last by Captain Delisle. Two volunteers, Lieutenants Murdock and Fickle, were to command the soldiers aboard. Paca wisely left the tactical details to Lynn. "I leave it to your Judgement and Discretion to secure the Enemy's Vessels, and to retreat with them to the Main, or to land on the Island, or to do both according to Circumstances." Should he find it proper to take the picaroons' vessels, "you can determine, after retreating with them to the Main, upon the Propriety of calling on the Militia to man the captured Vessels, and to return with them to the Island, to secure the Enemy, or to proceed with the Vessels up the Bay."[56]

Captain Frazier was ordered to leave with the flotilla from Annapolis on March 22 to rendezvous with Lynn at John Deal's on Herring Bay that evening. "As Capt[n] Lynn knows very little of Naval Affairs," Paca informed the bargeman, "we have directed him to consult and advise with you." The utmost secrecy was urged. The soldiers and sailors were only to be told that they were bound to Herring Bay to be placed under Lynn's command. No firing of salutes was to be carried out on departure lest the enemy be warned. Recalling the fatal accident at Cager's Strait, the Governor issued Frazier a particularly foreboding instruction: "Warned by Experience, I hope you will be particularly carefull of your Ammunition."[57]

The events surrounding the Lynn-Frazier expedition to Devil's Island were and forever will be surrounded by questions, owing to a total lack of documentation. Some historians, notably Scharf and Paullin, claim that the expedition was successful and resulted in the capture of a large quantity of enemy plunder and several barges. Others have suggested that the effort was abandoned almost as it was begun.[58] It would appear, however, that at least one barge, *Defence,* had put to sea and attacked somebody. On March 31, Captain Bryan and the barge's officers were charged in Annapolis "with great Misconduct in Boarding a Boat and seizing and Plundering and Detaining divers Articles therein found, and also with Plundering the Citizens of this State on some one of the Islands on the Bay of Chesapeak."[59]

Perhaps it had been Captain Bryan's misfortune to attack the enemy after the news of peace had reached all but the most isolated backwaters of the Bay country. Or perhaps Bryan had himself taken a rare opportunity offered by the confusions of the closing hours of the Revolution to seek personal profit. Whatever the realities of the intended sortie against Devil's Island, they were entirely overshadowed and abrogated by the news that reached a joyful and relieved Annapolis on March 29—that of "Peace being happily established."[60]

The war was over.

XXVII

Epilogue: A Plan of Piracy Broken Up

On August 16, 1807, the 280-ton Boston merchant ship *Othello,* Captain Russel Glover commanding, neared the Virginia Capes, totally innocent of the travails fate held in store for her. Having left Liverpool with a cargo of dry goods and clothing consigned to the firm of Harden and Wilson for the fall market at Baltimore, she had crossed the Atlantic without incident. She did so, however, at great risk, for the high seas had once more become a battleground between the European powers, this time England and Napoleonic France, and neutral shipping now ventured forth at great risk.[1]

As he spied the low-slung shoulders of the Capes, Captain Glover was unaware of the escalatory sequence of events that had immediately preceded his arrival in the area—events which sorely threatened to engage the infant United States in a war which nobody really wanted. On the morning of August 17, when he fell in with and enlisted the services of a capable tidewater pilot, Glover belatedly learned the tragic details. Within the previous nineteen months, three French Imperial Navy warships, *L'Eole, Cybelle,* and *Patriot,* had become blockaded within the confines of the Bay by a Royal Navy flotilla now commanded by Captain Lord Salisbury Pryce Humphreys. The blockade of foreign shipping in an American estuary during peacetime, and the occasional impressment of American seamen from incoming and outgoing merchant ships was bad enough, but when Royal Navy tars began to jump ship and enlist aboard United States warships, the situation was bound to degenerate. Though it was claimed by the United States that the seamen were actually American mariners illegally impressed into Royal Navy service, the British were stung and demanded the return of the deserters. When the United States frigate *Chesapeake* sailed from

Hampton Roads on June 22 with a number of purported Royal Navy
deserters aboard, Captain Humphreys, in command of HMS *Leopard*,
flagship of the blockading squadron, intercepted her off the Virginia
Capes and ordered their return. The commander of the American
frigate, Commodore James Barron, refused. *Leopard* opened fire and,
after killing three and wounding eighteen, forced *Chesapeake* to strike,
boarded her, and removed four alleged Royal Navy deserters (one of
whom, later proven to be a British subject, was hung). It had been an
attack on an American publicly-owned vessel, in American waters,
during peacetime, and the British had fired first. The United States
was enraged almost to the point of declaring war, and the nation was
already mobilizing. The French leviathans trapped in the Bay were
soon being considered, albeit without their consent, as an integral part
of the Chesapeake defense system.[2]

Glover was undoubtedly stunned by the turn of events, but now, so
close to his destination, he resolved to hazard the blockade and possible
search by the British. En route, he fell in with the schooner *Three Sisters*,
Matthias Rich master, which was bound from Cape Verde to Baltimore
with a cargo of salt and wine. Despite the presence of the strong force
of blockaders, the two merchantmen miraculously entered the Chesapeake unchallenged.[3]

With light and, frequently, contrary winds, *Othello* and *Three Sisters*
were somewhat delayed in their ascent to Baltimore. Not until August
22 did they reach the Patuxent River, the halfway point of their trip up
the Bay. As they entered the mouth of the river the wind again shifted,
and the two vessels came to anchor under Drum Point. Here they
discovered one of the French 74-gun warships, *Patriot*, riding grandly
at anchor. Commanded by Commodore Hiacinthe Krohm, Officer of
the Legion of Honor and Commandant of the French squadron on the
Bay, she was a friendly giant whose presence must have elicited sighs of
relief from the two merchant captains after their somewhat perilous
entry into the Chesapeake. Unfortunately, it was a false security at
best.[4]

In the course of *Othello*'s first evening anchored in the river, a small
pilot boat schooner was observed coming down the Bay. Soon she had
come to anchor in the river, squarely between the two merchantmen. A
congenial round of visitations between the four vessels was soon underway, and news and information were being exchanged. It was soon
learned that the pilot boat schooner was *General Massena*, a Frenchman
ostensibly bound from Baltimore for Santo Domingo. Captain Rich
was of the opinion that she was little more than a smuggler, and the
inquisitiveness of her crew regarding the lading of *Othello* was outright

suspicious. Captain Glover, however, seemed entirely unconcerned.[5]

On the afternoon of August 23 the breeze again became favorable, and *Othello* weighed anchor and pressed on up the Bay, coming to for the evening off Sharps Island. She was followed by *Three Sisters* and, curiously, *General Massena*, which should have been sailing south, not north. Late that night, even as her crew slept, *Othello*'s alert deck watch noticed the Frenchman quietly attempting to work around the ship and come alongside. "What do you want?" challenged the watch. The only reply was the lapping of water as the pilot boat sheered off and came to anchor under *Othello*'s stern.[6]

At daylight on August 24, the intentions of *General Massena* were finally revealed. Captain Glover, roused from his cabin by some commotion topside, rushed to the deck and discovered that the Frenchman's crew had opened fire upon his ship with pistols. It was all over in a few minutes, for the deeply-laden, unarmed merchantman stood little chance of outrunning her attacker or fending off a boarding.

"Are you a pirate?" Glover demanded.

"I am not a pirate, but a French privateer from Guadaloupe," lied the *General Massena*'s commander. "Has anyone been killed?"

Glover replied in the negative, and then boarded the schooner as ordered.[7] The pirate briefly examined his papers, and then declared *Othello* a legal prize for carrying British-manufactured goods on board. The prize was soon swarming with Frenchmen, her crew locked below decks under heavy guard, and her commander's great cabin wantonly plundered. Glover's pilot was summoned and ordered to take the ship past the British squadron skulking about the Capes and into the open Atlantic. He balked. An incentive of $400 was offered, but again he refused. Finally, threatened with death, he succumbed.[8]

The two vessels, predator and victim, were soon pressing down the Chesapeake. Upon reaching the mouth of the Potomac, however, they encountered a sudden and drastic shift in the wind, stalling further movement south. Unable to proceed, both captor and prize came to anchor off the sandy finger of Point Lookout. As the hours of enforced inaction ticked by, the French pirates became increasingly nervous. They were sadly aware that *Three Sisters* may have witnessed *Othello*'s seizure, and might even now be recounting the tale to authorities in Baltimore. Pursuit by the American authorities was a distinct likelihood, and successfully running the blockade suddenly loomed as a feat demanding inordinate good fortune. Escape from the confines of the Chesapeake seemed an impossibility.

The pirate chief, in a panic, attempted to backtrack by persuading Glover that the whole affair was a drastic mistake. He also sought to wrap himself in the mantle of immunity by implying the French Navy had been involved. Glover later testified that the pirate told him

> *that he had been supplied with fifteen men by the commander of the said ship* [Patriot], *being short of hands, which I believe to be correct, as one of the men told the mate and pilot that he was with the officer who boarded me from the ship. After apologising for firing on me, saying he could not prevent his men, lest they would use violence on himself and other officers. He proposed to liberate the ship, provided I would give him a certificate declaring he did not plunder or act improperly, which I refused; but finding I had no other alternative, was obliged to comply.*[9]

The certificate was attested to by a passenger named Harden (probably the buyer for the firm of Harden and Wilson), *Othello*'s papers were then delivered up, and after 28 hours' detention, the ship was released to proceed on to Baltimore.[10]

On August 25 the schooner *Three Sisters* reached Baltimore with a limited account of the capture of *Othello*. It was an account lacking in detail, but it was enough to whip Baltimoreans into a fine froth. When the victimized ship itself arrived the following day, all hell broke loose. Pro- and anti-French political factions hotly debated the issue of alleged French naval complicity. One charged that the warship *Patriot* had not only provided fifteen French seamen to the pirates, but had offered an additional hundred should they be needed. Another charge claimed the French warship had assisted in mending the pirate's rudder. A third charge implied that the attack was actually carried out within sight of *Patriot,* which failed to lift a hand in the merchantman's defense. Proponents supporting the French suggested that the rovers were but "a motley crew of all nations," and that the French Imperial Navy had nothing to do with the affair at all.[11]

French complicity being a possibility, and one which threatened to imperil Franco-American relations at a particularly critical juncture in history and cause the potential eviction of the French Navy from the Bay and into the arms of the waiting blockaders, the French Minister to the United States, General Turreau, was forced to act. Turreau immediately launched an investigation. To sidestep the potential accusation of a French whitewash of the incident, Captain John Comegys, an American officer commanding the Columbian Volunteers, a Baltimore militia unit, was requested to carry out the sensitive inquiry. Comegys's directions were explicit. If the commander of *Patriot* "had in any way connived at or aided in the attack on the *Othello,* the guilty should be immediately delivered up to the government of the United States, to be proceeded against agreeable to the laws of this country."[12]

On August 26, the first accounts of the *Othello* seizure sent ripples in ever-widening circles from the Baltimore waterfront. Within a short time, the news had reached Washington and the leaders of the nation. Orders were immediately dispatched to Norfolk on the speedy pilot boat *William Pitt* for Commodore Barron to take the frigate *Chesapeake,* still undergoing repairs after her engagement with *Leopard,* up the Bay in pursuit of the pirates. A second order was dispatched to Baltimore to Sailing Master David Porter to organize a move down the Bay, thereby squeezing the pirates in a pincers movement.[13]

In Baltimore, Colonel John Striker, commander of the Fifth Maryland Regiment of Volunteers, issued orders calling up two militia units, Captain John Sterret's Independent Company and Captain Joseph Sterret's Baltimore United Volunteers. Within hours of the call-up, fifty militiamen had assembled at the Baltimore waterfront. Even as the troops gathered, Captain Porter diligently recruited the services of more than fifteen masters of vessels and approximately thirty-five seamen to sail the pursuit vessel, a schooner volunteered by a public-spirited merchant named James Calwell. Hastily armed with four 6-pound cannons, the vessel, named, appropriately enough, *Volunteer,* set sail without further ado.[14]

David Porter was diligent in his search for the pirates, looking, as he cruised southward, into every inlet and harbor along the way. At 4:00 P.M. Friday, August 27, *Volunteer* encountered a sudden Chesapeake squall, but as she approached the entrance to the Patuxent, where it was supposed that the pirates might still be lurking, the skies cleared and the seas became calm.[15]

An hour later, *Volunteer* cautiously rounded the headland of Drum Point. There, lying close to shore and under the point, lay *General Massena.* Nearby, seemingly dormant and lifeless but within long-gun range of the pirate, lay the warship *Patriot.* Instantly, the order was given for the militiamen to load their weapons and to hold themselves in readiness to board. The troops were directed to conceal themselves below deck until the last second. Porter then moved to tack his vessel inshore of the pirate to cut her off from escape up the river or her men from putting ashore, but was unable to do so owing to the shallowness of the water. He thus directed his vessel to run straight for *General Massena.*[16]

Suddenly, the Baltimoreans discovered *General Massena*'s boat scurrying off for shore with four men aboard. One of *Volunteer*'s six-pounders, loaded with round and grape shot, was fired, peppering the waters about the fleeing craft, but with no effect. "The Volunteers," one participant of the expedition later recalled, *were then ordered on deck, ranged in Company, with fixed Bayonets ready to pour a Volley of Musketry if requisite. Our Boat was launched, the schooner brought to Anchor, within a short distance of the Pirate, a detachment from each Company with Lieut. Sullivan . . . and Capt. Cowper, a Sea Captain at their Head, with Orders to board the Prize. While they were proceeding we gave her another six Pounder with Grape, upon which they struck the French Flag. Capt. Porter then hailed, telling them, that if the least resistance was made to the Boat Crew going on board, that no quarters should be given. Our Boat took possession of her immediately, and she proved to be a small Pilot Boat schooner called the* General Massena, *with 50 Muskets ready loaded, with 18 Boarding Knives, &ca.—only 3 men were found on board, who were brought Prisoners on board us.*[17]

A boat was immediately sent in pursuit of the fugitive pirates, but just as the craft was putting off, an unidentified brig was spotted lying at anchor on the opposite side of the river. Suspecting her to be a prize to the pirate, Porter recalled the small boat and proceeded toward the brig. She proved to be an outward-bound merchantman which had been neither boarded nor molested by the buccaneers. Returning to *General Massena,* Porter toyed with the idea of again pursuing the fugitives, but with night coming on, and the intentions of the giant warship which had been a silent witness to the capture unpredictable, it was decided to head home with the prize.[18]

The following morning, while en route up the Chesapeake, *Volunteer* encountered the Baltimore schooner *Experiment* scudding down Bay with two militia companies under the command of Captains Woodland and Hyson aboard. *Experiment* had set off on August 28 in *Volunteer's* wake as a reinforcement. Porter directed the newcomer to continue on her voyage, and to land her men to scour the woods of Calvert County for the fugitives. Lieutenant James Calhoun, Jr., of the Independent Company was detached from *Volunteer* to assist in the landing, but, more importantly, to call upon Commodore Krohm and inquire whether any pirates had sought refuge aboard *Patriot.*[19]

On the morning of Sunday, August 30, *Volunteer* hove to off Annapolis. She was met by a delegation headed by the Governor of Maryland. Porter soon learned that five more pirates, who had gone to Annapolis to secure provisions for their nefarious undertakings, had been captured the day before and were at that moment incarcerated in the city jail. The Annapolitans had been as zealous in the search for the pirates as had been the Baltimoreans. Indeed, they had fitted out, on their own, the packet boat *Holy-Hawk,* a company of infantry under Captain

Duvall, and an artillery company under Captain Muir, to locate and capture the pirate ship themselves. They were aided in their search by a detachment from the French warship *L'Eole*, laid up in Annapolis, and a barge loaned out from the French contingent in the city. The expedition failed to encounter the pirates at sea. Ironically, those pirates who had been taken were captured ashore by an alert mounted detachment merely investigating suspicious persons near the town.[20]

The interrogation of the prisoners at Annapolis was attended by the local militia officers and several French naval officers, including Captain La Villeau of *Patriot*, who had been visiting in town. In the course of the interrogations, it was discovered that the pirates were, indeed, deserters from *L'Eole* and *Patriot* who had enlisted at Baltimore to go on a voyage to the West Indies, "but finding themselves deceived, had deserted." The officers of *General Massena* were all Frenchmen as well, but they were all from Baltimore and had no connection with *Patriot* or, for that matter, any ship at all![21]

Porter, pleased with the roundup of pirates underway, proceeded to Baltimore with his prisoners and *General Massena*. By early afternoon he had come to anchor off the Lazaretto and landed the freebooters amid a wildly ecstatic throng of welcomers. The pirate ship was left at Fells Point for the more curious citizens to view—and the citizens of Baltimore were indeed curious. They turned out by the thousands to welcome Baltimore's heroes who had rid the Chesapeake Bay of the curse of piracy. Cannons were discharged in joyous acclamation as Porter and the Captains Sterret marched their men through the city streets as conquering heroes.[22]

Far from the victory revelry in Baltimore, Lieutenant James Calhoun pointed out the landing and search areas on the banks of the Patuxent to Hyson's and Woodland's detachments, only to learn that the fugitives had fled aboard the warship *Patriot*. Cognizant of the delicate nature of the second part of his mission, the lieutenant turned to formally call upon the commander of the French squadron on the Chesapeake, Commodore Hiacinthe Krohm.[23]

Aboard *Patriot*, Calhoun was relieved to discover the four fugitives had indeed sought French protection, but upon boarding had been immediately thrown in irons. In discussing his mission with Krohm, the lieutenant learned that the commodore held himself personally responsible for the prisoners, but refused to answer to anyone but Ambassador Turreau. In the end, however, diplomacy and common sense won out. The prisoners, including the pirate commander, the owner of *General Massena*, and the mate, were handed over, albeit not to Calhoun, but to Turreau. The ambassador immediately "consigned them to the civil authorities, to be proceeded against agreeable to law." Twelve of the "desperadoes" were soon in confinement, thanks to the total cooperation of the French Imperial Navy.[24]

On August 29, news of *Othello*'s capture reached Norfolk aboard the pilot boat *William Pitt*. Commodore Barron, however, ignorant of the recent capture of *General Massena,* had no little difficulty in getting his warship to sea. Not until September 2 was *Chesapeake* ready to sail, accompanied by two gunboats, *No. 58* and *No. 67*. Three days later, off the mouth of the Potomac, Barron belatedly learned from a passing merchantman that the pirate had been taken. The commodore nevertheless proceeded to Annapolis, and then to Baltimore for a personal appraisal of the situation. On September 9, satisfied that Porter had handled the affair as efficiently as possible, he returned down the Bay to Norfolk.[25]

On September 2 Captain John Comegys returned from his own investigative mission to the Patuxent with news that relieved everyone. "The return of Captain Comegys," proclaimed the *American and Commercial Daily Advertiser,* "enables us to state that Commodore Krohm disclaims indignantly, all knowledge of the piratical attempt to seize the *Othello*." The pirate vessel, it was learned, had been independently purchased and fitted out at Baltimore by four Frenchmen and manned by a crew of deserters. Twenty-one conspirators were originally involved (though some sources indicated as many as twenty-five), and every effort was being strained to locate the few rascals thought to still be at large in Calvert County. Everyone seemed willing to accept the French Navy's claims of innocence in the affair. As a consequence, the military and political powderkeg that had threatened to explode into an international incident had been defused. "Thus," wrote the Sterrets in their final report of the operation, "has a plan of Piracy, which threatened serious injury to our commerce, been completely broken up."[26]

Public indignation against the French rapidly dissipated as other issues of national concern were forced to the forefront of attention. Though *Patriot* and *Cybelle* eventually left the Bay, and *L'Eole* was broken up at Annapolis, war clouds continued to blow in the direction of America. In less than six years the United States would find itself again embroiled in mortal combat with the British Empire, in an uneven struggle on land and sea that would, in time, come to be called the War of 1812. Unhappily, the Chesapeake was destined to serve as a major seat in that most vicious conflict, and the isolated little river upon which *General Massena* had been taken, the Patuxent, would become a focal point of naval contention and, ultimately, an avenue of British invasion and conquest.[27]

With time, the memory of the *Othello* affair, the last major act of classic buccaneering under sail on the Chesapeake, would grow dim and be forgotten, as would the deeds of the innumerable pirates and picaroons who had infested the Bay for nearly 200 years. For the most part, the blackest episodes of tidewater history, and the rascals and raiders who had perpetrated them, would fade into obscurity, while a few would become the grist of legend. Though the *General Massena* pirates, when compared to marauders like Ingle, Evertsen, Guittar, Teach, and Wheland, were but pale reflections of an earlier era, they were, fortunately, to be the last. The golden age of piracy on the Chesapeake was over.

Notes

The following abbreviations and short titles for the Notes follow the format established by E. G. Swem, *Virginia Historical Index*, in which the principal historical publications are cited in notes to this work by initials. In each such citation, the volume number precedes the initial or short title. The series number, if any, follows the initial or short title. In certain sections pertaining to *Acts of the Privy Council* and *Calendar of State Papers, Colonial Series*, page numbers are followed by item number. In several instances, multiple item numbers are further divided by paragraph or segment letters, presented herein as roman numerals within parentheses. Books are cited by author, or in collected documents by editor, and are preceded by volume number and followed by page number. For further particulars, complete citations may be found in the Bibliography.

APCC – *Acts of the Privy Council, Colonial Series.*

C.O. – Colonial Office Papers.

CHNY – *Documents Relative to the Colonial History of the State of New-York.*

Chronicles – *Chronicles of St. Mary's.*

CMSP – *Calendar of Maryland State Papers.*

CRNC – *Colonial Records of North Carolina.*

CSPC – *Calendar of State Papers, Colonial Series, America and West Indies.*

CVSP – *Calendar of Virginia State Papers.*

EJC – *Executive Journals of the Council of Colonial Virginia.*

Evertsen – *De Zeeuwsche Expeditie Naar De West Onder Cornelius Evertsen Den Jonge.*

JHB – *Journals of the House of Burgesses of Virginia.*

JCTP – *Journal of the Commissioners for Trade and Plantations.*

Md. Arch. – *Archives of Maryland.*

MHM – *Maryland Historical Magazine.*

Minutes – *Minutes of the Council and General Court of Colonial Virginia.*

NDAR – *Naval Documents of the American Revolution.*

NRAR – *Naval Records of the American Revolution.*

PRO Admiralty – Public Record Office, Admiralty Records.

Rawlinson – Rawlinson Collection.

Spotswood – Brock

T – *Tyler's Quarterly Historical and Genealogical Magazine.*

VMH – *Virginia Magazine of History and Biography.*

WMQ – *William and Mary Quarterly.*

I PROLOGUE: UNHALLOWED CREATURES

1. 2 Barbour, 255.
2. Rankin, 6.
3. Neill, 36.
4. Purchas, 15-16.
5. Smith, 175, and Stith, 117, note the date of the arrival of Gates and Newport as May 24, while Dabney, 19, and others note the date as May 23.
6. 2 Barbour, 286.

II GREVIOUS CRIMES OF PYRACIE AND MURTHUR

1. Claiborne, 44; Dabney, 27; Smith, 140.
2. 15 *VMH*, 31.
3. In the spring of 1623 *Tygre* was back in the tidewater with 26 men. Having ascended the Potomac to a point near the site of modern Washington, D.C. to trade for corn, she was attacked by Anacostan Indians. Those of her crew who were ashore were captured or killed. Among those taken prisoner were the trader Henry Fleet and Henry Spilman, son of Sir Henry Spilman. Five persons who had remained aboard repulsed the savages with cannon fire and escaped. 2 *T* (1), 128-29.
4. Smith, 128-30.
5. Ibid., 185; 24 *VMH*, 56.
6. Emory, 73; Claiborne, 45-47.
7. Emory, 75; Claiborne, 54.
8. 5 *Md. Arch.*, 158-59.
9. Ibid., 162.
10. Claiborne, 50; 1 Hening, 154.
11. Claiborne, 51-52.
12. Hall, 101; Andrews, 33.
13. Hall, 18-19.
14. Emory, 77.
15. Hall, 17, 39.
16. Ibid., 39.
17. Emory, 77.
18. Hall, 76.
19. Ibid., 56; Claiborne, 75; 5 *Md. Arch.*, 164-67.
20. Emory, 78; Claiborne, 78-79.
21. 5 *Md. Arch.*, 168

22. Emory, 79.
23. Hale, 79.
24. Emory, 79.
25. Hammett, 30.
26. Hall, 154.
27. Calvert Papers, no. 189; Hale, 200.
28. Hall, 148; Emory, 79; Hammett, 30; Claiborne, 140.
29. Hall, 148; Emory, 79, 88; Hammett, 30.
30. Hall, 148-49, 204; Emory, 79.
31. Hammett, 30.
32. Emory, 79; Claiborne, 83.
33. Hammett, 30; Claiborne, 87-88; Emory, 84.
34. Emory, 85; 5 *Md. Arch.*, 209.
35. Emory, 85-86; Claiborne, 88-91.
36. Hammett, 31.
37. Hall, 150-51.
38. Ibid.
39. Ibid., 152.
40. Ibid., 152-53.
41. Claiborne, 92; Hall, 154; Hammett, 31.
42. Hammett, 31; Claiborne, 90.
43. Emory, 90.
44. 3 *Md. Arch.*, 70.
45. Ibid., 65-72, 79-80.

III THE PLUNDERING TIME

1. Though *Eleanor of London* is not identified in Maryland records, she is documented in those of Massachusetts Bay. Winthrop writes in his *History of New England,* II, 75: "The ship Eleanor of London one Mr. Inglee master arrived at Boston she was laden with tobacco from Virginia, and having been about 14 days at sea she was taken with such a tempest, that though all her sails were down and made up, yet they were blown from the yards and she was laid over on one side two and a half hours, so low as the water stood upon her deck and the sea over-raking her continually and the day was so dark as if it had been night, and though they had cut her masts, yet she righted not till the tempest assuaged. She staid here till the 4th [June 4] and was well fitted with

masts, sails, rigging and victuals at such reasonable rates as that the master was much affected with his entertainment and professed that he never found the like usage in Virginia where he had traded these ten years."
2. Claiborne, 111; Ingle, 30.
3. *Reformation* is identified as a pinnace in the warrant issued for her seizure. 4 *Md. Arch.*, 231.
4. Ingle, 8-9.
5. 4 *Md. Arch.*, 233.
6. Ibid., 231.
7. Ibid.
8. The certificate admitted against Ingle on February 8 was dated as of that time. Edward Ingle claims it was dated after the fact. 4 *Md. Arch.*, 232, 251-52; Ingle, 14-15.
9. 4 *Md. Arch.*, 258.
10. Ibid., 248.
11. Ibid., 232, 234.
12. The charge, possibly suggested to reinforce the prosecution's case, was never proven. Ibid., 247.
13. Ibid., 231-32.
14. Ibid., 238, 247-48.
15. Ibid., 233-34.
16. Ibid., 237.
17. The Accomac incident reportedly occurred on February 22, 1642/43. The second incident charged was said to have occurred on November 20, 1642. The last incident was said to have taken place on or about April 15, 1643. 4 *Md. Arch.*, 238.
18. Ibid., 138-39.
19. Ibid., 239.
20. Ibid., 241.
21. Ibid., 197, 245, 247-48.
22. Ibid., 261, 263, 275.
23. Lewger testified later that the "sheriff and the guard were some of this deponent's family." *Chronicles*, 2-3; Ingle, 19; 4 *Md. Arch.*, 232-33, 249, 250, 258.
24. 4 *Md. Arch.*, 261; Ingle, 19.
25. Parr, 252.
26. Ibid.
27. Ibid., 252-53.
28. Dabney, 45; 2 Winthrop, 198; Ingle, 20-21.
29. Hammett, 32; Ingle, 21.
30. Cf. *Chronicles*, 7, for testimony regarding Calvert's willingness to per-

mit Ingle free trade in Maryland despite his earlier flight from charges against him.
31. *Chronicles*, 4; Hammett, 32.
32. Emory, 98.
33. Ibid.
34. *Chronicles*, 3.
35. Hammett, 32.
36. Ingle, 27.
37. *Chronicles*, 3-4.
38. Beitzell, *Jesuits*, 15, 20.
39. Emory, 98, relates a tradition which states that "an expedition was fitted out on the island of Kent which repaired to St. Mary's and captured the governor, carried him back with them, gave him a severe flogging and then expelled him from the island." True or not, on January 1, 1745, the governor ordered a proclamation published declaring William Claiborne and Richard Thompson enemies of the province and forbidding all correspondence with Kent Island.
40. *Chronicles*, 3-4; Hammett, 32.
41. If Brent was again seized at Kent Island, it seems possible that Claiborne may have been with Ingle.
42. One of the raiders, out of compassion for the nearly naked Lewger, gave him a pair of shoes and stockings from the plundered stock. Hammett, 32; Emory, 98.
43. *Chronicles*, 5-7.
44. Ibid., 4.
45. Ibid., 3-5.
46. Ibid., 3; Ingle, 28.
47. *Chronicles*, 4-7.
48. Ingle, 28-29; Hammett, 32.
49. *Chronicles*, 4.
50. Beitzell, *Jesuits*, 15.
51. Ibid., 21; 1 *MHM*, 135-40; 4 *Md. Arch.*, 178, 415; 10 *Md. Arch.*, 12; 40 *Woodstock Letters*, 72.
52. 1 *MHM*, 136-40.
53. 1 *Md. Arch.*, 270; 3 *Md. Arch.*, 214.
54. *Chronicles*, 3.
55. Ibid.; Beitzell, *Jesuits*, 22.
56. The departure date of Richard Ingle is based upon court testimony offered by John Lewger on September 26, 1645 in a suit brought against Ingle by Cornwaleys. Cornwaleys sought to obtain payment for damages incurred as a result of In-

gle's occupation of his property in Maryland. Lewger states Ingle arrived in Maryland waters on December 29, 1644 and fourteen weeks later departed, along with the Dutch ship *Speagle* as his prize. This would place the departure date on or about April 4. *Chronicles,* 3.

57. 1 *Md. Arch.,* 238.

IV   DUTCH CAPERS AND CRIMSON RAIDERS

1. *Minutes,* 484-85.
2. Montgomery, 287.
3. Ibid., 289.
4. *Minutes,* 484-85.
5. Ibid., 485.
6. Ibid.
7. Ibid.; Shea, 87.
8. Shea, 87-88; Thomas Ludwell to [Lord Culpepper] 9 August 1665, C. O. 1/19.
9. Middleton, 291; *Minutes,* 512.
10. *Minutes,* 511.
11. Ibid., 485.
12. Middleton, 290.
13. 1 *APCC,* no. 642, 389.
14. *Minutes,* 486.
15. 1 *APCC,* no. 690, 420.
16. *Minutes,* 487-88; Shea, 88.
17. *Minutes,* 487.
18. Ibid.
19. Ibid., 488-89.
20. Ibid.
21. Ibid., 489.
22. 1 *APCC,* no. 695, 422-23.
23. Middleton, 311.
24. Colledge, 186.
25. Wertenbaker, 127.
26. A typical culverin weighed 4,000 pounds and fired a fifteen pound shot; a demiculverin weighed 3,600 pounds and fired a nine pound shot; a saker weighed 2,500 pounds and fired a five and one-quarter pound shot. Marx, 102; Neill, 320.
27. Shea, 89; Wertenbaker, 127.
28. De Groot and Vorstman, 81, note that the trophy decoration of drum and flags on a Dutch vessel's sides indicated the vessel was equipped for war.
29. Shea, 89.

30. *Minutes,* 490.
31. Ibid.
32. Shea, 90; Wertenbaker, 128.
33. Ibid.
34. Ibid.
35. Ibid.
36. Shea, 91.
37. Ibid., 90.
38. Ibid., 91; Wertenbaker, 129.
39. Shea, 91.
40. Wertenbaker, 129.
41. Shea, 91.
42. Neill, 320, writes that on August 24, 1667, Captain White in the Royal Navy frigate *Oxford* gave chase to three Holland men-of-war. The Dutch admiral, said to have been the same that burned HMS *Elizabeth,* was killed.

V   CLEARE THEIR SHIPPS FOR FIGHT

1. *Minutes,* 490.
2. Ibid., 491.
3. Ibid.
4. Thomas Ludwell to William Berkeley, 7 November 1667, C. O. 1/21.
5. Shea, 92; Wertenbaker, 142.
6. An Answer to the Inquiries of the ... Lords Commissioners for Forreigne Plantations, 20 June 1671, C. O. 1/26.
7. Shea, 92.
8. *CSPC, 1669-1674* (no. 771), 335.
9. Ibid., (no. 1057), 474-75.
10. *Minutes,* 334; *CSPC, 1669-1674* (no. 1118), 508.
11. 1 *EJC,* 533-34.
12. Ibid., 534.
13. Ibid.; *CSPC, 1669-1674* (no. 1118), 508.
14. 1 *EJC,* 534.
15. *Minutes,* 334.
16. Ibid.
17. Ibid., 334, 342.
18. 1 *EJC,* 532-33.
19. Vere, 111, 143-44, 148, 152-53, 158, 172-74.
20. Evertsen died peacefully in his bed in 1679. Ibid., 158, 192.
21. *Evertsen,* 104, 105.
22. Vere, 165; *Evertsen,* Plate 67.
23. *Evertsen,* 33.

24. Ibid.
25. Ibid., 34.
26. Ibid.
27. 1 *EJC*, 532.
28. Ibid.; Wertenbaker, 129-30; *Evertsen*, 33-34. Evertsen saw thirteen ships on the first sighting, and apparently lumped both the Maryland fleet and Cotterell's forces as one, since both appeared to be coming down Bay.
29. *Evertsen*, 34; 1 *EJC*, 532.
30. *Evertsen*, 34.
31. Ibid., 35.
32. Ibid.
33. Ibid.; 1 *EJC*, 533.
34. *Evertsen*, 35.
35. Ibid.
36. Ibid., 37.
37. The vessels which grounded were commanded by Binkes, Evert Evertsen, and two officers noted only as Van Zijl, and Hanske Fockes. Ibid., 35.
38. Ibid., 35-36.
39. Ibid., 36.
40. Ibid., 36-37.
41. Ibid., 37. While Evertsen lay in the James, his flotilla of prize vessels, guarded by a small "setie," was attacked by two shallops. The prize flotilla lay at anchor in Hampton Roads, and would have been captured along with their guardship, which had not maintained a proper watch and was surprised, had not Evertsen dispatched *Suriname* to the rescue. Ibid., 36.
42. Ibid., 37.
43. 3 *CHNY*, 206; *Evertsen*, 37-38.
44. *Evertsen*, 38.
45. Ibid.
46. Ibid.
47. 3 *CHNY*, 206.
48. 1 *EJC*, 533.
49. Ibid., 534; *CSPC, 1669-1674* (no. 1118), 508.
50. Billings, 243-47.

VI COMMOTIONS, TUMULTS, AND DISTURBANCES

1. 1 *EJC*, 26, 38-39.
2. Ibid.
3. Colonel William Cole (1638-1694), of Warwick County, Virginia, was appointed to the Executive Council of Virginia in March 1674/5. In 1680 he was made Commander in Chief of Warwick County. He was appointed Secretary of State in January 1689/90, and the following year became President of the General Court and the Collector of Customs for the Lower James River District. In 1692, after many years of service to the Executive Council, he submitted his resignation "by reason of a deepe Melancholy that hath Seized him." The tomb and arms of Virginia's first appointed pirate fighter remain at "Bolthrope," or Boldrop, Warwick County. Ibid., 109, 173, 204, 249-50; 20 *VMH*, 7n.
4. 1 *EJC*, 26.
5. 7 *Md. Arch.*, 338, 385, 430.
6. 1 *EJC*, 39.
7. Ibid.
8. The issuance of "Hue & Cryes" was the formal spreading of an alarm. Ibid.
9. Ibid.
10. Ibid.
11. 3 *VMH*, 234.
12. 1 *EJC*, 497-98.
13. Dampier, 54.
14. 1 *EJC*, 40-41.
15. That Virginia was willing to foot the bill for the maintenance of the sloop *Katherine* established a precedent that was to last until the 1740s, and one which the Royal Navy frequently employed as an argument to secure naval assistance for guardships, but at colony expense.
16. 12 *VMH*, 319.
17. Ibid.; Rankin, 45.
18. The notorious practice of overdrawing salaries for seamen who were no longer living, or who were fictitious to begin with was rampant in the Royal Navy, and frequently employed by officers and naval supply contractors.
19. 1 *EJC*, 49.
20. Dampier, 55; Williams, 41.
21. Rankin, 45. The circumstances surrounding Jones's relationship with the pirates is clouded in mystery

owing to a lack of documentation.
That he struck to the pirates is probable. His crew was far inferior to
that of Cook's company, and his vessel was heavily outgunned by the
two ships in the pirate's hands. In
any event, his meeting with the buccaneers was on the friendly territory of the latter, for they had apparently been welcomed by the Virginians of the Eastern Shore. Dampier, 54, notes that he had remained
for some time in the colony, approximately 13 months, while Wafer's biographer, Joyce, has suggested that the pirates only departed out of boredom with the se-
rene Virginia environment. Jones
was never expelled from command,
and received full pay for his services
before returning to England. Thus,
most of the allegations against him
were apparently never proven.

22. Dampier, 55.
23. Ibid., 56.
24. 1 *EJC*, 50-51.
25. Ibid., 50.
26. Ibid., 53-54.
27. Ibid., 55.
28. Dabney, 72.
29. 2 *APCC* (no. 130), 54; *CPSC, 1681-
    1685* (no. 1273), 505; (no. 1335),
    529; (no. 1342), 531.
30. Colledge, 445.
31. 1 *EJC*, 62-63.
32. 17 *Md. Arch.*, 350.
33. Ibid., 350-51.
34. Ibid., 350.
35. Ibid.
36. Ibid.
37. Ibid., 350-51.
38. Ibid., 351.
39. Ibid.
40. Ibid.
41. Lacking an official, permanent
    council chamber to meet in, the Ex-
    ecutive Council of Virginia usually
    met either at Jamestown, or at the
    estate or plantation of various
    Council members.
42. Rankin, 46.
43. 1 *EJC*, 68-69.
44. Rankin, 46.
45. Little record has been encountered
    regarding Howard's execution of
    pirates in Virginia, although they

were the first such for piracy in the
colony. Normally, such brigands
were to be sent to England for trial,
but colonial governors, particularly
those of Virginia, occasionally
stretched their authority, as was the
case with Howard, and later
Nicholson.

46. Middleton, 315; Colledge, 159.
47. Rankin, 57-58.
48. 1 *EJC*, 90-91.
49. Rankin, 57-58.
50. Botting, 27.
51. 1 *EJC*, 89-90.

VII   PIECES OF EIGHT
AND SILVER PLATE

1. Admiral Holmes's effigy stands today at Yarmouth Church, on the
   Isle of Wight. Wafer, xliii.
2. Wafer, xliii.
3. Ibid., xliv; *CSPC, 1688,* 577-79.
4. Wafer, xliii; Rankin, 49.
5. Rankin, 49.
6. Colledge, 175, states the vessel was
   rated for 20 guns. Middleton, 315;
   20 *VMH,* 5-6.
7. John Hinson is also referred to as
   John Hincent, or Hingson. Peter
   Cloise is referred to as Peter Cleiss
   in some documents. Cloise, who was
   valued at £14 as a slave, died while
   in Virginia, perhaps, as Williams
   suggests, as a consequence of his
   damaging testimony against the
   three pirates. Wafer, xliv; Botting,
   26; Williams, 34.
8. Wafer, xliv-xlv; Botting, 26; Williams, 33-34.
9. Wafer, xlv.
10. Ibid.
11. Wafer, xlv-xlvi.
12. 1 *EJC,* 107, 112; Williams, 32; 20
    VMH, 6.
13. Ibid.
14. Rankin, 49.
15. Dampier, 54-55; Burney, 132.
16. Dampier, xxii, 8.
17. Dampier and several of his com-
    rades, most notably Basil Ringrose,
    William Ambrosia Cowley, Barthol-
    omew Sharp, John Cox, and, of
    course, Lionel Wafer, lived to write

of their adventures and discoveries in the South Seas. Their works have provided an invaluable insight into the operations of the English freebooters of the Americas, as well as considerable data on the natural history of much of the Caribbean, Central, and South America. Dampier, xxiii, xxvii-xxxii, 54.

18. Cf. Burney for a full account of the voyages of Edward Davis in the South Seas.
19. Wafer, 131.
20. 1 *EJC*, 107.
21. Ibid.; Wafer, xlvi.
22. Wafer, xlvi.
23. 1 *EJC*, 107-8.
24. Ibid.; Wafer, xlvi.
25. Wafer, xlvi.
26. Ibid., xlvii; 1 *EJC*, 107.
27. 1 EJC, 108.
28. Ibid.; Wafer, xlvii.
29. 1 *EJC*, 108-9.
30. Ibid.
31. Ibid., 112-13.
32. Wafer, xlvii.
33. 1 *EJC*, 114.
34. Ibid., 115.
35. Ibid., 124.
36. Ibid.
37. Wafer, 131.
38. Ibid., xlviii.
39. Ibid.
40. 9 *VMH*, 33.
41. 1 *EJC*, 172.
42. Ibid., 173.
43. Wafer, xlix; 9 *VMH*, 33.
44. Ibid.
45. Wafer, xlix.
46. Ibid.
47. Ibid.
48. 7 *WMQ* (I), 165; 8 *WMQ* (II), 220.

VIII   PROFLIGATE MEN

1. Rankin, 52; 1 *EJC*, 233.
2. 1 *EJC*, 194-95, 270, 275, 297.
3. Colledge, 263.
4. 1 *EJC*, 231-32.
5. Rankin, 52-53, notes the arrival of the guardship *Dover Prize* under the command of the ex-pirate Thomas Pound in Virginia waters, to replace or reinforce *Henry Prize* on April 17,

1691. Colledge, 263, indicates in his index of Royal Navy ships that this vessel was captured by the English in 1693, two years after its appearance in Virginia waters. No mention of the vessel appears in *EJC* for this period.
6. 1 *EJC*, 231-32.
7. Ibid., 232-33, 248-49.
8. Ibid., 274.
9. Ibid., 228-29.
10. Rankin, 53-54.
11. Ibid., 54-59.
12. Ibid., 58; Colledge, 539; 1 *EJC*, 378.
13. Rankin, 54-55.
14. 25 *Md. Arch.*, 554.
15. Ibid., 554-56.
16. Ibid., 557.
17. Ibid., 555, 560.
18. Ibid., 556-58.
19. Ibid., 565.
20. Ibid., 566-67.
21. Colledge, 169; Rankin, 53.
22. Admiralty to Aldred, 14 September 1697, C. O. 5/1411. Captain Bostock received his first set of sailing instructions on October 20, and his final set on October 30. Admiralty to Bostock, 30 October 1697, C. O. 5/1411.
23. Rankin, 60-61; 1 *EJC*, 422-23.
24. Lords Justices (directed to His Majesty's Governors of His Majesty's Colonies in America, undated), C. O. 5/1411; 1 *EJC*, 422-23.
25. 1 *EJC*, 422-23.
26. 8 *VMH*, 191-92; 25 *Md. Arch.* 97-98.
27. Thomas Wellburn to Nicholson, 29 June 1699, C. O. 5/1411.
28. 25 *Md. Arch.*, 77; Rankin, 61.
29. 25 *Md. Arch.*, 77.
30. Robert Quary to Commissioners of His Majesty's Customs, 6 June 1699, Blathwayth Papers, VII, f. 3.
31. Rankin, 61-62.

IX   THE PIRATE WITH THE GOLD TOOTHPICK

1. *CSPC, 1699* (no. 711), 390; (no. 989), 539.
2. Ibid. (no. 745), 414; (no. 802), 444; (no. 1001), 545.
3. William Rhett to Edmund Jennings,

1 July 1699, C. O. 5/1411; Nicholas Thomas Jones Deposition, 4 August 1699, C. O. 5/1411; *CSPC, 1699* (no. 1001), 542. James had taken a number of vessels, many of which have not been identified. He did, however, definitely take the *Trial* of Boston, John Green commanding, and while serving under Hynd, captured a 40-ton New England brigantine commanded by Edward Johnson.

4. Log of *Essex Prize,* 29 July 1699; C. O. 5/1411.
5. Ibid., 24 July 1699.
6. Ibid., 24-25 July 1699.
7. Ibid.
8. Ibid., 26 July 1699; John Aldred to Francis Nicholson, 26 July 1699, C. O. 5/1411.
9. John Martin to Nicholson, 29 July 1699, C. O. 5/1411; Log of *Essex Prize,* 26 July 1699.
10. Ibid.
11. Ibid.
12. Log of *Essex Prize,* 26 July 1699.
13. Ibid.; Aldred to Nicholson, 26 July 1699, C. O. 5/1411. *Essex Prize* fired "minion Guns with shot" 138 times, "falcon [guns] 6 with shot their cases 39 barrs 32 fired."
14. Aldred to Nicholson, 26 July 1699, C. O. 5/1411.
15. *CSPC, 1699* (no. 711), 390.
16. Ibid.
17. John Martin to Nicholson, 29 July 1699, C. O. 5/1411. Rankin, 66, notes the prize cargo included only nine pipes of water, 100 casks of bread, rigging, and a new hawser cable. He also states that seven, not eight, crew members signed the pirate articles.
18. *CSPC, 1699* (no. 711), 390.
19. *Maryland Merchant* was later freed from the shoals with the aid of *Essex Prize* and on August 5 set sail for London. Log of *Essex Prize,* 2, 3, 4, 5 August 1699.
20. *CSPC, 1699* (no. 898(I)), 539; Jones Deposition, 4 August 1699, C. O. 5/1411.
21. Jones Deposition, 4 August 1699, C. O. 5/1411.
22. Ibid.
23. Ibid.; *CSPC, 1699* (no. 746 (XVI and XVII)), 415.
24. Ibid. Jones states the commander of *Charles* was a certain Captain Sears. However, depositions taken regarding the capture of the vessel near Cape Sable by John James were provided by Captain Joseph Baker.
25. Jones Deposition, 4 August 1699.
26. Ibid.
27. Ibid.
28. Ibid.
29. Ibid.
30. Ibid.; Log of *Essex Prize,* 27 July 1699.
31. Jones Deposition, 4 August 1699.
32. John Martin to Nicholson, 29 July 1699.
33. Jones Deposition, 4 August 1699.
34. Log of *Essex Prize,* 27-28 July 1699.
35. Ibid., 29 July 1699.
36. "Certificate of Ye Weakness and insufficiency of his ship," 30 July 1699, C. O. 5/1411.
37. Ibid.
38. Order of Governor and Council, 3 August 1699, C. O. 5/1411.
39. Ibid.
40. Ibid.
41. Ibid., 9 August 1699, C. O. 5/1411.
42. Custis to Nicholson, 16 August 1699, C. O. 5/1411.
43. Ibid. Smith's Island River is not recorded on maps of either the seventeenth or early eighteenth centuries. It is believed by the author that the "river," frequently referred to in documents of these centuries, was actually the sound between the island and the mainland of the Eastern Shore, a sheltered area which provided a relatively suitable deepwater anchorage, refuge from weather, and a convenient gathering and trading place for vessels entering and departing the Chesapeake.
44. Ibid.
45. Nicholson to Custis, 24 October 1699, C. O. 5/1411.
46. 21 *VMH,* 256.

X   THE WINTER OF DISCONTENT

1. Rankin, 67.

2. 2 *EJC*, 9.
3. Aldred was originally supposed to submit his report on October 15, but apparently failed to appear. On October 17 he was sternly directed to make his presentation the following day. 2 *EJC*, 9-10.
4. Ibid., 13.
5. Ibid., 16.
6. Ibid., 15-16.
7. Ibid., 16.
8. Ibid.
9. Ibid., 18.
10. Ibid., 38.
11. The pirates included: Edward Buckmaster, escapee from New York City; one Guilliam, escapee from Rhode Island; James How, Nicholas Churchill, Daniel Dooley, John Eldridge, James Holstead, and Robert Hickman, escapees from New Jersey. Guilliam was reportedly the pirate leader. Ibid., 29-30.
12. Ibid., 19-20.
13. Ibid., 24.
14. Ibid.
15. Ibid.
16. Ibid.
17. Ibid.
18. HM Advice Boat *Messenger* was a vessel of six guns and 73 tons, built at Plymouth, England and commissioned in 1694. She foundered in the Atlantic on November 30, 1701 on her homeward journey from Virginia. Colledge, 360; 2 *EJC*, 32.
19. Ibid., 43.
20. 2 *EJC*, 43.
21. Ibid., 33.
22. Aldred to Nicholson, 3 March 1700, C. O. 5/1411.
23. Aldred to Nicholson, 11 March 1700, C. O. 5/1411.
24. Nicholson Orders, 9 March 1700, C. O. 5/1411; 2 *EJC*, 43.
25. The items sent included: "Rice, Barley, Mace, Cinnamon, and Nutmegs, one quarter of what his Excellency at present has, being two ounces of Cinnamon, two ounces of Mace, four ounces of Nutts, fifteen pounds of Rice, and Seventeen pounds & an half of barley." Several of these items, such as cinnamon, nutmeg, and mace were expensive rarities in the colonies, often avail-

able only through apothecaries or in medical kits of the upper class. Jonathan Keate Receipt, 30 March 1700; Nicholson to Aldred, 30 March 1700; Aldred to Nicholson (undated ca. March 1700), C. O. 5/1411.
26. Petition of Israel Voss (undated), C. O. 5/1411.
27. Aldred to Nicholson (undated but probably 29 March 1700); Nicholson to Aldred, 30 March 1700, C. O. 5/1411.
28. Nicholson to Aldred, 9 April 1700, C. O. 5/1411.
28. Nicholson to Aldred, 9 April 1700, C. O. 5/1411.
29. Nicholson to Aldred, 30 March 1700, C. O. 5/1411.
30. Nicholson to Aldred, 9 April 1700, C. O. 5/1411.
31. 2 *EJC*, 47-48.
32. Nicholson to Joseph [Josiah] Burchett, 11 April 1700, C. O. 5/1411.

XI   BLOODY *PEACE*

1. The history of the rampage of the pirate Lewis Guittar has been drawn from the extensive manuscript materials in the microfilm collections of the Virginia Colonial Records Project housed at Colonial Williamsburg. The proceedings of the Court of Oyer and Terminer of May 13, 1700, as well as numerous letters, and the inventory of the ship *La Paix*, taken after her capture by the Royal Navy, are included in the Rawlinson manuscripts of the Bodleian Library at Oxford, England. Additional data has been extracted from the proceedings of the Virginia General Court of May 14, 15, and 16, 1700, in which the pirates Houghling, Delaunee, and Frank were tried and condemned. Transcriptions of this material, C. O. 5/647, are housed in the Manuscript Division of the Library of Congress, Washington, D.C.
2. Guittar related to the Court of Admiralty the following details of his initiation into piracy: "he was living att Petty Gavous [Pointe a Gravois,

on the southwest coast of Hispanio-la] where [he] took a Canew wth his Servt to go see a friend 6. or 7 leagues off And as he was comeing downe a little River these men that were the pyrates sent another Canoe to him they being in a Sloop and told him he must come on board & at last they forc'd him being unwilling when he was on board they told him they wanted a Captaine and would make him theirs so would not let him go but staved his Canoe and kept him on board and thus he came Engaged wth them."

3. John Houghling Testimony, C. O. 5/647.
4. Joseph Wood Testimony, C. O. 5/647.
5. Joseph Maunsaged Testimony, Rawlinson.
6. Josiah Burchett to Nicholson, 5 December 1699, C. O. 5/1411; Joshia Burchett to John Aldred, 5 December 1699, C. O. 5/1411.
7. Nicholson to [Aldred] 16 April 1700, C. O. 5/1411. A survey of *Essex Prize* revealed, among other things, that her bottom was defective, she needed caulking inside and out, her pump needed repairs, her shrouds of spun yarn were useless, and she needed a few new knees. Survey Report, 19 April 1700, C. O. 5/1411.
8. Aldred to Nicholson, 24 April 1700, C. O. 5/1411.
9. 2 *EJC*, 57; Colledge, 506.
10. 2 *EJC*, 58-59.
11. 2 *EJC*, 72; Joseph Maunsaged Testimony, Rawlinson; Rankin, 68-69; Williams, 59. Captain Passenger had requested a press of nine men and a pilot familiar with Virginia waters on April 15, 1700, but was apparently less irritating in his appeal than Aldred had been. Nicholson was more concerned with pirates than civil rights. He approved of the press, and offered a reward of £20 sterling for every pirate taken ashore.
12. Williams, 59; Rankin, 72.
13. There is disagreement, even among participants, as to when the battle began and ended. Many testified it ended at 4:00 P.M., while others indicate it lasted between seven and

eight hours. If the engagement started at 5:00 A.M. as Rankin, 72, states, it would have ended at 1:00 P.M. at the latest. Others state the fight began at 7:00 A.M., thus making 3:00 P.M. a more plausible time for its conclusion. Cf. testimonies of Joseph Bigges, Thomas Watt, John Calwell, George Levingston, and Joseph Maunsaged, in Rawlinson.
14. The church site where Peter Heyman was interred was near Hampton in what later became known as Pembrooke Farm. 11 *VMH*, 158-59.

XII   THREE GIBBETS

1. The proceedings of the trial are excerpted from the court records, PRO Admiralty 1/647, transcripts of which are in the Manuscript Division of the Library of Congress.
2. 2 *EJC*, 94.
3. Ibid., 76-77.
4. Ibid., 76-77, 81, 82-84.
5. Rankin, 74; 2 *EJC*, 80.
6. 2 *EJC*, 88.
7. Rankin, 76.
8. 2 *EJC*, 71, 92.
9. Ibid., 141.

XIII   NO FARTHER THAN YE SOUNDINGS

1. Nicholson to Passenger, 4 May 1700, Rawlinson.
2. 2 *EJC*, 66-67, 69.
3. Daniel Thorogood to Nicholson, 3 May 1700; Benjamin Harrison to Nicholson, 4 May 1700, Rawlinson.
4. Ibid.; Williams, 56.
5. 2 *EJC*, 69-70.
6. Ibid., 85-86, 105.
7. Ibid., 91-92.
8. Middleton, 318.
9. 2 *EJC*, 106-7.
10. Ibid., 119-20.
11. Ibid., 120; Middleton, 318.
12. 2 *EJC*, 139-40, 142.
13. Ibid.; Colledge, 319, 515; Middleton, 318.

14. Similar dispatches were sent to the governors of New England, Rhode Island, New Jersey, Connecticut, Barbados, the Leeward Islands, Maryland, and the Carolinas (through Virginia). *CSPC, 1701* (no. 104), 59.
15. Rankin, 78.
16. *CSPC, 1701* (no. 573), 313.

XIV   THE GUARDSHIPS

1. 2 *EJC*, 146.
2. *CSPC, 1701* (no. 566), 309.
3. HM Advice Boat *Eagle* was built at Arundel in 1696. She mounted 10 guns, all six-pounders, and was manned by a crew of 50. She was 153 tons burthen, 76 feet in length, and 21 feet abeam. *Eagle* was wrecked on the Sussex Coast on November 27, 1703. Colledge, 180; *CSPC, 1701* (no. 859), 519-20; *1702* (no. 911), 561.
4. *CSPC, 1701* (no. 893), 539.
5. 2 *EJC*, 198.
6. Ibid., 198-201, 214-15.
7. Ibid., 204-5.
8. Ibid., 215.
9. *CSPC, 1702* (no. 793), 492; *1702-1703* (no. 77), 59; 2 *APCC*, 385.
10. *CPSC, 1702* (no. 210), 141-42.
11. 2 *APCC*, 417-18.
12. 2 *EJC*, 219.
13. Ibid., 237-38.
14. The anchorages selected were: in the James River at Jamestown; in the Elizabeth River as high as the town (presumably Norfolk); above the fort on the Nansemond River; at the head of Pagan Creek; in the Warwick River above Sandy Point; in the Hampton River off Towne Point; in the York River above King's Creek; in all the rivers flowing into Mobjack Bay as high as the water would permit; as high up the Rappahannock as possible; above the fort on Corotoman River; in the Potomac River as high up as "Appamatock Creek"; and in the Yeocomico and Lower Machodoc as far up as possible. 2 *EJC*, 239.
15. *CSPC, 1702* (no. 1174), 652.
16. Captain Bostock, commander of *Eagle,* was instructed by the Admiralty to attend to Maryland and to follow the orders of Governor Blackiston. Yet he was also directed to facilitate the desires of the Governor of Virginia as well. Thus, the yoke of decision was placed squarely on the shoulders of the field commander. He was also directed to take, burn, or sink all pirates but those of Sallee. *CSPC, 1702* (no. 1029), 653; (no. 1174), 734; 22 *VMH*, 124-25.
17. 2 *APCC*, 425-26.
18. Middleton, 296.
19. *CSPC, 1702-1703* (no. 171), 117.
20. 3 *EJC*, 1, 7.
21. 3 Hening, 335-42, 362-67.
22. 3 *EJC*, 3.
23. Ibid., 9.
24. Ibid., 17.
25. Ibid., 8-9, 17.
26. Ibid., 88.
27. Ibid., 89-91.
28. Ibid., 94-96, 97.
29. Ibid., 96.
30. Ibid., 28-29; 16 *VMH*, 76; 25 *Md. Arch.*, 185, 188; 26 *Md. Arch.*, 379, 450-51, 453; 27 *Md. Arch.*, 23, 26, 31, 33.
31. 3 *EJC*, 69.
32. 16 *VMH*, 76; 25 *Md. Arch.*, 240-41, 262-63, 265.
33. 27 *Md. Arch.*, 21.
34. Rankin, 79-81.
35. 3 *EJC*, 102.
36. HMS *Triton's Prize* was originally the French privateer *Royal* captured by the English on March 3, 1705 and taken into the Royal Navy as a sixth-rate man-of-war. Armed with 28 guns, she was 274 tons burthen, 75 feet long, and 26½ feet abeam. She was sold out of service on November 26, 1713. Colledge, 571; 3 *EJC*, 102, 103-4, 113.
37. 3 *EJC*, 150.
38. HMS *Garland* was a fifth-rate man-of-war of 496 tons burthen. Built at Woolwich Dockyard on the Thames River, she was commissioned on April 28, 1703. Colledge, 228; Middleton, 320.
39. 3 *EJC*, 169-70; *JCTP, 1704-1708/09,*

409.

40. 3 *EJC*, 170-71, 174, 175.
41. Ibid., 208; Middleton, 320; *CSPC, 1706-1708*, xxviii; (no. 137), 96; (no. 1570), 760.
42. *CSPC, 1708-1709* (no. 421), 254; 3 *EJC*, 205-6.
43. 3 *EJC*, 205, 206, 210.
44. Ibid., 208-11; *CSPC, 1708-1709* (no. 765), 480.
45. *CSPC, 1708-1709*, xxviii; (no. 137), 96; (no. 254), 185.
46. Tancred Robinson to Josiah Burchett, 6 July 1709, Letters, Tancred Robinson Collection; Middleton, 321-22.
47. 3 *EJC*, 228-30; Middleton, 322; Spotswood to Robinson, 27 July 1710, Tancred Robinson Papers.
48. HMS *Enterprize* was a fifth-rate, 44-gun warship of 531 tons burthen. Built at Plymouth, this vessel was 118 feet in length and 32 feet abeam. She was commissioned on April 28, 1709. In 1718 she was rebuilt at Chatham as a 700-ton warship. In September 1745 she was hulked, and on April 3, 1749 the hulk was sold. Colledge, 191; 4 *EJC*, 229; *CSPC, 1710-1711* (no. 208), 84; *1710-1711* (no. 263), 114.
49. *CSPC, 1710-1711* (no. 263), 114.
50. The 372-ton, 34-gun, fifth-rate warship *Bedford Galley* was 103 feet in length, and 29 feet abeam. Built in New England in 1697, she was purchased the same year for the Royal Navy. In 1709 she was rebuilt at Plymouth, England as a 410-ton man-of-war. In 1716 she was converted to a fireship. On May 3, 1725 she was scuttled as a foundation at Sheerness. Colledge, 69; Admiralty Orders, 31 March 1710, Tancred Robinson Papers; Robinson to Burchett, 10 July 1710, Letters, Tancred Robinson Collection (cf. 3 April 1710 Line-of-Battle in same place); Dabney, 76.
51. 2 *Spotswood*, 11, 12, 88; *CSPC, 1710-1711* (no. 349), 171; (no. 363), 177; (no. 441), 242-43; *JHB, 1702-1712*, 249.
52. Spotswood to Robinson, 18 September 1710, Tancred Robinson Papers; Dodson, 210-11; *CSPC, 1711-*

1712 (no. 42), 25; 2 *Spotswood*, 91.
53. 3 *EJC*, 282; 2 *Spotswood*, 99.
54. 3 *EJC*, 282-83.
55. The spyboat is also referred to as *Jenny and Mary*. The magazine which Spotswood had erected in Williamsburg stands today as the famous Powder Horn. *CSPC, 1711-1712* (no. 120), 112; 26 *VMH*, 54; Middleton, 324.
56. *JHB, 1702-1712*, 302.
57. Middleton, 324-25.

XV WE PLUNDER THE RICH

1. Rankin, 81; 2 *Spotswood*, 168; 6 *APCC*, Unbound Papers (no. 251), 103; *CSPC, 1714-1715* (no. 449), 199; (no. 520), 232; Colledge, 583.
2. Middleton, 341.
3. Rankin, 82; Lee, 10-11; 2 *Spotswood*, 169.
4. Marx, 206-9.
5. Rankin, 86.
6. Depositions of John Vickers and Alexander Stockdale, C. O. 5/1317.
7. 2 *Spotswood*, 168-69.
8. Ibid., 170-71; 4 *EJC*, 427-28; 3 *VMH*, 176; Rankin, 85.
9. Botting, 138.
10. Rankin, 85-86.
11. Rankin, 86; Dodson, 216; 2 *Spotswood*, 168-71; 3 *EJC*, 428.
12. 2 *Spotswood*, 250-51, 259; 3 *VMH*, 176; Rankin, 86-88.
13. Dethlefsen, 15, 20.
14. Johnson, 480.
15. Dethlefsen, 22-23.
16. Ibid., 24-25; Johnson, 480; *The Boston News-Letter*, 6 May to 13 May 1717.
17. Rankin, 89, indicates she carried 12 guns and 40 men. Dethlefsen, 26; Depositions of Andrew Tarbett and Robert Gilman, C. O. 5/1342; 4 *EJC*, 443-44.
18. Johnson, 482.
19. Depositions of Andrew Tarbett and Robert Gilman, C. O. 5/1342; Johnson, 480; Dethlefsen, 27.
20. Rankin, 89.
21. Rankin, 89-90, claims Bellamy captured one more sloop off the Vir-

ginia Capes, a claim which is ignored by some, such as Dethlefsen.
Cf. *The Boston News-Letter*, 6 May to
13 May 1717.
22. 3 *EJC*, 443-44; Depositions of Andrew Tarbett and Robert Gilman,
C. O. 5/1342.
23. 2 *Spotswood*, 249.
24. Ibid., 246, 249-50.
25. Ibid., 255; Colledge, 335.
26. Log of HMS *Pearl;* Colledge, 410.
27. 2 *APCC*, 723-25.
28. 2 *CVSP*, 193; 3 *EJC*, 469.

XVI   A FURY FROM HELL

1. Johnson, 57.
2. Rankin, 106; 9 *VMH*, 95; Lee, 4.
3. Johnson, 57.
4. Ibid., 58.
5. Ibid.
6. Ibid., 45.
7. Ibid.
8. Ibid.; Rankin, 107.
9. Johnson, 45.
10. Williams, 80.
11. Ibid., 80-81.
12. Johnson, 45; Lee, 18.
13. Johnson, 45-46.
14. Ibid., 67.
15. Ibid., 46.
16. Ibid.
17. Ibid., 46-47; Williams, 90-93.
18. Governor Bennet of Bermuda, in a
    letter to the Commissioners of
    Trade and Plantations dated May
    31, 1718, elucidates the danger and
    strength of Teach's force while in
    the West Indies. His letter, though
    only symptomatic of the panic felt
    by many, served to instill in the Brit-
    ish government a resolve to deal
    with the problem of piracy in the
    Americas. Cf. *CSPC, 1717-1718* for
    the growing governmental con-
    cerns and the actions taken.
19. Johnson, 47-48; Williams, 93-98;
    Lee, 39-48.
20. Lee, 51.
21. Johnson, 48; Williams, 99.
22. Johnson claimed that 17 men were
    marooned by Teach, but one of
    their number, Ned Patterson of
    Aberdeen, Scotland, testified at his
    trial that their number was 25.
    Johnson, 48; Howell, 1254.
23. Johnson, 69.
24. Ibid., 70.
25. Ibid.
26. Lee, 53-54.
27. Ibid., 62; Johnson, 48.
28. Johnson, 49; Williams, 101.
29. Johnson, 48, 64; 2 *Spotswood*, 273.
30. Johnson, 64.
31. Ibid., 48; Williams, 101.
32. Lee, 78; Rankin, *PCNC*, 53.
33. Johnson, 48.
34. Ibid., 58.
35. Ibid., 49; 2 *CRNC*, 341.
36. Johnson, 49.
37. Ibid., 49-50.
38. Ibid., 56.
39. Ibid., 50; 2 *Spotswood*, 273.
40. Rankin, 105.
41. 2 *Spotswood*, 294.
42. Rankin, 106.
43. Lee, 90; Pringle, 202; Johnson, 107-
    8.
44. Rankin, 116.
45. Ibid.; Lee, 99; 2 *Spotswood*, 354.
46. Williams, 77.
47. Rankin, 116; Lee, 99; 2 *Spotswood*,
    351-54.
48. Williams, 80-81.
49. Ibid., 78; Rankin, 116-17; 2 *Spots-
    wood*, 351-54. Cf. Spotswood's letter
    to the Council of Trade, December
    22, 1718, in *CSPC, 1717-1718.*
50. Howard also retained one Richard
    Fitzwilliams, an influential lawyer,
    to assist him. Fitzwilliams later
    served as chief counsel to the pirate
    John Vidal in 1727.
51. *CSPC, 1717-1718* (no. 10), 800.
52. Williams, 80-82.
53. 2 *Spotswood*, 351-61; Lee, 104.
54. 2 *Spotswood*, 351-54.
55. Williams, 79; Lee, 105.
56. Rankin, 118.

XVII   CUT THEM
TO PIECES

1. Johnson, 265.
2. Ibid., 269; Lee, 106.
3. *CSPC, 1717-1718* (no. 800), 432.
4. Ibid., 431.
5. Ibid.

6. Lee, 109-10.
7. 2 *Spotswood*, 306; *JHB, 1718*, 223-24.
8. *JHB, 1718*, 224-28.
9. Ibid., 233.
10. Ibid.
11. Valuable data regarding the Royal Navy's participation in the effort to subdue Blackbeard is contained in the log of HMS *Lyme*, which identifies *Jane* as Maynard's command sloop. The log, however, was poorly maintained, and many notations are made after the fact, some entries having apparently been made several days later than the events noted. Some documentation of the expedition is occasionally inadequate owing to late reportage. Captain Brand, in a letter to the Admiralty dated February 6, 1719, written well after the conclusion of the expedition, indicates Maynard sailed at 3:00 P.M. on November 17. Since the letter was written several months after the event, the data might be considered potentially suspect. The log of HMS *Lyme*, though perhaps inaccurate regarding dates, is quite probably more accurate on the number of men participating. Maynard's vessel employed on the expedition has only been named in the ship logs of *Lyme* and *Pearl* but appears nowhere else in the literature of the expedition histories. Log of HMS *Lyme*, November 15, 1718; Johnson, 52
12. Letters of Brand to Admiralty, 6 February and 12 March 1719.
13. Johnson, 52; Rankin, 119.
14. Log of HMS *Lyme*, 20 November 1718.
15. Lee, 146.
16. Johnson, 52; Rankin, 119; Lee, 114.
17. Log of HMS *Lyme*, 20 November 1718.
18. Ibid.; Johnson, 53, 58.
19. Rankin, 120.
20. Log of HMS *Lyme*, 20 November 1718.
21. Williams, 109; Johnson, 53; Rankin, 120.
22. Johnson, 53.
23. Ibid.
24. Ibid., 53; Lee, 118.
25. Johnson, 54.
26. Ibid.
27. Ibid.
28. Ibid., 54-55; Williams, 111.
29. Johnson, 54-55.
30. Ibid., 55; Letters of George Gordon to Admiralty, 14 September 1721.
31. Johnson, 55.
32. Ibid.
33. Ibid., 55-56; Williams, 111.
34. 2 *CRNC*, 341-49; Johnson, 55-56; Letters of George Gordon to Admiralty, 14 September 1721.
35. Log of HMS *Pearl*, 1 January 1718/19.
36. Ibid., 2 January 1718/19.
37. Johnson, 59.
38. Ibid., 56-57; Lee, 138; Williams, 117. Johnson lists fourteen pirates hung. These were: John Carnes, Joseph Brooks, Jr., James Blake, John Gills, Thomas Gates, James White, Richard Stiles, Caesar, Joseph Philips, James Robbens, John Martin, Edward Salter, Stephen Daniel, and Richard Greensail. Johnson contradicts himself by also stating that there were fifteen prisoners carried to Virginia, thirteen of whom were hung. The disparity has been attributed by Williams to an error by Johnson, who may have included one of the pirates killed at Ocracoke among those who were later hung. The confusion may also be caused by the hanging of two pirates, as noted in the log of HMS *Pearl*, on January 28, 1718/19, at Hampton, but not cited elsewhere.
39. Log of HMS *Pearl*, 28 January 1719.
40. *Boston News-Letter*, 16 February to 23 February 1719; Johnson, 56; Lee, 125.

XVIII   GOLDEN LUGGAGE

1. 1 Byrd, 326.
2. Rankin, 132.
3. Johnson, 167-68.
4. Ibid., 176-77.
5. Johnson, 177, suggests Roberts' selection of Devil's Island was made because the place was a "safe retreat where they might hive (*sic*) them-

selves up to all the pleasures that luxury and wantonness could bestow."

6. It has been suggested that Roberts drank great quantities of tea and disdained liquor because he believed strong drink impaired efficiency. Botting, 162.
7. Johnson, 168, 178, 179.
8. Ibid., 178.
9. Ibid.
10. Ibid., 168, 179.
11. Ibid., 179.
12. 2 *Spotswood,* 340.
13. *The Supplement to The Boston Gazette,* 21 March to 22 March 1719.
14. 2 *Spotswood,* 338.
15. *The Supplement to The Boston Gazette,* 21 March to 22 March 1719.
16. *Boston News-Letter,* 20 February to 27 February, 1720.
17. The date given is approximated from the Philadelphia *American Weekly Mercury* account of 17 March 1720 which noted the arrival of *West River Merchant* at the Virginia Capes "The beginning of last Month." Williams, 119, claims the vessel was out of Barbados, basing his comment on Johnson. Rankin, 132, claims the vessel was from London. The Philadelphia newspaper account supports Rankin's statement.
18. *American Weekly Mercury,* 17 March 1720.
19. 4 *EJC,* 521.
20. 2 *Spotswood,* 338, 342.
21. *American Weekly Mercury,* 17 March 1720.
22. Johnson, 179.
23. *American Weekly Mercury,* 17 March 1720.
24. Ibid. The women were apparently indentured servants whose time of service the pirates were able to purchase from their masters.
25. Johnson, 179, indicates the pirates found "good Entertainment among the Planters."
26. *American Weekly Mercury,* 17 March 1720.
27. The pirates were taken into custody by Thomas Wythe and four companions. Rankin, 133; Johnson, 180.
28. *American Weekly Mercury,* 17 March

1720.
29. Ibid.
30. Ibid.
31. 4 *EJC,* 522.
32. 2 *Spotswood,* 338.
33. Ibid., 338, 342.
34. 4 *EJC,* 522; *The Boston News-Letter,* 7 March to 14 March 1720.
35. Williams, 122; 2 *Spotswood,* 338.
36. *American Weekly Mercury,* 17 March 1720.
37. Ibid.
38. 2 *Spotswood,* 338, 342.
39. Ibid.; Williams, 123.
40. 2 *Spotswood,* 338, 342.
41. Irwin had once been charged with fraudulent practices in office by Richard Fitzwilliams, the same attorney who had served as a consultant to the pirate Howard, but was cleared on all counts. 4 *EJC,* 492; 10 *VMH,* 216.
42. 2 *Spotswood,* 342.
43. Ibid., 338-39, 343.
44. Rankin, 134.
45. Johnson, 85-86.
46. Ibid., 142.
47. Rankin, 135; 2 *Spotswood,* 339.
48. 2 *Spotswood,* 339.
49. Ibid., 340.
50. 4 *EJC,* 5-6; Rankin, 135.
51. Rankin, 134.
52. 2 *Spotswood,* 349; Williams, 123.
53. 2 *Spotswood,* 349; Rankin, 136; Williams, 123-24.
54. 2 *Spotswood,* 349-50; Williams, 124.
55. Rankin, 137.
56. Ibid., 138.

XIX TOES TIED TOGETHER

1. Dodson, 221.
2. *American Weekly Mercury,* 2 June 1720; 2 *Spotswood,* 341.
3. *American Weekly Mercury,* 2 June 1720.
4. Ibid., 19 May 1720; 2 *Spotswood,* 341.
5. *American Weekly Mercury,* 9 June 1720.
6. Ibid., 23 June 1720.
7. Ibid., 30 June 1720.
8. Ibid., 14 July 1720.
9. Ibid., 3 November 1720; 4 *EJC,* 529;

2 *Spotswood*, 347.
10. *American Weekly Mercury*, 17 January 1721.
11. 2 *Spotswood*, 346; 4 *EJC*, 529-30.
12. Ibid.; *American Weekly Mercury*, 3 November 1720.
13. 2 *Spotswood*, 346; 4 *EJC*, 529-30.
14. *American Weekly Mercury*, 17 January 1721.
15. Ibid.
16. Ibid.; 2 *Spotswood*, 346-48.
17. *American Weekly Mercury*, 17 January 1721.
18. Ibid.
19. *JHB, 1712-1726*, 304-9; 3 *EJC*, 536, 538, 540; 4 *EJC*, 43.

XX   I NEVER INTENDED TO GO A PIRATING

1. 2 *Spotswood*, 350.
2. Ibid., 351-52; 4 *EJC*, 550; Colledge, 191.
3. 4 *EJC*, 550.
4. Rankin, 152.
5. Ibid., 153.
6. Ibid.; *CSPC, 1730* (no. 375), 229-30.
7. Rankin, 153.
8. Ibid., 155; 4 *EJC*, 144.
9. 32 *VMH*, 242.
10. 1 *CVSP*, 211-12.
11. *CSPC, 1726-1727* (no. 707), 353.
12. 32 *VMH*, 242-45.
13. *CSPC, 1726-1727* (no. 707), 353.
14. 4 *EJC*, 170-71; Colledge, 75.

XXI   PESTS OF TRADE

1. Middleton, 330.
2. 5 *EJC*, 57-59.
3. Ibid., 71.
4. Middleton, 330.
5. 1 *CVSP*, 235.
6. HMS *Hector* was built at Rotherhithe by Josiah Burchett. Her original tonnage was placed at 493. She was 116½ feet in length and 31 feet abeam. She was commissioned on February 13, 1703. In 1721 she was rebuilt at Plymouth. In 1742 she was ordered broken up. Colledge, 261.

7. 3 *APCC* (no. 590), 777.
8. C. O. 5/1326; C. O. 5/1327, 173-74.
9. HMS *Hastings* was constructed at Liverpool as *Endymion* and renamed in 1739. She was originally 682 tons, 124 feet in length, and 36 feet abeam. She was rebuilt at Liverpool and recommissioned on March 7, 1740. On September 19, 1763 she was broken up at Sheerness. Colledge, 256; C. O. 5/1326, 11-12.
10. Middleton, 343-44.
11. *Maryland Gazette*, 17 May 1745.
12. Ibid., 23 May 1745.
13. *Virginia Gazette*, 23 May 1745.
14. Ibid.
15. Ibid., 13 June 1745.
16. *Maryland Gazette*, 17 May 1745; 12 July 1745.
17. *Virginia Gazette*, 20 June 1745; 4 July 1745.
18. *Maryland Gazette*, 1 June 1745.
19. Ibid., 26 July 1745; *Virginia Gazette*, 12 September 1745.
20. *Maryland Gazette*, 16 August 1745.
21. Ibid., 13 May 1746; *Virginia Gazette*, 12 September 1745.
22. *Virginia Gazette*, 12 September 1745.
23. Ibid.
24. Ibid., 24 April 1746; 3 July 1746.
25. *Maryland Gazette*, 2 December 1746.
26. Ibid.
27. Middleton, 299-300.
28. *Maryland Gazette*, 20 January 1748; 18 May 1748.
29. HMS *Looe* was built in 1745 at Liverpool and commissioned on August 17, 1745. In 1759 she was sunk as a breakwater at Harwich. HMS *Hector*, the second vessel bearing that name to serve on the Chesapeake, was built in 1743 as a fifth-rate, 44-gun man-of-war. She was 720 tons, 126 feet in length, 36½ feet abeam, and served until 1762 when she was broken up. Colledge, 261, 328.
30. *Maryland Gazette*, 8 June 1748.
31. This incident is reported as two separate actions, but a close reading of contemporary news accounts suggests they were varied reports of the same action. *Maryland Gazette*, 22 June 1748; 6 July 1748.
32. Ibid., 6 July 1748.
33. Ibid., 20 July 1748.

34. Ibid.
35. Ibid., 6 July 1748.
36. One of the French vessels taken was *Cul de Sac*, laden with sugar and indigo. She sailed from Philadelphia, probably as a flag of truce vessel. She was taken by *Otter*, although the capture was attributed to HMS *Hector*, from which the complement of *Otter* had been made up. Ibid.; 20 July 1748; 10 August 1748; 28 September 1748.
37. Ibid., 10 August 1748.
38. Ibid., 7 September 1748.
39. Middleton, 333.
40. Ibid.

XXII TORY VILLAINS

1. 5 *MHM*, 129.
2. Eller, 381.
3. 5 *NDAR*, 742, 839.
4. Ibid., 742.
5. 12 *Md. Arch.*, 151-56.
6. 5 *NDAR*, 996, 1050, 1078-79, 1094-96; *Virginia Gazette* (Purdie), 12 July 1776; *Pennsylvania Packet*, 22 July 1776.
7. 5 *NDAR*, 1247-48.
8. Ibid.
9. Ibid., 1296.
10. 12 *Md. Arch.*, 151-56, 166.
11. *CMSP, Executive Miscellanea, No. 5* (no. 426), 57; (nos. 428, 429), 58.
12. *CMSP, The Red Books, No. 4, Part 1* (no. 612), 106.
13. *CMSP, The Red Books, No. 4, Part 3* (nos. 376, 377), 58.
14. Ibid. (no. 388), 58.
15. Eller, 391-92; 21 *Md. Arch.*, 333; 43 *Md. Arch.*, 247; Eller, 391-92.
16. *CMSP, The Red Books, No. 4, Part 3* (no. 405), 63.
17. Ibid.
18. 45 *Md. Arch.*, 10, 23, 55, 56.
19. Ibid., 77, 78, 113, 115.
20. Ibid., 113.
21. *CMSP, The Brown Books, No. 3* (no. 393), 74-75.
22. *CMSP, The Red Books, No. 4, Part 3* (no. 696), 110; (no. 699), 111.
23. Ibid. (no. 697), 110; (no. 699), 111.
24. Ibid. (no. 699), 111.

XXIII FANGS OF THE SAME VULTURE

1. Willcox, 472.
2. Eller, 233-34; 47 *Md. Arch.*, 585.
3. 45 *Md. Arch.*, 143; *Maryland Gazette*, 17 November 1780. It is noteworthy that a number of loyalists who had failed to show their political leanings, such as James Lowder and Andrew Wilson, threw in with the King's men when the picaroons made a show of strength in the Patuxent on this occasion.
4. 45 *Md. Arch.*, 256; 47 *Md. Arch.*, 2.
5. *CMSP, The Red Books, No. 3, Part 4* (no. 757), 119.
6. Footner, 50-51.
7. *CMSP, The Red Books, No. 3, Part 4* (no. 758), 119.
8. *CMSP, Executive Miscellanea*, no. 1010, 137; *The Red Books, No. 3, Part 4* (no. 758), 119.
9. 47 *Md. Arch.*, 334; Eller, 393.
10. *CMSP, The Red Books, No. 3, Part 4* (no. 757), 119.
11. *Pennsylvania Gazette*, 22 November 1780.
12. 47 *Md. Arch.*, 37-38.
13. Ibid., 38, 39, 41.
14. Ibid., 103-4.
15. Ibid., 104.
16. Ibid.
17. Ibid., 118, 120-23.
18. Ibid., 122-23.
19. *CMSP, The Red Books, No. 4, Part 3* (no. 860), 135.
20. *CMSP, The Red Books, No. 4, Part 2* (no. 1759), 276; 47 *Md. Arch. No. 4, Part 3* (no. 1034), 162; 47 *Md. Arch.* 131-32, 133, 138-39.
21. 47 *Md. Arch.*, 177.
22. Ibid., 177-78.
23. Ibid., 170, 177, 184, 198.
24. Ibid., 22-23.
25. Ibid., 140-41.
26. Ibid., 389-90, 402-3, 584-85; Eller, 235-36.
27. Ibid., 178. The first plan for naval defense of the Patuxent was suggested by Stephen West, an Upper Marlboro merchant, on April 1, 1781. West noted that there were several vessels at Nottingham and Pig Point which might be armed

with four short French three-pounders belonging to a Mr. Kerban of Alexandria, Virginia, which were then in Upper Marlboro. Together with armed detachments from the surrounding country, the picaroon raiders would not dare to penetrate higher than Benedict, if they dared to enter the river at all. Ibid., 157-58; 6 *MHM*, 305-6.

28. 47 *Md. Arch.*, 214; *New Jersey Gazette*, 16 May 1781.
29. 6 *MHM*, 306-17.
30. Ibid.
31. Footner, 57.
32. 47 *Md. Arch.*, 338.
33. Ibid., 339.
34. Ibid., 361.
35. Ibid., 334.
36. *Maryland Journal and Baltimore Advertiser*, 14 August 1781; Eller, 236; 2 Tilghman, 126-27.
37. 47 *Md. Arch.*, 462; Footner, 53.
38. Footner, 53.
39. 2 *CVSP*, 174; Eller, 399-400.
40. Willcox, Part 3, 79.

XXIV   A SET OF GALLOWS-MARKED RASCALS

1. 5 *MHM*, 123.
2. Ibid.
3. Ibid., 123-25.
4. Ibid., 125.
5. Ibid., 125-26.
6. Ibid., 126.
7. Ibid.
8. Ibid., 126-27.
9. Ibid., 127.
10. Ibid.
11. Ibid., 128.
12. Ibid.
13. Ibid.
14. Ibid.
15. Ibid., 128-29.
16. Ibid., 129.
17. Ibid.
18. Ibid., 129-30.
19. Ibid.
20. Ibid., 130.
21. Ibid.
22. Ibid.

XXV   SIGNAL ACTS OF VALOUR

1. 48 *Md. Arch.*, 107; Footner, 54-55.
2. Eller, 280.
3. 48 *Md. Arch.*, 97.
4. Ibid., 106-7.
5. Ibid.
6. *CMSP, Brown Book* (no. 571), 110; (no. 572), 111; (no. 591), 115.
7. 48 *Md. Arch.*, 116.
8. Ibid., 130-31.
9. Ibid., 48-49.
10. Ibid., 151.
11. *Maryland Journal and Baltimore Advertiser*, 14 May 1782.
12. Eller, 238-39.
13. 48 *Md. Arch.*, 179.
14. *CMSP, Brown Book* (no. 591), 115. The privateer *Ranger* received her commission as a letter of marque and reprisal vessel on October 9, 1781 in Massachusetts. She is noted as a brigantine with a crew of 15 under the command of Thomas Simmons. She was owned by Daniel Sargent and others of Boston. *NRAR*, 430.
15. Beitzell, *Life on the Potomac River*, 22; Eller, 393; *CMSP, No. 4, Part 3* (no. 1034), 162; Footner, 56; *Maryland Gazette*, 18 July 1782.
16. Beitzell, *Life on the Potomac River*, 22; Footner, 56; *Maryland Gazette*, 18 July 1782.

XXVI   A SHOWER OF MUSKET BALLS

1. 48 *Md. Arch.*, 226, 227, 229.
2. *Maryland Journal and Baltimore Advertiser*, 17 September 1782.
3. 48 *Md. Arch.*, 252-53.
4. Ibid., 253.
5. Eller, 240.
6. 48 *Md. Arch.*, 267, 269.
7. Ibid., 271.
8. Ibid., 266, 267, 292-94, 296.
9. Walley reports sixteen men and their commander were taken, but a list later submitted to the government names seventeen prisoners

plus a commander. 4 *MHM*, 115, 133.

10. Ibid., 116, 133.
11. Ibid., 115.
12. Ibid., 115, 128. Captain Levin Handy of the marines implied that their intentions were to push for the enemy, but they were delayed by adverse winds.
13. Ibid., 128.
14. Ibid., 128-29.
15. Ibid., 129.
16. Ibid., 116, 124.
17. Ibid., 117.
18. Ibid., 126, 129. The Council of War is not documented, but is strongly implied by the various records and testimony provided later. Such a conference would have been normal procedure in any event.
19. Ibid., 116, 117, 124, 130.
20. Frazier places the time at 9:00 A.M. Ibid., 117, 130.
21. Ibid., 117, 119, 122, 124, 130. Dashiell claimed after the battle that Walley had no battle plan. Such a laxity, however, and in view of his previous record, seems improbable for a man such as Walley, and the charge may have stemmed from Dashiell's desire to make his own subsequent actions seem less demeaning than they really were.
22. Ibid., 117-19, 122.
23. Ibid., 118, 122, 124, 130; Smith and Earle in Eller, 243. Smith and Earle suggest the reason for the *Terrible's* dropping back was to protect the schooner from an end run by the enemy. Frazier claimed that Captain Speedin occupied the center and Walley the left. However, Speedin could not bring his 12-pounders to bear owing to Walley's position, suggesting that Walley did indeed occupy the center.
24. Ibid., 119.
25. Ibid., 120, 122.
26. Ibid., 118, 120-21, 125.
27. Ibid., 118.
28. Ibid., 125, 130-31.
29. Ibid., 127; Eller, 244.
30. 4 *MHM*, 118, 120.
31. Ibid., 119-21.
32. Ibid., 119, 122.
33. Ibid., 121, 125, 127.
34. Eller, 244.
35. Footner, 63.
36. 48 *Md. Arch.*, 328-29.
37. 4 *MHM*, 124.
38. 48 *Md. Arch.*, 312-13.
39. Ibid., 322.
40. Ibid., 322-23, 336, 360.
41. Ibid., 336.
42. Ibid., 361.
43. Governor Paca gives the date as February 13, a Thursday. Wheland's flotilla was identified at Benedict as consisting of four barges, but these may have been either sloop or schooner rigged. Ibid., 357, 360; *CMSP, The Red Books, No. 4, Part 1* (nos. 1226, 1227), 211.
44. *CMSP, The Red Books, No. 3, Part 4* (nos. 1301, 1302, 1303, 1304, 1305), 202; 48 *Md. Arch.*, 366.
45. *CMSP, The Red Books, No. 3, Part 4* (nos. 1301, 1303), 202.
46. 48 *Md. Arch.*, 366.
47. Ibid., 365-66.
48. Eller, 245.
49. 48 *Md. Arch.*, 361.
50. Ibid., 365.
51. Ibid., 364.
52. Ibid., 379-80.
53. *CMSP, The Red Books, No. 4, Part 3* (no. 1312), 203.
54. 48 *Md. Arch.*, 388.
55. Ibid., 387-88.
56. Ibid., 388.
57. Ibid., 387.
58. Eller, 245.
59. 48 *Md. Arch.*, 392.
60. Ibid., 391.

XXVII EPILOGUE: A PLAN OF PIRACY BROKEN UP

1. *American and Commercial Daily Advertiser*, 26 August 1807; 29 August 1807; 5 *MHM*, 175.
2. Cf. Emmerson.
3. *American and Commercial Daily Advertiser*, 29 August 1807.
4. Ibid., 29 August 1807.
5. Ibid., 26 August 1807; 29 August 1807.
6. Ibid., 29 August 1807.
7. Ibid., 26 August 1807; 29 August

1807.

8. Ibid., 29 August 1807.

9. Ibid.; *Federal Gazette*, 27 August 1807.

10. Ibid.

11. *American and Commercial Daily Advertiser*, 26 August 1807; 29 August 1807; *Federal Gazette*, 27 August 1807.

12. *American and Commercial Daily Advertiser*, 3 September 1807.

13. Log of USF *Chesapeake*, 29 August 1807.

14. *American and Commercial Daily Advertiser*, 3 September 1807; 5 *MHM*, 175. The number of actual participants varies with the source. James R. Caldwell notes the force consisted of "Capt. Samuel, and Capt. Jos. Sterrets Companies, to the number of 50 men, Capt. Porter of the U.S. Navy, 15 masters of Vessels and Crews, consisting of 100 men in all . . ." The *Advertiser* notes there were 19 "Master Mariners and others" that volunteered.

15. *American and Commercial Daily Advertiser*, 3 September 1807; 5 *MHM*, 175.

16. Ibid.

17. 5 *MHM*, 176.

18. *American and Commercial Daily Advertiser*, 3 September 1807.

19. Ibid.; 5 *MHM*, 176.

20. 5 *MHM*, 176; Riley, 226-27.

21. Ibid.

22. 5 *MHM*, 177.

23. *American and Commercial Daily Advertiser*, 2 September 1807; 3 September 1807.

24. Ibid., 1 September 1807; 3 September 1807.

25. Log of USF *Chesapeake*, 29 August-10 September 1807.

26. 5 *MHM*, 176; *American and Commercial Daily Advertiser*, 2 September 1807.

Bibliography

Acts of the Privy Council, Colonial Series. Edited by William L. Grant and James Munro. 6 vols. Hereford, England, 1908-19.

American and Commercial Daily Advertiser (Baltimore).

American Weekly Mercury (Philadelphia).

Andrews, Matthew Page. *The Founding of Maryland.* Baltimore, 1933.

Archives of Maryland. Baltimore, 1833-date.

Barbour, Philip L., ed. *The Jamestown Voyages Under the First Charter 1606-1609.* 2 vols. Cambridge, 1969.

Beitzell, Edwin W. *The Jesuit Missions of St. Mary's County, Maryland.* Abell, Maryland, 1960.

————. *Life on the Potomac River.* Abell, Maryland, 1968.

Billings, Warren M., ed. *The Old Dominion in the Seventeenth Century: A Documentary History of Virginia, 1606-1689.* Chapel Hill, 1979.

Blathwayth Papers, vol. VII. Colonial Williamsburg, Inc., Williamsburg, Virginia.

Boston News-Letter (Boston).

Botting, Douglas. *The Pirates.* Alexandria, Virginia, 1978.

Brock, Robert A., ed. *The Official Letters of Alexander Spotswood, Lieutenant Governor of the Colony of Virginia, 1710-1722.* 2 vols. Richmond, 1882.

Burney, James. *History of the Buccaneers of America.* London, 1816.

Byrd, William. *The Correspondence of the Three William Byrds of Westover, Virginia 1684-1776.* Charlottesville, Virginia, 1977.

Calendar of Maryland State Papers. Annapolis, Maryland.

Calendar of State Papers, Colonial Series, America and West Indies. 40 vols. London, 1860-date.

Calendar of Virginia State Papers. Edited by William P. Palmer. 11 vols.

Richmond, 1875-1893.

Calvert Papers. Maryland Historical Society, *Fund-Publications,* no. 189. Baltimore, 1889-1899.

Chronicles of St. Mary's, vol. 26, no. 2. St. Mary's, Maryland, 1978.

Claiborne, John Herbert. *William Claiborne of Virginia With Some Account of His Pedigree.* New York and London, 1917.

Colledge, J. J. *Ships of the Royal Navy: An Historical Index,* vol. 1. New York, 1969.

Colonial Office Papers, Public Record Office. Transcripts in Library of Congress, Washington, D. C.

Colonial Records of North Carolina. Edited by William P. Palmer and others. Raleigh, 1886-1890.

Dabney, Virginius. *Virginia: The New Dominion.* Garden City, New York, 1971.

Dampier, William. *A New Voyage Round the World.* New York, 1968.

De Groot, Irene, and Vorstman, Robert, eds. *Sailing Ships: Prints by the Dutch Masters from the Sixteenth to the Nineteenth Century.* New York, 1980.

Dethlefson, Edwin. *Whidah: Cape Cod's Mystery Treasure Ship.* Woodstock, Vermont and Key West, Florida, 1984.

De Zeeuwsche Expeditie Naar De West Onder Cornelius Evertsen Den Jonge 1672-1674. Edited by C. De Waard. Gravenhage, Netherlands, 1928.

Documents Relative to the Colonial History of the State of New-York; Procured in Holland, England and France, vol. 3. Edited and compiled by John Romeyn Brodhead. Albany, 1853.

Dodson, Leonidas. *Alexander Spotswood, Governor of Colonial Virginia, 1710-1722.* Philadelphia, 1932.

Eller, Ernest McNeill, ed. *Chesapeake Bay in the American Revolution.* Centreville, Maryland, 1981.

Emmerson, John C., Jr., comp. *The Chesapeake Affair of 1807: An objective account of the attack by HMS Leopard, upon the U. S. frigate Chesapeake, off Cape Henry, Va., June 22, 1807, and its repercussions; compiled from contemporary newspaper accounts, official documents, and other authoritative sources.* Portsmouth, Virginia, 1954.

Emory, Frederic. *Queen Anne's County, Maryland: Its Early History and Development.* Queenstown, Maryland, 1981.

Esquemeling, John. *The Buccaneers of America: A true account of the most remarkable assaults committed of late years upon the coasts of the West Indies by the Buccaneers of Jamaica and Tortuga (both English and French).* New York, 1967.

Executive Journals of the Council of Colonial Virginia, 1680-1754. Edited by Henry R. McIlwaine and Wilmer L. Hall. 5 vols. Richmond,

1925-1945.

Federal Gazette (Baltimore).

Footner, Hulbert. *Rivers of the Eastern Shore: Seventeen Maryland Rivers.* New York and Toronto, 1944.

Force, Peter, ed. *American Archives,* 4th Series. Washington, D. C., 1837-1853.

Hale, Nathan C. *Virginia Venturer: A Historical Biography of William Claiborne 1600-1677.* Richmond, 1951.

Hall, Clayton C., ed. *Narratives of Early Maryland, 1633-1684,* in Frankin Jameson, ed., *Original Narratives of Early American History.* New York, 1910.

Hammett, Regina Combs. *History of St. Mary's County, Maryland.* Ridge, Maryland, 1977.

Hening, William Waller, ed. *The Statutes-at-Large, Being a Collection of All the Laws of Virginia.* 13 vols. Richmond, 1819-1823.

Howell, Thomas Bayly. *State Trials,* vol 15. London, 1811.

Ingle, Edward. *Captain Richard Ingle, The Maryland "Pirate and Rebel," 1642-1653.* Baltimore, 1884.

Johnson, Captain Charles. *A General History of the Robberies and Murders of the Most Notorious Pirates.* London, 1926.

Journal of the Commissioners for Trade and Plantations, April 1704-1782. 14 vols. London, 1920-1938.

Journals of the House of Burgesses of Virginia, 1619-1776. Edited by John P. Kennedy and Henry R. McIlwaine. 13 vols. Richmond, 1905-1915.

Lee, Robert E. *Blackbeard the Pirate: A Reappraisal of His Life and Times.* Winston-Salem, North Carolina, 1974.

Letters, Tancred Robinson Collection, Public Record Office, Admiralty 1/2377. London, England.

Letters of Captain Ellis Brand to the Lords of Admiralty, Public Record Office, Admiralty 1/1472. London, England.

Letters of Captain George Gordon to the Lords of Admiralty, Public Record Office, Admiralty 1/1826. London, England.

Log of HMS *Essex Prize.* Colonial Office Transcript, Admiralty 5/1441. Library of Congress, Washington, D. C.

Log of HMS *Lyme.* Public Record Office, Admiralty 51/4250. London, England.

Log of HMS *Pearl.* Public Record Office, Admiralty 51/627. London, England.

Log of USF *Chesapeake.* Library of Congress, Washington, D. C.

Marx, Robert F. *Shipwrecks of the Western Hemisphere: 1492-1825.* New York, 1971.

Maryland Gazette (Annapolis).

Maryland Historical Magazine. Baltimore, 1906-date.

Maryland Journal and Baltimore Advertiser (Baltimore).

Middleton, Arthur Pierce. *Tobacco Coast: A Maritime History of Chesapeake Bay in the Colonial Era.* Newport News, 1953.

Minutes of the Council and General Court of Colonial Virginia 1622-1632, 1670-1676 With Notes and Excerpts from the Original Council and General Court Records, Into 1683, Now Lost. Edited by H. R. McIlwaine. Richmond, 1924.

Montgomery of Alamein, Field-Marshal Viscount. *A History of Warfare.* Cleveland and New York, 1968.

Naval Documents of the American Revolution. Edited by William Bell Clark and William James Morgan. 8 vols. to date. Washington, D. C., 1964-date.

Naval Records of the American Revolution 1775-1788. Washington, D. C., 1906.

Neill, Edward D. *Virginia Carolorum: The Colony Under the Rule of Charles the First and Second A.D. 1625-A.D. 1685, Based Upon Manuscripts and Documents of the Period.* Albany, New York, 1886.

New Jersey Gazette (Trenton).

Parr, Charles McKew. *The Voyages of David de Vries.* New York, 1969.

Pennsylvania Gazette (Philadelphia).

Pennsylvania Packet (Philadelphia).

Pringle, Patrick. *Jolly Roger, the Story of the Great Age of Piracy.* New York, 1953.

Proceedings of the Trial of the Pirates John Houghling, Francois Delaunee, and Cornelius Frank. Colonial Office Transcript, 5/647. Library of Congress, Washington, D. C.

Purchas, Samuel. *Hakluytus Posthumas, or Purchas his Pilgrimes.* Glasgow, 1905-1907.

Rankin, Hugh. *The Golden Age of Piracy.* Williamsburg, Virginia, 1969.

———. *The Pirates of Colonial North Carolina.* Raleigh, 1976.

Rawlinson Collection. Bodleian Library, Oxford, England.

Riley, Elihu S. *"The Ancient City." A History of Annapolis, in Maryland 1649-1887.* Annapolis, 1887.

Shea, William L. *The Virginia Militia in the Seventeenth Century.* Baton Rouge and London, 1983.

Smith, John. *The General Historie of Virginia, New-England, and the Summer Isles.* London, 1624.

Stith, John. *The History of the First Discovery and Settlement of Virginia; Being an Essay Towards a General History of This Colony.* London, 1743.

Supplement to the Boston Gazette (Boston).

Tancred Robinson Papers. Virginia Colonial Records Project, Williamsburg, Virginia.

Tyler's Quarterly Historical and Genealogical Magazine. Richmond, 1919-1952.

Vere, Francis. *Salt in Their Blood: The Lives of the Famous Dutch Admirals.* London, 1955.

Virginia Gazette (Williamsburg).

Virginia Magazine of History and Biography. Richmond, 1893-date.

Wafer, Lionel. *A New Voyage and Description of the Isthmus of America.* Edited by L. E. Elliott Joyce. Oxford, 1934.

Wertenbaker, Thomas J. *Virginia Under the Stuarts, 1607-1688.* Princeton, 1914.

Whipple, Addison B. C. *Pirate Rascals of the Spanish Main.* New York, 1957.

Willcox, William B. *American Rebellion: Sir Henry Clinton's Narrative of his Campaigns, 1775-1782; with an Appendix of Original Documents.* New Haven, 1954.

William and Mary Quarterly. 1st ser., July 1892-April 1919; 2d ser., January 1921-October 1943; 3d ser., January 1944-date.

Williams, Lloyd Haynes. *Pirates of Colonial Virginia.* Richmond, 1937.

Winthrop, John. *Winthrop's Journal: History of New England 1630-1649.* Edited by James Kendall Hosmer. New York, 1908.

Woodstock Letters. Baltimore, Maryland.

Index

Ships by name are indexed under "Vessels"